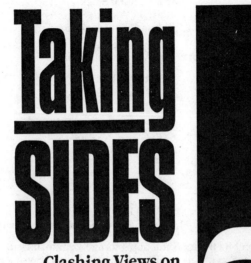

Taking
SIDES

Clashing Views on Controversial Environmental Issues

Seventh Edition

Edited, Selected, and with Introductions by

Theodore D. Goldfarb

State University of New York at Stony Brook

Dushkin/McGraw-Hill
A Division of The McGraw-Hill Companies

This book is dedicated to my children and all other children for whom the successful resolution of these issues is of great urgency.

Photo Acknowledgments

Part 1   Environmental Protection Agency
Part 2   Digital Stock
Part 3   Alcoa
Part 4   Colorado Tourism Board

Cover Art Acknowledgment

Charles Vitelli

Manufactured in the United States of America

Seventh Edition

10   9   8   7   6   5   4   3   2   1

Library of Congress Cataloging-in-Publication Data

Main entry under title:
    Taking sides: clashing views on controversial environmental issues/edited, selected, and with introductions by Theodore D. Goldfarb.—7th ed.
    Includes bibliographical references and index.
    1. Environmental policy. 2. Environmental protection. I. Goldfarb, Theodore D., *comp.*

363.7

0-697-37536-6   ISSN: 1091-8825

PREFACE

For the past 20 years I have been teaching an environmental chemistry course, and my experience has been that the critical and complex relationship we have with our environment is of vital and growing concern to students, regardless of their majors. Consequently, for this seventh edition, I again sought to shape issues and to select readings that do not require a technical background or prerequisite courses in order to be understood. In addition to the sciences, this volume would be appropriate for such disciplines as philosophy, law, sociology, political science, economics, and allied health—any course where environmental topics are addressed.

Faculty are divided about whether or not it is appropriate to use a classroom to advocate a particular position on a controversial issue. Some believe that the proper role of a teacher is to maintain neutrality in order to present the material in as objective a manner as possible. Others, like myself, find that students rarely fail to recognize their instructors' points of view. Rather than reveal which side I am on through subtle hints, I prefer to be forthright about it, while doing my best to encourage students to develop their own positions, and I do not penalize them if they disagree with my views. No matter whether the goal is to attempt an objective presentation or to encourage advocacy, it is necessary to present both sides of any argument. To be a successful proponent of any position, it is essential to understand your opponents' arguments. The format of this text, with 36 essays arranged in pro and con pairs on 18 environmental controversies, is designed with these objectives in mind.

In the *introduction* to each issue, I present the historical context of the controversy and some of the key questions that divide the disputants. The *postscript* that follows each pair of essays includes comments offered to provoke thought about aspects of the issue that are suitable for classroom discussion. A careful reading of my remarks may reveal the positions I favor, but the essays themselves and the *suggestions for further reading* in each postscript should provide the student with the information needed to construct and support an independent perspective. Also, when applicable, I have provided Internet site addresses (URLs) in the postscripts that should prove useful as starting points for further research.

Changes to this edition   This seventh edition has been extensively revised and updated. There are three completely new issues: *Should Environmental Regulations Be Replaced by Market-Based Strategies?* (Issue 1); *Do Environmental Estrogens Pose a Potentially Serious Health Threat?* (Issue 8); and *Is Rapid Introduction of Electric Cars a Good Strategy for Reducing Air Pollution?* (Issue 10). For four of the issues retained from the previous edition, the issue question has been significantly modified and both selections have been replaced in order to focus the debate more sharply and bring it up to date: Issue 3 on the Endangered Species Act; Issue 4 on environmental justice; Issue 13 on waste recycling; and Issue 15 on saving tropical rain forests. Additionally, the following selections have been replaced: the YES selection for Issue 6 on property rights; the NO selection for Issue 11 on the use of agricultural chemicals; the YES selection for Issue 16 on ozone-depleting chemicals; both selections for Issue 17 on, global warming; and the YES selection for Issue 18 on the threat of a global environmental crisis. The result is that 20 of the 36 selections in this seventh edition are new.

A word to the instructor   An *Instructor's Manual With Test Questions* (multiple-choice and essay) is available through the publisher for the instructor using *Taking Sides* in the classroom. Also available is a general guidebook, called *Using Taking Sides in the Classroom,* which has general suggestions for adapting the pro-con approach in any classroom setting. An on-line version of *Using Taking Sides in the Classroom* and a correspondence service for Taking Sides adopters can be found at www.cybsol.com/usingtakingsides/.

Taking Sides: Clashing Views on Controversial Environmental Issues is only one title in the Taking Sides series; the others are listed on the back cover. If you are interested in seeing the table of contents for any of the other titles, please visit the Taking Sides Web site at http://www.dushkin.com/takingsides/.

Acknowledgments   I received many helpful comments and suggestions from friends and readers across the United States and Canada. Their suggestions have markedly enhanced the quality of this edition and are reflected in the new issues and the updated selections.

Special thanks go to those who responded to the questionnaire with specific suggestions for the seventh edition:

Duane Bartak
University of Northern Iowa

John Bumpus
University of Northern Iowa

Kathleen Carroll
University of Maryland–
  Baltimore City

R. Laurence Davis
University of New Haven

Anne L. Day
Clarion University of
  Pennsylvania

Elizabeth A. Desy
Southwest State University

Charles Garraway
Hardin-Simmons University

Ruthie Hefner
Clovis Community College

Louis R. Hellwig
University of Northern Iowa

Nan Ho
Las Positas College

Alison Hoffmann
University of Tennessee–
  Chattanooga

Nayyer Hussain
Tougaloo College

Kate Inman
University of Georgia

William T. Jordan
Pacific University

Mark A. Kelso
University of Nevada–
  Las Vegas

Priscilla Mattson
Middlesex Community
  College

Joy McKenna
Southern Vermont College

Rebecca Monhardt
University of Iowa

Gregory Nishiyama
University of Southern
  California

Robert E. Reiman
Pembroke State University

Don Rodriguez
Colorado State University

Thomas E. Shriver
Oklahoma State University

Donald Spano
University of Southern
  Colorado

Thomas H. Tietenberg
Colby College

Donald Vance
Baldwin-Wallace College

Aaron Wolf
University of Alabama–
  Tuscaloosa

Finally, I am grateful to David Dean, list manager for the Taking Sides program, for his assistance.

Theodore D. Goldfarb
State University of New York at Stony Brook

CONTENTS IN BRIEF

CONTENTS

Reason Foundation vice president Lynn Scarlett argues that traditional "top-down environmental regulation" should be replaced by decentralized bargaining and market-based approaches. Environmental activist Brian Tokar maintains that pollution credits and other market-oriented environmental protection policies do nothing to reduce pollution.

Wilderness magazine poetry editor John Daniel asserts that wilderness is a valuable resource that must be protected. William Tucker, a writer and social critic, asserts that wilderness areas are elitist preserves designed to keep people out.

David Langhorst, executive board member of the Idaho Wildlife Federation, asserts that the Endangered Species Act has saved hundreds of plant and animal species that were in serious decline and that reauthorization of the act is in the public interest. Mark L. Plummer, an environmental economist, argues that the act's goal of bringing listed species to full recovery is not achievable.

History professor Ruth Rosen argues that racial discrimination has resulted in minorities' being exposed to the highest levels of industrial pollution, and she supports demands for corrective action. American business researchers Christopher Boerner and Thomas Lambert favor compensating those who are impacted by polluting facilities to achieve environmental justice.

Author Paul Harrison argues that family planning programs should be implemented to prevent world population from exceeding carrying capacity. Betsy Hartmann, director of the Hampshire College Population and Development Program, argues that the real problem is not how many people there are but that controls over resource consumption are inadequate.

Ed Carson, a reporter for *Reason* magazine, argues that property owners should be compensated when the state restricts the uses of their land. *Business Week* correspondent Doug Harbrecht claims that it is absurd to have to pay owners of private property for obeying environmental regulations.

Greenpeace research coordinator Joe Thornton asserts that chlorinated organic compounds should be phased out to protect humans and animals from the toxic effects of these chemicals. Science writer Ivan Amato states that only a few chlorinated compounds are proven health threats and that no adequate substitutes for chlorine exist.

Environmental journalist Jon R. Luoma asserts that pollutants that mimic estrogens have caused reproductive problems in wildlife and are considered by many researchers to threaten humans as well. Toxicologist Stephen H. Safe argues that industrial estrogenic compounds do not contribute to increased cancer incidence and reproductive problems in humans.

Environmental health and policy professor Jeffery A. Foran and Clean Water Project director Robert W. Adler argue that revisions to the Clean Water Act should aim for the goal of zero discharge of toxic pollutants. American Enterprise Institute scholar Robert W. Hahn advocates a market-based approach to water regulation based on cost-benefit analyses.

Environmental engineering professor Daniel Sperling argues that speedy introduction of electric vehicles would be the most effective way of combating air pollution. Technology and Policy Program chair Richard de Neufville and several of his MIT colleagues oppose electric vehicle mandates, claiming that they will not significantly improve air quality.

Environmental journalist Ronald Bailey asserts that intensive farming, relying on pesticides and fertilizers, is needed to feed the world's people. Katherine R. Smith, policy studies director at the Henry A. Wallace Institute for Alternative Agriculture, asserts that use of chemicals is causing serious environmental problems that could be solved if subsidies were redirected to promote "green" alternatives.

DuPont corporate counsel Bernard J. Reilly argues that the Superfund legislation has led to unfair standards and waste cleanup cost delegation. *Audubon* contributing editor Ted Williams warns against turning Superfund into a public welfare program for polluters.

Researcher John E. Young argues that recycling has become an economically
viable waste management option. Engineering and economics researchers
Chris Hendrickson, Lester Lave, and Francis McMichael assert that ambitious
recycling programs are of dubious environmental value.

Nuclear waste researcher Nicholas Lenssen asserts that the search for a permanent nuclear waste repository should be delayed until the future of nuclear
power is decided. Science writer Luther J. Carter argues that now is the time to
begin using the proposed Yucca Mountain site for surface and underground
storage of nuclear waste.

Economics professors Thomas A. Carr and Sunder Ramaswamy and mathematics teacher Heather L. Pedersen maintain that sustainable use of rain
forest products helps to preserve the forest. Reporter Jon Entine asserts that
most green marketing programs do nothing to slow forest destruction.

Amicus Journal contributing editor Don Hinrichsen argues that chlorofluorocarbons (CFCs) are a serious threat to terrestrial life and that immediate
action is needed to protect the ozone layer. *Garbage* magazine's editor and
publisher Patricia Poore and associate publisher Bill O'Donnell argue that
ozone depletion is not a crisis requiring an outright ban on CFCs.

Interdisciplinary studies professor Moti Nissani argues that action should be
taken to reduce the potentially grave impacts of greenhouse-induced global
warming. Economist Thomas Gale Moore maintains that it makes no sense
to invest in expensive efforts to reduce greenhouse gas emissions.

Senior researcher Hilary F. French calls for an international effort to stabilize the planet by switching to sustainable technologies before environmental deterioration becomes irreversible. Professor of economics and business
administration Julian L. Simon predicts that over the long term enhanced
brainpower will lead to a healthier environment.

INTRODUCTION

The Environmental Movement

Theodore D. Goldfarb

ENVIRONMENTAL CONSCIOUSNESS

In June 1992 Rio de Janeiro was the site of the United Nations Conference on Environment and Development (UNCED), popularly billed as the Earth Summit. UNCED, which was the follow-up to a much more modest United Nations conference held 20 years earlier, consisted of two massive, global conferences—one of official government delegations and the other of a diverse array of nongovernmental organizations (NGOs)—as well as a separate "Earth Parliament" comprised of 800 delegates of indigenous peoples. The most far-reaching outcome of UNCED was a 600-page agreement called Agenda 21, which sets guidelines for how, under UN leadership, the governments and businesses of the world should attempt to achieve economic growth, while maintaining environmental quality. Two years prior to the Earth Summit, on April 22, 1990, 200 million people in 140 countries around the world participated in a variety of activities to celebrate Earth Day. It was also a follow-up to an event that took place two decades earlier, the first Earth Day (celebrated only in the United States), which many social historians credit with spawning the ongoing global environmental movement.

Comparing the enormous increase in size, complexity, range of issues, and diversity of participation in either UNCED or Earth Day 1990 with its predecessor event reveals the explosive growth in political, scientific and technical, regulatory, financial, industrial, and educational activity related to an expanding list of environmental problems that has developed in the intervening years. Industrial development has reached a level at which pollutants threaten not only local environments but also the global ecosystems that control the Earth's climate and the ozone shield that filters out potentially lethal solar radiation. The elevation of environmental concern to a prominent position on the international political agenda persuaded commentators on Earth Day 1990 events to speculate that the world was entering "the decade —or even era—of the environment." The initial attention given to UNCED and the ongoing activities it spawned at first appeared to confirm this prediction. However, as concern about future worldwide economic prosperity has grown, there has been an increase in resistance from the international industrial community to the imposition of further environmental regulations and restrictions. Thus, for example, the unprecedented and surprising progress made in controlling the release of pollutants that threaten stratospheric ozone has not resulted in similar, rapid progress in reducing the emission of "greenhouse gases" that threaten global climatic stability.

THE HISTORY OF ENVIRONMENTALISM

The current interest in environmental issues in the United States has its historical roots in the conservation movement of the late nineteenth and early twentieth centuries. This earlier, more limited, recognition of the need for environmental preservation was a response to the destruction wrought by uncontrolled industrial exploitation of natural resources in the post–Civil War period. Clear-cutting forests, in addition to producing large devastated areas, resulted in secondary disasters. Bark and branches left in the cutover areas caused several major midwestern forest fires. Severe floods were caused by the loss of trees that previously had helped to reduce surface water runoff. The Sierra Club and the Audubon Society, the two oldest environmental organizations still active today, were founded around the turn of the century and helped to organize public opposition to the destructive practice of exploiting resources. Mining, grazing, and lumbering were brought under government control by such landmark legislation as the Forest Reserve Act of 1891 and the Forest Management Act of 1897. Schools of forestry were established at several of the land grant colleges to help develop the scientific expertise needed for the wise management of forest resources.

The present environmental movement can be traced back to 1962, when Rachel Carson's book *Silent Spring* appeared. The book's emotional warning about the inherent dangers in the excessive use of pesticides ignited the imagination of an enormous and disparate audience who had become uneasy about the proliferation of new synthetic chemicals in agriculture and industry. The atmospheric testing of nuclear weapons began to cause widespread public concern about the effects of nuclear radiation. City dwellers began to recognize the connection between the increasing prevalence of smoky, irritating air and the daily ritual of urban commuter traffic jams. The responses to Carson's book included not only a multitude of scientific and popular debates about the issues she had raised, but also a ground swell of public support for increased controls over all forms of pollution.

The rapid rise in the United States of public concern about environmental issues is apparent from the results of opinion polls. Similar surveys taken in 1965 and 1970 showed an increase from 17 to 53 percent in the number of respondents who rated "reducing pollution of air and water" as one of the three problems they would like the government to pay more attention to. By 1984 pollster Louis Harris was reporting to Congress that 69 percent of the public favored making the Clean Air Act more stringent. A CBS News/*New York Times* survey revealed that 74 percent of respondents in 1990 (up from 45 percent in 1981) supported protecting the environment *regardless of the cost.*

The growth of environmental consciousness in the United States swelled the ranks of the older voluntary organizations, such as the national Wildlife

Federation, the Sierra Club, the Isaac Walton League, and the Audubon Society, and has led to the establishment of more than 200 new national and regional associations and 3,000 local ones. Such national and international groups as the Environmental Defense Fund, Friends of the Earth, the National Resources Defense Council, Environmental Action, the League of Conservation Voters, and Zero Population Growth have become proficient at lobbying for legislation, influencing elections, and litigating in the courts.

Environmental literature has also grown exponentially since the appearance of *Silent Spring*. Many popular magazines, technical journals, and organizational newsletters devoted to environmental issues have been introduced, as well as hundreds of books, some of which, like Paul Ehrlich's *The Population Bomb* (1968) and Barry Commoner's *The Closing Circle* (1972), have become best-sellers.

CLASHING VIEWS FROM CONFLICTING VALUES

As with all social issues, those on opposite sides of environmental disputes have conflicting personal values. On some level, almost everyone would admit to being concerned about threats to the environment. However, enormous differences exist in individual perceptions about the seriousness of some environmental threats, their origins, their relative importance, and what to do about them. In most instances, very different conclusions, drawn from the same basic scientific evidence, can be expressed on these issues.

What are these different value systems that produce such heated debate? Some are obvious: An executive of a chemical company has a vested interest in placing greater value on the financial security of the company's stockholders than on the possible environmental effects of the company's operation. He or she is likely to interpret the potential health effects of what comes out of the plant's smokestacks or sewer pipes differently than would a resident of the surrounding community. These different interpretations need not involve any conscious dishonesty on anyone's part. There is likely to be sufficient scientific uncertainty about the pathological and ecological consequences of the company's effluents to enable both sides to reach very different conclusions from the available "facts."

Less obvious are the value differences among scientists that can divide them in an environmental dispute. Unfortunately, when questions are raised about the effects of personal value systems on scientific judgments, the twin myths of scientific objectivity and scientific neutrality get in the way. Neither the scientific community nor the general population appear to understand that scientists are very much influenced by subjective, value-laden considerations and will frequently evaluate data in a manner that supports their own interests. For example, a scientist employed by a pesticide manufacturer may be less likely than a similarly trained scientist working for an environmental organization to take data that show that one of the company's products is a low-level carcinogen in mice and interpret those data to mean that the product therefore poses a threat to human health.

Even self-proclaimed environmentalists frequently argue over environmental issues. Hunters, while supporting the prohibition of lumbering and mining on their favorite hunting grounds, strongly oppose the designation of these regions as wilderness areas because that would result in their being prohibited from using their vehicles to bring home their bounty. Also opposed to wilderness designation are foresters, who believe that forest lands should be scientifically managed rather than left alone to evolve naturally.

Political ideology can also have a profound effect on environmental attitudes. Those critical of the prevailing socioeconomic system are likely to attribute environmental problems to the industrial development supported by that system. Others are likelier to blame environmental degradation on more universal factors, such as population growth.

Changes in prevailing social attitudes influence public response to environmental issues. The American pioneers were likely to perceive their natural surroundings as being dominated by hostile forces that needed to be conquered or overcome. The notion that humans should conquer nature has only slowly been replaced by the alternative view of living in harmony with the natural environment, but the growing popularity of the environmental movement evinces the public's acceptance of this goal.

PROTECTING THE ENVIRONMENT

There has always been strong resistance to regulatory restraints on industrial and economic activity in the United States. The most ardent supporters of America's capitalist economy argue that pollution and other environmental effects have certain costs and that regulation will take place automatically through the marketplace. Despite mounting evidence that the social costs of polluted air and water are usually external to the economic mechanisms affecting prices and profits, prior to the 1960s, Congress imposed very few restrictions on the types of technology and products industry could use or produce.

As noted above, the turn-of-the-century conservation movement did result in legislation restricting the exploitation of lumber and minerals on federal lands. Similarly, in response to public outrage over numerous incidents of death and illness from adulterated foods, Congress established the Food and Drug Administration (FDA) in 1906.

Regulatory Legislation

The environmental movement of the 1960s and 1970s produced a profound and controversial change in the political climate concerning regulatory legislation. Concerns such as the proliferation of new synthetic chemicals in industry and agriculture, the increased use of hundreds of inadequately tested additives in foods, and the effects of automotive emissions were pressed on

Congress by increasingly influential environmental organizations. Beginning with the Food Additives Amendment of 1958, which required FDA approval of all new chemicals used in the processing and marketing of foods, a series of federal and state legislative and administrative actions resulted in the creation of numerous regulations and standards aimed at reducing and reversing environmental degradation.

Congress responded to the environmental movement with the National Environmental Policy Act of 1969. This act pronounced a national policy requiring an ecological impact assessment for any major federal action. The legislation called for the establishment of a three-member Council on Environmental Quality to initiate studies, make recommendations, and prepare an annual Environmental Quality Report. It also requires all agencies of the federal government to prepare a detailed environmental impact statement (EIS) for any major project or proposed legislation in which they are involved. Despite some initial attempts to evade this requirement, court suits by environmental groups have forced compliance, and now, new facilities like electrical power plants, interstate highways, dams, harbors, and interstate pipelines can proceed only after preparation and review of an EIS.

Another major step in increasing federal antipollution efforts was the establishment in 1970 of the Environmental Protection Agency (EPA). Many programs previously administered by a variety of agencies, such as the departments of the Interior, Agriculture, Health, Education, and Welfare, were transferred to this new, central, independent agency. The EPA was granted authority to do research, propose new legislation, and implement and enforce laws concerning air and water pollution, pesticide use, radiation exposure, toxic substances, solid waste, and noise abatement. The year 1970 also marked the establishment of the Occupational Safety and Health Administration (OSHA), the result of a long struggle by organized labor and independent occupational health organizations to focus attention on the special problems of the workplace.

The first major legislation to propose the establishment of national standards for pollution control was the Air Quality Act of 1967. The Clean Air Act of 1970 specified that ambient air quality standards were to be achieved by July 1, 1975 (a goal that was not met and remains elusive), and that automotive hydrocarbon, carbon monoxide, and nitrogen oxide emissions were to be reduced by 90 percent within five years—a deadline that has been repeatedly extended. Specific standards to limit the pollution content of effluent wastewater were prescribed in the Water Pollution Control Act of 1970. The Safe Drinking Water Act of 1974 authorized the EPA to establish federal drinking water standards, applicable to all public water supplies. The Occupational Safety and Health Act of 1970 allowed OSHA to establish strict standards for exposure to harmful substances in the workplace. The Environmental Pesticide Control Act of 1972 gave the EPA authority to regulate pesticide use and to control the sale of pesticides in interstate commerce. In 1976 the EPA was authorized to establish specific standards for the disposal of hazardous industrial wastes under the Resource Conservation and Recovery Act—but it was not until 1980 that the procedures for implementing this legislative mandate were announced. Finally, in 1976, the Toxic Substance Control Act became law, providing the basis for the regulation of public exposure to toxic materials not covered by any other legislation.

All of this environmental legislation in such a short time span produced a predictable reaction from industrial spokespeople and free-market economists. By the late 1970s attacks on what critics referred to as overregulation appeared with increasing frequency in the media. Antipollution legislation was criticized as a principal contributor to inflation and a serious impediment to continued industrial development.

One of the principal themes of Ronald Reagan's first presidential campaign was a pledge to get regulators off the backs of entrepreneurs. He interpreted his landslide victory in 1980 to mean that the public supported a sharp reversal of the federal government's role as regulator in all areas, including the environment. Two of Reagan's key appointees were Interior Secretary James Watt and EPA Administrator Ann Gorsuch Burford, both of whom set about to reverse the momentum of their agencies with respect to the regulation of pollution and environmental degradation. It soon became apparent that Reagan and his advisers had misread public attitudes. Sharp staffing and budget cuts at the EPA and OSHA produced a counterattack by environmental organizations whose membership rolls had continued to swell. Mounting public criticism of the neglect of environmental concerns by the Reagan administration was compounded by allegations of misconduct and criminal activity against environmental officials, including Ms. Burford, who was forced to resign. President Reagan attempted to mend fences with environmentalists by recalling William Ruckelshaus, the popular, first EPA administrator, to again head the agency. But throughout Reagan's presidency, few new environmental initiatives were carried out.

Despite campaign promises to return to vigorous efforts to curb pollution, President George Bush received poor grades for the overall environmental policies of his administration. However, he can be credited with providing the support that resulted in the enactment of the long-stalled 1990 Clean Air Act amendments. Despite some criticisms concerning compromises with the automobile and fossil fuel industries, most environmentalists were pleased with many aspects of the new law, particularly its provisions designed to decrease the threat of acid rain. This early optimism was soon negated by what many perceived to be weak efforts to implement and enforce this legislation. Bush has also been faulted for his failure to implement an environmentally sound energy policy and his refusal to support other industrial nations' proposed initiatives to slow global warming and deforestation.

Once again a new president, Bill Clinton, was elected in 1992 on a platform that pledged to reverse the environmental neglect of his predecessors. This pledge was reinforced by the fact that his choice for vice president, Al Gore, had gained a reputation as an environmental activist. The administration failed to make much headway in fulfilling its campaign promises during its first two years in office, despite the appointment of committed environmentalist Carol Browner to head the EPA. Initially encouraged by the selection of environmental advocate Bruce Babbitt as secretary of the interior, environmentalists were soon disheartened by his failure to successfully press for restrictions on the ecological damage that results from the commercial exploitation of public lands. The 1994 elections resulted in a Congress dominated by legislators who once again echoed Reagan's promise to reduce the burden of environmental restrictions on industry and commerce. This doomed any encouraging prospects for the Endangered Species Act, the Clean Water Act, or the Resource Conservation and Recovery Act, all of which remain stalled in Congress, awaiting revision and reauthorization. In their successful 1996 reelection campaign, Clinton and Gore once again promised vigorous promotion of an environmental protection agenda, but their failure to promote the defeat of antienvironmental legislators provides little hope that they will be able to satisfy those critics who support legislative prescriptions for environmental ailments.

RECENT DEVELOPMENTS

The 1990 Earth Day celebration prompted the publication of two articles that are critical of the mainstream environmental movement in the April 1990 issue of *The Nation*. In the first, "Ending the War Against the Earth," Barry Commoner summarizes the principal theme of his book *Making Peace With the Planet* (Pantheon Books, 1990). He argues that attempts to merely limit pollution due to existing inappropriate technology are doomed to failure. He calls for a program that would redesign industrial, agricultural, and transportation systems so that they will be environmentally benign and harmonious with the ecosphere. The other article, "The Trouble With Earth Day," by author and social critic Kirkpatrick Sale, presents four fundamental criticisms of the program organized by the planners of Earth Day. Sale contends that the focus on individual action is misguided because most environmental problems are a result of inappropriate systems of production or policies of governments or institutions that cannot be altered or reversed by each of us acting individually to adopt a more ecological lifestyle. Second, he complains about the decision to use most of the $3 million and unlimited publicity to put on a "week-long media bash" rather than to organize a long-range campaign with a continuing political thrust. Third, he accuses the organizers of having added support by accepting as partners many of the corporations, politicians, and lobbyists who have helped create existing problems. Finally, Sale points to the narrow anthropocentric focus on human peril and argues that it would be more appropriate to adopt an ecocentric perspective that would identify the solutions as those that would begin to restore the balance of the Earth's natural systems.

Sale's third complaint was amplified by a dispute over the agenda for the 25th anniversary of Earth Day in April 1995. Many prominent individuals and environmental organizations were displeased by the extent to which self-proclaimed "green" corporations used their wealth to sponsor and coopt the event in order to serve a developmental agenda that does not meet the criteria of sustainability.

Much concern in the environmental community has resulted from the emergence of what has been popularly labeled the "environmental backlash movement." With considerable funding and support from regulated industries, organizations like Wise Use/Property Rights, the Council on Energy Awareness, and the Information Council on the Environment have rallied together to oppose environmental regulations. Some of these groups go so far as to claim that environmental problems like ozone depletion, global warming, and acid rain are nonexistent. A strategy of these groups that has had some success is to fight restrictions on land development on the basis of the constitutional prohibition against the "taking" of private property, which they claim applies to any governmental action that restricts the freedom of a property owner. Many moderate members of this backlash movement claim to be deeply concerned about environmental degradation but argue that protection should be achieved by strategies involving the economic marketplace or by encouraging voluntary environmentalism, rather than by means of legislation.

GLOBAL DEVELOPMENTS

Although initially lagging behind the United States in environmental regulation, other developed industrial countries have been moving rapidly over the past decade to catch up. In a few European countries where "green parties" have become influential participants in the political process, certain pollutant emission standards are now more stringent than their U.S. counterparts. A uniform system of environmental regulations and controls is prominent among the controversial issues being planned and implemented by the nations of the European Economic Community.

Although the feeding and clothing of their growing populations continue to be the dominant concerns of developing countries, they too are paying increasing attention to environmental protection. Suggestions that they forgo the use of industrial technologies that have resulted in environmental degradation in developed countries are often viewed as an additional obstacle to the goal of raising their standard of living.

During the past decade, attention has shifted from a focus on local pollution to concern about global environmental degradation. Studies of the potential effects of several gaseous atmospheric pollutants on the Earth's climate and its protective ozone layer have made it apparent that human activity has reached a level that can result in major impacts on the planetary ecosystems. A series of major international conferences of political as well as scientific leaders have been held with the goal of seeking solutions to threatening worldwide environmental problems. The "North-South" disputes that limited the agreements reached at the Rio Earth Summit were about how to promote future industrial development so as to avert or minimize the threats to the world's ecosystems, while satisfying the frequently conflicting socioeconomic needs of the developed and developing nations.

New Approaches

An evaluation of the apparent failure to control environmental decay in the past two decades has given rise to demands for new approaches. Environmental policy analysts have proposed that regulatory agencies adopt a more holistic approach to environmental protection, rather than continue their attempts to impose separate controls on what are actually interconnected problems. The use of economic strategies, such as pollution taxes or the sale of licenses to those who wish to produce limited quantities of pollutants, has received increasing support as potentially more effective than regulatory emission standards. Such schemes continue to enrage many environmentalists who consider the sale of pollution rights to be unethical. Environmental activists point out that both population growth and increasing worldwide industrial development will result in increasing total quantities of pollutants released despite attempts to reduce the impact of pollution from current, specific sources. Such concerns have resulted in intensive discussion about the concept of "sustainable development," whose advocates propose replacing our entire system of energy production, transportation, and industrial technology with systems that are designed from the start to produce minimal cumulative environmental degradation. An excellent introduction to this concept is included in the 1987 World Commission on the Environment report *Our Common Future* (often referred to as the *Brundtland Report* after its principal author, commission chairperson Gro Harlem Brundtland).

A new militant wing, spearheaded by Greenpeace, has sprung up within the environmental movement. As a result of highly successful membership recruiting and fund-raising efforts, it has become the most powerful international grassroots environmental organization. More radical still are the politics and tactics of other "green" organizations such as Earth First! During a 1990 campaign that they called Redwood Summer, members chained themselves to trees to prevent the cutting of redwood trees in the ancient forests of northern California. The eco-radicals who constitute the small, but growing, extreme fringe of the environmental movement advocate such policies as a drastic reduction in the world's population and a return to much simpler, less materialistic lifestyles.

ECOLOGY AND ENVIRONMENTAL STUDIES

Efforts to protect the environment from the far-reaching effects of human activity require a detailed understanding of the intricate web of interconnected cycles that constitute our natural surroundings. The recent blossoming of ecology and environmental studies into respectable fields of scientific study has provided the basis for such an understanding. Traditional fields of scientific endeavor such as geology, chemistry, or physics are too narrowly focused to successfully describe a complex ecosystem. Thus, it is not surprising that chemists who helped to promote the use of DDT and other pesticides failed to predict the harmful effects that accumulation of these substances in biological food chains had on birds and marine life.

Ecology and environmental studies involve a holistic study of the relationships among living organisms and their environment. It is clearly an ambitious undertaking, and ecologists are only beginning to advance our ability to predict the effects of human intrusions into natural ecosystems.

It has been suggested that our failure to recognize the potentially harmful effects of our activities is related to the way we lead our lives. Industrial development has produced lifestyles that separate most of us from direct contact with the natural systems upon which we depend for sustenance. We buy our food in supermarkets and get our water from a kitchen faucet. We tend to take the availability of these essentials for granted until something threatens the supply.

SOME THOUGHTS ON ARMED CONFLICT AND INTERNATIONAL COOPERATION

It has long been recognized that a major nuclear war would produce devastating environmental consequences. In *The Fate of the Earth* (Alfred A. Knopf, 1982), Jonathan Schell provides a chilling analysis of the likely effects of radioactive fallout, including destruction of the ozone layer and radioactive contamination of the food chain. In 1983 a group of eminent scientists initiated a controversial debate by predicting that a "nuclear winter" that could threaten the continued existence of human civilization might result from even a limited nuclear conflict.

Perhaps, as some political analysts suggest, the realignment of power following the demise of the Soviet Union has reduced the threat of nuclear war. Unfortunately, we have recently learned from the Persian Gulf War that modern, *conventional*, nonnuclear war can also produce catastrophic ecological damage. The intentional release of huge quantities of petroleum into the Persian Gulf and the ignition of the vast Kuwaiti oil fields produced severe water and air pollution problems whose long-term effects are still being assessed. Several analysts have suggested that environmental factors will figure prominently as both causes and effects of future armed conflicts. Whether or not this proves to be the case, it is beyond doubt that solutions to the growing list of threats to global and regional ecosystems will require unprecedented efforts toward international cooperation.

PART 1

General Philosophical and Political Issues

People who regard themselves as environmentalists can be found on both sides of all the issues in this section. But the participants in these debates nonetheless strongly disagree —due to differences in personal values, political beliefs, and what they perceive as their own self-interests—on how best to prevent environmental degeneration.

Understanding the general issues raised in this initial section is useful preparation for examining the more specific controversies that follow in later sections.

- Should Environmental Regulations Be Replaced by Market-Based Strategies?

- Does Wilderness Have Intrinsic Value?

- Is the U.S. Endangered Species Act Fundamentally Sound?

- Should Environmental Policy Be Redesigned to Cure Environmental Racism?

- Is Limiting Population Growth a Key Factor in Protecting the Global Environment?

- Should Property Owners Be Compensated When Environmental Restrictions Limit Development?

1

ISSUE 1

Should Environmental Regulations Be Replaced by Market-Based Strategies?

YES: Lynn Scarlett, from "Evolutionary Ecology," *Reason* (May 1996)

NO: Brian Tokar, from "Trading Away the Earth: Pollution Credits and the Perils of 'Free Market Environmentalism,'" *Dollars and Sense* (March/April 1996)

ISSUE SUMMARY

YES: Reason Foundation vice president and environmental researcher Lynn Scarlett argues that traditional "top-down environmental regulation" does not serve the public interest and should be replaced by decentralized bargaining and market-based approaches.

NO: Author, college teacher, and environmental activist Brian Tokar maintains that pollution credits and other market-oriented environmental protection policies do nothing to reduce pollution; rather, they transfer the power to protect the environment from the public to large corporate polluters.

Following World War II, the United States and other developed nations experienced an explosive period of industrialization accompanied by an enormous increase in the use of fossil fuel energy sources and a rapid growth in the manufacture and use of new synthetic chemicals. Unfortunately, insufficient attention was paid to the release of combustion products and the safe disposal of waste materials. In response to growing public concern about the pollution and other forms of environmental deterioration resulting from this largely unregulated activity, the U.S. Congress passed the National Environmental Policy Act of 1969. This legislation included a commitment on the part of the government to take a much more active and aggressive role in protecting the environment. The next year, the Environmental Protection Agency was established to coordinate and oversee this effort. During the next two decades an unprecedented series of legislative acts and administrative rules were promulgated, placing stringent restrictions on industrial and commercial activities that might result in the pollution, degradation, or contamination of land, air, water, food, and the workplace.

This regulatory onslaught was strongly opposed by the affected business interests, who were not accustomed to such far-reaching restraints on their activities. The popularity of the environmental movement, however, precluded any serious political response to cries of overregulation until the very end of the 1970s, when Ronald Reagan took up the cause of getting the regulators off the backs of entrepreneurs in his first presidential campaign. Despite this rhetoric, Reagan's two terms in office were marked not by a repeal of environmental statutes but by a slowdown in the enactment of new restrictions and less vigorous enforcement of the laws that were already on the books.

Having failed to persuade the U.S. public that the movement to protect the environment has gone too far, those who believe that antipollution legislation seriously impedes industrial development have adopted a new set of strategies. The common theme is that what they refer to as "top-down, federal, command-and-control legislation" is not an appropriate or effective means of preventing ecological degradation. They propose instead a wide range of alternative tactics, many of which are designed to operate through the economic marketplace. The first significant congressional response to these proposals was the incorporation of tradeable pollution emission rights into the 1990 Clean Air Act amendments as an acceptable means for achieving the goals set for reducing acid rain–causing sulfur dioxide emissions.

Recognizing past difficulties in obtaining compliance with strict statutory pollution limits, some major mainstream environmental organizations have partly accepted the idea of using market-based schemes, such as the trading of pollution control credits or the imposition of pollution taxes. Many environmentalists, however, continue to oppose the idea of allowing anyone to pay to pollute, either on moral grounds or because they doubt that these tactics will actually control pollution. Supporters of the antiregulatory backlash movement have made more drastic proposals, such as increasing reliance on voluntary pollution controls by "green" corporations that are attempting to appeal to concerned consumers, or the radical decentralization of environmental preservation efforts. These have failed to gain either organizational or public support within the environmental community.

In the following selections, political scientist Lynn Scarlett argues that the public needs to be given greater opportunity to balance environmental protection goals against other personal and public needs and desires. She advocates decentralized decision making and the replacement of top-down regulation by a combination of voluntarism and market-based strategies. Environmental activist Brian Tokar uses the experience with sulfur dioxide pollution credit trading since 1993 to argue that such "free market environmentalism" tactics fail to reduce pollution and turn environmental protection into a commodity that corporate powers can manipulate for private profit.

YES
Lynn Scarlett

EVOLUTIONARY ECOLOGY

The 25th anniversary of Earth Day came and went last year, with little fanfare and no public demand for more environmental laws. The new Republican Congress tried, and mostly failed, to enact reforms designed to lessen the burden of environmental regulation. Behind the scenes and in public forums, various schools of environmental reform debated and discussed. They talked cost-benefit analysis and "takings" compensation, emissions trading and "win-win" environmentalism. They disagreed about many things, including basic principles. But there was general consensus about two ideas: that environmental goals are important, and that the current structure of regulation isn't that great.

Environmental policy is finally growing up. But to make genuine improvements, rather than merely tinker around the edges, we first need to understand where the demand for environmental regulation comes from, and where it went wrong. And we need a vision of how environmental policy might be set right—of the general principles and concepts that might guide a new environmentalism.

Environmentalism is not, as its critics sometimes portray it, simply a New Age ideology foisted upon an unwilling public. The environmental *movement* has important ideological components, but the demand for cleaner air and water or for wilderness and species preservation is not that different from the demand for any other good. As living standards rise, people want to buy more environmental "goods." Pollution is as old as human activity, but only recently have we been rich enough to worry about it.

Looking across countries, University of Chicago economist Don Coursey finds a clear correlation between increased wealth, measured by per capita GDP, and increased allegiance to environmental protection. As incomes rise, per capita expenditures on pollution control increase—a phenomenon Coursey observes in most advanced industrialized nations. The amount of land set aside for protection also rises with GDP. Green groups may decry economic growth, but it is growth itself that makes environmental protection possible and popular.

Coursey's work also points up a fact often forgotten in public discussions: "The environment" is not an all-or-nothing good, but a bundle of different goods. In surveys, he asks people to indicate how much they'd be willing to spend to preserve different species. The results are wildly varied. Animals like the bald eagle and grizzly bear consistently rank high, while spiders, beetles, snakes, and snails are barely valued. The varied costs of real-world regulations reflect this distinction: Coursey calculates the amount spent to preserve a single Florida panther at $4.8 million, compared to a mere $1.17 to preserve a single Painted Snake Coil Forest Snail.

Political maneuvering may produce such disparate results, but the law does not actually recognize such distinctions, or the implicit tradeoffs they express. It declares species protection, like many other environmental goods, an absolute. Early environmentalist thinking—influential to this day—did not recognize environmental values as some goods among many but rather proclaimed them preeminent: Earth First! A California regulator describes his state's water policy this way: "If Mother Nature didn't put it in, you had to take it out—everything—that was the goal. This drove us to rigid, grossly exuberant attempts at clean up."

This absolutism suggests one way that environmental policy went wrong. It did not recognize that quality of life resides in pursuit of multiple values. People seek shelter, nourishment, health, security, learning, fairness, companionship, freedom, and personal comfort together with environmental protection. They even seek many, sometimes competing, environmental goals. They don't agree on how to marshal their resources (and time) in pursuit of these many goals.

And it is often difficult for outsiders—or even individuals themselves—to know in advance how they would prefer to trade off among different values.

Competing values are not unique to the environmental arena. In fact, people make such tradeoffs every day. They also deal with another conundrum of environmental policy: the "knowledge problem."

On the one hand, environmental problems involve matters of "general" knowledge, scientific knowledge of facts that are constant across time and space. In some cases, the general knowledge is a matter of settled understanding: the boiling point of water, for instance, or the bonding patterns of chemicals. In others, it is a matter of ongoing research and scientific contention. General knowledge includes such still-controversial issues as the health hazards of various substances or the effects of CFCs [chlorofluorocarbons] on the ozone layer. Much environmental debate takes place over issues of general knowledge, and these questions are important. But they aren't the whole story.

* * *

Environmental problems and problem solving also often involve "specific" knowledge—the knowledge of time, place, and experience described by Nobel laureate F.A. Hayek in "The Use of Knowledge in Society." This information varies by circumstance and location and may change over time. Specific knowledge is decentralized—it resides on the factory floor, at a particular Superfund site, or on a specific farm.

The impacts of a landfill in a desert will differ from those near the Florida Everglades. Emitting effluent into a fast-moving stream is different from emitting waste into a pond. Using two coats of paint will have different effects than using just one coat. Resource use and emissions associated with cloth and disposable diapers will depend on how many are used each day, what kinds of disposal systems are available, and where those systems are located. Nor are environmental effects the only important specific knowledge relevant to environmental issues—tradeoffs between environmental goods and other goods may vary from situation to situation. These kinds of details do not reside in the minds of bureaucrats in Washington. Yet it is this kind of knowledge that is often most relevant to understanding environmental problems and possible remedies.

Again, there is nothing unique to environmental issues about the knowledge problem. It is a fundamental aspect of human life, something people cope with all the time.

If, for instance, an environment-loving outdoorsman wishes to equip himself for mountain climbing, he may need to buy a special jacket (among much other gear). Deciding what to buy requires tradeoffs: First, he's devoting his financial resources to a jacket, rather than to something else, and his free time to mountain climbing. Then he must decide what characteristics he wants: how much insulation, how much durability, what sort of pockets or hood, and so on—all keeping in mind the continuing tradeoff between money he spends on the jacket and money he could spend on something else. He looks at brand names and reputations. He finds out what sort of return policies and customer service the jacket maker has.

The outdoorsman has specific knowledge. He knows what mountains he wishes to climb, and at what time of year. He knows whether he's an occasional climber, or a devotee. He knows whether he wants a lot of help from a sales clerk, or simply the best price. He knows his size and his favorite color. The jacket maker, too, has specific knowledge: of supplies, of tradeoffs between design features and costs, of distribution channels, of changing patterns of demand. No one centrally decides a single jacket policy for all U.S. mountain climbers....

Environmental goods present special challenges because of the characteristics of these goods. But meeting those challenges has been unnecessarily difficult. For too long environmental policy has been shaped by people who demanded that environmental values trump all other considerations and who assumed that a regulatory elite possessed all necessary knowledge. Rather than figuring out how to perfect or create institutions that would allow a market for environmental goods to develop and flourish, they have been bent on opposing and destroying markets. They have seen markets not as processes for addressing values and conveying knowledge but as symbols of base commercialism and greed. This moralistic approach is finally fading. We can now begin to examine what sorts of institutions different environmental goods require—to explore a new environmental vision.

* * *

For 20 years, some of the most effective proponents of "free market environmentalism" have come out of the New Resource Economics school of thought. These economists, mostly based in the Western United States, focus on the environmental goods most easily incorporated into traditional institutions of property rights—and, perhaps not coincidentally, the oldest areas of U.S. environmental policy, dating back to the Progressive Era. Their starting premise is that individuals are predominantly self-interested. New Resource Economics then explores how different ownership settings and decision-making institutions shape incentives for stewardship.

"Actual or potential owners have incentives to use their resources efficiently," write economists Richard Stroup and John Baden, neatly summing up their thesis. Owners enjoy the fruits of efficient resource use and land stewardship through enhanced returns on their investment and maintenance of their property's value over time.

Environmental problems arise, in this model, when resources are unowned. This is the famous "tragedy of the commons," in which resources are "owned" by everyone and thus effectively by no one, because they can be used indiscriminately by everyone. Each person has an incentive to consume as much as possible, as fast as possible, rather than to preserve and protect resources for future use. According to this view, institutions, not perverse people, are the genesis of environmental problems.

"The same people who nearly destroyed the buffalo population," write Stroup and Baden, "posed no threat to the more valuable beef cattle raised on the western range. In that instance more clearly defined property rights resulted in the proliferation of beef cattle while the imperfect, if not altogether absent, property rights to the buffalo led to its near elimination."

Translated into policy, the insights of these economists encourage experiments in market creation. Environmental writer Tom Wolf describes a "Ranching for Wildlife" program in Colorado that borrows from the ideas of New Resource Economists. In the Sangre de Cristo Mountains, elk on public and private lands compete with cattle for forage. The challenge, suggests Wolf, is "to figure out how ranchers can capture value from the elk."

Hunters will pay as much as $8,000 for a license to hunt a trophy elk. But until Colorado passed its Ranching for Wildlife program, landowners were unable to take part in potential revenue from sale of hunting licenses. To cattle ranchers, then, elk were merely pests. Under Ranching for Wildlife, the state still "owns" the wildlife, but owners of large ranches can auction off, at whatever price the market will bear, a designated number of hunting licenses that guarantee trophy elk. The program, in effect, has partially privatized elk-hunting rights. Participating ranch owners now manage their lands to provide suitable habitat for elk. They also guard vigilantly against poaching of young bull elk.

One of the advantages of "privatizing" resource and land-use decisions through various property rights arrangements is that these arrangements reduce the need for consensus. Goals, such as wilderness preservation, can be pursued through private land purchases that, unlike public preservation activities, do not require majority voter approval.

Wedding their work to the pioneering work of Nobel laureate economist James Buchanan and Gordon Tullock on "public choice theory," the New Resource Economists are also able to explain some of the perversities that keep surfacing in public lands management. The U.S. Forest Service, for instance, has incentives enshrined in law that encourage it to allow large-scale timber cutting even when the logging costs more than the Forest Service takes in. Because bureaucrats have no rights to the resources they manage, Stroup and Baden argue, "Even when [they] are highly trained, competent, and well intended, the information and incentives they face do not encourage either sensitive or efficient resource management."

* * *

Most environmental issues are not, however, quite that simple. Incentives and self-interest are always present, but they are not the whole story.

Markets work for jackets and, with a little work, for elk because these goods have certain characteristics that make transactions relatively simple. It's possible to clearly specify who owns what, to identify buyers and sellers, and to convey all the necessary information for trades to take place. As a result, the market operates as a discovery process to address the knowledge and value problems—and to encourage improvements over time, such as better jacket brands or improved elk forage.

In other cases, however, things aren't so clearly defined. There are frictions: hard-to-divide goods, parties too numerous or scattered to be identified, vital information that isn't easily shared or easily known, blurry property lines. Institutions must evolve to deal with these hard cases.

One such institution is the common law. The common-law approach asks, "What happens when one person's sphere of activity conflicts with another person's?" The result is a focus on the concepts of liability, nuisance, and trespass; the role of courts in evaluating harms and benefits; and their role in resolving conflicts by clarifying the scope of different intersecting rights.

This blurry realm is not confined to a few difficult air pollution problems

(and, in fact, common law may not work well for air pollution). Anywhere people congregate, conflicts emerge over sights, smells, and physical invasions that include everything from factory smoke to ugly houses to one neighbor's leaves falling on another's yard. They also include potentially big nuisances such as toxic air emissions or discharges of waste into water bodies.

The common-law framework offers a means of further clarifying rights and refining just what "enjoyment and use" of one's property means. It is thus both a mechanism for conflict resolution and a means of discovering the scope and limit of rights.

Consider an apartment building with a noisy air-conditioning unit that disturbs a neighbor. Asked for injunctive relief, one tool of common law, the court may emphasize the neighbor's rights, requiring the apartment owner to eliminate the air conditioner noise—unless the neighbor agrees to some other arrangement. Or it may assign the owner the rights, declaring that the neighbor must put up with the noise unless he can make a deal with the owner. In actual conflicts, injunctive relief usually balances the two interests. "The law of nuisance," says Chicago economist Coursey, "actually would tend to use a rule that looked like a combination...: the apartment owner may make noise with impunity up to some critical level, and, if the apartment owner makes more than the critical level of noise, the single family may obtain an order of the court directing the apartment owner to reduce the noise down to the critical level." ...

Common-law tradition embodies a discovery process that clarifies and refines rights boundaries and obligations in those blurry realms where different sets of rights intersect. Common law tends to follow precedent, and precedent can only be disturbed by private parties bringing new cases with slightly different circumstances or new arguments. As the law gets better and better at maximizing the welfare of the parties in a particular kind of case, fewer and fewer such cases will be brought. As a result, the common law tends to settle on fairly efficient rules—those that make the value pie larger. Private parties then bargain "in the shadow" of settled law, dividing a larger pie than they would under rules not tested over time.

Common law, write economists Bruce Yandle and Roger Meiners, "continues to evolve. Changing preferences and improved understanding of pollution problems continuously enter the arena of law." And, unlike statutes, common law takes into account the particular circumstances of specific situations.

* * *

The common law can work to mediate disputes between discrete, identifiable parties. But, concede Yandle and Meiners, "It is hard to imagine how common law could address urban auto emission control, ozone layer problems, and global warming, to the extent that the science of those problems becomes more settled." In such cases, it is much too difficult to identify a clear-cut "polluter" and a clear-cut "plaintiff." Either most people fall simultaneously into both categories or the cost of dividing the environmental good—clean air, an undisturbed ozone layer, etc.—is much too high (sometimes approaching infinity).

Yet the problems of knowledge and values remain, and so does the demand for environmental goods. The trick for environmental reformers is to develop a vision of evolving institutions that permits different sorts of institutions to address different kinds of issues, and to do so at the appropriate decision-making level. It helps to think of this challenge as a sequence of interrelated questions, a decision tree based on the characteristics of the particular environmental goods involved.

In some cases, what is needed is not political rule making but business institutions, analogous to standard sizes and outdoor-equipment trade shows. In these cases, environmental goods are divisible, rights are assignable, and we are in the ordinary realm of markets, where entrepreneurs are rewarded for finding ways to address the knowledge and value problems effectively. Here the only issue is allowing time for institutions to evolve on their own.

Markets for some recyclables, for instance, are hampered because buyers and sellers sometimes lack information about available supplies and demand, and uniform quality is not guaranteed. These problems resemble those of many farm commodities in the 1800s. One remedy is to mimic the experience of corn farmers a century ago: Establish a coordinated process for trading in recyclables. The recent creation of electronic listing of some recyclables with the Chicago Board of Trade is a first step in this direction.

This approach differs markedly from political activists' calls to mandate recycled content in products. Those proposed mandates simply override the specific knowledge of circumstances so critical to efficient resource use. For example, mandating high levels of recycled content in certain paperboard products can require adding extra virgin (nonwaste) fiber to maintain adequate strength of the paperboard. The result is a heavier product that uses more total fiber.

Often, however, environmental goods are indivisible and present challenges to ordinary markets. Faced with these "market failures," the traditional response from the green movement has been to substitute government coercion for individual choice. Yet absolutist regulation that suppresses knowledge and imposes a single value hierarchy is not the only way to achieve such goals as clean air. It is possible to create evolvable institutions that, while they are not as simple or politically neutral as traditional markets, capture much relevant information about knowledge and values.

Traditional regulations, such as technology prescriptions and resource-use mandates, ignore the location-specific and ever-changing information critical to all production and consumption decisions. Performance standards, by contrast, allow individuals and firms to figure out how best to achieve the stated standards: to lower overall air pollution to a certain level, for instance. This is the central insight of economists who have articulated the case for market-oriented regulations like the tradeable permits scheme set forth in the 1990 Clean Air Act Amendments.

Tradeable permit schemes and pollution charges provide flexibility to producers (and consumers, in the case of vehicle emission charges) that should, in the long run, result in more efficient responses to air pollution problems. These approaches still require top-down goal-setting, and they are still therefore subject to political pressures that don't affect the market for jackets. In setting such standards, general scientific knowledge is critical, and often a matter of dispute.

But the problem of indivisibility— especially in the case of air pollution— makes some sort of collective goal-setting inevitable. The number of affected parties makes common-law approaches or voluntary bargaining cumbersome, given today's technologies. What is attractive about tradeable permit schemes is their potential to prepare the groundwork for creating enforceable "clean air rights" over time. For this to happen, however, legislators need to eliminate all the current language that insists these pollution credits are not rights—language that renders investment in such credits uncertain.

* * *

Tradeable permits and pollution charges are promising mechanisms. But even if we decide they are the right mechanisms to address a certain environmental problem, we still must ask who the affected parties are—who is breathing the air in question—and where, then, the goal-setting ought to be done. For three decades, we've taken for granted the idea that there should be one single environmental standard for the whole nation. But understanding the roles of knowledge and values in defining and pricing environmental goods suggests that that may not be the case. For some problems, impacts are strictly local and narrowly circumscribed. Other environmental problems may impose regional, or even global, impacts. The locus of impact should help determine where decision-making authority resides.

If most relevant knowledge is location-specific and dynamic, decisions about "how clean is clean" and what remedies to use should take place closest to where the problem occurs. For air-emission problems, that might mean a local air basin. For decisions about siting a hazardous waste facility, that might mean bargaining between landowners adjacent to the site and the site owner.

The rationale for using decentralized bargaining approaches to address environmental problems lies not with any mystical faith that small is always beautiful, nor with the now-faddish notion that all that is good must come from communities. The rationale for these approaches builds, instead, on two premises. One is the importance of decentralized information in understanding and remedying environmental problems. The other is the importance of finding ways for real people affected by real conflicts of social space to undertake their own balancing act among competing values....

Political edicts directing communities to site landfills are one possible remedy. But such edicts simply override the concerns and preferences of affected individuals. Bargaining between would-be landfill operators and local communities offers another option—one already used by waste management companies. Sometimes called YIMBY-FAP (yes, in my backyard, for a price), these arrangements involve negotiations in which landfill operators offer a package of protections and benefits, including compensation, to affected landowners—or sometimes entire communities—in exchange for permission to site a landfill. The costs of the landfill are thus borne by all its customers, rather than only the property owners in the surrounding area. (The same principle applies in legal reforms aimed at requiring government "takings" compensation to landowners who bear the cost of such policies as wetlands protection. Society as a whole is buying an environmental good, and all the "purchasers" should bear the cost.)...

Technocratically minded environmental reformers fear that public perceptions will yield irrational demands, driving up costs to solve environmental problems—whether those problems involve building landfills or cleaning up Superfund sites. Those fears do not appear to be justified in circumstances where citizens face *both* the risks associated with a facility and enjoy directly the benefits—in the form of lower costs or higher compensation—associated with a particular remedy. Bargaining itself may serve as a discovery process, revealing more accurate information about both risks and benefits.

Unbounded fears may, in fact, be more likely to drive decisions toward "zero risk" in centralized decision processes. There, the costs of decisions are spread over an entire population, while the benefits from pursuing pristine clean-ups are enjoyed by those few near a particular site. The few then have an incentive to invest heavily in lobbying, while the many do not—with obvious results. Experience with many EPA regulations, and the very high cost per year of life saved associated with those regulations, confirms this observation.

The contrast between costly Superfund site clean-ups, which have occurred in a top-down, regulatory framework directed by the EPA, and more recent local remediation of abandoned industrial sites, through negotiated settlements offers further testament to this point. Processes that create closer links between those who pay for clean-up costs and those who enjoy the benefits of clean-up offer a discipline missing from traditional top-down approaches. The locally negotiated clean-ups have, in general, been achieved at a fraction of the cost for Superfund sites.

* * *

Not all indivisible environmental problems will be well-suited to collective-negotiation processes, however. In a very imperfect world, sometimes national, state, or local restrictions may be the best we can do.

What distinguishes these circumstances? They involve a high degree of public consensus—even among the regulated parties—that limits or "injunctions" against the activity are appropriate. These are those very rare cases in which everyone would be better off if an environmentally damaging practice were ended, but where there will always be incentives to "cheat" unless a restriction can be enforced by law.

Most environmental problems do not share these characteristics, but some problems may come close—as in the use and discharge of acute, well-understood toxins into the air or water. Consider two examples: the case of the "mad hatter" and the problem of cadmium discharges into water in Japan. The term "mad hatter" came from the severe effects of using mercury in the hatter's trade to make felt hats. And in 1950s Japan, mining operations discharged cadmium into water that eventually found its way into the food supply, causing Itai-Itai ("ouch-ouch") disease that results in demineralization of bones. When the source of the disease was pinpointed in 1968, the Japanese government set strict effluent standards for cadmium and prohibited consumption of rice with cadmium concentrations above a specific standard.

In each of these cases, uniform standards on the handling, use, or disposal of these materials might reduce harm, coincide with broad-based public values, and lessen transaction costs associated with case-by-case bargaining or court remedies. In effect, a legal ban enforces a cartel, in which everyone in the industry is able to stop using the dangerous chemicals because they know their competitors will have to stop, too.

Such standards need not always emerge through government actions. When acute problems of this kind become known, the marketplace itself sometimes moves to eliminate use of the offending toxins. For example, after it became clear that vapors from chromium-plating processes resulted in serious health problems for workers, the costs from worker compensation claims drove industries to find ways of safely containing the vapors.

The same kind of evolution occurred among dentists in their use of mercury amalgams. The government did not ban the use of such amalgams. However, dentists found ways of minimizing exposures to the mercury vapors created during the preparation of amalgams, and some dentists turned to substitutes. Trade associations, trade unions, professional organizations, and consumer groups often promote these kinds of changes by monitoring safety issues relevant to their members.

Whether uniform standards ought to be considered will be a function of the level of consensus regarding whether some action should be taken; the clarity of knowledge about the causation of a problem; and the level of risk associated with the problem. Where problems are indivisible, risks posed by the problem are extremely high, and causes of those risks are well-understood, public rules offer a plausible solution.

* * *

Clearly, an environmental vision based on evolving institutions will not please everyone. It acknowledges tradeoffs among values, and it admits both the necessity and the limits of political decision making—positions guaranteed to upset both traditional environmentalists and free market absolutists. It does not promise a perfect world, merely a slowly improving one. And it faces squarely the underlying problem with current environmental regulations: Centralized, top-down rule making is ill-suited to addressing environmental problems in a complex, dynamic world in which most relevant information is location-specific and different people have very different priorities.

Applying such a vision cannot be a matter of waving a single legislative wand. Three decades of statutes have created layer upon layer of regulations. But Congress could start with a few basic reforms. The National Environmental Policy Institute is exploring ways to craft a single statute that would phase in devolution of most environmental decisions to states. The concept is worth pursuing. Devolution to states does not really go far enough, since, ultimately, what is needed is further decentralization to local communities and, where feasible, privatization of environmental decisions. But devolution to the states is a good place to start in any reform agenda.

Similarly, Congress needs to get the EPA out of the business of prospectively approving state and local environmental protection programs. Under the Clean Air Act, for example, Congress sets air-emission standards and states are delegated responsibility for developing State Implementation Plans. Using computer models and other criteria, the EPA assesses those plans to determine whether they comply with federal law. States get full emission-reduction "credits" when the EPA's computer models show a state program achieving over time some estimated pollution reduction. But this means the EPA's assumptions about everything from population growth to commuting patterns, not actual pollution levels, determine the outcome. The process prevents experimentation. It locks states into using technologies or programs that the EPA thinks—but has not necessarily demonstrated—will work. Eliminating the prospective approval process would give states the latitude to design programs they believe will achieve emission reductions, and to evaluate and adjust those programs based on real-world data.

Above all, what is needed is a fundamental shift away from an approach that is primarily regulatory and punitive to one that emphasizes bargaining, improvement in information flows, and incentives for stewardship. The 1995 House proposals regarding takings compensation are essential to realigning the incentive equation.

Turning environmental policy in the direction of more bargaining is likely to require experimentation and many varied measures. But a place to start is in revising approaches to environmental enforcement. Current approaches have blurred any distinctions between intent and accident; the line between civil and criminal cases is not always clear; sentencing guidelines bear little logical relationship to the scope of alleged crimes.

In recent soul-searching, business leaders and legislators who led the 1995 regulatory reform effort of the 104th Congress opined that their reform vision was the right one. It was, they concluded, only their message that was inadequate. This self-appraisal is too generous.

Their message was inadequate *because* their vision was not well thought out. Pieces of that vision—such as the need to realign private incentives through takings compensation—were on target. But bills to require cost-benefit analysis and risk assessment really targeted only a symptom—high costs and skewed goals—without looking at the more fundamental problem. Would-be reformers adopted a mirror image of their opponents' technocratic, top-down approach without thinking seriously about how to ensure environmental protection in a world in which environmental goods are widely valued.

The movement toward environmental reform will not, however, disappear. And, in the long run, the past year's setbacks may provide an important opportunity: an occasion to reflect seriously not only on the politics of environmental regulation but on the alternatives to traditional methods. We have a chance to get it right this time, but only if we are willing to invest in developing a dynamic vision.

NO

Brian Tokar

TRADING AWAY THE EARTH: POLLUTION CREDITS AND THE PERILS OF "FREE MARKET ENVIRONMENTALISM"

The Republican takeover of Congress has unleashed an unprecedented assault on all forms of environmental regulation. From the Endangered Species Act to the Clean Water Act and the Superfund for toxic waste cleanup, laws that may need to be strengthened and expanded to meet the environmental challenges of the next century are instead being targeted for complete evisceration.

For some activists, this is a time to renew the grassroots focus of environmental activism, even to adopt a more aggressively anti-corporate approach that exposes the political and ideological agendas underlying the current backlash. But for many, the current impasse suggests that the movement must adapt to the dominant ideological currents of the time. Some environmentalists have thus shifted their focus toward voluntary programs, economic incentives and the mechanisms of the "free market" as means to advance the cause of environmental protection. Among the most controversial, and widespread, of these proposals are tradeable credits for the right to emit pollutants. These became enshrined in national legislation in 1990 with President George Bush's amendments to the 1970 Clean Air Act.

Even in 1990, "free market environmentalism" was not a new phenomenon. In the closing years of the 1980s, an odd alliance had developed among corporate public relations departments, conservative think tanks such as the American Enterprise Institute, Bill Clinton's Democratic Leadership Council (DLC), and mainstream environmental groups such as the Environmental Defense Fund. The market-oriented environmental policies promoted by this eclectic coalition have received little public attention, but have nonetheless significantly influenced debates over national policy.

Glossy catalogs of "environmental products," television commercials featuring environmental themes, and high profile initiatives to give corporate officials a "greener" image are the hallmarks of corporate environmentalism in the 1990s. But the new market environmentalism goes much further

From Brian Tokar, "Trading Away the Earth: Pollution Credits and the Perils of 'Free Market Environmentalism,'" *Dollars and Sense* (March/April 1996). Copyright © 1996 by Economic Affairs Bureau, Inc. Reprinted by permission. *Dollars and Sense* is a progressive economics magazine published six times a year. First-year subscriptions cost $18.95 and may be ordered by writing to *Dollars and Sense*, One Summer St., Somerville, MA 02143.

than these showcase efforts. It represents a wholesale effort to recast environmental protection based on a model of commercial transactions within the marketplace. "A new environmentalism has emerged," writes economist Robert Stavins, who has been associated with both the Environmental Defense Fund and the DLC's Progressive Policy Institute, "that embraces... market-oriented environmental protection policies."

Today, aided by the anti-regulatory climate in Congress, market schemes such as trading pollution credits are granting corporations new ways to circumvent environmental concerns, even as the same firms try to pose as champions of the environment. While tradeable credits are sometimes presented as a solution to environmental problems, in reality they do nothing to reduce pollution—at best they help businesses reduce the costs of complying with limits on toxic emissions. Ultimately, such schemes abdicate control over critical environmental decisions to the very same corporations that are responsible for the greatest environmental abuses.

HOW IT WORKS, AND DOESN'T

A close look at the scheme for nationwide emissions trading reveals a particular cleverness; for true believers in the invisible hand of the market, it may seem positively ingenious. Here is how it works: The 1990 Clean Air Act amendments were designed to halt the spread of acid rain, which has threatened lakes, rivers and forests across the country. The amendments required a reduction in the total sulfur dioxide emissions from fossil fuel burning power plants, from 19 to just under 9 million tons per year by the year 2000. These facilities were targeted as the largest contributors to acid rain, and participation by other industries remains optional. To achieve this relatively modest goal for pollution reduction, utilities were granted transferable allowances to emit sulfur dioxide in proportion to their current emissions. For the first time, the ability of companies to buy and sell the "right" to pollute was enshrined in U.S. law.

Any facility that continued to pollute more than its allocated amount (roughly half of its 1990 rate) would then have to buy allowances from someone who is polluting less. The 110 most polluting facilities (mostly coal burners) were given five years to comply, while all the others would have until the year 2000. Emissions allowances were expected to begin selling for around $500 per ton of sulfur dioxide, and have a theoretical ceiling of $2000 per ton, which is the legal penalty for violating the new rules. Companies that could reduce emissions for less than their credits are worth would be able to sell them at a profit, while those that lag behind would have to keep buying credits at a steadily rising price. For example, before pollution trading every company had to comply with environmental regulations, even if it cost one firm twice as much as another to do so. Under the new system, a firm could instead choose to exceed the mandated levels, purchasing credits from the second firm instead of implementing costly controls. This exchange would save money, but in principle yield the same overall level of pollution as if both companies had complied equally. Thus, it is argued, market forces will assure that the most cost-effective means of reducing acid rain will be implemented first, saving the economy billions of dollars in "excess" pollution control costs.

Defenders of the Bush plan claimed that the ability to profit from pollution credits would encourage companies to invest more in new environmental technologies than before. Innovation in environmental technology, they argued, was being stifled by regulations mandating specific pollution control methods. With the added flexibility of tradeable credits, companies could postpone costly controls—through the purchase of some other company's credits—until new technologies became available. Proponents argued that, as pollution standards are tightened over time, the credits would become more valuable and their owners could reap large profits while fighting pollution.

Yet the program also included many pages of rules for extensions and substitutions. The plan eliminated requirements for backup systems on smokestack scrubbers, and then eased the rules for estimating how much pollution is emitted when monitoring systems fail. With reduced emissions now a marketable commodity, the range of possible abuses may grow considerably, as utilities will have a direct financial incentive to manipulate reporting of their emissions to improve their position in the pollution credits market.

Once the EPA actually began auctioning pollution credits in 1993, it became clear that virtually nothing was going according to their projections. The first pollution credits sold for between $122 and $310, significantly less than the agency's estimated minimum price, and by 1995, bids at the EPA's annual auction of sulfur dioxide allowances averaged around $130 per ton of emissions. As an artificial mechanism superimposed on existing regulatory structures, emissions allowances have failed to reflect the true cost of pollution controls. So, as the value of the credits has fallen, it has become increasingly attractive to buy credits rather than invest in pollution controls. And, in problem areas air quality can continue to decline, as companies in some parts of the country simply buy their way out of pollution reductions.

At least one company has tried to cash in on the confusion by assembling packages of "multi-year streams of pollution rights" specifically designed to defer or supplant purchases of new pollution control technologies. "What a scrubber really is, is a decision to buy a 30-year stream of allowances," John B. Henry of Clean Air Capital Markets told the *New York Times,* with impeccable financial logic. "If the price of allowances declines in future years," paraphrased the *Times,* "the scrubber would look like a bad buy."

Where pollution credits have been traded between companies, the results have often run counter to the program's stated intentions. One of the first highly publicized deals was a sale of credits by the Long Island Lighting Company to an unidentified company located in the Midwest, where much of the pollution that causes acid rain originates. This raised concerns that places suffering from the effects of acid rain were shifting "pollution rights" to the very region it was coming from. One of the first companies to bid for additional credits, the Illinois Power Company, canceled construction of a $350 million scrubber system in the city of Decatur, Illinois. "Our compliance plan is based almost totally on purchase of credits," an Illinois Power spokesperson told the *Wall Street Journal.* The comparison with more traditional forms of commodity trading came full circle in 1991, when the government announced that the entire system for trading and auctioning emissions allowances would be administered by the Chicago Board of Trade, long famous for its ever-frantic markets in everything from grain futures and pork bellies to foreign currencies.

Some companies have chosen not to engage in trading pollution credits, proceeding with pollution control projects, such as the installation of new scrubbers, that were planned before the credits became available. Others have switched to low-sulfur coal and increased their use of natural gas. If the 1990 Clean Air Act amendments are to be credited for any overall improvement in the air quality, it is clearly the result of these efforts and not the market in tradeable allowances.

Yet while some firms opt not to purchase the credits, others, most notably North Carolina-based Duke Power, are aggressively buying allowances. At the 1995 EPA auction, Duke Power alone bought 35% of the short-term "spot" allowances for sulfur dioxide emissions, and 60% of the long-term allowances redeemable in the years 2001 and 2002. Seven companies, including five utilities and two brokerage firms, bought 97% of the short term allowances that were auctioned in 1995, and 92% of the longer-term allowances, which are redeemable in 2001 and 2002. This gives these companies significant leverage over the future shape of the allowances market.

The remaining credits were purchased by a wide variety of people and organizations, including some who sincerely wished to take pollution allowances out of circulation. Students at several law schools raised hundreds of dollars, and a group at the Glens Falls Middle School on Long Island raised $3,171 to purchase 21 allowances, equivalent to 21 tons of sulfur dioxide emissions over the course of a year. Unfortunately, this represented less than a tenth of one percent of the allowances auctioned off in 1995.

Some of these trends were predicted at the outset. "With a tradeable permit system, technological improvement will normally result in lower control costs and falling permit prices, rather than declining emissions levels," wrote Robert Stavins and Brad Whitehead (a Cleveland-based management consultant with ties to the Rockefeller Foundation) in a 1992 policy paper published by the Progressive Policy Institute. Despite their belief that market-based environmental policies "lead automatically to the cost-effective allocation of the pollution control burden among firms," they are quite willing to concede that a tradeable permit system will not in itself reduce pollution. As the actual pollution levels still need to be set by some form of regulatory mandate, the market in tradeable allowances merely gives some companies greater leverage over how pollution standards are to be implemented.

Without admitting the underlying irrationality of a futures market in pollution, Stavins and Whitehead do acknowledge (albeit in a footnote to an Appendix) that the system can quite easily be compromised by large companies' "strategic behavior." Control of 10% of the market, they suggest, might be enough to allow firms to engage in "price-setting behavior," a goal apparently sought by companies such as Duke Power. To the rest of us, it should be clear that if pollution credits are like any other commodity that can be bought, sold and traded, then the largest "players" will have substantial control over the entire "game." Emissions trading becomes yet another way to assure that large corporate interests will remain free to threaten public health and ecological survival in their unchallenged pursuit of profit.

TRADING THE FUTURE

Mainstream groups like the Environmental Defense Fund (EDF) continue to throw their full support behind the trading of emissions allowances, including the establishment of a futures market in Chicago. EDF senior economist Daniel Dudek described the trading of acid rain emissions as a "scale model" for a much more ambitious plan to trade emissions of carbon dioxide and other gases responsible for global warming. This plan was unveiled shortly after the passage of the 1990 Clean Air Act amendments, and was endorsed by then-Senator Al Gore as a way to "rationalize investments" in alternatives to carbon dioxide-producing activities.

International emissions trading gained further support via a U.N. Conference on Trade and Development study issued in 1992. The report was co-authored by Kidder and Peabody executive and Chicago Board of Trade director Richard Sandor, who told the *Wall Street Journal*, "Air and water are simply no longer the 'free goods' that economists once assumed. They must be redefined as property rights so that they can be efficiently allocated."

Radical ecologists have long decried the inherent tendency of capitalism to turn everything into a commodity; here we have a rare instance in which the system fully reveals its intentions. There is little doubt that an international market in "pollution rights" would widen existing inequalities among nations. Even within the United States, a single large investor in pollution credits would be able to control the future development of many different industries. Expanded to an international scale, the potential for unaccountable manipulation of industrial policy by a few corporations would easily compound the disruptions already caused by often reckless international traders in stocks, bonds and currencies.

However, as long as public regulation of industry remains under attack, tradeable credits and other such schemes will continue to be promoted as market-savvy alternatives. Along with an acceptance of pollution as "a by-product of modern civilization that can be regulated and reduced, but not eliminated," to quote another Progressive Policy Institute paper, self-proclaimed environmentalists will call for an end to "widespread antagonism toward corporations and a suspicion that anything supported by business was bad for the environment." Market solutions are offered as the only alternative to the "inefficient," "centralized," "command-and-control" regulations of the past, in language closely mirroring the rhetoric of Cold War anticommunism.

While specific technology-based standards can be criticized as inflexible and sometimes even archaic, critics choose to forget that in many cases, they were instituted by Congress as a safeguard against the widespread abuses of the Reagan-era EPA. During the Reagan years, "flexible" regulations opened the door to widely criticized—and often illegal—bending of the rules for the benefit of politically favored corporations, leading to the resignation of EPA administrator Anne Gorsuch Burford and a brief jail sentence for one of her more vocal legal assistants.

The anti-regulatory fervor of the present Congress is bringing a variety of other market-oriented proposals to the fore. Some are genuinely offered to further environmental protection, while others are far more cynical attempts to replace public regulations with virtual blank checks for polluters. Some have proposed a direct charge for pollution, modeled after the comprehensive pollution taxes that have proved popular in Western Europe. Writers as diverse as Supreme Court Justice Stephen Breyer, American Enterprise Institute economist Robert Hahn and environmental business guru Paul Hawken have defended pollution taxes as an ideal market-oriented approach to controlling pollution. Indeed, unlike tradeable credits, taxes might help reduce pollution beyond regulatory levels, as they encourage firms to control emissions as much as possible. With credits, there is no reduction in pollution below the threshold established in legislation. (If many companies were to opt for substantial new emissions controls, the market would soon be glutted and the allowances would rapidly become valueless.) And taxes would work best if combined with vigilant grassroots activism that makes industries accountable to the communities in which they operate. However, given the rapid dismissal of Bill Clinton's early plan for an energy tax, it is most likely that any pollution tax proposal would be immediately dismissed by Congressional ideologues as an outrageous new government intervention into the marketplace.

Air pollution is not the only environmental problem that free marketeers are proposing to solve with the invisible hand. Pro-development interests in Congress have floated various schemes to replace the Endangered Species Act with a system of voluntary incentives, conservation easements and other schemes through which landowners would be compensated by the government to pro-tect critical habitat. While these proposals are being debated in Congress, the Clinton administration has quietly changed the rules for administering the Act in a manner that encourages voluntary compliance and offers some of the very same loopholes that anti-environmental advocates have sought. This, too, is being offered in the name of cooperation and "market environmentalism."

Debates over the management of publicly-owned lands have inspired far more outlandish "free market" schemes. "Nearly all environmental problems are rooted in society's failure to adequately define property rights for some resource," economist Randal O'Toole has written, suggesting a need for "property rights for owls and salmon" developed to "protect them from pollution." O'Toole initially gained the attention of environmentalists in the Pacific Northwest for his detailed studies of the inequities of the U.S. Forest Service's long-term subsidy programs for logging on public lands. Now he has proposed dividing the National Forest system into individual units, each governed by its users and operated on a for-profit basis, with a portion of user fees allocated for such needs as the protection of biological diversity. Environmental values, from clean water to recreation to scenic views, should simply be allocated their proper value in the marketplace, it is argued, and allowed to out-compete unsustainable resource extraction. Other market advocates have suggested far more sweeping transfers of federal lands to the states, an idea seen by many in the West as a first step toward complete privatization.

Market enthusiasts like O'Toole repeatedly overlook the fact that ecological values are far more subjective than the market value of timber and minerals removed from public lands. Efforts to quantify these values are based on various sociological methods, market analysis and psychological studies. People are asked how much they would pay to protect a resource, or how much money they would accept to live without it, and their answers are compared with the prices of everything from wilderness expeditions to vacation homes. Results vary widely depending on how questions are asked, how knowledgeable respondents are, and what assumptions are made in the analysis. Environmentalists are rightfully appalled by such efforts as a recent Resources for the Future study designed to calculate the value of human lives lost due to future toxic exposures. Outlandish absurdities like property rights for owls arouse similar skepticism.

The proliferation of such proposals—and their increasing credibility in Washington—suggest the need for a renewed debate over the relationship between ecological values and those of the free market. For many environmental economists, the processes of capitalism, with a little fine tuning, can be made to serve the needs of environmental protection. For many activists, however, there is a fundamental contradiction between the interconnected nature of ecological processes and an economic system which not only reduces everything to isolated commodities, but seeks to manipulate those commodities to further the single, immutable goal of maximizing individual gain. An ecological economy may need to more closely mirror natural processes in their stability, diversity, long time frame, and the prevalence of cooperative, symbiotic interactions over the more extreme forms of competition that thoroughly dominate today's economy. Ultimately, communities of people need to reestablish social control over economic markets and relationships, restoring an economy which, rather than being seen as the engine of social progress, is instead, in the words of economic historian Karl Polanyi, entirely "submerged in social relationships."

Whatever economic model one proposes for the long-term future, it is clear that the current phase of corporate consolidation is threatening the integrity of the earth's living ecosystems—and communities of people who depend on those ecosystems—as never before. There is little room for consideration of ecological integrity in a global economy where a few ambitious currency traders can trigger the collapse of a nation's currency, its food supply, or a centuries-old forest ecosystem before anyone can even begin to discuss the consequences. In this kind of world, replacing our society's meager attempts to restrain and regulate corporate excesses with market mechanisms can only further the degradation of the natural world and threaten the health and well-being of all the earth's inhabitants.

POSTSCRIPT

Should Environmental Regulations Be Replaced by Market-Based Strategies?

Scarlett admits that her vision of a process whereby informed citizens can negotiate for the degree of environmental protection they desire, based on balancing ecological values against their other needs and concerns, requires a set of institutions and mechanisms that have not yet evolved. Even if we concur that such an evolution is a practical possibility, she still does not make it clear how we can prevent ecological degradation while her "dynamic vision" materializes. Although she advocates a common-law approach to resolve environmental disputes, Scarlett fails to acknowledge that in many rural jurisdictions, justices of the peace, often acting out of ignorance, rarely give any credence to environmental concerns in challenges to property rights claims. There are practical problems with the proposal to decentralize environmental decision making to state and local jurisdictions. Manufacturers of products that are sold regionally or nationally are more opposed to a patchwork of differing local regulations than to a single uniform set of restrictions. Furthermore, much of the environmental research needed to make scientifically valid decisions is beyond the resource capabilities of villages, towns, or even individual states. The evidence that Tokar cites, primarily based on short-term experience with trading in sulfur dioxide pollution credits, does not appear to justify the broad generalizations he makes about the inherent perils in market-based regulatory plans.

For two reports on the antienvironmental backlash by the majority party in the 104th Congress and the response by environmental activists, read "Anti-Environmental Blitzkrieg," by Cam Duncan, *Dollars and Sense* (March/April 1996) and "Greens vs. Congress: A Play-by-Play," by Phillip Shabecoff, *The Amicus Journal* (Fall 1996). Vicki Monks gives a strong defense of environmental regulations in "Environmental Regulations: Who Needs Them?" in the February/March 1996 issue of *National Wildlife,* whereas Fred L. Smith, Jr., in his speech "Survival Lessons," *Vital Speeches of the Day* (July 15, 1996), touts the free market while depicting environmentalism as an attack on industrial development.

In "Selling Air Pollution," *Reason* (May 1996), Brian Doherty supports the concept of pollution rights trading but argues that politics is interfering with its successful implementation. A strong denunciation of a specific pollution rights program is the subject of the December 8, 1994, news release "Environmentalists Reject Faulty Pollution Trading Program," available from the Environmental Defense Fund. Cautious support for the use of environmental taxes is the theme of Richard Morgenstern's article in the April 1996 issue of *Environment*. Voluntary industry environmental protection efforts like the Chemical Manufacturers Association's "Responsible Care" program, the Coalition for Environmentally Responsible Economies' (CERES) principles, and the International Chamber of Commerce's ISO 14000 program are presented in a favorable light by Jennifer Nash and John Ehrenfeld in the January/February 1996 issue of *Environment*. Conversely, in a feature article in the Summer 1996 issue of *The Amicus Journal*, David Helvarg cautions that corporate environmental programs often amount to meaningless public relations efforts.

The antienvironmental backlash has been promoted by several organizations with deceptive names, the most prominent of which is "Wise Use," which is heavily funded by forest products, mining, agricultural, and real estate interests. In his article "Determined Opposition," *Environment* (October 1995), Phil Brick argues that the populist appeal of such organizations represents a serious threat to environmentalism, and he suggests a strategy that the environmental movement should adopt as a response to this threat. The acceptance of large industrial contributions by major environmental organizations has a divisive effect on the environmental movement; Margaret Morgan Hubbard, director of the Environmental Action Foundation, discusses this concern in her article in the July/August 1996 issue of *Dollars and Sense*.

For an Internet site related to this issue, see http://www.nrdc.org/ bkgrd/lelawhis.html, which contains an essay by the Natural Resources Defense Council on the history of environmental regulation entitled "E-law: What Started It All?"

ISSUE 2

Does Wilderness Have Intrinsic Value?

YES: John Daniel, from "Toward Wild Heartlands," *Audubon* (September/October 1994)

NO: William Tucker, from "Is Nature Too Good for Us?" *Harper's Magazine* (March 1982)

ISSUE SUMMARY

YES: *Wilderness* magazine poetry editor John Daniel philosophizes that wilderness may help us to discern "the rightful limits of our place on this continent."

NO: William Tucker, a writer and social critic, asserts that wilderness areas are elitist preserves designed to keep people out.

The environmental destruction that resulted from the exploitation of natural resources for private profit during the founding of the United States and its early decades gave birth after the Civil War to the progressive conservation movement. Naturalists such as John Muir (1839–1914) and forester and politician Gifford Pinchot (1865–1946) worked to gain the support of powerful people who recognized the need for resource management. Political leaders such as Theodore Roosevelt (1858–1912) promoted legislation during the last quarter of the nineteenth century that led to the establishment of Yellowstone, Yosemite, and Mount Rainier national parks and the Adirondack Forest Preserve. This period also witnessed the founding of the Sierra Club and the Audubon Society, whose influential, upper-class members worked to promote the conservationist ethic.

Two conflicting positions on resource management emerged. Preservationists, like Muir, argued for the establishment of wilderness areas that would be off-limits to industrial or commercial development. Conservationists, like Roosevelt and Pinchot, supported the concept of "multiple use" of public lands, which permitted limited development and resource consumption to continue. The latter position prevailed and, under the Forest Management Act of 1897, mining, grazing, and lumbering were permitted on U.S. forest lands and were regulated through permits issued by the U.S. Forestry Division.

The first "primitive areas," where all development was prohibited, were designated in the 1920s. Aldo Leopold and Robert Marshall, two officers in the Forest Service, helped establish 70 such areas by administrative fiat. Leopold and Marshall did this in response to their own concerns about the failure of some of the National Forest Service's management practices. Many preservationists were heartened by this development, and the Wilderness Society was organized in 1935 to press for the preservation of additional undeveloped land.

It became increasingly apparent during the 1940s and 1950s that the administrative mechanism whereby land was designated as either available for development or off-limits was vulnerable. Because of pressure from commercial interests (lumber, mining, and so on), an increasing number of what were then called wilderness areas were lost through reclassification. This set the stage for an eight-year-long campaign that ended in 1964 with the passage of the Federal Wilderness Act. But this was by no means the end of the struggle. The process of implementing this legislation and determining which areas to set aside has been long and tortuous and will probably continue into the next century.

There are more clear-cut differences between values espoused by the opposing factions in the battle over wilderness preservation than in many other environmental conflicts. On one side are the naturalists who see undeveloped "wild" land as a precious resource, where people can go to seek solace and solitude—provided they do not leave their mark. On the opposite extreme are the entrepreneurs whose principal concern is the profit that can be made from utilizing the resources on these lands.

One consequence of the environmental movement has been the proliferation of studies that explore the impact of human developmental activities on remote, isolated regions of the globe. It has become apparent that industrial pollutants move through the air and water and find their way into every nook and cranny of the ecosphere. The notion of totally protecting any area of the Earth from contamination is an ideal that cannot be fully realized. This knowledge has increased the zeal of wilderness advocates who wish to minimize the impact of pollution on the few remaining relatively pristine ecosystems.

Advocates of wilderness preservation have also gained support from the growing recognition that protecting areas that are the habitats of many threatened species from destructive development may be the most effective means of achieving the vital goal of preserving biodiversity.

John Daniel is an award-winning essayist and the poetry editor of *Wilderness* magazine. In the following essay, written to celebrate the 30th anniversary of the enactment of the U.S. Wilderness Act, he warns that the preservation of wild places will ultimately depend on how we choose to live our lives. He questions the wisdom of defining as progress any technology that threatens to replace a real experience of nature with an artificial image. William Tucker, a writer who is critical of environmentalism, views the wilderness movement as elitist and the idea of excluding most human activity from wilderness areas as a consequence of a misguided, romantic, ecological ethic.

YES
John Daniel

TOWARD WILD HEARTLANDS

It has been 30 years since President Lyndon B. Johnson signed into law the most generous gesture we Americans have made toward the wild nature of this continent. The Wilderness Act of 1964 gave Congress the authority to declare certain unspoiled lands permanently off-limits to human occupation and development. Thus was born the National Wilderness Preservation System, which did the national park system one better. Wilderness allows no roads or vehicles—you enter on your own two feet, as explorers and settlers once entered the greater wilderness that was North America.

The wilderness system stands as a landmark of collective self-restraint on the part of the American people and the human species. Yet three decades after its inception, the most notable feature of the system—aside from the remarkable fact of its existence—is the meagerness of its size. Our subduing of the continent has been so extensive and thorough that all lands designated as wilderness constitute less than 4 percent of the United States; more than half of those are in Alaska. In the 48 contiguous states, the National Wilderness Preservation System amounts to 1.8 percent of our territory. It will grow in years to come, but not by much. Little undeveloped land remains, and efforts to designate new wilderness areas are met, unfailingly, by fierce and often overpowering resistance from those who have different ideas about the value of land.

Their ideas go back to the very beginnings of our history and culture. Europeans came to the New World not as hikers or nature lovers but as homemakers, community builders, land developers. They took freely of the continent's plenty and turned it to their uses. "In Europe," wrote Alexis de Tocqueville in the 1830s, "people talk a great deal of the wilds of America, but the Americans themselves never think about them; they are insensible to the wonders of inanimate nature and they may be said not to perceive the mighty forests that surround them till they fall beneath the hatchet."

There were those along the way who warned against excess. William Penn ordered an acre of woods left standing for every four cut. William Bartram catalogued the natural history of the Southeast and railed against early plantation agribusiness. Henry David Thoreau envisioned a 500- to 1,000-acre wilderness in every township. John Wesley Powell tried to show that the arid West couldn't support large populations or midwestern land-use practices. John Muir declaimed against commercial vandals in the temples of the wild. But those voices, to the extent they were heard at all, ran mostly against the American grain, ran counter to the spirit and even the common sense of a westering people who saw boundlessness before them.

And so we are left with a few hundred remnants of untamed land, most in the mountain West and most very small, which we call the National Wilderness Preservation System. Those remnants aren't nearly as secure as the ringing language of the Wilderness Act would seem to suggest. The act had holes in it to begin with, and its insufficiencies are becoming more evident as pressure builds against the last wild places. The pressure comes most obviously from extractive industries that value the land for what it can be made to produce, but they are only surrogates for a far more powerful force that will not be stopped by a line on a map or a sign at a trailhead. Ultimately, the fate of wilderness will be determined not by Congress or the President or any government agency, but by the way we live.

*   *   *

Climb Mount Hood, Mount Jefferson, or Mount Washington in the Oregon Cascades, and you will see the situation of American wilderness in microcosm. To the east, on the semiarid steppe that begins the Great Basin, you'll look out on irrigated pasture and alfalfa fields, a few pine-covered hills and volcanic outcrops, thin highways slanting off into distance. Looking west, through a haze of auto smog and smoke from field burning,

you'll see the Willamette Valley, the paradise at the end of the Oregon Trail, bright green with pasture and orchards and fields of hay. You'll see towns and small cities, Interstate 5 with its continual glint of traffic, a network of highways and roads.

North and south along the wavy green Cascades going blue in the distance, you'll enjoy the sight of an occasional solitary volcano like the one you're standing on and a smattering of small lakes. But you'll find yourself staring at something else: an irregular patchwork of sheared ground along both flanks of the range, at some points reaching the crest, with white road-squiggles threading through it. The overall effect may suggest to you what it once suggested to me—mange on the sides and back of a dog. But mange is scraggly, uneven. These clearcut barrens are geometric, made with fine precision. Mange doesn't know what it's doing to the dog. What's working on these mountains knows exactly what it's doing.

Standing on that peak, you should be aware that almost every acre in your view, stripped or still wooded, is land you own. It's national forest land, part of a system of federal reserves we set aside a century ago, or thought we did, for wise future use. You should also know that up to one-fifth of the standing forest you see has been marked with flags and spray paint for timber sales or is planned for marking. The Northwest timber pipeline has been frozen for the past three years by conservationist lawsuits. It may reopen soon, at some reduced rate.

And what of wilderness in the scene before you? Is the mostly intact crest of the range protected as wilderness? Not much. The U.S. Forest Service currently manages the higher country for recreation and wildlife; but if its fir and lodgepole pine become valuable to the nation, it can be managed differently. The only congressionally protected wilderness within your view is a spare archipelago of little islands around the range's solitary volcanoes—Hood, Jefferson, Three-Fingered Jack, Washington, the Three Sisters, Diamond Peak. Those islands, the Wilderness Act has decreed, shall remain untrammeled by man.

We have protected those mountain islands in part because we love alpine scenery. But we love other terrains and biomes too. We love big trees, for instance —groves of centuries-old Douglas firs, their pocked and furrowed trunks as much as 15 feet around and 200 feet tall, their great broken crowns filtering sunlight to a muted clarity. Very few such groves stand within wilderness areas. Very few such groves stand at all. They yield the best and most timber, and so they are gone to clearcuts now, and we in the Pacific Northwest are fighting bitterly over the scraps of old-growth forest that remain. We wouldn't be having that fight, or not so bitterly, if a fair representation of old growth had been included in the wilderness system, but it was too commercially valuable for that.

The wilderness mountain on which you're standing, on the other hand, like most parcels in the system, is mostly rock and ice and straggly trees. It has scant commodity value at present. But the logic of the scraped and battered ground that surrounds you isn't hard to read, and if you love your mountain, it should make you nervous.

You can read the same logic, if not always so boldly written, in most any American landscape. You can read it in California's great Central Valley, for example, where 95 percent of the original wetlands have been lost to agribusiness and development. In the Southwest and the intermountain West, where little more than a century of stock grazing has set loose more soil erosion than occurred in the previous 10,000 years. In the Mississippi-Missouri river drainage, where half the original topsoil, the best in the world, has gone to sea, and the other half is going at a faster rate. In the ravaged hills and poisoned waters of West Virginia and eastern Kentucky, where coal has been ripped from the ground to give us power. You can read it, too, in skeletal forests and sterile lakes in the Smokies and Alleghenies and Adirondacks, where the coal has returned in precipitation as much as 400 times more acidic than ordinary rain.

This is the logic of the American chapter of the world economy, a living organism composed of us and all that we do. It is a beast more fearsome than any the Pilgrims could have imagined when they gazed on the wild shore of North America four centuries ago. What other creature could have silenced forever the raucous hordes of passenger pigeons that once streamed through the sky for days at a time? Or stripped the continent of 60 million buffalo and routed wolf and grizzly into a few remote strongholds? Or driven the great thunderbird of the California hills into zoos and the merest glimmer of its ancient life in the wild?

All humans exert control on wild nature to feed, clothe, and shelter themselves, but we are especially ambitious and gifted controllers. We take more and more from the land, and not only what we need—we take what our increasingly powerful technologies allow us to take, and what we take we learn to need, and our numbers grow, and we need more, and we take more.

We have begun to see how dangerous we are to the natural world, and so we have enacted a few restraints such as the Wilderness Act. But compromises were required to get the act through Congress. Stock grazing was grandfathered into many western wilderness areas, resulting in cropped grasslands and mucked-up springs and streams. Mining also was grandfathered in, and existing and potential areas were open to new claims until 1984. Claims have been filed in most wilderness areas in the West. And it's perfectly plausible that the Oregon mountain you're standing on may harbor a mineral that will become valuable in the 21st century. Will the stirring phrases of the Wilderness Act save it from harm? Maybe. But it would not be too surprising if the same regard for nature that surgically mutilated those forested slopes someday pushes up the mountain and starts blasting the rock beneath you.

In fact, the invasion is already under way, by proxy. The acid precipitation that is ruining lakes and forests in the East is now occurring in the West too, at lower but rising levels. Auto smog from the urban centers of the Pacific Coast has been drifting into the Cascades and the Sierra Nevada for years, passing freely across wilderness boundaries, disrupting photosynthesis in trees and weakening their resistance to disease. Unless our habits of energy consumption change, these effects will only increase. If we don't consume our wilderness for its raw materials, we may yet poison it to death.

* * *

No wild place will be safe from us until we reconsider our devout belief that economic growth is always and limitlessly good and examine our equally devout belief in the unlimited use of technology. Taken together, these two articles of faith compose a modern secular orthodoxy that pervades our culture. The object of its worship is the future—a future, we are told, in which our lives will be made safer, longer, healthier, better informed, and far more pleasurable. A new and improved future. And a future—this isn't in the advertising —that threatens not only the wild places of our continent but the very quality of wildness itself.

In the chorus of boosterism for a new technology, little is ever heard of its potential dangers, in part because the most significant dangers associated with any profound tampering with nature can't be foreseen. The nuclear enthusiasts of the 1950s promised that energy would be too cheap to meter, that radiation was containable and virtually harmless anyway. Forty years later, as the downwinders in Utah and Washington State have learned in the cruelest way, the costs and benefits of splitting the atom figure differently.

At this point in our technological history, it can only be naive to expect a different result from genetic engineering, which is currently the most prominent of our manipulative interventions into the life of the wild universe. The paradox of our obsessive urge to control is that we invariably release forces that will not *be* controlled, or that can be controlled only with great difficulty and at great expense.

But to judge genetic engineering by its possible effects is to judge it by an insufficient standard. It is necessary to ask not only whether it is wise, but also whether it is right. To revise in a laboratory what evolution has spent 4 billion years making must be an exhilarating experience. But for all our prodigious technical abilities, we cannot manufacture so much as one gene, one paramecium, one nerve fiber in the brain of a blue whale. We do not know how it happened that this rock-and-water planet stirred in its sleep and woke into sentient life, or how one fertile cell becomes an elephant, or how the uncountable lives we live among twine together in the wild mysteries we call ecosystems. Jack Ward Thomas, the new chief of the Forest Service, put it this way at last year's Northwest forest conference: "Ecosystems are more complex than we think. They're more complex than we *can* think."

We tend to revere technological inventors and interveners as heroes, as modern woodsmen penetrating the frontiers of human knowledge. I think we need a new kind of hero, one whose mission is not to breach limits but to understand them and to show us how to abide by those that are necessary and just—a hero capable of restraining what he *can* do in favor of what he *ought* to do for the good of the entire community. Some scientists, most corporate executives, and all members in good standing of the economic-technological orthodoxy will characterize this idea as a travesty, a capitulation of the questing human spirit. I call it growing up. As a child matures, he learns he is but one rightful member of a human community that sets limits on the satisfaction of his wishes. He then learns, I hope, what Aldo Leopold sketched as the "land ethic"— that his community extends beyond the human and includes other forms of life. And he also needs to learn that his known community opens around him into mysteries both beautiful and sacred, mysteries to which he belongs, mysteries which do not belong to him.

There is something in us deeply intolerant of mystery, something that drives us to prod and probe the natural world and crack open more and more of its secrets and tinker with its deepest workings. We open darknesses to the light of rationality as relentlessly as the early settlers once opened the eastern forests. We do this in the name of knowledge, but our knowledge is too often a knife—it cuts the world into pieces, wonders where its life and spirit have gone, and cuts again.

I don't mean to indict science in general. Many of the foremost champions of wild nature are scientists, and their work has done much to warn us of the environmental limits we are transgressing. I am arguing only against interventionist science that wants to splice genes, split atoms, or otherwise manipulate the wild—science aimed more at control than understanding, science that assumes ownership of the natural mysteries. When technological specialists come to believe that nature is answerable to their own prerogatives, they are not serving but endangering the greater community.

The same reasoning is evident in our seemingly boundless interest in a kind of pseudoknowledge its devotees call information. The "Information Superhighway" is being readied to convey us into our future, and to travel it, evidently, we need only buy the right machines and connections to machines. I hear little news about where the Superhighway is expected to lead us, and why. Apparently it will take us by means of information into a condition of more information for the reason that information is good for us.

We will have 500 channels of interactive television, it seems. A few of those channels will feed us "information" about weather and animals and natural landscapes, for which some of us will be hungry. Old proclivities die hard. But if we travel the highway far enough, we are bound to arrive at the condition for which television has been preparing us for decades—the electronic image of a redwood will replace the natural experience of a redwood, and so the real tree with roots in the ground will logically become expendable. In the evermore-real-seeming ghosts that haunt our screens, in the video-game sensory immersion of virtual reality, the new technology promises to complete the procedure of controlling nature, finally, by becoming it.

*   *   *

The psychologist and writer James Hillman has said that our inability to experience the beautiful is what separates us from the world. We are sick and therefore the land is sick because we no longer know its beauty, and our love for it has withered. His diagnosis may seem unlikely, given that we in America flock by the millions to the scenic splendors of our national parks and other natural areas. But there is something rote and decidedly passionless in our experience of natural beauty. I feel it whenever I stop at a scenic overlook, and I see it in other watchers. I rarely see enthusiasm or even animation, but mostly bored children and impassive parents showing the scenery to their cameras and video recorders. Though drawn to nature, we are still somehow insensible to it. Our lives are so removed from the land that it's become just a scene for us, an image to be captured and taken home. As tourists we don't damage the land as a mining or timber corporation would, but essentially we do what they do—we value the land for one of its extractable qualities. We have reduced nat-

ural beauty to postcard prettiness, another commodity for our consumption.

It's a different beauty of the land, a deeper and far more lively beauty, that we have largely forfeited. To know this beauty requires more than eyes and can't be done at a distance. It takes legs and sweat, hard breathing, and sometimes pain. It requires that we approach the land on its own terms, that we enter it respectfully and yield ourselves to its presence. The beauty I'm speaking of is simply the beauty of the given world—the land as it is, with its particular lives, its various weathers, its dynamic and singular wholeness. All of us feel some stirring for this beauty, some twitch or flood of yearning. Any scrap of nature provides a portion of it; but only our wild places can give us its full measure, and renew our love for it, and show us how it lives within ourselves.

Wilderness, the word, shares roots with *willfulness,* the condition of being ungovernable, beyond authority and control. When I ask myself what wilderness most truly is, what its beauty is most made of, willfulness is what I find—a vast, unconscious willfulness that bodies forth mountains from seas of magma, dreams the dark chaos of soil into forests of spiring trees, fashions meadowlarks and black bears from the long weaving strands of evolutionary time. In this willfulness I am something small—rightfully, refreshingly small. In the wild I experience myself and my kind in something like actual scale. And except perhaps for one willful mosquito or one paramount pebble beneath my sleeping bag, I am happy.

In our restless sight-seeing of nature, skimming down the road from one view to another, we see much more than we can absorb. In wilderness, we absorb much more than we see. We walk to rhythms longer than the conscious mind can know—the rhythm of sequoias rising, the Escalante carving its canyon, the slow titanic stirring of this crust of earth that bears us. The rhythm of the wild carries through shimmering aspen leaves and the blast of Mount St. Helens, through the boom of surf at Cape Perpetua and the hoarse whistle of a red-tailed hawk adrift in the summer sky. Life and death both dance to it—the browsing deer, the cougar that snaps the deer's neck and rips its belly, and the good carrion eaters that ultimately transform the cougar.

First and finally, wilderness is what we are. "Talk of mysteries!" wrote Thoreau. "Think of our life in nature,—daily to be shown matter, to come in contact with it,—rocks, trees, wind on our cheeks! the *solid* earth! the *actual* world!" If you follow the physicists, the actual world is made of willful little particles with names like *quark* and *gluon* that dodge in and out of existence, enlivening a universe born some 15 billion years ago, a form-seeking universe that has organized itself into nebulas, stars, planets, and Thoreau with wind on his cheeks. If you follow others, you find other accounts. There are many good books, but even the book you most believe in can tell no more than a glancing passage of the actual story of being. We want to understand, we want to know how it begins and ends and why, but the story, not our knowing, is what matters most. To be part of this—to rest in a mesa still warm with sun and watch the stars brighten to their fierce glitter, the little wind smelling of sage, while far away a coyote loosens his wail.... In this beauty, this mystery, I am glad to be alive. This beautiful mystery makes me whole.

If the sickness of the land is our sickness, its health can be our health. True empowerment comes from membership in the wild matrix that gave birth to us and sustains us even in our distance and contempt. We have much to learn from other members, if we can stop ourselves from destroying them. Much to learn from wild salmon, who leap the rapids with a faithfulness to home we have scarcely begun to imagine for ourselves. Much to learn from old-growth forest, how its diverse and vigorous commonwealth sustains itself through time. We might learn patience from the bristlecones, fortitude from monarch butterflies, the dignity of space and breathing room from junipers and saguaros.

When I spend too many hours reading newspapers or watching television, too many weeks breathing city air and hardening my ears to city noises, I don't believe we as a people are capable of learning anything more than how to operate the next machine. But wilderness, as Wallace Stegner wrote, is the geography of hope. When I'm able to pry myself out of town and let the land inform me, an unreasonable optimism comes over me. The land lets me feel no other way. It's been getting by for a long time, after all, and I expect it will outlive us and the worst we can do.

At our best, there is sanity among us, and it may prosper. There is a passionate caring for the wild in many of our younger people. If, with the help of the Wilderness Act and the system it created, we can nurse our wild remnants a few decades into the next century, we may see the emergence of the new heroism we need, a heroism capable of discerning the rightful and necessary limits of our place on this continent.

The Wilderness Act was a beginning, a momentous first step, but it accepts the premise of our unhealthy culture, fencing off only a few scraps of unspoiled land. The next step is to redefine wilderness according to the premise of nature's health—as entire, vigorous ecosystems and landscapes in the full array of their diversity. To define wilderness, in other words, as wilderness defines itself, and in that way restore and perpetuate the biotic well-being of our homeland.

That step will take centuries to complete. It means withdrawing ourselves a respectful distance, voluntarily closing roads and removing habitations, so that nature can expand and join some of the remnants into greater wilderness heartlands, large enough for grizzlies and wolves and wolverines to thrive, and those members of our own species who require a lot of room to get lost in. Wild heartlands not only of the western mountains, but heartlands of deserts and plains and prairies, heartlands of the southern and eastern forests. Regions outside those wildlands will be farmed and managed for multiple use—not as we have mismanaged our public and private lands, but with regard for the wildness that is the land's long-term health and fertility. And outside the buffer zones of multiple use will be the places where most of us live, in such numbers and economies as the vitality of the entire community will permit.

Maybe we are not capable of such a change. But if we can make that step, if we can find the generosity to give back a fair portion of all we have taken, then we will have a National Wilderness Preservation System worthy of this generous, beautiful, and hard-used continent. Then we may find ourselves members at last of the American land.

NO

William Tucker

IS NATURE TOO GOOD FOR US?

Probably nothing has been more central to the environmental movement than the concept of wilderness. "In wildness is the preservation of the world," wrote Thoreau, and environmental writers and speakers have intoned his message repeatedly. Wilderness, in the environmental pantheon, represents a particular kind of sanctuary in which all true values—that is, all nonhuman values—are reposited. Wildernesses are often described as "temples," "churches," and "sacred ground"—refuges for the proposed "new religion" based on environmental consciousness. Carrying the religious metaphor to the extreme, one of the most famous essays of the environmental era holds the Judeo-Christian religion responsible for "ecological crisis."

The wilderness issue also has a political edge. Since 1964, long-standing preservation groups like the Wilderness Society and the Sierra Club have been pressuring conservation agencies like the National Forest Service and the Bureau of Land Management to put large tracts of their holdings into permanent "wilderness designations," countering the "multiple use" concept that was one of the cornerstones of the Conservation Era of the early 1900s.

Preservation and conservation groups have been at odds since the end of the last century, and the rift between them has been a major controversy of environmentalism. The leaders of the Conservation Movement—most notably Theodore Roosevelt, Gifford Pinchot, and John Wesley Powell—called for rational, efficient development of land and other natural resources: multiple use, or reconciling competing uses of land, and also "highest use," or forfeiting more immediate profits from land development for more lasting gains. Preservationists, on the other hand, the followers of California woodsman John Muir, have advocated protecting land in its natural state, setting aside tracts and keeping them inviolate. "Wilderness area" battles have become one of the hottest political issues of the day, especially in western states—the current "Sagebrush Revolt" comes to mind—where large quantities of potentially commercially usable land are at stake.

The term "wilderness" generally connotes mountains, trees, clear streams, rushing waterfalls, grasslands, or parched deserts, but the concept has been institutionalized and has a careful legal definition as well. The one given

From William Tucker, "Is Nature Too Good for Us?" *Harper's Magazine* (March 1982). Adapted from William Tucker, *Progress and Privilege: America in the Age of Environmentalism* (Doubleday, 1982). Copyright © 1982 by William Tucker. Reprinted by permission.

by the 1964 Wilderness Act, and that most environmentalists favor, is that wilderness is an area "where man is a visitor but does not remain." People do not "leave footprints there," wilderness exponents often say. Wildernesses are, most importantly, areas in which *evidence of human activity is excluded;* they need not have any particular scenic, aesthetic, or recreational value. The values, as environmentalists usually say, are "ecological"—which means, roughly translated, that natural systems are allowed to operate as free from human interference as possible.

The concept of excluding human activity is not to be taken lightly. One of the major issues in wilderness areas has been whether or not federal agencies should fight forest fires. The general decision has been that they should not, except in cases where other lands are threatened. The federal agencies also do not fight the fires with motorized vehicles, which are prohibited in wilderness areas except in extreme emergencies. Thus in recent years both the National Forest Service and the National Park Service have taken to letting forest fires burn unchecked, to the frequent alarm of tourists. The defense is that many forests require periodic leveling by fire in order to make room for new growth. There are some pine trees, for instance, whose cones will break open and scatter their seeds only when burned. This theoretical justification has won some converts, but very few in the timber companies, which bridle at watching millions of board-feet go up in smoke when their own "harvesting" of mature forests has the same effect in clearing the way for new growth and does less damage to forest soils.

The effort to set aside permanent wilderness areas on federal lands began with the National Forest Service in the 1920s. The first permanent reservation was in the Gila National Forest in New Mexico. It was set aside by a young Forest Service officer named Aldo Leopold, who was later to write *A Sand County Almanac,* which has become one of the bibles of the wilderness movement. Robert Marshall, another Forest Service officer, continued the program, and by the 1950s nearly 14 million of the National Forest System's 186 million acres had been administratively designated wilderness preserves.

Leopold and Marshall had been disillusioned by one of the first great efforts at "game management" under the National Forest Service, carried out in the Kaibab Plateau, just north of the Grand Canyon. As early as 1906 federal officials began a program of "predator control" to increase the deer population in the area. Mountain lions, wolves, coyotes, and bobcats were systematically hunted and trapped by game officials. By 1920, the program appeared to be spectacularly successful. The deer population, formerly numbering 4,000, had grown to almost 100,000. But it was realized too late that it was the range's limited food resources that would threaten the deer's existence. During two severe winters, in 1924-26, 60 percent of the herd died, and by 1939 the population had shrunk to only 10,000. Deer populations (unlike human populations) were found to have no way of putting limits on their own reproduction. The case is still cited as the classic example of the "boom and bust" disequilibrium that comes from thoughtless intervention in an ecological system.

The idea of setting aside as wilderness areas larger and larger segments of federally controlled lands began to gain more support from the old preservationists' growing realizations, during the 1950s, that they had not won the battle during the Conservation Era, and that the national forests were not parks that would be protected forever from commercial activity.

Pinchot's plan for practicing "conservation" in the western forests was to encourage a partnership between the government and large industry. In order to discourage overcutting and destructive competition, he formulated a plan that would promote conservation activities among the larger timber companies while placing large segments of the western forests under federal control. It was a classic case of "market restriction," carried out by the joint efforts of larger businesses and government. Only the larger companies, Pinchot reasoned, could generate the profits that would allow them to cut their forest holdings *slowly* so that the trees would have time to grow back. In order to ensure these profit margins, the National Forest Service would hold most of its timber lands out of the market for some time. This would hold up the price of timber and prevent a rampage through the forests by smaller companies trying to beat small profit margins by cutting everything in sight. Then, in later years, the federal lands would gradually be worked into the "sustained yield" cycles, and timber rights put up for sale. It was when the national forests finally came up for cutting in the 1950s that the old preservation groups began to react.

The battle was fought in Congress. The 1960 Multiple Use and Sustained Yield Act tried to reaffirm the principles of the Conservation Movement. But the wilderness groups had their day in 1964 with the passing of the Wilderness Act. The law required all the federal land-management agencies—the National Forest Service, the National Park Service, and the Fish and Wildlife Service—to review all their holdings, keeping in mind that "wilderness" now constituted a valid alternative in the "multiple use" concept—even though the concept of wilderness is essentially a rejection of the idea of multiple use. The Forest Service, with 190 million acres, and the Park Service and Fish and Wildlife Service, each with about 35 million acres, were all given twenty years to start designating wilderness areas. At the time, only 14.5 million acres of National Forest System land were in wilderness designations.

The results have been mixed. The wilderness concept appears valid if it is recognized for what it is—an attempt to create what are essentially "ecological museums" in scenic and biologically significant areas of these lands. But "wilderness," in the hands of environmentalists, has become an all-purpose tool for stopping economic activity as well. This is particularly crucial now because of the many mineral and energy resources available on western lands that environmentalists are trying to push through as wilderness designations. The original legislation specified that lands were to be surveyed for valuable mineral resources before they were put into wilderness preservation. Yet with so much land being reviewed at once, these inventories have been sketchy at best. And once land is locked up as wilderness, it becomes illegal even to explore it for mineral or energy resources.

Thus the situation in western states—where the federal government still owns 68 percent of the land, counting Alaska—has in recent years become a race between mining companies trying to prospect under severely restricted conditions, and environmental groups trying to lock the doors to resource development for good. This kind of permanent preservation —the antithesis of conservation—will probably have enormous effects on our future international trade in energy and mineral resources.

At stake in both the national forests and the Bureau of Land Management holdings are what are called the "roadless areas." Environmentalists call these lands "de facto wilderness," and say that because they have not yet been explored or developed for resources they should not be explored and developed in the future. The Forest Service began its Roadless Area Resources Evaluation (RARE) in 1972, while the Bureau of Land Management began four years later in 1976, after Congress brought its 174 million acres under jurisdiction of the 1964 act. The Forest Service is studying 62 million roadless acres, while the BLM is reviewing 24 million.

In 1974 the Forest Service recommended that 15 million of the 50 million acres then under study be designated as permanent wilderness. Environmental groups, which wanted much more set aside, immediately challenged the decision in court. Naturally, they had no trouble finding flaws in a study intended to cover such a huge amount of land, and in 1977 the Carter administration decided to start over with a "RARE II" study, completed in 1979. This has also been challenged by a consortium of environmental groups that includes the Sierra Club, the Wilderness Society, the National Wildlife Federation, and the Natural Resources Defense Council. The RARE II report also recommended putting about 15 million acres in permanent wilderness, with 36 million released for development and 11 million held for further study. The Bureau of Land Management is not scheduled to complete the study of its 24 million acres until 1991.

The effects of this campaign against resource development have been powerful. From 1972 to 1980, the price of a Douglas fir in Oregon increased 500 percent, largely due to the delays in timber sales from the national forests because of the battles over wilderness areas. Over the decade, timber production from the national forests declined slightly, putting far more pressure on the timber industry's own lands. The nation has now become an importer of logs, despite the vast resources on federal lands. In 1979, environmentalists succeeded in pressuring Congress into setting aside 750,000 acres in Idaho as the Sawtooth Wilderness and National Recreational Area. A resource survey, which was not completed until *after* the congressional action, showed that the area contained an estimated billion dollars' worth of molybdenum, zinc, silver, and gold. The same tract also contained a potential source of cobalt, an important mineral for which we are now dependent on foreign sources for 97 percent of what we use.

Perhaps most fiercely contested are the energy supplies believed to be lying under the geological strata running through Colorado, Wyoming, and Montana just east of the Rockies, called the Overthrust Belt. Much of this land is still administered by the Bureau of Land Management for multiple usage. But with the prospect of energy development, environmental groups have been rushing to try to have these high-plains areas designated as wilderness areas as well (cattle grazing is still allowed in wilderness tracts). On those lands permanently withdrawn from commercial use, mineral exploration will be allowed to continue until 1983. Any mines begun by then can continue on a very restricted basis. But the exploration in "roadless areas" is severely limited, in that in most cases there can be no roads constructed (and no use of off-road vehicles) while exploration is going on. Environmentalists have argued that wells can still be drilled and test mines explored using helicopters. But any such exploration is likely to be extraordinarily expensive and ineffective. Wilderness restrictions are now being drawn so tightly that people on the site are not allowed to leave their excrement in the area.

IMPOSSIBLE PARADISES

What is the purpose of all this? The standard environmental argument is that we have to "preserve these last few wild places before they all disappear." Yet it is obvious that something more is at stake. What is being purveyed is a view of the world in which human activity is defined as "bad" and natural conditions are defined as "good." What is being preserved is evidently much more than "ecosystems." What is being preserved is an *image* of wilderness as a semisacred place beyond humanity's intrusion.

It is instructive to consider how environmentalists themselves define the wilderness. David Brower, former director of the Sierra Club, wrote in his introduction to Paul Ehrlich's *The Population Bomb* (1968):

> Whatever resources the wilderness still held would not sustain (man) in his old habits of growing and reaching without limits. Wilderness could, however, provide answers for questions he had not yet learned how to ask. He could predict that the day of creation was not over, that there would be wiser men, and they would thank him for leaving the source

of those answers. Wilderness would remain part of his geography of hope, as Wallace Stegner put it, and could, merely because wilderness endured on the planet, prevent man's world from becoming a cage.

The wilderness, he suggested, is a source of peace and freedom. Yet setting wilderness aside for the purposes of solitude doesn't always work very well. Environmentalists have discovered this over and over again, much to their chagrin. Every time a new "untouched paradise" is discovered, the first thing everyone wants to do is visit it. By their united enthusiasm to find these "sanctuaries," people bring the "cage" of society with them. Very quickly it becomes necessary to erect bars to keep people *out*—which is exactly what most of the "wilderness" legislation has been all about.

In 1964, for example, the Sierra Club published a book on the relatively "undiscovered" paradise of Kauai, the second most westerly island in the Hawaiian chain. It wasn't long before the island had been overrun with tourists. When *Time* magazine ran a feature on Kauai in 1979, one unhappy island resident wrote in to convey this telling sentiment: "We're hoping the shortages of jet fuel will stay around and keep people away from here." The age of environmentalism has also been marked by the near overrunning of popular national parks like Yosemite (which now has a full-time jail), intense pressure on woodland recreational areas, full bookings two and three years in advance for raft trips through the Grand Canyon, and dozens of other spectacles of people crowding into isolated areas to get away from it all. Environmentalists are often critical of these inundations, but they must recognize that they have at least contributed to them.

I am not arguing against wild things, scenic beauty, pristine landscapes, and scenic preservation. What I am questioning is the argument that wilderness is a value against which every other human activity must be judged, and that human beings are somehow unworthy of the landscape. The wilderness has been equated with freedom, but there are many different ideas about what constitutes freedom. In the Middle Ages, the saying was that "city air makes a man free," meaning that the harsh social burdens of medieval feudalism vanished once a person escaped into the heady anonymity of a metropolitan community. When city planner Jane Jacobs, author of *The Death and Life of Great American Cities*, was asked by an interviewer if "overpopulation" and "crowding into large cities" weren't making social prisoners of us all, her simple reply was: "Have you ever lived in a small town?"

It may seem unfair to itemize the personal idiosyncrasies of people who feel comfortable only in wilderness, but it must be remembered that the environmental movement has been shaped by many people who literally spent years of their lives living in isolation. John Muir, the founder of the National Parks movement and the Sierra Club, spent almost ten years living alone in the Sierra Mountains while learning to be a trail guide. David Brower, who headed the Sierra Club for over a decade and later broke with it to found the Friends of the Earth, also spent years as a mountaineer. Gary Snyder, the poet laureate of the environmental movement, has lived much of his life in wilderness isolation and has also spent several years in a Zen monastery.

All these people far outdid Thoreau in their desire to get a little perspective on the world. There is nothing reprehensible in this, and the literature and philosophy that merge from such experiences are often admirable. But it seems questionable to me that the ethic that comes out of this wilderness isolation—and the sense of ownership of natural landscapes that inevitably follows—can serve as the basis for a useful national philosophy.

THAT FRONTIER SPIRIT

The American frontier is generally agreed to have closed down physically in 1890, the year the last Indian Territory of Oklahoma was opened for the settlement. After that, the Conservation Movement arose quickly to protect the remaining resources and wilderness from heedless stripping and development. Along with this came a significant psychological change in the national character, as the "frontier spirit" diminished and social issues attracted greater attention. The Progressive Movement, the Social Gospel among religious groups, Populism, and Conservation all arose in quick succession immediately after the "closing of the frontier." It seems fair to say that it was only after the frontier had been settled and the sense of endless possibilities that came with open spaces had been constricted in the national consciousness that the country started "growing up."

Does this mean the new environmental consciousness has arisen because we are once again "running out of space"? I doubt it. Anyone taking an airplane across almost any part of the country is inevitably struck by how much greenery and open territory remain, and how little room our towns and cities really occupy. The amount of standing forest in the country, for example, has not diminished appreciably over the last fifty years, and is 75 percent of what it was in 1620. In addition, as environmentalists constantly remind us, trees are "renewable resources." If they continue to be handled intelligently, the forests will always grow back. As farming has moved out to the Great Plains of the Middle West, many eastern areas that were once farmed have reverted back to trees. Though mining operations can permanently scar hillsides and plains, they are usually very limited in scope (and as often as not, it is the roads leading to these mines that environmentalists find most objectionable).

It seems to be that the wilderness ethic has actually represented an attempt psychologically to reopen the American frontier. We have been desperate to maintain belief in unlimited, uncharted vistas within our borders, a preoccupation that has eclipsed the permanent shrinking of the rest of the world outside. Why else would it be so necessary to preserve such huge tracts of "roadless territory" simply because they are now roadless, regardless of their scenic, recreational, or aesthetic values? The environmental movement, among other things, has been a rather backward-looking effort to recapture America's lost innocence.

The central figure in this effort has been the backpacker. The backpacker is a young, unprepossessing person (inevitably white and upper middle class) who journeys into the wilderness as a passive observer. He or she brings his or her own food, treads softly, leaves no litter, and has no need to make use of any of the resources at hand. Backpackers bring all the necessary accouterments of civilization with them. All their needs have been met by the society from which they seek temporary release. The backpacker is freed from the need to support itself in order to enjoy the aesthetic and spiritual values that are made available by this temporary *removal* from the demands of nature. Many dangers—raging rivers or precipitous cliffs, for instance—become sought-out adventures.

Yet once the backpacker runs out of supplies and starts using resources around him—cutting trees for firewood, putting up a shelter against the rain—he is violating some aspect of the federal Wilderness Act. For example, one of the issues fought in the national forests revolves around tying one's horse to a tree. Purists claim the practice should be forbidden, since it may leave a trodden ring around the tree. They say horses should be hobbled and allowed to graze instead. In recent years, the National Forest Service has come under pressure from environmental groups to enforce this restriction.

Wildernesses, then, are essentially parks for the upper middle class. They are vacation reserves for people who want to rough it—with the assurance that few other people will have the time, energy, or means to follow them into the solitude. This is dramatically highlighted in one Sierra Club book that shows a picture of a professorial sort of individual backpacking off into the woods. The ironic caption is a quote from Julius Viancour, an official of the Western Council of Lumber and Sawmill Workers: "The inaccessible wilderness and primitive areas are off limits to most laboring people. We must have access...." The implication for Sierra Club readers is: "What do these beer-drinking, gun-toting, working people want to do in *our* woods?"

This class-oriented vision of wilderness as an upper-middle-class preserve is further illustrated by the fact that most of the opposition to wilderness designations comes not from industry but from owners of off-road vehicles. In most northern rural areas, snowmobiles are now regarded as the greatest invention since the automobile, and people are ready to fight rather than stay cooped up all winter in their houses. It seems ludicrous to them that snowmobiles (which can't be said even to endanger the ground) should be restricted from vast tracts of land so that the occasional city visitor can have solitude while hiking past on snowshoes.

The recent Boundary Waters Canoe Area controversy in northern Minnesota is an excellent example of the conflict. When the tract was first designated as wilderness in 1964, Congress included a special provision that allowed motorboats into the entire area. By the mid-1970s, outboards and inboards were roaming all over the wilderness, and environmental groups began asking that certain portions of the million-acre preserve be set aside exclusively for canoes. Local residents protested vigorously, arguing that fishing expeditions, via motorboats, contributed to their own recreation. Nevertheless, Congress eventually excluded motorboats from 670,000 acres to the north.

A more even split would seem fairer. It should certainly be possible to accommodate both forms of recreation in the area, and there is as much to be said for canoeing in solitude as there is for making rapid expeditions by powerboat. The natural landscape is not likely to suffer very much from either form of recreation. It is not absolute "ecological" values that are really at stake, but simply different tastes in recreation.

NOT ENTIRELY NATURE

At bottom, then, the mystique of the wilderness has been little more than a revival of Rousseau's Romanticism about the "state of nature." The notion that "only in wilderness are human beings truly free," a credo of environmentalists, is merely a variation on Rousseau's dictum that "man is born free, and everywhere he is in chains." According to Rousseau, only society could enslave people, and only in the "state of nature" was the "noble savage"—the preoccupation of so many early explorers—a fulfilled human being.

The "noble savage" and other indigenous peoples, however, have been carefully excised from the environmentalists' vision. Where environmental efforts have encountered primitive peoples, these indigenous residents have often proved one of the biggest problems. One of the most bitter issues in Alaska is the efforts by environmentalist groups to restrict Indians in their hunting practices.

At the same time, few modern wilderness enthusiasts could imagine, for example, the experience of the nineteenth-century artist J. Ross Browne, who wrote in *Harper's New Monthly Magazine* after visiting the Arizona territories in 1864:

> Sketching in Arizona is . . . rather a ticklish pursuit. . . . I never before traveled through a country in which I was compelled to pursue the fine arts with a revolver strapped around my body, a double-barreled shot-gun lying across my knees, and half a dozen soldiers armed with Sharpe's carbines keeping guard in the distance. Even with all the safeguards . . . I am free to admit that on occasions of this kind I frequently looked behind to see how the country appeared in its rear aspect. An artist with an arrow

in his back may be a very picturesque object... but I would rather draw him on paper than sit for the portrait myself.

Wilderness today means the land *after* the Indians have been cleared away but *before* the settlers have arrived. It represents an attempt to hold that particular moment forever frozen in time, that moment when the visionary American settler looked out on the land and imagined it as an empty paradise, waiting to be molded to our vision.

In the absence of the noble savage, the environmentalist substitutes himself. The wilderness, while free of human dangers, becomes a kind of basic-training ground for upper-middle-class values. Hence the rise of "survival" groups, where college kids are taken out into the woods for a week or two and let loose to prove their survival instincts. No risks are spared on these expeditions. Several people have died on them, and a string of lawsuits has already been launched by parents and survivors who didn't realize how seriously these survival courses were being taken.

The ultimate aim of these efforts is to test upper-middle-class values against the natural environment. "Survival" candidates cannot hunt, kill, or use much of the natural resources available. The true test is whether their zero-degree sleeping bags and dried-food kits prove equal to the hazards of the tasks. What happens is not necessarily related to nature. One could as easily test survival skills by turning a person loose without money or means in New York City for three days.

I do not mean to imply that these efforts do not require enormous amounts of courage and daring—"survival skills." I am only suggesting that what the backpacker or survival hiker encounters is not entirely "nature," and that the effort to go "back to nature" is one that is carefully circumscribed by the most intensely civilized artifacts. Irving Babbitt, the early twentieth-century critic of Rousseau's Romanticism, is particularly vigorous in his dissent from the idea of civilized people going "back to nature." This type, he says, is actually "the least primitive of all beings":

> We have seen that the special form of unreality encouraged by the aesthetic romanticism of Rousseau is the dream of the simple life, the return to a nature that never existed, and that this dream made its special appeal to an age that was suffering from an excess of artificiality and conventionalism.

Babbitt notes shrewdly that our concept of the "state of nature" is actually one of the most sophisticated productions of civilization. Most primitive peoples, who live much closer to the soil than we do, are repelled by wilderness. The American colonists, when they first encountered the unspoiled landscape, saw nothing but a horrible desert, filled with savages.

What we really encounter when we talk about "wilderness," then, is one of the highest products of civilization. It is a reserve set up to keep people *out*, rather than a "state of nature" in which the inhabitants are "truly free." The only thing that makes people "free" in such a reservation is that they can leave so much behind when they enter. Those who try to stay too long find out how spurious this "freedom" is. After spending a year in a cabin in the north Canadian woods, Elizabeth Arthur wrote in *Island Sojourn:* "I never felt so completely tied to *objects*, resources, and the tools to shape them with."

What we are witnessing in the environmental movement's obsession with purified wilderness is what has often been called the "pastoral impulse." The image of nature as unspoiled, unspotted wilderness where we can go to learn the lessons of ecology is both a product of a complex, technological society and an escape from it. It is this undeniable paradox that forms the real problem of setting up "wildernesses." Only when we have created a society that gives us the leisure to appreciate it can we go out and experience what we imagine to be untrammeled nature. Yet if we lock up too much of our land in these reserves, we are cutting into our resources and endangering the very leisure that allows us to enjoy nature.

The answer is, of course, that we cannot simply let nature "take over" and assume that because we have kept roads and people out of huge tracts of land, then we have absolved ourselves of a national guilt. The concept of stewardship means taking responsibility, not simply letting nature take its course. Where tracts can be set aside from commercialism at no great cost, they should be. Where primitive hiking and recreation areas are appealing, they should be maintained. But if we think we are somehow appeasing the gods by *not* developing resources where they exist, then we are being very shortsighted. Conservation, not preservation, is once again the best guiding principle.

The cult of wilderness leads inevitably in the direction of religion. Once again, Irving Babbitt anticipated this fully.

When pushed to a certain point the nature cult always tends toward sham spirituality.... Those to whom I may seem to be treating the nature cult with undue severity should remember that I am treating it only in its pseudo-religious aspect.... My quarrel is only with the asthete who assumes an apocalyptic pose and gives forth as a profound philosophy what is at best only a holiday or weekend view of existence....

It is often said that environmentalism could or should serve as the basis of a new religious consciousness, or a religious "reawakening." This religious trend is usually given an Oriental aura. E. F. Schumacher has a chapter on Buddhist economics in his classic *Small Is Beautiful*. Primitive animisms are also frequently cited as attitudes toward nature that are more "environmentally sound." One book on the environment states baldly that "the American Indian lived in almost perfect harmony with nature." Anthropologist Marvin Harris has even put forth the novel view that primitive man is an environmentalist, and that many cultural habits are unconscious efforts to reduce the population and conserve the environment. He says that the Hindu prohibition against eating cows and the Jewish tradition of not eating pork were both efforts to avoid the ecological destruction that would come with raising these grazing animals intensively. The implication in these arguments is usually that science and modern technology have somehow dulled our instinctive "environmental" impulses, and that Western "non-spiritual" technology puts us out of harmony with the "balance of nature."

Perhaps the most daring challenge to the environmental soundness of current religious tradition came early in the environmental movement, in a much quoted paper by Lynn White, professor of the history of science at UCLA. Writing in *Science* magazine in 1967, White traced "the historical roots of our ecological crisis" directly to the Western Judeo-

Christian tradition in which "man and nature are two things, and man is master." "By destroying pagan animism," he wrote, "Christianity made it possible to exploit nature in a mood of indifference to the feelings of natural objects." He continued:

Especially in its Western form, Christianity is the most anthropocentric religion the world has seen.... Christianity, in absolute contrast to ancient paganism and Asia's religions (except, perhaps, Zoroastrianism), not only established a dualism of man and nature but also insisted that it is God's will that man exploit nature for his proper ends.... In antiquity every tree, every spring, every stream, every hill had its own *genius loci*, its guardian spirit.... Before one cut a tree, mined a mountain, or dammed a brook, it was important to placate the spirit in charge of that particular situation, and keep it placated.

But the question here is not whether the Judeo-Christian tradition is worth saving in and of itself. It would be more than disappointing if we canceled the accomplishments of Judeo-Christian thought only to find that our treatment of nature had not changed a bit.

There can be no question that White is onto a favorite environmental theme here. What he calls the "Judeo-Christian tradition" is what other writers often term "Western civilization." It is easy to go through environmental books and find long outbursts about the evils that "civilization and progress" have brought us. The long list of Western achievements and advances, the scientific men of genius, are brought to task for creating our "environmental crisis." Sometimes the condemnation is of our brains, pure and simple. Here, for example, is the opening statement from a book about pesticides, written by the late Robert van den Bosch, an outstanding environmental advocate:

Our problem is that we are too smart for our own good, and for that matter, the good of the biosphere. The basic problem is that our brain enables us to evaluate, plan, and execute. Thus, while all other creatures are programmed by nature and subject to her whims, we have our own gray computer to motivate, for good or evil, our chemical engine.... Among living species, we are the only one possessed of arrogance, deliberate stupidity, greed, hate, jealousy, treachery, and the impulse to revenge, all of which may erupt spontaneously or be turned on at will.

At this rate, it can be seen that we don't even need religion to lead us astray. We are doomed from the start because we are not creatures of *instinct*, programmed from the start "by nature."

This type of primitivism has been a very strong, stable undercurrent in the environmental movement. It runs from the kind of fatalistic gibberish quoted above to the Romanticism that names primitive tribes "instinctive environmentalists," from the pessimistic predictions that human beings cannot learn to control their own numbers to the notion that only by remaining innocent children of nature, untouched by progress, can the rural populations of the world hope to feed themselves. At bottom, as many commentators have pointed out, environmentalism is reminiscent of the German Romanticism of the nineteenth century, which sought to shed Christian (and Roman) traditions and revive the Teutonic gods because they were "more in touch with nature."

But are progress, reason, Western civilization, science, and the cerebral cortex really at the root of the "environmental crisis"? Perhaps the best answer comes from an environmentalist himself, Dr. Rene Dubos, a world-renowned microbiologist, author of several prize-winning books on conservation and a founding member of the Natural Resources Defense Council. Dr. Dubos takes exception to the notion that Western Christianity has produced a uniquely exploitative attitude toward nature:

> Erosion of the land, destruction of animal and plant species, excessive exploitation of natural resources, and ecological disasters are not peculiar to the Judeo-Christian tradition and to scientific technology. At all times, and all over the world, man's thoughtless interventions into nature have had a variety of disastrous consequences or at least have changed profoundly the complexity of nature.

Dr. Dubos has catalogued the non-Western or non-Christian cultures that have done environmental damage. Plato observed, for instance, that the hills in Greece had been heedlessly stripped of wood, and erosion had been the result; the ancient Egyptians and Assyrians exterminated large numbers of wild animal species; Indian hunters presumably caused the extinction of many large paleolithic species in North America; Buddhist monks building temples in Asia contributed largely to deforestation. Dubos notes:

> All over the globe and at all times... men have pillaged nature and disturbed the ecological equilibrium... nor did they have a real choice of alternatives. If men are more destructive now... it is because they have at their command more powerful means of destruction, not because they have been influenced by the Bible. In fact, the Judeo-Christian peoples were probably the first to develop on a large scale a pervasive concern for land management and an ethic of nature.

The concern that Dr. Dubos cites is the same one we have rescued out of the perception of environmentalism as a movement based on aristocratic conservatism. That is the legitimate doctrine of *stewardship* of the land. In order to take this responsibility, however, we must recognize the part we play in nature—that "the land is ours." It will not do simply to worship nature, to create a cult of wilderness in which humanity is an eternal intruder and where human activity can only destroy.

"True conservation," writes Dubos, "means not only protecting nature against human misbehavior but also developing human activities which favor a creative, harmonious relationship between man and nature." This is a legitimate goal for the environmental movement.

POSTSCRIPT

Does Wilderness Have Intrinsic Value?

Daniel's rhapsodic descriptions of the beauty and wonder of wild areas would surely qualify him as a member of what Tucker refers to as the "cult of wilderness," but his preservationist motives include such practical ecological goals as preserving biodiversity, which Tucker does not discuss.

Despite the increasing popularity of backpacking, Tucker is correct in maintaining that it is still primarily a diversion of the economically privileged. Indeed, a lack of financial resources and leisure time prevents the majority of U.S. citizens from taking advantage of the tax-supported parks that multiple-use conservationists such as Tucker support, as well as from enjoying a small fraction of the acreage that has been set aside as protected wilderness.

The controversies over oil development on Alaska's coastal plain and mineral exploitation in Utah's vast red rock region are currently the two most bitterly contested struggles concerning U.S. wilderness areas. Although the huge 1989 oil spill in Prince William Sound by the supertanker *Exxon Valdez* dealt a temporary setback to proponents of oil exploration in the Alaskan wilderness, the development lobby has renewed its efforts. President Bill Clinton's recent executive action to protect a large part of the Utah wilderness is being challenged by congressional opponents. For information about the Alaskan wilderness controversy, see articles by Duncan Frazier in *National Parks* (November/December 1987), George Laylock in *Audubon* (May 1988), and Douglas Kuzmiak in *The Geographical Magazine* (April 1994). Daniel Glick presents a strong argument for preserving Utah's wilderness region in the Winter 1995 issue of *Wilderness*.

A moving and thought-provoking commemoration of the 30th anniversary of the U.S. Wilderness Act is the essay "An Enduring Wilderness," by Bruce Hamilton, in the September/October 1994 issue of *Sierra*. For a comprehensive collection of essays on the subject, see *Voices for the Wilderness* edited by William Schwartz (Ballantine Books, 1969).

Those who are sympathetic to the concerns raised by Daniel would probably find Bill McKibben's controversial book *The End of Nature* (Random House, 1990) both moving and deeply disturbing. More upbeat is the essay "The Heart and Soul of Culture," by Wilbur LaPage and Sally Ranney, *Parks and Recreation* (July 1988), which illustrates the profound influence of America's wild country on its writers, artists, andmusicians. For a description of the transformation of wilderness preservation from an esoteric concern into a pragmatic international priority, see "Wilderness International: The New Horizon," by Robert K. Olson, *Wilderness* (Fall 1990).

For an Internet site related to this issue, see `http://www.law.cornell.edu/uscode/16/1131.html`, which contains a concise description of the U.S. National Wilderness Preservation System.

ISSUE 3

Is the U.S. Endangered Species Act Fundamentally Sound?

YES: David Langhorst, from "Is the Endangered Species Act Fundamentally Sound? Pro," *Congressional Digest* (March 1996)

NO: Mark L. Plummer, from "Is the Endangered Species Act Fundamentally Sound? Con," *Congressional Digest* (March 1996)

ISSUE SUMMARY

YES: David Langhorst, executive board member of the Idaho Wildlife Federation, asserts that the Endangered Species Act has saved hundreds of plant and animal species that were in serious decline, in a manner sensitive to economic concerns, and that reauthorization of the act is in the public interest.

NO: Mark L. Plummer, an environmental economist and fellow of the Discovery Institute, denies that species extinction is a catastrophe. He argues that the act's goal of bringing listed species to full recovery is not achievable.

Extinction of biological species is not necessarily a phenomenon initiated by human activity. Although the specific role of extinction in the process of evolution is still being researched and debated, it is generally accepted that the demise of any biological species is inevitable. Opponents of special efforts to protect endangered species invariably point this out. They also suggest that the role of *Homo sapiens* in causing extinction should not be distinguished from that of any other species.

This position is contrary to some well-established facts. Unlike other creatures that have inhabited the Earth, human beings are the first to possess the technological ability to cause wholesale extermination of species, genera, or even entire families of living creatures. This process is accelerating. Between 1600 and 1900, humans hunted about 75 known species of mammals and birds to extinction. Wildlife management efforts initiated during the twentieth century have been unsuccessful in stemming the tide, as indicated by the fact that the rate of extinction of species of mammals and birds has jumped to approximately one per year.

In 1973 the Endangered Species Act was adopted, and an international treaty was negotiated, in an effort to combat this worldwide problem. This act united a variety of industrial and business interests with the commercial hunters and trappers who traditionally objected to efforts to restrict their activities. Opposition developed because the act prohibited construction projects that threatened to cause the extinction of any species. The most celebrated example of a confrontation brought about under this act was an effort by environmentalists to halt construction of the Tellico Dam in Loudon County, Tennessee, on the Little Tennessee River, because it threatened a small fish called the snail darter. Much publicity has also been given to the lumber industry's opposition to efforts to protect the spotted owl, whose habitat is in valued timber areas in the U.S. Northwest. Opponents of the act cite such controversies as evidence that the nation's economic well-being is undermined by species preservation efforts. The act's supporters counter by claiming that the number of serious conflicts between development and species protection have been very few and that despite the uncompromising language of the law, no major project has been prevented because of its enforcement.

Scientists fear that the vitality of our ecology may be undermined by the reduction of biodiversity resulting from genetic resources lost through species extinction. The ability of species to evolve and adapt to environmental change depends on a vast pool of genetic material. The present principal human threat to species survival is habitat destruction, rather than hunting or trapping. This links the issues of wilderness preservation and endangered species protection.

The authorization of the Endangered Species Act expired on October 1, 1992; the appropriation of funds for the act's enforcement, however, has been extended. The battle over reauthorization continues to be one of the key unresolved environmental questions before the U.S. Congress. In 1995 a moratorium was imposed on the listing of new endangered or threatened species. In 1996 President Bill Clinton vetoed a bill that would have extended the moratorium for another year. A coalition of environmental organizations has proposed an Endangered Natural Heritage Act that would broaden and strengthen the present law while requiring a modest increase in funding. Several bills introduced, but not passed, in the 104th Congress, however, would have significantly weakened the act through such provisions as requiring compensation for property owners who are affected by habitat protection restrictions and imposing costly and problematic cost/benefit analyses to justify the protection of endangered species.

The following arguments are from testimony before a congressional committee hearing on the Endangered Species Act. David Langhorst, a member of the Idaho Wildlife Federation executive board, presents the position of the National Wildlife Federation, which is that the act is an effective and vital tool for the preservation of biodiversity. He describes six examples of how protecting endangered species helps people. Langhorst argues strongly against using cost/benefit analysis to decide which species to protect. Economist Mark L. Plummer argues that the goal of the act, which is to bring endangered species to recovery, is not achievable and results in species remaining on the list for an indefinite time. Plummer does not consider individual species extinction a catastrophe and believes that the costs of wildlife protection should be balanced against other social goals.

YES   David Langhorst

IS THE ENDANGERED SPECIES ACT FUNDAMENTALLY SOUND? PRO

I am here to testify on behalf of the National Wildlife Federation [NWF], the Nation's largest conservation education organization. I serve as Executive Board member of the Idaho Wildlife Federation, one of NWF's 45 affiliated conservation organizations throughout the United States.

The ESA [Endangered Species Act] has produced a remarkable string of successes. In its 23-year history, it has stabilized or improved the conditions of hundreds of plant and animal species that had been in serious decline. In my own work, I have seen large numbers of concerned citizens work with the ESA to help bring about the recovery of the gray wolf in the Northern Rockies ecosystem. By educating communities about the importance of the wolf to the health of the ecosystem and using the ESA's flexible provisions, we are successfully restoring this wonderful animal to the wild in a manner sensitive to local economic interests.

The gray wolf recovery effort is a model of how diverse groups of local citizens can work together to achieve results using the ESA. However, as a result of delaying tactics by narrow ranching interests, wolf recovery is taking too many years and is generating inordinate costs to the Federal taxpayer. Meanwhile, during the period of the wolf recovery effort, the recovery of numerous other listed species is being neglected.

Certain regulated industry groups are now advocating that the ESA's goal of protecting and recovering all of the Nation's imperiled plant and animal species be abandoned and that the fate of each species be left to the discretion of the Secretaries of Interior and Commerce. Such an abandonment of the ESA's goal would be unwise for at least two reasons. First, conserving the fullest extent of our natural heritage provides enormous benefits to people, benefits that greatly exceed the costs of protection measures. Second, the alternative—separately deciding the fate of each species using a cost/benefit analysis—is simply unnecessary, unworkable, and would be extremely wasteful considering the numerous ESA procedures already in place to ensure that economic consequences are considered before the law is implemented.

From David Langhorst, "Is the Endangered Species Act Fundamentally Sound? Pro," in "Saving Endangered Species: Wildlife Conservation and Property Rights," *Congressional Digest*, vol. 75, no. 3 (March 1996). Copyright © 1996 by The Congressional Digest Corp., Washington, DC (202) 333-7332. Reprinted by permission.

Congress established the goal of protecting and recovering all imperiled species when it first enacted the ESA in 1973. This ambitious goal was not chosen carelessly, but was arrived at after Congress determined that the rapid loss of biodiversity in the U.S. and abroad posed a direct threat to the well-being of the American people. When the law was reauthorized in 1978, 1982, and 1988, Congress reaffirmed that recovering all threatened and endangered species was essential.

The scientific evidence that motivated previous Congresses to set the goal of recovering all species has only strengthened in recent years. Today there is no dispute in the scientific community that human activity has brought about a loss of biodiversity not witnessed since the cataclysmic changes ending the dinosaur era 65 million years ago. Edmund O. Wilson, the eminent Harvard biologist, estimates that the current extinction rate in the tropical rain forests is somewhere between 1,000 to 10,000 times the rate that would exist without human disturbances of the environment. According to the recent study of the ESA by the National Academy of Sciences, the "current accelerated extinction rate is largely human-caused and is likely to increase rather than decrease in the near future."

This rapid loss of biodiversity is occurring not just in the tropical rain forests. In the nearly 400 years since the Pilgrims arrived to settle in North America, about 500 extinctions of plant and animal species and subspecies have occurred—a rate of extinction already much greater than the natural rate. According to recent calculations by Peter Hoch of the Missouri Botanical Garden, over the next five to 10 years, another 4,000 species in the U.S. alone

could become extinct. This evidence of increased extinctions provides sad testimony to the need for improving the ESA rather than scaling back its fundamental goal.

Species are essential components of natural life-support systems that provide medicines, food, and other essential materials, regulate local climates and watersheds, and satisfy basic cultural, aesthetic, and spiritual needs. Below are six examples of how endangered species protections help people.

New Medicines to Respond to the Health Crises of Tomorrow. Wild plant and animal species are an essential part of the $79 billion annual U.S. pharmaceutical industry. One-fourth of all prescriptions dispensed in the U.S. contain active ingredients extracted from plants. Many other drugs that are now synthesized such as aspirin, were first discovered in the wild.

Researchers continue to discover new potential applications of wild plants and animals for life-saving or life-enhancing drugs. In fact, many pharmaceutical companies screen wild organisms for their medicinal potential. Yet, to date, less than 10 percent of known plant species have been screened for their medicinal values, and only 1 percent have been intensively investigated. Thus, species protections are essential to ensure that the full panoply of wild plants and animals remains available for study and future use.

Wild Plant Species That Safeguard Our Food Supply. The human population depends upon only 20 plant species, out of over 80,000 edible plant species, to supply 90 percent of its food. These plants are the product of centuries of genetic cross-breeding among various strains of wild plants. Continual cross-breeding enables these plant species to withstand ever-evolving new diseases, pests, and changes in climatic and soil conditions. According to a recent study, the constant infusion of genes from wild plant species adds approximately $1 billion per year to U.S. agricultural production.

If abundant wild plant species were unavailable to U.S. agriculture companies for crossbreeding, entire crops would be vulnerable to pests and disease, with potentially devastating repercussions for U.S. farmers, consumers, and the economy.

Renewable Resources for a Sustainable Future. At existing levels of consumption, nonrenewable resources such as petroleum will inevitably become increasingly costly and scarce in the coming decades. To prepare the U.S. for the global economy's certain transition toward renewable resources, Congress must ensure the health of the U.S. biological resource base. Fish, wildlife, and plant species could potentially supply the ingredients for the products that drive the U.S. economy of the 21st century. The substance that holds mussels to rocks through stormy seas, for example, may hold clues for a better glue to use in applications from shipbuilding to dentistry.

Early Warning of Ecosystem Decline. Scientists have long known that the loss of any one species is a strong warning sign that the ecosystem that supported the species may be in decline. A recent study reported that loss of species could directly curtail the vital services that ecosystems provide to people. A subsequent study suggests that destruction of habitat could lead to the selective extinction of an ecosystem's "best competitors," causing a more substantial loss of ecosystem functions than otherwise would be expected.

Negative impacts in wild species often portend negative impacts for human health and quality of life. For example, some animal species are critical indicators of the harm that heavy chemicals can cause in our environment.

Ecosystems: Life-Support Systems for People. Our society has become so alienated from nature that sometimes we forget that we rely on ecosystems for our survival. Ecosystems carry out essentially natural processes, such as those that purify our water and air, create our soil, protect against floods and erosion, and determine our climate.

For example, the Chesapeake Bay, the Nation's largest estuary, not only supports 2,700 plant and animal species, but also plays a major role in regulating environmental quality for humans. Rapid development around the Bay has sent countless tons of sediment downstream, landlocking communities that were once important ports. The construction of seawalls and breakwaters in some areas has led to rapid beach erosion in others.

Ecosystems: Industries and Jobs Depend on Them. Healthy ecosystems enable multi-billion dollar, job-intensive industries to survive. Examples of industries that are dependent on the health of ecosystems are: tourism, commercial fishing, recreational fishing, hunting, and wildlife watching.

When ecosystems are degraded, the result is economic distress. Destruction of salmon runs on the Columbia and Snake river systems in the Pacific Northwest led to the near collapse of that region's multi-billion dollar commercial and sport fishing industries.

Anti-ESA advocates propose to replace the goal of saving all species with a cost/benefit analysis to determine whether to save each species. Such cost/benefit analysis would likely produce an extinction of hundreds of endangered species due to human disturbances of habitat.

In the absence of any legal obligation to recover species, the Secretary of Interior could ultimately succumb to political pressures and choose meager objectives for any species that dare to get in the way of industry or development. For most species, any objective short of full recovery would effectively perpetuate the continued slide toward extinction.

Even if the cost/benefit analysis could somehow be insulated from political manipulation, its outcome would still be totally unreliable. The information available to the Secretary about the costs of protecting the species in question would be extremely incomplete, because no one could know at the time of the cost/benefit analysis what human activities would ultimately threaten the species and whether those activities could be modified through the ESA consultation process to avoid or reduce economic losses.

Equally important, the Secretary would also have incomplete information about the benefits to people provided by the species. Despite years of research and development, we have only just begun to discover the beneficial uses of species. Of the estimated five to 30 million species living today on Earth, scientists have identified and named only about 1.6 million species, and most of these have never been screened for beneficial uses. As species become extinct, we simply don't know what we are losing. The species that become extinct today might have provided the chemical for a miracle cancer treatment or the gene that saves the U.S. wheat crop from the next potentially devastating disease. A cost/benefit analysis of the penicillin fungus in the years prior to the discovery of its antibiotic qualities would have been a surefire recipe for extinction because no one could foresee its future role in the development of wonder drugs that would save and enhance the lives of millions of people.

There is yet another reason why we should not attempt to decide the fate of species based on a prediction of their future benefits. Species within an ecosystem are interdependent, and thus the extinction of one species potentially disrupts other species and the functioning of the entire ecosystem. As reported by the Missouri Botanical Garden, the loss of one plant species can cause a chain reaction leading to the extinction of up to 30 other species, including insects, higher animals, and other plants. Like pulling a single bolt from an airplane wing, we cannot know beforehand what effect the loss of a single species might have on the entire ecosystem.

A final flaw with the cost/benefit approach is that it is based on a false premise that the ESA lacks opportunities for consideration of economic and social impacts of listings. In fact, numerous ESA provisions require that economic and social consequences be balanced with species protection goals. Once a species is listed, the ESA provides for the consideration of socioeconomic factors in the designation of critical habitat, the development of special regulations for threatened species and experimental populations, the issuance of incidental take permits, the development of reasonable and prudent alternatives during Federal agency consultations, and the existence of the Endangered Species Committee to resolve any conflicts between conservation and economic goals.

Reauthorization of an effective Endangered Species Act is in the best interest of everyone involved. Species provide untold benefits to humans and are essential to our quality of life. By making thoughtful improvements to the ESA, we can enable private landowners and other stakeholders to take a greater conservation role and thereby provide for both species conservation and sustainable development —for the benefit of each of us and generations to come.

NO

Mark L. Plummer

IS THE ENDANGERED SPECIES ACT FUNDAMENTALLY SOUND? CON

In 1973, when Congress passed the Endangered Species Act, its Members believed the goal of banishing extinction was imperative and within quick reach. The assumption, echoed by many conservationists today, was that endangered species can be saved without significant sacrifice. If development affects a species here, we can just move the development or the species somewhere else—an easy thing to do.

Over the past 21 years, it has become increasingly clear that the opposite is the case. From loggers in the Pacific Northwest to orange growers in Florida, from backyard barbecuers in upper-State New York to real estate developers in southern California, it is ordinary men and women doing ordinary things that threaten species, not trivialities. Still, the good reasons for endangering biodiversity might still not be enough if losing even one species would indeed "tinker with our future."

Yet that belief also stands in ruins. Losing a species may be tragic, but the result is rarely, if ever, catastrophic.

The problem of endangered species, then, presents us with few automatic solutions. As uncomfortable as facing the prospect may be, we must make choices that will have profound consequences for the future of our natural heritage. Ignoring this necessity, as the Endangered Species Act does, will not make the difficult choices go away. Instead, we will make them poorly.

The goal of the Endangered Species Act is to bring species to 'recovery," which the Act defines as the point "at which the measures provided pursuant to this Act are no longer necessary." If a species attains recovery, Fish and Wildlife is supposed to remove it from the official list. At the end of 1973, the list consisted of 122 species. By the end of 1994, 21 years later, the agency had added another 833 domestic species, an average of almost 40 species a year. In that time, the agency delisted 21 species, an average of one species a year.

In fact, the 40 to 1 ratio of listings to delistings overstates the progress rate, because few of the latter were due to recovery. Seven species left the list when Fish and Wildlife declared them extinct. Of these, only one species with a good chance of survival—the dusky seaside sparrow—disappeared

From Mark L. Plummer, "Is the Endangered Species Act Fundamentally Sound? Con," in "Saving Endangered Species: Wildlife Conservation and Property Rights," *Congressional Digest*, vol. 75, no. 3 (March 1996). Copyright © 1996 by The Congressional Digest Corp., Washington, DC (202) 333-7332. Reprinted by permission.

on the agency's watch. The others were either on the verge of extinction at the time of listing because of their extreme rarity, or long thought to be extinct, but placed on the endangered list in the hope that the action would spur biologists to discover new populations.

Another eight of the 21 delisted species were removed because they should not have been on it to begin with. The data on which the agency decided to list them turned out to be mistaken.

Finally, even the remaining balance of six domestic species delisted by Fish and Wildlife because their status had improved did not always owe that improvement to the Endangered Species Act. Consider the arctic peregrine falcon, which Fish and Wildlife struck from the list in October 1995. Although the Endangered Species Act banned hunting the falcon or harming its habitat, these actions, according to the official notice of delisting, were not "pivotal" to its recovery. Instead, the bird owes its improvement largely to the ban on pesticides like DDT [dichloro-diphenyl-trichloroethane]—an action that predated the Endangered Species Act.

By other measures of success, the Act shows similarly poor results. Reclassifying species from endangered to threatened has occurred less often than delisting: Between 1973 and 1994, Fish and Wildlife reclassified 13 species. And according to the 1992 biennial report from Fish and Wildlife on the recovery of listed species, the latest available, only 69 of the 711 species then listed—not quite 10 percent of the total—could be described as "improving," indicating active progress toward full recovery. Twenty-eight percent had "stable" populations, a sign that their declines had been halted. But a full 33 percent were "declining"; another 27 percent were "unknown." (The remaining 2 percent were believed to be extinct.) And species with stable populations were being held in a precarious position: almost three-fifths had achieved fewer than 25 percent of their recovery objectives.

The failure of the law to achieve full recovery means that once a species joins the list, it is almost certain to remain there for an indefinite period of time. Any private or public action that threatens the species no matter how praiseworthy in other circumstances, becomes tainted. Private landowners and Federal agency managers live under the perpetual shadow of the Endangered Species Act. In this way, an endangered species becomes a permanent liability for anyone unlucky enough to be host to one.

Understandably, landowners have responded by trying to free themselves from these restraints, sometimes in ways that work against the goal of protecting biodiversity. In the Austin area, for example, some landowners keep their property clear of the vegetation that could provide homes for the black-capped vireo or the golden-cheeked warbler, two endangered birds. In the Pacific Northwest, some timber owners have adopted forest practices that ensure conditions inimical to the northern spotted owl.

Most perverse of all is the fight over the attempts by the Department of Interior to launch a nationwide biological survey. What possible objection could landowners have to this survey? The answer is simple. The knowledge that a parcel of land houses a listed or potentially listable species puts that land under a cloud. The better course of action is to keep the government in the dark, and quietly scrape the land bare of vegetation.

These responses point to a central defect in the current law. In principle, the Endangered Species Act creates a two-step process. Science is the first step, policy is the second—except that the second step admits only one goal, full recovery. The scientific determination that a species is endangered effectively locks in the duty to save it, almost no matter what.

Because full recovery has turned out to be an impossibly difficult task, the political conflicts that should naturally be resolved in the second step find their expression instead in the first, where they cannot be debated on any but scientific grounds. Biologists, not government or elected officials, are the ones who set policy, assuming the role of economic mandarins with the power to bless or condemn a wide variety of land uses. In this way, science becomes embroiled in what are essentially policy questions, and the actions of scientists, just like those of landowners, are greeted with suspicion, fostered by a belief that their values, not their data, hold sway.

Reforming the Endangered Species Act must begin with restoring the separate domains of science and policy. The endangered list should remain as a scientific tally of this Nation's threatened wildlife. But it should no longer be tied to the single goal of full recovery for each of its entries. Instead, we must acknowledge that the choices of how much and what forms of protection an endangered species receives profoundly affect people's lives, and are therefore inherently political.

Crying "no more extinctions" produces a noble sound, but it does nothing to ensure that extinction will stop. And it has the potential for worsening the status of biodiversity, because aspiring to the perfect may prevent us from obtaining the merely good. The absolute duty of the Federal Government to stop any action that threatens a listed species must be relinquished. Otherwise, attempts to resolve conflicts between species and humans will wither under the eternal shadow of the Endangered Species Act.

POSTSCRIPT

Is the U.S. Endangered Species Act Fundamentally Sound?

A 1995 Supreme Court decision upheld regulations that interpret the Endangered Species Act (ESA) as prohibiting the destruction of habitat necessary to sustain a species, as well as prohibiting actions that directly kill or harm members of the species. This decision has heightened the concern of those who claim that the sanctions against habitat destruction should require compensation to any property owner whose economic interests are negatively impacted by them. Opponents of compensation claim that such a requirement would make wildlife protection prohibitively expensive and that there is no obligation to pay property owners to act in the public interest.

Langhorst's support for the ESA implies that the goal of protecting all species is achievable. Most defenders of the act admit that this is not actually possible and that decisions do have to be made about the most effective way to spend funds allocated for wildlife protection. Plummer's negative assessment of the ESA is based on its failure to bring listed species to full recovery. The National Research Council recently released a generally favorable evaluation of the act based on a review of its overall impact rather than on the overly ambitious initial legislative goal. Like many proponents of the use of cost/benefit analysis as a means to decide which species to protect, Plummer fails to explain how the benefits of preventing the extinction of any particular plant or animal species could possibly be scientifically evaluated. Some policy analysts who support the goal of preserving biodiversity argue that the government should protect critical ecosystems rather than focus on near-extinct species. One such proposal is described by Suzanne Winckler in "Stopgap Measures," in the January 1992 issue of *The Atlantic Monthly*. Critics of such proposals argue that deciding which ecosystems to protect would be even more problematic than making decisions about individual species and that implementation of such a plan would be very costly.

The March 1996 issue of *Congressional Digest* contains the testimony of several additional supporters and opponents of the ESA. For additional arguments favoring reauthorization, see "A Tough Law to Solve Tough Problems," by Frances Hunt and William Robert Irvin, *Journal of Forestry* (August 1992); "Making Room in the Ark," by John Volkman, *Environment* (May 1992); articles by Ted Williams and Paul Rauber in the January/February 1996 issue of *Sierra*; and the article by T. H. Watkins in the January/February 1996 issue of *Audubon*. Arguing that the act is economically too costly are John Heissenbuttel and William Murray in "A Troubled Law in Need of Revision," *Journal of Forestry* (August 1992).

For an Internet site related to this issue, see http://www.nesarc.org/ endang.htm, which contains a legislative history of the U.S. Endangered Species Act, from its enactment to the present.

ISSUE 4

Should Environmental Policy Be Redesigned to Cure Environmental Racism?

YES: Ruth Rosen, from "Who Gets Polluted? The Movement for Environmental Justice," *Dissent* (Spring 1994)

NO: Christopher Boerner and Thomas Lambert, from "Environmental Injustice: Industrial and Waste Facilities Must Consider the Human Factor," *USA Today Magazine* (March 1995)

ISSUE SUMMARY

YES: History professor and author Ruth Rosen argues that racial discrimination is a significant factor in further burdening impoverished groups by exposing them to the highest levels of industrial pollution. She supports the demands of the environmental justice movement for corrective action.

NO: American business researchers Christopher Boerner and Thomas Lambert maintain that studies attributing environmental inequities to racism are flawed. They favor compensating those who are impacted by polluting facilities to achieve environmental justice.

The environmental movement has often been described as reflecting the idealist aspirations of white middle- and upper-income people. Indeed, poor people and minority groups were not well represented among those who gathered for the teach-ins and other events organized to celebrate the first Earth Day in April 1970. Only later did some of the growing environmental organizations even begin to discuss the need to reach out in their organizing efforts to low-income communities and ethnic minority neighborhoods.

The dearth of African Americans, Native Americans, Hispanics, and poor white people among the early environmental activists was passed off as a reflection of the pressing need such people felt to pay attention to more "basic" social concerns such as hunger, homelessness, and safety.

Until very recently, little media attention has been given to publicizing the fact that, after a slow start, the involvement of poor and minority people in grassroots environmental organizing has been growing dramatically for more than a decade. The movement for environmental justice was triggered in 1982 by demonstrations to protest the decision to locate a poorly planned PCB disposal site adjacent to impoverished African American and Native American communities in Warren County, North Carolina. Since then, the movement has grown to encompass local, regional, and national groups organized to protest the systematic discrimination of environmental goals and the siting of polluting industries and waste disposal facilities in their backyards.

Recognition of the demands of this movement by mainstream environmental organizations and government officials has been slow in coming. It was not until 1990 that the Environmental Protection Agency (EPA) issued the report *Environmental Equity: Reducing Risks for All Communities,* which acknowledged the need to pay attention to many of the concerns being raised by environmental justice activists. In that same year leaders of the Southwest Organizing Project sent a letter demanding a dialogue with U.S. environmental organizations, which, they charged, "emphasize the cleanup and preservation of the environment on the backs of working people in general and people of color in particular." At the 1992 United Nations Earth Summit in Rio de Janeiro, a set of "Principles of Environmental Justice" was widely circulated and discussed. In 1993 the EPA opened an Office of Environmental Equity with plans for cleaning up sites in several poor communities, and in 1994 President Bill Clinton made the cause of environmental equity a national priority by issuing a sweeping Executive Order on Environmental Justice.

The environmental justice movement has given rise to several controversies. Critics of the charges of environmental racism assert that inequities in the siting of sources of pollution are simply the result of market forces that make the poor neighborhoods where minorities live the economically logical choice for the location of such facilities, or that apparent inequities result because once these facilities are built, they depress real estate values, turning the neighborhoods into poor and minority communities. A more fundamental concern is whether or not simplistic efforts to combat environmental racism will simply shift pollution to poor white neighborhoods. To avoid this consequence, some environmentalists have suggested that the principal demand of the environmental justice movement should be general pollution reduction.

In the following selections, Ruth Rosen presents a history of the environmental justice movement, stressing how it has woven together strands of the civil rights and environmental struggles. She argues that racial discrimination plays a significant role in the unusually intense exposure to industrial pollutants experienced by disadvantaged minorities, and she expresses the hope that "greening the ghetto will be the first step in greening our entire society." Christopher Boerner and Thomas Lambert raise technical questions about the validity of studies that appear to show a racial component to environmental injustice. They reject proposals to eliminate environmental inequities or to substitute nonpolluting technologies in favor of offering economic compensation to those who are potentially exposed to excessive industrial emissions.

YES
Ruth Rosen

WHO GETS POLLUTED? THE MOVEMENT FOR ENVIRONMENTAL JUSTICE

"All communities are not created equal."

—Robert Bullard, Sociologist, U.C. Riverside

During the last decade, a grass-roots, minority-led movement against environmental racism (more recently described as the movement for environmental justice) has been spreading across urban America. Led largely by local women of color, the movement for environmental justice has received scant national attention. Yet these activists, by weaving together ideas and tactics of the civil rights and environmental movements, are creating one of the most potentially radical movements in recent American history.

What is environmental injustice? Let me begin with a true story, an incident that escaped most of the country's attention.

On July 26, 1993, while the rest of the nation watched the rising waters of the Mississippi drown people's homes and dreams, a ruptured railroad car at General Chemical's plant in North Richmond, California, spewed a fifteen-mile long toxic plume of sulfuric acid through surrounding residential communities. People wheezed and coughed, their eyes and lungs scorched by the toxic cloud. Three hours passed before the explosion could be capped. Over the next few days, more than twenty thousand residents sought medical treatment from nearby hospitals.

Disaster and trauma are nothing new to the residents of North Richmond, California, one of the poorest and most devastated African-American neighborhoods in the United States. It is a community whose history stretches back to slavery. Many residents are descendants of former southern sharecroppers, lured to Richmond during World War II by the higher paid skilled jobs created by the defense industry. On recent weekends, drive-by shootings have routinely injured as many as twenty people. The community has the highest rate of HIV-infected African-American drug users in the state. It is a community injured every day by the effects of poverty. "Unemployment, in fact, is the greatest public health problem," says Dr. Wendel Brunner, county director of public health. People hold their families and lives together with faith and a prayer.

After the accident, community and environmental activists asked questions that never seemed to get answered. Why did the General Chemical plant's accident prevention plan—required by law but barred from public scrutiny—fail to identify such a possible incident? Its "worst case" scenario predicted that a toxic plume would not extend further than its property line—a preposterous assumption. Why hadn't General Chemical installed safety technology so that, if an accident occurred, toxic emissions would be vented into alternative containment systems, rather than into the atmosphere? And why, asked residents, had neither industry nor county government established a siren warning system?

Several weeks later, the community of North Richmond gathered to hear a lame apology from a General Chemical representative, and to testify about the trauma they suffered. Much of the local media trivialized their complaints, accusing residents of seeking to establish fake liability claims, as though they hadn't been injured or traumatized. If the wind had driven the plume south into Berkeley's white middle-class gourmet ghetto, where activists sit in cafes sipping cafe latte discussing environmental racism, would the media have minimized the terror of a toxic cloud gassing an entire community?

As residents testified before an open microphone in a cavernous church, I heard little grandstanding, just the voices of people who felt hurt and frightened. Still hoarse and coughing, mothers described the terror they felt as they watched their families and homes gassed. They asked public health officials

when their children's asthma would improve. After speaking, one woman sat down beside me, still gasping for breath. "I'm afraid to go home," she said crying softly. "When I look outside the window, how will I know if it's another toxic cloud or just summer fog?"

It could have been worse; North Richmond is a disaster waiting to happen. Fifteen serious industrial accidents at Contra Costa county's chemical plants and refineries in the past five years have endangered this area. At least thirty-eight industrial sites store as much as ninety-four million pounds of forty-five different chemicals, including some of the most dangerous—ammonia, chlorine, hydrogen fluoride and nitric acid. About 500,000 pounds of ammonia is stored at Chevron's fertilizer plant in Richmond, for example, just two miles from schools and homes. Had a toxic cloud of ammonia erupted, it would have left hundreds, if not thousands, of dead bodies on the ground.

As the journalists who briefly parachuted into North Richmond all reported, the residents were lucky this time.

* * *

North Richmond, California is only one of dozens of low-income communities that feel victimized by industrial pollution and have organized a grass-roots movement to fight for what they call environmental justice.

It's no accident that the nation's most toxic sites are surrounded by black and Latino communities. Most minority communities in the United States are poor, and low income people can't vote with their feet and move wherever they choose. Nor do the poor have the political clout to challenge the local zoning boards that protect wealthy communities.

Environmental injustice, then, refers to the fact that poor communities are disproportionately harmed by industrial toxic pollution and that corporations and government—intentionally or unintentionally—build their worst toxic sites and store their most hazardous chemicals in and around these low-income neighborhoods. It also refers to the well-documented fact that local governments have excluded minority communities from environmental planning and that toxic sites have destroyed many traditional minority communities.

Some companies, like North Richmond's Chevron, defensively point out that they built their plants long before the growth of a residential community. True enough. But Chevron's plants are the exception, not the rule. Some local government agencies argue that it is zoning, not racism, that has dumped the worst toxic substances into minority communities. Yes, but who sits on—or influences—the local city councils and county boards that carve out industrial zones? Housing developers and their friends, not the residents whose homes are just across the street from refineries and landfills.

* * *

Awareness of environmental discrimination has grown in fits and starts. Some minority activists trace their movement to 1982, when North Carolina decided to build a PCB (polychlorinated biphenyl) disposal site in Warren County. For unexplained reasons, government officials allowed waste to be stored only fifteen feet above the water table, instead of the usual fifty feet required for PCBs. Outraged by what they viewed as racial discrimination, sixteen thousand residents, mostly African Americans and Native Americans, organized a series of marches and protests that resulted in over five hundred arrests. Although they lost the battle, the Warren County residents may have begun the battle against environmental racism.

The tragedy of Bhopal, India, on December 3, 1984 intensified American minorities' awareness of environmental dangers. When a toxic gas known as MIC leaked from a Union Carbide pesticide plant in Bhopal, the poisonous cloud killed close to four thousand people and permanently disabled another fifty thousand residents.

The magnitude of the chemical nightmare of Bhopal captured international attention and cast the media's spotlight on the predominantly African-American community of Institute, West Virginia, the site of the only Union Carbide plant in the United States that manufactured MIC. West Virginia's Kanawha Valley—dubbed by residents "the chemical capital of the world"—would never be the same.

Soon after the Bhopal tragedy, conflict broke out between those Union Carbide workers who feared for their jobs and those who feared for their lives. A documentary film titled *Chemical Valley* (1991) recounts how Union Carbide blackmailed the community with loss of jobs and how both the company *and* the federal Environmental Protection Agency (EPA) stonewalled efforts to investigate the community's health complaints. The film also traces the community's growing political sophistication, including its awareness of its collusion in the creation of an endangered valley. In one interview, an African-American male worker sadly concedes, "I sold my soul to Union Carbide."

When community residents demanded an explanation for the chemical odors that saturated the valley's air, company inspectors somehow couldn't detect the same odors. Even more frustrating was the fact that the EPA kept revising its risk assessment methods until no health hazard could be determined. Angry but determined, one African-American woman turned organizer tells the filmmaker, "I often wonder, if it had been a white neighborhood, would they have done the same thing?" Then, without skipping a beat, she quickly adds that Union Carbide and the government probably would have treated poor—but not affluent—whites with the same indifference.

She is right. Environmental pollution is not merely a problem that effects people of color; it disproportionately threatens the poor in general. Ask the poor white citizens in Yellow Creek, Kentucky, who formed Concerned Citizens to stop a tannery from dumping toxic wastes into the creek that flowed through their community. After documenting a series of health problems and unraveling ties between local government and industry, a slate of concerned citizens successfully took over the city council.

Still, people of color are likely to be endangered because their neighborhoods are not only poor but also relatively politically powerless. To outsiders, the siting of toxic waste facilities or refineries in minority communities may seem like a coincidence, or the consequences of the poor's political marginality. To people who live in these communities, however, the very decisions that dump toxics in and around their homes seem, at best, like de facto racism. The citizens of North Richmond, for example, know that it is their poverty and political vulnerability that allow their neighborhood to be polluted. But they also know that authorities would address any middle-class white community's complaints more seriously. They feel dispensable—and discriminated against—as African Americans, not only as poor people.

* * *

Over the last decade, a series of studies and reports have amply documented the fact that impoverished racial groups —Native Americans, Mexican migrant workers, and African-American and Hispanic inner city residents—have endured the greatest industrial pollution. In 1986, for example, the Center for Third World Organizing in Oakland, California issued a report called "Toxics and Minority Communities." Among its most important findings were that two million tons of radioactive uranium tailings had been dumped on Native American lands and that cancers of the reproductive organs among Navajo teenagers had climbed to seventeen times the national average.

In April 1987, the United Church of Christ Commission for Racial Justice released a widely quoted study that documented environmental racism throughout the United States. Spearheaded by Ben Chavis, now the executive director of the National Association for the Advancement of Colored People, the study discovered that three of five African Americans live in communities endangered by abandoned toxic waste sites and commercial hazardous waste landfills. The report also revealed that the nation's largest hazardous waste landfill, which receives toxics from forty-five states, is situated in Emelle, Alabama, whose population is 78.9 percent African American. The study further demonstrated that the greatest concentration of hazardous-waste sites in the United States is in the predominately black and Latino South

Side of Chicago. In some cases, minority communities agreed to accept such facilities in return for jobs and contracts that never appeared.

During the last decade, scholars, journalists, and activists have been busy proving—and tracking the impact of—environmental injustice. In 1983, Robert Bullard, a sociologist at the University of California, Riverside and author of *Dumping in Dixie*, demonstrated that, from the late 1920s to the late 1970s, Houston placed all of its city-owned landfills and six of its eight incinerators in largely African-American neighborhoods. Investigative journalists have publicized the fact that the dirtiest ZIP code in California, a one square mile section of Los Angeles County, is filled with waste dumps, smokestacks and wastewater pipes from polluting industries. Environmental activists charge that it's no accident that the population in this ZIP code, where eighteen companies discharge five times as much as pollution as they emit in the next worst ZIP code, is 59 percent African American and 38 percent Hispanic.

A more recent study published by the *National Law Journal* in 1992 concluded that government agencies treat polluters based in minority areas less severely than those in largely white communities and that toxic cleanup programs under the federal Superfund law take longer and are less thorough in minority neighborhoods.

A series of "smoking gun" leaks to the public have helped make charges of environmental injustice credible. In 1984, Cerell Associates, a private consulting firm hired by the California Waste Management Board, issued a report titled "Political Difficulties Facing Waste-to-Energy Conversion Plant Siting." The report concluded that all socioeconomic groups resent and resist the siting of hazardous wastes in their neighborhoods (NIMBYism or Not In My Backyard Syndrome) but that lower income groups have fewer resources to fight government decisions. Hardly a startling conclusion, but when leaked to the public, the study helped galvanize the growing environmental justice movement in California.

Activists had longed suspected—and in some cases documented—that the industrialized world intentionally dumped toxic wastes in third world countries. When an internal memo written by a chief economist from the World Bank was leaked to the public in 1991, it touched off a global scandal. The candor of the memo —"Just between you and me, shouldn't the World Bank be encouraging MORE migration of the dirty industries to the LDCs [Less Developed Countries]?"—revealed the kind of cavalier cynicism the World Bank expresses toward third world countries. The memo offered further ammunition to activists because the author cited three reasons for dumping toxics in Third World nations: the fact that their citizens already had a lower life expectancy; that such countries were relatively still "under-polluted;" and that impairing the health of people with the lowest wages made the "greatest economic sense."

* * *

The environmental movement used to conjure up an image of white middle-class people concerned with conserving a pristine wilderness, backpackers seeking to protect a contemplative sanctuary, and conservationists who sought to protect the forests, rivers, and species of the Earth.

No more. From farm-worker communities to Native American reservations, from urban landfills to waste dumps, minority activists are expanding environmentalism to include the protection of urban and rural communities endangered by industrial toxic substances. Until recently, many minority communities had been willing to choose between jobs and environmental pollution. Poor people worry more about starving to death from unemployment than about the health risks they may face from industrial pollution. Robert Bullard, whose most recent book *Confronting Environmental Racism* provides an excellent overview of the movement for environmental justice, explains, "These [communities] are ideal because of their powerlessness and their lack of education and vulnerability. It's the path of least resistance whether it's a municipal landfill, an incinerator, a toxic-waste dump or a chemical plant. It's exploiting the fears of communities that have a high unemployment rate. Any job is better than no job."

In the last decade, however, a growing number of minority communities have refused to choose between jobs and the environmental health of their families and communities. In a study of nine of these community resistance movements, Bullard found that eight of them began as environmental groups and that six were led by women who were grass-roots activists. Their tactics focused on local targets: they demonstrated and marched, held hearings and public workshops, initiated fact-finding research, and filed suits against local and state governments. Not content to fight against health hazards, most of the groups embraced a multi-issue agenda, organized around the principles of social justice and economic equity.

North Richmond, California, for example, has developed an intricate infrastructure of community organizations that is challenging industry's ability to threaten their community. In the last decade, minority-led groups like the North Richmond West County Toxics Coalition have redefined environmentalism to emphasize the protection of urban residents from toxic pollution. Both Citizens for a Better Environment and the Sierra Club have offered their assistance to these groups.

Other communities, too, have begun to challenge corporate and government environmental discrimination. In 1985, Concerned Citizens of South Central (Los Angeles), one of the nation's first African-American environmental groups, defeated an effort by a manufacturer to build one of the country's fourteen toxic waste incinerators in their neighborhood. When another manufacturer tried to construct it a few miles away in a large Latino community, Concerned Citizens joined with the largely Latino Concerned Mothers of East L.A., sued the government and won. In the Los Angeles struggle, the wilderness-focused group Earth First! joined with community organizations.

Although largely ignored by the national media, the leaders of this grassroots movement have quietly challenged the corporate right to endanger the health of poor people. *Vogue* magazine recently featured a rare profile of one of these unsung heroines.

Patsy Ruth Oliver was a former resident of Carver Terrace, a polluted black suburb in Texarkana. African American families began to notice dark patches of "gunk" seeping through their withered lawns, around puddles and into the cracked center of the street. An unusual cluster of medical problems further terrified the residents of this community.

The truth did not emerge until 1979, one year after residents discovered leaking barrels of dioxin beneath Love Canal, New York. Congress ordered the country's biggest chemical firms to identify their hazardous waste sites, and the Pittsburgh-based Koppers Company placed Carver Terrace high on its list. For half a century, it turned out, Koppers' old treatment plant had used creosote (a known carcinogen) to coat railroad ties. When Koppers Company closed the plant in 1961, it bulldozed over most of the operation, including the creosote tanks. African-American families who had scrimped and saved to own their own homes happily bought up the plots in the new suburb.

In 1984, Texas officials asked the federal EPA to place Carver Terrace on the Superfund list, the $1.3 billion trust that congress established in 1980 to clean up toxic waste dumps. The EPA brought in a small army of scientists, outfitted in full protective gear, who declared the soil contaminated, but then, in an arcane and baffling twist, concluded that the area posed no immediate danger to residents' health. The EPA never even bothered to interview the residents.

Outraged, Oliver and her neighbors formed the Carver Terrace Community Action group, and with the assistance of local environmentalists, residents soon discovered that the EPA had failed to inform them of two other studies that showed that Carver Terrace did indeed pose immediate risks to the community's health. The community group decided that its members—like the residents of Love Canal—wanted the government to buy them out. Oliver knew that it was racism, not the soil, that distinguished

Carver Terrace from Love Canal. "If there's one thing I know," she said, "it's racism; I have a master's degree in Jim Crow."

Eventually, over the objections of the EPA, Patsy Ruth Oliver and her neighbors forced the government to buy them out. The neighbors dispersed. In the process, a budding suburban African American community was saved, but also destroyed. Robert Bullard, who has studied the local leadership of these campaigns, explains that "Patsy typifies what's happening in the environmental justice movement in communities of color. It's mostly women who get involved to protect family, home, and community. These are not traditional environmentalists. These are people talking about survival."

Oliver, who joined the board of Friends of the Earth, then went on to publicize the environmental hazards faced by poor communities in the Southwest. On December 17, 1993, the day demolition of homes began in Carver Terrace, Patsy Ruth Oliver died of a heart attack.

"Crack babies are the spotted owl of East Oakland. They're an indicator species of the health of the community."

—Carl Anthony,
Director of Urban Habitat

The movement for environmental justice, led by grassroots activists like Pasty Ruth Oliver, is offering a serious challenge to government and corporate environmental policies. But the obstacles are daunting.

The national media, for example, haven't grasped that all these local organizations constitute a new movement —despite the large number of citizens who have marched, demonstrated and been arrested. True, local media arrive in herds when a toxic explosion threatens lives. Journalists dutifully interview leaders for the evening news, but they leave as soon as they count the bodies and collect their sound bites. What they fail to report is that the community's demonstrations, marches and meetings are part of a movement that transcends traditional civil rights or environmental concerns.

In part, one can blame the media's racist and sexist attitudes for this truculent indifference. Community leaders, after all, are often local women who speak on behalf of minority populations. Without a high-profile national reputation that can capture the media's attention, they are easily ignored. Nor do these women actively seek media attention. They want results, not public glory. As mothers and grandmothers of the community—often veterans of the civil rights movement—they organize to protect the health of their families and communities. What motivates these women is an outrage born of the desperate desire to hold together already fragile families and communities.

The federal government offers yet more obstacles. Rather than protecting these communities, the Environmental Protection Agency has been slow to acknowledge the existence of environmental injustice or to investigate minority communities' health hazards. In its 1990 report, "Environmental Equity: Reducing Risks for All Communities," the EPA finally agreed that minority communities have borne more than their share of environmentally undesirable hazards. The EPA's office of Environmental Equity, which opened just last year, now plans to initiate several demonstration projects at cleanup sites in poor communities. The agency also promised to launch a public awareness campaign targeted at minor-

ity groups. Minority activists, however, aren't holding their breath; they have observed the EPA's grudging interest in the Kanawha Valley and other community battles against industrial pollution.

Another serious problem is the way the EPA evaluates health hazards. Community activists believe that higher rates of asthma, cancer, and respiratory diseases in poor neighborhoods may be linked to air, water and soil pollution from industries. But the EPA investigates specific causation, rather than evaluating the aggregate risks that assault a community. Employing a "scientific" method of risk assessment—which selects from dozens of variables—EPA environmental epidemiologists invariably fail to demonstrate a link between a particular pollutant and a specific disease. "Risk assessment," says Dr. Wendel Brunner, public health director of the county in which North Richmond's refineries are located, "is the only thing that makes economics look like a science."

Arguing against risk-assessment methods, Robert Bullard proposes that the burden of proof should shift from communities, which now have to prove the existence of health hazards, to industry, which should have to prove that their operations do no harm. Bullard also proposes a Fair Environmental Protection Act to redress the intended and unintended effects of public and industrial policies. Based on the precedents of the Civil Rights Act of 1964 and the Fair Housing Act of 1968, such federal and state legislation would prohibit environmental discrimination based on race and class.

One sign of the movement's success came in February 1993, when the Clinton administration issued an Executive Order requiring federal agencies to "make environmental justice a part of all they do." Under the order, every agency would have to consider the impact of its policies on minority communities. In addition, the initiative sets in motion an unprecedented data-gathering effort across the federal government to document the impact of pollution on low-income and minority communities. Some movement activists hailed the executive order as a great success; others thought the order evaded the need for an environmental justice impact statement to accompany every agency's policy.

The movement for environmental justice has also had more success in forging a multiracial coalition among community groups than in joining forces with established labor organizations or national environmental groups. In April 1990, for example, the SouthWest Organizing Project drew together thirty organizations from the Southwest, mostly minority representatives involved in environmental and economic justice issues.

Job blackmail, which has hit most American workers, makes efforts to organize against industrial pollution particularly difficult. In response to the demand for healthy jobs as well as a clean environment, many American companies have chosen to relocate. Labor organizers and environmental activists have been seeking ways to unite their movement on the issue of removing toxics from the workplace. The Oil, Chemical and Atomic Workers International, for example, proposed a new federal "superfund" for workers displaced by the removal of toxics from the workplace. Such workers would receive displacement benefits while training to reenter the work force with new skills. But such joint efforts are few and far between, particularly in minority communities.

Although mainstream environmental organizations have occasionally provided minority organizations with invaluable expert testimony, research, technical assistance and legal advice, no real coalition between the established national groups—whose membership is largely white and middle class—and minority community organizations has so far developed.

In a very real sense, these activists come from different worlds and are concerned about different worlds. At best, the large, mainstream environmental groups focus on the health of the planet—the wildernesses, forests and oceans that cannot protect themselves. In contrast, the movement for environmental justice, led by the poor, is not concerned with overabundance, but with the environmental hazards and social and economic inequalities that ravage their communities.

Some mainstream environmentalists charge that minority grass-roots organizations aren't sufficiently concerned with the environment, that they seek only a fairer distribution of environmental dangers—"environmental equity." And when poor communities accept monetary reparations from polluting industries, mainstream environmental activists sometimes charge them with being "bought off" by industry.

Such allegations, however, miss the radical potential of grass-roots environmental activism. Poor communities, already ravaged by drugs, violence, and unemployment, have only the slimmest resources to protect their own health from industrial waste. But their insistence upon decent jobs as well as a clean environment is a legitimate *and* radical demand that challenges the distribution of wealth and racial discrimination in America. Furthermore, by promoting their own NIMBYism, minority communities offer a profound challenge to past corporate and governmental environmental practices. For if industrial America cannot dump its waste in minority communities, or if these communities exact too high a price, Americans must decide what kinds of toxics they will tolerate anywhere.

As one community activist recently said about a proposed waste incinerator: "I don't want these things in my back yard, and I don't want them in any back yard." Peter L. Reich, a legal expert on environmental race discrimination, argues—perhaps a bit optimistically—that "When the pollution costs of industrial development can no longer be shifted to the powerless, greening the ghetto will be the first step in greening our entire society."

Let's hope he's right.

* * *

POSTSCRIPT: The residents of North Richmond have patiently waited. State and local officials, after all, appeared to listen attentively to their complaints.

Four months after the toxic emission, California state health environmental epidemiologists called a community meeting at which they announced that they had changed their minds and could not design a study to measure the health impact of the toxic release.

Five months after the incident, the county office of emergency services still had not designed a long-promised evacuation plan for North Richmond residents.

Six months later, industry still had not installed an early warning siren system.

Bureaucratic bumbling, environmental racism, or environmental injustice? Which words most accurately describe the casual indifference authorities have demonstrated? The community of North Richmond will, no doubt, hand down its own verdict.

Meanwhile, their organized movement has won one major victory: As reparations, General Chemical has agreed to build and support a medical clinic in the community. A small but important triumph in the long struggle for environmental justice.

NO

Christopher Boerner and Thomas Lambert

ENVIRONMENTAL INJUSTICE: INDUSTRIAL AND WASTE FACILITIES MUST CONSIDER THE HUMAN FACTOR

Eliminating "environmental racism" has become one of the premier civil rights and ecological issues of the 1990s. Over the past 15 years, what began as a modest grassroots social movement has expanded to become a national issue, combining environmentalism's sense of urgency with the ethical concerns of the civil rights movement. According to "environmental justice" advocates, discrimination in the siting and permitting of industrial and waste facilities has forced minorities and the poor disproportionately to bear the ill effects of pollution, compared to more affluent whites. What is more, they contend, the discriminatory application of environmental regulations and remediation procedures essentially has let polluters in minority communities off the hook.

To remedy this perceived imbalance, policymakers in Washington have mounted a full-court press. On Feb. 11, 1994, Pres. Clinton issued an executive order on environmental justice, requiring Federal agencies to demonstrate that their programs and policies do not inflict environmental harm unfairly on the poor and minorities. The order also creates an interagency task force to inform the President of all Federal environmental justice policies and to work closely with the Environmental Protection Agency's Office of Environmental Equity as well as other government agencies to ensure that those policies are implemented promptly. In addition to the President's executive order, Congress is debating several bills designed to guarantee environmental equity. These proposals would affect the location of industrial facilities.

With charges of racism, discrimination, and social negligence being bantered about, discussions of the environmental justice issue often are passionate and, occasionally, inflammatory. Behind the emotion, however, two critical questions arise: Does the existing evidence justify such a high-level commitment of resources to addressing environmental justice claims, and what reasonable steps should society take to ensure that environmental policies are enacted and implemented fairly?

Contrary to conventional wisdom, the answers to these questions are not simple or readily apparent. While it certainly seems noncontroversial to assert that environmental officials ought to enforce existing laws equally, the question of siting and permitting reforms is not so clear-cut. Before approving additional regulations on facility siting and permitting, policymakers would be well-advised to assess candidly the quality of the existing environmental racism research as well as the likely costs and benefits of proposed solutions. Only with such a critical eye can legislators be certain that the measures ultimately enacted are cost-effective and successful in addressing the equity concerns of minority and low-income communities.

The call for environmental justice first surfaced during the late 1970s with the work of grassroots organizations such as the Mothers of East Los Angeles and Chicago's People for Community Recovery. While ostensibly formed to combat specific local environmental problems, each of these groups seemingly shared one unifying belief: that the poor and minorities are systematically discriminated against in the siting, regulation, and remediation of industrial and waste facilities. Through social and political protest, these neighborhood organizations aggressively challenged local developments they considered undesirable, becoming an effective voice for the concerns of inner-city residents. In the absence of detailed research, however, the evidence for their claims of discrimination remained largely anecdotal. As a result, their influence on policy was limited. Not until several studies appeared to sub-stantiate their assertions did the movement gain national attention.

The first major attempt to provide empirical support for environmental justice claims was conducted by Robert D. Bullard, a sociologist at the University of California, Riverside, in the late 1970s. Examining population data for communities hosting landfills and incinerators in Houston, Tex., he found that, while African-Americans made up 28% of the city's population, six of its eight incinerators and 15 of its 17 landfills were located in predominantly black neighborhoods. The presence of these facilities, Bullard suggests, not only makes black Houston the "dumping grounds for the city's household garbage," but compounds the myriad of social ills (*e.g.*, crime, poverty, drugs, unemployment, etc.) that already plague poor, inner-city communities. While limited in scope, Bullard's research has helped shape the policy debate surrounding environmental justice. His Houston study played a central role in one of the first, though unsuccessful, legal cases involving environmental discrimination, *Bean v. Southwestern Waste Management Corp.*, and forms the basis for two often-cited books, *Invisible Houston* and *Dumping in Dixie*.

The second widely discussed study examining community demographics near commercial waste treatment, storage, and disposal facilities (TSDFs) was conducted by the U.S. General Accounting Office (GAO) in 1983. The purpose was to "determine the correlation between the location of hazardous waste landfills and the racial and economic status of surrounding communities." Examining data from four facilities in EPA Region IV (Southeast region), government researchers found that the populations in three of the four surrounding areas primarily were black. African-Americans comprised 52, 66, and 90% of the population, respectively, in those three communities. In contrast, blacks made up no more than 30% of the general population of the states involved. In addition, the study found that the communities hosting waste facilities were disproportionately poor, when local poverty levels were compared to state averages.

The third, and the most often cited, study, published in 1987 by the Commission for Racial Justice (CRJ) of the United Church of Christ, had two important components: an analytical survey of commercial waste TSDFs and a descriptive analysis of uncontrolled toxic waste sites. Both statistical studies were designed to determine the extent to which African-Americans and other minority groups are exposed to hazardous wastes in their communities. By using population data (based on five-digit ZIP codes) as well as information gathered from the U.S. Environmental Protection Agency (EPA) and other sources, CRJ researchers isolated three variables: the percentage of minority population, mean household income, and mean value of owner-occupied housing.

The study revealed a correlation between the number of commercial waste facilities in a given community and the percentage of minority residents in that community. Specifically, it found that the percentage of nonwhites within ZIP codes with one waste plant was approximately twice that of ZIP codes without such a facility. For areas with more than one waste plant, the percentage of minority residents on average was three times greater than that of communities with no facilities. The CRJ found that race was statistically more significant than either mean household income or mean value of

owner-occupied housing. This suggested that race was more likely determinant of where noxious facilities were located than socioeconomic factors.

A final study deserving mention was published by the *National Law Journal* in September, 1992. Unlike the research above, which focused on the location of industrial and waste facilities, it examined racial disparities in EPA enforcement and remediation procedures. The findings indicate that significant differences exist in the fines levied against polluters in white communities and those in minority areas. The study also found that EPA took longer to clean up waste sites in poor and minority communities than in more affluent neighborhoods.

RESEARCH FLAWS

While these studies have been cited widely by environmental justice advocates, all suffer from serious methodological difficulties. Defining minority communities as those areas where the percentage of nonwhite residents exceeds that of the entire population means that a community may be considered "minority" even if the vast majority of its residents are white. For example, Staten Island, N.Y.—home of the nation's largest landfill—is considered a minority community even though more than 80% of its residents are white.

A second, but related, issue is that these studies ignore population densities. Merely citing the proportion of minority or low-income residents in a given community does not provide information about how many people actually are exposed to environmental harms. For instance, given that blacks presently comprise approximately 16% of the nation's population, a host community of 1,000 residents, 20% of whom are black, would be considered minority, while one of 6,000 residents, 15% of whom are black, would not. By overlooking population density, the studies fail to point out that more blacks (900 vs. 200) would be exposed to the pollution in the second, "non-minority," community than in the first.

In addition to the problems associated with proportionality and population density, environmental justice studies often define the affected area in geographic terms that are too broad. Much of the prior research is based on ZIP-code areas—frequently large units—established by the U.S. Postal Service. As a result, the data likely suffer from what statisticians call "aggregation errors"—i.e., the studies reach conclusions from ZIP-code data that would not be valid if a smaller, more consistent geographic unit were examined.

A third flaw is that they imply, rather than explicitly state, the actual risk presented by commercial TSDFs. While the research attempts to disclose the prevalence of commercial waste plants in poor and minority communities, there is no corresponding information about the dangers associated with living near such facilities. The regulatory requirements regarding the building and operation of industrial and waste facilities in the U.S. are among the most stringent of any industrialized country in the world. These requirements, along with the voluntary efforts of industry, significantly reduce the noxious emissions of commercial waste plants and other facilities.

Moreover, health risks are a function of actual exposure, not simply proximity to a waste facility. Environmental justice advocates' claims of negative health effects are not substantiated by scientific studies. In fact, many of the legislative proposals

to combat environmental inequities may result in greater harm to minority and poor residents than the emissions from noxious facilities themselves. By reducing the incentives for businesses to locate in poor and minority areas, these measures may exacerbate local conditions of poverty and unemployment—conditions far more unhealthy than the minute risks associated with waste disposal facilities and industrial plants.

Finally, and most critically, existing research on environmental justice fails to establish that discriminatory siting and permitting practices caused present environmental disparities. While the studies match the location of industrial and waste facilities with the current socioeconomic and racial characteristics of the surrounding neighborhoods, they do not consider community conditions when the facilities were sited. They also fail to explore alternate or additional explanations for higher concentrations of minority and low-income citizens near undesirable facilities. Thus, none prove that the siting process actually caused the disproportionate burden poor and minority communities purportedly now bear. These gaps leave open the possibility that other factors, such as the dynamics of the housing market, may lead minorities and the poor to move into areas of high industrial activity.

Clearly, there are reasons to question the validity of much of the research surrounding environmental justice. Nevertheless, there well may be room for policymakers to reform environmental laws in a manner that would prevent future environmental inequities without discouraging the siting and operation of any socially beneficial projects. Crafting such policies requires understanding pollution from an economic perspective. Such an awareness gets at the very heart of the environmental justice issue and provides a theoretical framework for dealing with the perceived problem.

Economists refer to pollution as an "external cost" or a "negative externality." Pollution is negative because it is undesirable, and it is an externality because it affects those who are outside of (*i.e.*, who have no control over) the process that creates it. Air and water pollution are examples of costs involuntarily borne by individuals outside the production process. Similarly, industrial and hazardous waste facilities may impose external costs on the host communities in the form of unpleasant noise, foul odors, increased traffic, or greater health risk.

The crux of environmental justice concerns is that particular communities (chiefly those composed of minorities and the poor) have been forced to bear disproportionately the external costs of industrial processes. It follows, then, that one way of achieving environmental equity is to ensure that these costs are borne proportionately by all who reap the benefits of these processes. Society essentially has three options for accomplishing this: eliminate all external costs of industrial processes; allocate the external costs evenly through the political system; or fairly compensate the individuals who bear these costs.

THE "BANANA" PRINCIPLE

Many environmental justice advocates appear to desire above all else the complete elimination of pollution, so that *no* community has to bear the external costs of industrial processes. This goes beyond the familiar NIMBY ("not in my backyard"). They instead are crying BANANA ("build absolutely nothing anywhere near anything") or, as one activist insisted, NOPE ("not on planet Earth"). Eliminating pollution, of course, would eradicate the problem of disproportionately distributed pollution, an issue at the heart of environmental justice. However, a moment of reflection on the BANANA principle, or a policy of complete waste elimination, reveals that such a course ultimately is not feasible. Manufacturers simply can not reduce pollution indefinitely without eliminating many valuable goods and processes Americans take for granted. In most cases, phasing out particular products is much more costly to society than accepting and treating the pollution required to create them.

Consider, for instance, pesticide utilization. In Congressional testimony on environmental justice in 1993, activist Pat Bryant demanded action "at all levels" to stop the use of pesticides. He was correct in asserting that high dosages may be harmful, but, when *properly* used, chemical pesticides produce net social benefits in the form of higher per-acre crop yields and lower food prices. Eliminating these chemicals would impose costs on society far greater than those the substances themselves do. Thus, total pollution elimination is not an optimal solution.

Pollution reduction likewise has obvious limits. As pollution is cut further and further, the incremental cost of scaling back each unit of pollution tends to rise and the incremental benefit associated with each unit of reduction falls. The optimal level of pollution reduction occurs at the point at which the incremental cost of abating an additional unit of pollution equals the incremental benefit of such abatement. Eliminating units of pollution beyond this point imposes costs on society greater than those incurred by the pollution.

Because some pollution is inevitable in modern society, policymakers may decide that the best way to ensure environmental justice is to have the government determine which communities must host undesirable facilities. Thus, a purely political solution whereby those in power simply decide where polluting and waste facilities should be located probably is not in the best interest of minorities and the economically disadvantaged, as these groups typically are underrepresented in the government. Most of those who advocate a political solution to environmental inequity argue instead for the establishment of nebulous legal and regulatory mechanisms that would force those in power to allocate pollution "fairly."

It is difficult to pinpoint exactly what those legal and regulatory mechanisms are, though. For the most part, environmental justice advocates have refrained from proposing concrete political remedies for ecological inequities. While activists often suggest creating various offices, councils, and task forces, they rarely detail how these entities should influence the pollution allocation process. While they advocate increased community involvement in siting decisions, they have yet to propose specific policies delineating how public participation is to be improved.

The few legal and regulatory mechanisms that have been suggested to remedy disparity in the allocation of pollution essentially boil down to two devices: regulations that directly would limit or prohibit future industrial siting in minority and disadvantaged communities; and penalties against presently active polluting and waste facilities that disproportionately impact minorities. The threat of such penalties, of course, would motivate facility owners to relocate or site future developments in non-minority neighborhoods.

Several proposals to prohibit siting in particular communities have been introduced in Congress and have garnered significant support from environmental justice proponents. One. by Rep. Cardiss Collins (D.-Ill.), would allow citizens to challenge and prohibit the construction of waste facilities in "environmentally disadvantaged communities." By definition, an environmentally disadvantaged community contains a higher than average percentage of low-income or minority residents and already hosts at least one waste facility, superfund site, or facility that releases toxics. Any citizen of the state in which the facility has been proposed for siting may introduce a challenge; the challenger need not reside in the affected community.

Under the Collins bill, a challenge would be granted and the proposed facility's construction and operating permits denied unless its proponent demonstrated that there is no alternative location in the state that poses fewer risks and that the proposed facility neither will release contaminants nor increase the impact of present contaminants. Even if every resident of the potential host community desired that the facility be constructed and the sole challenger lived on the opposite end of the state, construction would be forbidden as long as the challenger demonstrated that the proposed community was, in fact, an environmentally disadvantaged community and that alternative locations were available.

Grassroots activists are joining legislators in calling for prohibitions on new industry in certain communities. In Congressional testimony in 1993, Hazel Johnson of Chicago's People for Community Recovery called upon lawmakers to "place a moratorium on landfills and incinerators in residential areas." Pat Bryant, representing the Gulf Coast Tenants Association, called on "the Congress, state legislatures, and local government[s] to legislate... an immediate moratorium on the siting of all hazardous waste facilities... and the placing of polluting and nuclear industries in the South."

On the regulatory front, the EPA already is making attempts to incorporate racial and socioeconomic considerations into permitting and siting programs. EPA Administrator Carol Browner has promised to "weave environmental justice concerns throughout all aspects of EPA policy and decision-making." According to Clarice Gaylord, director of the agency's Office of Environmental Equity, "EPA offices are re-evaluating how the siting and permitting process is used to determine where hazardous and solid waste facilities are placed." She insists, "Concerted efforts are being taken to work with state and local governments to incorporate socioeconomic factors into these decisions."

The legislative proposals and the suggestions of grassroots activists are clear— the government must actively take steps to prohibit the siting of locally undesirable facilities in minority and low-income neighborhoods. EPA's initiatives are a bit more ambiguous. It is not immediately obvious how the agency will "weave environmental justice concerns" throughout all aspects of its decision-making. Specifics aside, any re-evaluation of siting and permitting processes to "incorporate socioeconomic factors" likely will have the effect of prohibiting the construction or operation of polluting and waste facilities in minority and low-income communities.

DISCOURAGING CONSTRUCTION

The second method of politically allocating pollution does not directly prohibit or limit siting in minority and disadvantaged neighborhoods. Instead, it strongly discourages the construction of polluting and waste facilities in such areas.

At the urging of environmental justice advocates, the EPA opened investigations of environmental agencies in several states for allegedly violating Title VI of the 1964 Civil Rights Act. Under Title VI, which bans discrimination by Federally funded programs, plaintiffs may prove discrimination by demonstrating that a Federal program (*e.g.*, a siting or permitting program) disproportionately impacts minorities. Plaintiffs need not establish that there was any intent to discriminate. These cases are on hold pending separate litigation.

While EPA's decision to open investigations under Title VI was somewhat controversial, Sen. Paul Wellstone (D.-Minn.) introduced legislation that would have cleared up any controversy surrounding the law's use. Explicitly applying Title VI to environmental agencies, the Public Health Equity Act of 1994 would have guaranteed that discrimination judgments against siting and permitting agencies could be based solely upon a demonstration of disparate impact. This bill never got out of committee.

Merely by demonstrating that differences in exposure exist, Title VI enables the government to deny companies needed building and operating permits and to withhold Federal money destined for offending states. The threat of discrimination suits discourages government officials from permitting and fa-cility owners from operating industrial plants in communities where such suits are likely to occur. Title VI effectively en-courages facility owners to build away from poor and minority neighborhoods.

The various proposed political solution to environmental inequity increase gov-ernment control over the siting and per-mitting of locally undesirable facilities. The idea is that, if the government has more influence in deciding where pollut-ing and waste facilities operate, it better can assure that their negative externali-ties are distributed fairly.

Eliminating environmental inequity will not be quite so simple, though. Proposals to prohibit, limit, or discour-age polluting facilities from locating in minority and low-income communities deny those areas the economic benefits associated with hosting industrial and waste plants. In many cases, these bene-fits far outweigh the costs of hosting such facilities. Affected communities should be allowed to make tradeoffs and de-cide for themselves whether or not to accept approved industrial activities. Policies arbitrarily prohibiting or dis-couraging facility owners from siting in minority and low-income neighborhoods effectively preclude residents from decid-ing to accept comparatively small risks and inconveniences in exchange for sub-stantial economic benefits.

It is possible for potential host com-munities to work out profitable agree-ments with polluting and waste facilities. To the extent that current environmental standards ensure minimal exposure risks, the primary costs associated with host-ing a polluting or waste facility are "in-conveniences" (*i.e.*, odors, increased traf-fic, unpleasant noise, etc.). Community residents might find it in their best inter-est to endure these nuisances and min-imal health risks in exchange for sub-stantial economic benefits. By denying the much-needed economic opportuni-ties, such policies exacerbate the social ills plaguing many minority and low-income neighborhoods. Even if increased siting restrictions were able to achieve a more racially balanced distribution of polluting and waste facilities, such poli-cies still would not ensure environmental justice. In essence, environmental justice rests upon two issues: that a few indi-viduals (the residents of the community hosting a polluting or waste facility) are forced to bear the external costs of in-dustrial processes from which the public at large receives benefits, and that a dis-proportionate percentage of these indi-viduals are minority or low-income citi-zens. Political solutions that simply inject racial and socioeconomic considerations into siting and permitting procedures ad-dress the latter concern, but not the for-mer. These proposals seek to guarantee that the few individuals who are affected adversely are not minority or poor resi-dents. The measures, however, do noth-ing to alleviate the first concern—the very fact that a few citizens disproportionately must bear the costs of processes that ben-efit everyone.

A third possible solution attempts to eliminate the primary environmental in-justice by "diffusing" the concentrated external costs associated with a pollut-ing or waste facility and compensating those individuals disproportionately im-pacted by the facility. There primarily are two methods of accomplishing both cost diffusion and residential compensation. If the beneficiaries of a facility are some-what well-defined (*e.g.*, the residents of a multi-county region that shares a waste disposal facility), the government may use tax revenue from those citizens to compensate the host community. Alternatively, the undesirable facility could compensate local residents directly, reflecting the cost of doing so in the prices charged to those who utilize the facility's services. Under both schemes, the external expenses of the facility are dispersed so that all who share its benefits also bear a portion of its costs. The fundamental difference between the two scenarios is that, in the former case, beneficiaries bear these costs wearing their taxpayer hat, while in the latter, they do so as consumers.

Economists refer to the procedure embodied in the second scheme as the "internalization" of external costs. Under such an approach, facility owners view the adverse local impact of their plant as part of their operating expenses and charge prices sufficiently high to cover them, using the added revenue to compensate local residents. As a result, pollution costs no longer are borne solely by those "outside" of the production process, but are dispersed equitably among those utilizing the facility's services. Due to offsetting benefits, residents of the host communities, on balance, are no worse off than they would be without the facilities.

The specific nature of these offsetting benefits may vary and should remain in the purview of the potential host community and the prospective developer. Some possible forms of compensation include direct payments to affected landowners, "host fees" paid into a community's general revenue fund that may be used to finance a variety of public projects or lower property taxes, grants for improving local health-care delivery and education, and providing parks and other recreational amenities.

Many may argue that it is immoral to pay individuals to expose themselves to health risks. Critics should keep in mind the regulatory environment in which compensation agreements are negotiated. Ecological standards are designed to guarantee a base level of environmental protection whereby the exposure risks associated with polluting and waste facilities are minor. For instance, the risk of developing cancer from living at the fence line of a properly constructed solid waste landfill is estimated to be one in a million.

While many environmental justice advocates recite anecdotes of health problems in communities adjacent to licensed facilities and claim that present regulations are inadequate, they can produce no scientific data tying these alleged ailments to pollution exposure. Should such a relationship ever be established, the appropriate policy response would be to raise the inadequate environmental standards, not to prevent individuals and facility owners from negotiating compensation agreements. As long as environmental regulations guarantee minimal risk, there should be no moral difficulties with compensating individuals for voluntarily accepting the nuisances associated with waste and polluting facilities.

In fact, agreeing to host an industrial facility in exchange for compensating benefits may *improve* a community's public health. Often, the physical ailments that seem to plague low-income communities in industrial areas stem from inadequate nutrition and health care. In such cases, the best way to alleviate them is to provide the community with economic opportunities and a better health-care system. While compensating agreements can be negotiated to include job opportunities and funding for improved health services, political solutions that force industrial facilities out of low-income and minority areas only will increase rates of unemployment and poverty—conditions proven to impose significant health risks.

SOCIAL COSTS

A second advantage of compensation approaches is that they are more likely to guarantee a socially optimal level of pollution. Since both extremes—complete pollution elimination and reckless polluting—are undesirable, society must attempt to determine the optimal level of abatement. Doing so requires a clear understanding of the full costs and benefits associated with a proposed facility. By negotiating compensation arrangements, the developer and the host community illuminate social costs, which otherwise would remain unaccounted for. As such, compensation arrangements better enable decision-makers to determine when and where to reduce pollution.

Consider, for example, the negotiations surrounding the siting of a hypothetical solid waste incinerator. Throughout the negotiating proceedings, the proposed host community gathers information concerning the local impact of the incinerator's operations. Using this data, it determines the minimum compensation required to host the facility. The developer then must decide whether to accept the community's compensation demands, implement additional abatement devices so as to reduce the level of pollution exposure and the consequent compensation requirement, or focus on an alternative host site. In some instances, the external costs associated with a proposed facility may be so high as to make it unprofitable in any location. A com-

pensation approach helps weed out such ill-conceived industrial projects.

Increasingly, private developers are using negotiated compensation as a mechanism for diffusing local opposition. Nevertheless, a number of obstacles remain in the way of widespread compensation agreements. A brief examination of one case demonstrates how legislators can encourage the use of such agreements.

Wisconsin's landfill negotiation/arbitration statute was adopted in 1981 with the intent not only to make the siting of waste facilities more efficient, but to accommodate the legitimate concerns of local residents and municipalities. The principal mechanism by which the legislation accomplishes both of these goals is the requirement that any developer wishing to site a landfill first must establish negotiations with the affected municipalities. During these negotiations, any subject is open for discussion "except the need for the facility and any proposal that would make the [developer's] responsibilities less stringent than required by the Department of Natural Resources." In principle, negotiations can continue until all of the parties' concerns are resolved. If a settlement has not been reached after a "reasonable period," one or both of the parties can request that the case be turned over to binding arbitration.

Thus far, the Wisconsin program seemingly has worked very well. Since the law took effect in 1982, just three of over 150 submitted permit applications have been arbitrated. Officials with waste management organizations apparently are quite happy with the landfill arbitration/negotiation statue. According to Joe Suchechi, manager of government affairs for WMX Technologies, Inc., requiring compensation negotiations makes it "much easier" to site and expand waste facilities in Wisconsin than in other states, where developers and potential host communities often are polarized. By involving the local community and formalizing negotiation procedures, the Wisconsin law creates a "process that gets everyone to the right place."

The virtue of the Wisconsin legislation as a model is that it includes several principles necessary for compensation agreements to be successful. First, it clearly specifies "the players of the game" —who negotiates with whom. Both developers and potential host communities are required to establish negotiating committees, with the rules regarding these representatives explicitly set forth in the statute. Second, the legislation assures that these "players" not only will negotiate, but that the results of their negotiations will be legally binding. The fulcrum of the legislation is its prohibition against constructing or operating a new facility without a siting agreement, which records the conditions and compensation to be exacted by the community from the developer, as well as the promises made by local government officials. Without such legally binding authority, the parties have fewer incentives to negotiate in good faith. Finally, the Wisconsin statute provides a way to arbitrate siting decisions should negotiations fail or should one party refuse to cooperate. Each of these criteria is crucial if negotiated compensation agreements are to be applied successfully to environmental justice issues.

POSTSCRIPT

Should Environmental Policy Be Redesigned to Cure Environmental Racism?

After describing the evidence and consequences of environmental injustice, as well as the vigorous grassroots movement it has spawned, Rosen focuses on the concern that efforts designed to achieve environmental equity may simply shift the burdens of pollution resulting from the use of inappropriate technology from one population group to another. She details the daunting obstacles that face minority activists who are guided by this fundamental concern.

Boerner and Lambert, on the other hand, assert that pollution reduction is only justified if the benefits outweigh the costs. They then suggest that such an assessment would show pollution reduction to be very costly and to have little benefit. The example they choose to support their case is the demand from environmental justice activists in the early 1990s that the use of pesticides be drastically reduced. However, their claim that chemical pesticides produce benefits such as higher crop yields and lower food prices that outweigh the environmental and human health costs they impose is contrary to the conclusions reached by many environmental, agricultural, and health care experts.

A student of the environmental justice movement would do well to read some of the many articles and books written or edited by Robert D. Bullard. His most recent book is *Unequal Protection: Environmental Justice and Communities of Color* (Sierra Club Books, 1994). Regina Austin and Michael Schill, in "Black, Brown, Red and Poisoned," *The Humanist* (July/August 1994), discuss the elitism and racism that many minority activists perceive as existing in the mainstream environmental movement. In "Waste Management and Risk Assessment: Environmental Discrimination Through Regulation," *Urban Geography* (vol. 17, no. 5, 1996), Michael Heiman describes aspects of U.S. regulatory policy that may contribute to environmental injustice and proposals by local activists for reform. The suggestion that environmental inequity may be the result of normal market dynamics rather than racism or discrimination is explored by Robert Braile in "Is Racism a Factor in Siting Undesirable Facilities?" *Garbage* (Summer 1994).

For an Internet site related to this issue, see http://www.igc.apc.org/envjustice/. This is the site for the EcoJustice Network, which addresses environmental issues facing communities of color in the United States.

ISSUE 5

Is Limiting Population Growth a Key Factor in Protecting the Global Environment?

YES: Paul Harrison, from "Sex and the Single Planet: Need, Greed, and Earthly Limits," *The Amicus Journal* (Winter 1994)

NO: Betsy Hartmann, from "Population Fictions: The Malthusians Are Back in Town," *Dollars and Sense* (September/October 1994)

ISSUE SUMMARY

YES: Author and Population Institute medal winner Paul Harrison argues for family planning programs that take into account women's rights and socioeconomic concerns in order to prevent world population from exceeding carrying capacity.

NO: Betsy Hartmann, director of the Hampshire College Population and Development Program, argues that the "real problem is not human *numbers* but undemocratic human *systems* of labor and resource exploitation, often backed by military repression."

The debate about whether human population growth is a fundamental cause of ecological problems and whether population control should be a central strategy in protecting the environment has long historical roots.

Those seriously concerned about uncontrolled human population growth are often referred to as "Malthusians" after the English parson Thomas Malthus, whose "Essay on the Principle of Population" was first published in 1798. Malthus warned that the human race was doomed because geometric population increases would inexorably outstrip productive capacity, leading to famine and poverty. His predictions were undermined by technological improvements in agriculture and the widespread use of birth control (rejected by Malthus on moral grounds), which brought the rate of population growth in industrialized countries under control during the twentieth century.

The theory of the demographic transition was developed to explain why Malthus's dire predictions had not come true. This theory proposes that the first effect of economic development is to lower death rates. This causes a population boom, but stability is again achieved as economic and social changes lead to lower birth rates. This pattern has indeed been followed in Europe, the United States, Canada, and Japan. The less-developed countries of the Third World have more recently experienced rapidly falling death rates. Thus far, the economic and social changes needed to bring down birth rates have not occurred, and many countries in Asia and Latin America suffer from exponential population growth. This fact has given rise to a group of neo-Malthusian theorists who contend that it is unlikely that Third World countries will undergo the transition to lower birth rates required to avoid catastrophe due to overpopulation.

Biologist Paul Ehrlich's best seller *The Population Bomb* (Ballantine Books, 1968) popularized his view that population growth in both the developed and developing world must be halted to avert worldwide ecological disaster. Ecologist Garrett Hardin extended the neo-Malthusian argument by proposing that some Third World nations have gone so far down the road of population-induced resource scarcity that they are beyond salvation and should be allowed to perish rather than possibly sink the remaining world economies.

Barry Commoner, a prominent early critic of the neo-Malthusian perspective, argues in *The Closing Circle* (Alfred A. Knopf, 1971) and his subsequent popular books and articles that inappropriate technology is the principal cause of local and global environmental degradation. While not denying that population growth is a contributing factor, he favors promoting ecologically sound development rather than population-control strategies that ignore socioeconomic realities.

Enthusiasts for population control as a sociopolitical and environmental strategy have always been opposed by religious leaders whose creeds reject any overt means of birth control. Recently, the traditional population control policy planners have also been confronted with charges of sexism and paternalism by women's groups, minority groups, and representatives of developing nations who argue that the needs and interests of their constituencies have been ignored by the primarily white, male policy planners of the developed world. At the September 1994 World Population Conference in Cairo, organizers and spokespeople for these interests succeeded in promoting policy statements that reflected sensitivity to many of their concerns.

In the following selections, Paul Harrison, who won a Population Institute Global Media award for his book *The Third Revolution* (Penguin Books, 1993), argues that "population growth combined with ... consumption and technology damages the environment." He proposes "quality family planning and reproductive health services, mother and child health care, women's rights and women's education" as a four-point program to rapidly decrease population growth. Betsy Hartmann, who directs the Hampshire College Population and Development Program, claims that "the threat to livelihoods, democracy and the environment posed by the fertility of poor women hardly compares to that posed by the consumption patterns of the rich or the ravages of militaries." She proposes greater democratic control over resources rather than narrow population control as an environmental strategy.

YES
Paul Harrison

SEX AND THE SINGLE PLANET:
NEED, GREED, AND EARTHLY LIMITS

Population touches on sex, gender, parenthood, religion, politics—all the deepest aspects of our humanity. Start a debate on the topic, and the temperature quickly warms up. In the preparations for next year's World Population Conference in Cairo, the link between population growth and environmental damage is one of the hottest topics.

The sheer numbers involved today make it hard to ignore the link. The last forty years saw the fastest rise in human numbers in all previous history, from only 2.5 billion people in 1950 to 5.6 billion today. This same period saw natural habitats shrinking and species dying at an accelerating rate. The ozone hole appeared, and the threat of global warming emerged.

Worse is in store. Each year in the 1980s saw an extra 85 million people on earth. The second half of the 1990s will add an additional 94 million people per year. That is equivalent to a new United States every thirty-three months, another Britain every seven months, a Washington every six days. A whole earth of 1800 was added in just one decade, according to United Nations Population Division statistics. After 2000, annual additions will slow, but by 2050 the United Nations expects the human race to total just over 10 billion —an extra earth of 1980 on top of today's, according to U.N. projections.

If population growth does not cause or aggravate environmental problems, as many feminists, socialists, and economists claim, then we do not need to worry about these numbers. If it does, then the problems of the last decade may be only a foretaste of what is to come.

At the local level, links between growing population densities and land degradation are becoming clearer in some cases. Take the case of Madagascar. Madagascar's forests have been reduced to a narrowing strip along the eastern escarpment. Of the original forest cover of 27.6 million acres, only 18.8 million acres remained in 1950. Today this has been halved to 9.4 million acres—which means that habitat for the island's unique wildlife has been halved in just forty years. Every year some 3 percent of the remaining forest is cleared, almost all of that to provide land for populations expanding at 3.2 percent a year.

The story of one village, Ambodiavi-avy, near Ranomafana, shows the process at work. Fifty years ago, the whole area was dense forest. Eight families, thirty-two people in all, came here in 1947, after French colonials burned down their old village. At first they farmed only the valley bottoms, which they easily irrigated from the stream running down from the hilltops. There was no shortage of land. Each family took as much as they were capable of working. During the course of the next forty-three years, the village population swelled ten times over, to 320, and the number of families grew to thirty-six. Natural growth was supplemented by immigration from the overcrowded plateaus, where all cultivable land is occupied. By the 1950s, the valley bottom lands had filled up completely. New couples started to clear forest on the sloping valley sides. They moved gradually uphill; today, they are two-thirds of the way to the hilltops.

Villager Zafindraibe's small paddy field feeds his family of five for only four months of the year. In 1990 he felled and burned five acres of steep forest land to plant hill rice. The next year cassava would take over. After that the plot should be left fallow for at least six or seven years.

Now population growth is forcing farmers to cut back the fallow cycle. As land shortage increases, a growing number of families can no longer afford to leave the hillsides fallow long enough to restore their fertility. They return more and more often. Each year it is cultivated, the hillside plot loses more topsoil, organic matter, nutrients.

* * *

The debate over this link between population growth and the environment has raged back and forth since 1798. In that year Thomas Malthus, in his notorious *Essay on Population*, suggested that population tended to grow faster than the food supply. Human numbers would always be checked by famine and mortality.

Socialists from William Cobbett to Karl Marx attacked Malthus's arguments. U.S. land reformer Henry George, in *Progress and Poverty* (1879), argued that the huge U.S. population growth had surged side by side with huge increases in wealth. Poverty, said George, was caused not by overpopulation, but by warfare and unjust laws. Poverty caused population growth, not the other way around.

In modern times, U.S. ecologist Paul Ehrlich has played the Malthus role. "No geological event in a billion years has posed a threat to terrestrial life comparable to that of human overpopulation," he argued back in 1970, urging compulsion if voluntary methods failed. His early extremism (such as suggesting cutting off aid to certain Third World countries) has mellowed into a more balanced analysis (for example, he acknowledges the need for more than just contraceptives to attack the problem). But doomsday rhetoric remains in his 1990 book, *The Population Explosion*, which predicts "many hundreds of millions" of famine deaths if we do not halt human population growth.

Today's anti-Malthusians come in all shades, from far left to far right. For radical writers Susan George and Frances Moore Lappé, poverty and inequality are the root causes of environmental degradation, not population. For Barry Commoner the chief threat is misguided technology. Economist Julian Simon sees moderate population growth as no problem at all, but as a tonic for economic growth. More people mean more brains to think up more solutions. "There is no meaningful limit to our capacity to keep growing forever," he wrote in 1981 in *The Ultimate Resource.*

Other voices in the debate focus on ethics and human rights. Orthodox Catholics and fundamentalist Muslims oppose artificial contraception or abortion. A wide range of feminists stress women's rights to choose or refuse and downplay the impact of population growth. "Blaming global environmental degradation on population growth," argued the Global Committee on Women, Population and the Environment before Rio, "stimulates an atmosphere of crisis. It helps lay the groundwork for an intensification of top-down population control programs that are deeply disrespectful of women."

There is no debate quite like this one for sound and fury. As the forgoing examples show, positions are emotional and polarized. Factions pick on one or two elements as the basic problem, and ignore all the others. Thinking proceeds in black-and-white slogans.

Often debaters seem to be locked into the single question: Is population growth a crucial factor in environmental degradation—or not? However, if we frame our inquiry in this simplistic way, only two answers are possible—yes or no —and only two conclusions—obsession with family planning, or opposition to family planning. Both of these positions lead to abuse or neglect of women's rights.

There has to be a way out of this blind alley. Perhaps we can make a start by accepting that *all* the factors mentioned by the rival schools are important. All interact to create the damage. Sometimes one factor is dominant, sometimes another. Population is always there. In some fields it plays the lead role, in others no more than a bit part.

Most observers agree that it is not just population growth that damages the environment. The amount each person consumes matters too, and so does the technology used in production and waste disposal. These three factors work inseparably in every type of damage. Each of them is affected by many other factors, from the status of women to the ownership of land, from the level of democracy to the efficiency of the market. If we adopt this complex, nuanced view, much of the crazy controversy evaporates, and the hard work of measuring impact and designing policy begins.

A number of success stories have emerged. One hallmark of these successes is the recognition that population should be an integral part of long-range resource management.

* * *

Take a snapshot at one particular moment, and there is no way of saying which of the three factors carries the main blame for damage. It would be like asking whether brain, bone, or muscle plays the main role in walking. But if we compare changes over time, we can get an idea of their relative strengths. Results vary a lot, depending on which country or which type of damage we are looking at.

In Madagascar, population growth bears the main blame for deforestation and loss of biodiversity. As described before, the island's rain forests have shrunk to a narrow strip. Increased consumption—a rise in living standards —and technology tend to play less and less of a role in this devastation. Incomes and food intake today are lower than thirty years ago. Farming methods have not changed in centuries.

Population growth is running at 3 percent a year. When technology is stagnant, every extra human means less forest and wildlife.

By contrast, population growth played only a minor role in creating the ozone hole. The main blame lay with rising consumption and technology change. Between 1940 and 1980, world chlorofluorocarbon (CFC) emissions grew at more than 15 percent a year. Almost all of this was in developed countries, where population grew at less than 1 percent a year. So population growth accounted for less than 7 percent (one-fifteenth) of increased CFC emissions.

A central issue in the controversy is whether we are on course to pass the earth's carrying capacity—the maximum population that the environment can support indefinitely. Malthusians like Dennis and Donnella Meadows suggest in their book *Beyond the Limits* that we have already passed the limits in some areas such as alteration of the atmosphere. Anti-Malthusians like Julian Simon insist that we can go on raising the limits through technology.

Here, too, a compromise comes closer to reality. Humans *have* raised the ceiling on growth many times in the past. When hunter-gatherers ran short of wild foods, they turned to farming. When western Europeans started to run out of wood in the seventeenth century, they turned to coal. The process continues today. When one resource runs down, its price changes, and we increase productivity or exploration, bring in substitutes, or reduce use. In other words, we do not just stand by and watch helplessly while the world collapses. We respond and adapt. We change our technology, our consumption patterns, even the number of children we have. It is because we can adapt so fast that we are the dominant species on earth.

So far adaptation has kept us well stocked with minerals despite rising use. It has proved Malthus wrong by raising food production roughly in line with the five-and-a-half-fold growth in population since his time. But it has not worked at all well in maintaining stocks of natural resources like forests, water, sea fish, or biodiversity, nor with preserving the health of sinks for liquid and gaseous wastes such as lakes, oceans, and atmosphere. These are common property resources—no one owns them—so what Garrett Hardin called the "tragedy of the commons" applies. Everyone overuses or abuses the source or sink, fearing that if they hold back others will reap the gains.

Problems like erosion, acid rain, or global warming are not easy to diagnose or cure. Sometimes we do not even know they are happening until they are far advanced, as in the case of the ozone hole. Like cancer, they build up slowly and often pass unseen till things come to a head. Farmers in Burkina Faso did not believe their land was eroding away until someone left a ruler stuck into the soil; then they saw that the level had gone down an inch in a year.

Environmental quality follows a U-shaped curve. Things get worse before they get better, on everything from biodiversity and soil erosion to air and water quality. But everything hinges on how long the downswing lasts—and how serious or irreversible are the problems it gives rise to. Given time we will develop institutions to control overfishing or ocean pollution, stop acid rain or halt global warming. But time is the crux of the matter. Adaptable though we are, we rarely act in time to prevent severe damage. In one area after another, from whales to ozone holes, we have let crises happen before taking action.

Over the next few decades we face the risk of irreversible damage on several fronts. If we lose 10 or 20 percent of species, we may never restore that diversity. If the global climate flips, then all our ability to adapt will not stave off disaster. Rather than wait for global crisis, prudence dictates that we should take action now.

However, the way we look at causes deeply affects the search for solutions. That is why the debate on population and environment matters. If we say that damage results only from technology, only from overconsumption, only from injustice, or only from population, we will act on only one element of the equation. But damage results from population, consumption, and technology multiplied together, so we must act on all three. And we cannot neglect the many factors from inequality to women's rights and free markets that influence all others.

* * *

Consumption will be the hardest nut to crack. Reducing overconsumption may be good for the soul, but the world's poorest billion must *increase* their consumption to escape poverty. The middle 3 billion will not willingly rein in their ambitions. The middle classes in India and China are already launched on the consumer road that Europe took in the 1950s. They are moving faster down that road, and their consumer class probably outnumbers North America's already. Even in the rich countries, consumption goes on growing at roughly 2 percent a year, with hiccups during recession. Consumption can be cut if consumers and producers have to pay

for the damage they do through higher prices or taxes—but, politically, it is not easy. Politicians who threaten to raise taxes risk electoral defeat.

So technological change must reduce the *impact* of consumption. But it will be a Herculean task for technology to do the job alone. The massive oil price rises of 1973 and 1979–80 stimulated big advances in energy efficiency. Between 1973 and 1988 gasoline consumption per mile in western countries fell by 29 percent. But this technology gain was wiped out by a rise in car numbers of 58 percent, due to the combined growth of population and consumption. The result was a rise in gasoline consumption of 17 percent.

Population and consumption will go on raising the hurdles that technology must leap. By 2050, world population will have grown by 80 percent, on the U.N. medium projection. Even at the low 1980s growth rate of 1.2 percent a year, consumption per person will have doubled. Technology would have to cut the damage done by each unit of consumption by 72 percent, just to keep total damage rising at today's destructive rate.

Yet the International Panel on Climate Change says we ought to *cut* carbon dioxide output by 60 percent from today's levels. If incomes and population grow as above, technology would have to cut the emissions for each unit of consumption by a massive 89 percent by 2050. This would require a 3.8 percent reduction every year for fifty-seven years.

Such a cut is not utterly impossible, but it would demand massive commitment on all sides. Introducing the 85 miles-per-gallon car could deliver a cut of almost exactly this size in the transport sector, if it took ten years to go into mass production, and another fifteen years to saturate the market. But the combined growth of population and car ownership could easily halve the gain.

Technology change will have a far easier job if it is backed by action on the population front. Population efforts are slow-acting at first: for the first fifteen years the difference is slight. The U.N.'s low population projection points to what might be achieved if all countries did their best in bringing birth rates down. Yet for 2010, the low projection for world population is only 1.2 percent less than the medium projection. Over the longer term, though, there are big benefits. By 2025 the low projection is 7.3 percent less than the medium—621 million fewer people, or a whole Europe plus Japan. By 2050 the low figure is 22 percent or 2.206 billion people less—equal to the whole world's population around 1930.

With a concerted effort in all countries (including the United States), world population could peak at 8.5 billion or less in 2050 and, after that, come down. And it is clear that this would reduce environmental impact and lower the hurdles that improved technology will have to leap.

What do we need to do to bring it about? Here, too, the debate rages. Diehard Malthusians talk of the need for crash programs of "population control." Horrified feminists answer that a woman's fertility is her own business, not a target for male policy measures. The objective should be reproductive health and choice, not simply bringing numbers down, they argue.

Yet this conflict, too, is an artificial one. The best way to bring numbers down fast is to pump resources not into crash or compulsory programs narrowly focused on family planning, but into broad women's development programs that most feminists would welcome. How do we get enough resources out of male governments to do this properly? Only by using the arguments about environment and economy that feminists do not allow.

Coercion and crash programs defeat their own aims. "Population control" is impossible without killing people: the term implies coercion and should be dropped forthwith. Coercion rouses protests that sooner or later bring it to an end. India's brief and brutal experiment with forced sterilization in 1975–76 led within a year to the fall of Indira Gandhi's government. The progress of family planning in India was set back a decade.

Mass saturation with just one or two family planning methods is equally doomed to failure. With female contraceptives, side-effects are common: women need good advice and medical backup to deal with them or avoid them. Left to handle them alone, they will stop using contraceptives and go on having five children each. Once mistrust has been aroused, it will make the job harder even when better programs are finally brought in.

If we want to bring population growth rates down rapidly, we must learn from the real success stories like Thailand. In the early 1960s, the average Thai woman was having 6.4 children. Today she is having only 2.2. This represents a drop of 3.5 percent per year—as speedy as the fastest change in technology.

Such success was achieved, without a whiff of coercion, by universal access to a wide and free choice of family planning methods, with good-quality advice and medical backup. Mother and child health was improved, women's rights were advanced, and female education leveled up with male.

All these measures are worthwhile in their own right. They improve the quality of life for women and men alike. And there are economic spin-offs. Thai incomes grew at 6 percent a year in the 1980s. A healthy and educated work force attracts foreign investment and can compete in the modern high-tech world.

Quality family planning and reproductive health services, mother and child health, women's rights, and women's education—this four-point program is the best way to achieve a rapid slowdown in population growth. It can improve the quality of life directly, through health and education benefits, and it improves the status of women. It creates a healthy and educated work force. It gives people the knowledge with which they can fight for their own rights. It might also help to raise incomes, and it will certainly help to slow environmental damage.

With its human, economic, and environmental benefits, there are few programs that will offer better value for money over the coming decades.

NO

Betsy Hartmann

POPULATION FICTIONS: THE MALTHUSIANS ARE BACK IN TOWN

In the corridors of power, the tailors are back at work, stitching yet another invisible robe to fool the emperor and the people. After 12 years in which the Reagan and Bush administrations downplayed population control as a major aim of U.S. foreign policy, the Clinton administration is playing catch-up. World attention will focus on the issue this month in Cairo, when leaders from the United States and abroad gather at the United Nations' third International Conference on Population and Development. Cloaked in the rhetoric of environmentalism and—ironically—women's rights, population control is back in vogue.

At the UN's second International Conference on Population in Mexico City in 1984, the Reagan administration asserted that rapid population growth is a "neutral phenomenon" that becomes a problem only when the free market is subverted by "too much governmental control of economies." Under the Republicans, the U.S. withdrew funding from any international family planning agencies that perform abortions or even counsel women about them. Aid was cut off to the International Planned Parenthood Foundation as well as the UN Fund for Population Activities (UNFPA).

The Clinton administration, by contrast, is requesting $585 million for population programs in fiscal year 1995, up from $502 million the year before. This aid is channelled through the U.S. Agency for International Development (USAID), which has made population control a central element of its new "Sustainable Development" mission for the post Cold War era. The USAID's draft strategy paper of October 1993 identifies rapid population growth as a key "strategic threat" which "consumes all other economic gains, drives environmental damage, exacerbates poverty, and impedes "democratic governance."

Clinton's more liberal stand on abortion is certainly welcome, but even that has yet to translate into effective Congressional action or foreign policy. Announced in April, USAID's new policy on abortion funding overseas is still very restrictive: It will finance abortion only in cases of rape, incest, and life endangerment, the same conditions the Hyde amendment puts on

From Betsy Hartmann, "Population Fictions: The Malthusians Are Back in Town," *Dollars and Sense* (September/October 1994). Copyright © 1994 by Economic Affairs Bureau, Inc. Reprinted by permission. *Dollars and Sense* is a progressive economics magazine published six times a year. First-year subscriptions cost $18.95 and may be ordered by writing to *Dollars and Sense*, 1 Summer St., Somerville, MA 02143.

federal Medicaid funds. Along with the mainstream environmental movement, the administration pays lip service to women's rights but continues to back practices—such as promoting long-acting contraceptive methods like Norplant without follow-up medical care—that are actually harmful to women's health.

POPULATION MYTHS

It is true that population growth (which is actually slowing in most areas of the world) can put additional pressure on resources in specific regions. But the threat to livelihoods, democracy and the global environment posed by the fertility of poor women is hardly comparable to that posed by the consumption patterns of the rich or the ravages of militaries.

The industrialized nations, home to 22% of the world's population, consume 60% of the world's food, 70% of its energy, 75% of its metals, and 85% of its wood. They generate almost three-quarters of all carbon dioxide emissions, which in turn comprise nearly half of the manmade greenhouse gases in the atmosphere, and are responsible for most of the ozone depletion. Militaries are the other big offenders. The German Research Institute for Peace Policy estimates that one-fifth of all global environmental degradation is due to military activities. The U.S. military is the largest domestic oil consumer and generates more toxic waste than the five largest multinational chemical companies combined.

What about the environmental degradation that occurs within developing countries? The UNFPA's *State of World Population 1992* boldly claims that population growth "is responsible for around 79% of deforestation, 72% of arable land expansion, and 69% of growth in livestock numbers." Elsewhere it maintains that the "bottom billion," the very poorest people in developing countries, "often impose greater environmental injury than the other 3 billion of their citizens put together."

Blaming such a large proportion of environmental degradation on the world's poorest people is untenable, scientifically and ethically. It is no secret that in Latin America the extension of cattle ranching —mainly for export, not domestic consumption—has been the primary impetus behind deforestation. And it is rich people who own the ranches, not the poor, as most countries in Latin America have a highly inequitable distribution of land. In Southeast Asia the main culprit is commercial logging, again mainly for export.

In developing countries, according to USAID, rapid population growth also "renders inadequate or obsolete any investment in schools, housing, food production capacity and infrastructure." But are increasing numbers of poor people really the main drain on national budgets? The UN's 1993 *Human Development Report* estimates that developing countries spend only one-tenth of their national budgets on human development priorities. Their military expenditures meanwhile soared from 91% of combined health and education expenditures in 1977 to 169% in 1990. And in any case, the social spending that there is often flows to the rich. A disproportionate share of health budgets frequently goes to expensive hospital services in urban areas rather than to primary care for the poor, and educational resources are often devoted to schools for the sons and daughters of the wealthy.

The "structural adjustment" programs imposed by the World Bank have not helped matters, forcing Third World countries to slash social spending in order to service external debts. The burden of growing inequality has fallen disproportionately on women, children, and minorities who have borne the brunt of structural adjustment policies in reduced access to food, health care and education. But in USAID's view, population growth is at the root of their misery: "As expanding populations demand an even greater number of jobs, a climate is created where workers, especially women and minorities, are oppressed."

A COSTLY CONSENSUS

In the collective psyche of the national security establishment, population growth is now becoming a great scapegoat and enemy, a substitute for the Evil Empire. A 1992 study by the Carnegie Endowment for International Peace warned that population growth threatens "international stability" and called for "a multilateral effort to drastically expand family planning services." A widely cited February 1993 *Scientific American* article by Thomas Homer-Dixon, Jeffrey Boutwell and George Rathjens identifies rapidly expanding populations as a major factor in growing resource scarcities that are "contributing to violent conflicts in many parts of the developing world."

In the pages of respectable journals, racist metaphors are acceptable again, as the concept of noble savage gives way to post-modern barbarian. In an *Atlantic Monthly* article on the "coming anarchy" caused by population growth and resource depletion, Robert Kaplan likens poor West African children to ants.

Their older brothers and fathers (and poor, nonwhite males in general) are "re-primitivized" men who find liberation in violence, since their natural aggression has not been "tranquilized" by the civilizing influences of the Western Enlightenment and middle-class existence.

The scaremongering of security analysts is complemented by the population propaganda of mainstream environmental organizations. U.S. environmentalism has long had a strong neo-Malthusian wing which views Man as the inevitable enemy of Nature. The Sierra Club backed Stanford biologist Paul Ehrlich's 1968 tract *The Population Bomb*, which featured lurid predictions of impending famine and supported compulsory sterilization in India as "coercion in a good cause."

By the late 1980s, population growth had transformed from just one of several preoccupations of the mainstream environmental movement into an intense passion. Groups such as the National Wildlife Federation and the National Audubon Society beefed up their population programs, hoping to attract new membership. Meanwhile, population lobbyists such as the influential Population Crisis Committee (renamed Population Action International) seized on environmental concerns as a new rationale for their existence.

The marriage of convenience between the population and environment establishments led to many joint efforts in advance of the 1992 UN Conference on Environment and Development (UNCED) in Rio de Janeiro. In 1990, Audubon, National Wildlife, Sierra Club, Planned Parenthood Federation of America, and the Population Crisis Committee began a joint Campaign on Population and the Environment. Its major objective was "to expand public awareness of the link between population growth, environmental degradation and the resulting human suffering."

Despite their efforts, the U.S. population/environment lobby had a rude awakening at Rio. In the formal intergovernmental negotiations, many developing nations refused to put population on the UNCED agenda, claiming it would divert attention from the North's responsibility for the environmental crisis. At the same time the nongovernmental Women's Action Agenda 21, endorsed by 1500 women activists from around the world, condemned suggestions that women's fertility rates were to blame for environmental degradation.

In the aftermath of Rio, "the woman question" has forced the population/environment lobby to amend its strategy. Many organizations are emphasizing women's rights in their preparations for the Cairo conference. Women's empowerment—through literacy programs, job opportunities, and access to health care and family planning—is now seen as a prerequisite for the reduction of population growth.

While this is a step forward, the population/environment lobby largely treats the protection of women's rights as a means to population reduction, rather than as a worthy pursuit in itself. Its inclusion—and co-optation—of feminist concerns is part of a larger strategy to create a broad population control "consensus" among the American public. Behind this effort is a small group of powerful actors: the Pew Charitable Trusts Global Stewardship Initiative; the U.S. State Department through the office of Timothy Wirth, Undersecretary for Global Affairs; the UNFPA; and Ted Turner of the powerful Turner Broadcasting System, producer of CNN.

Although the Pew Initiative's "White Paper" lists "population growth and unsustainable patterns of consumption" as its two targets, population growth is by far its main concern. Among Pew's explicit goals are to "forge consensus and to increase public understanding of, and commitment to act on, population and consumption challenges." Its targeted constituencies in the United States are environmental organizations, religious communities, and international affairs and foreign policy specialists.

Pew and the Turner Foundation have sponsored "high visibility" town meetings on population around the country, featuring Ted Turner's wife Jane Fonda, who is also UNFPA's "Goodwill Ambassador." At the Atlanta meeting, covered on Turner's CNN, Fonda attributed the collapse of two ancient Native American communities to overpopulation.

To prepare for the Cairo conference, the Pew Initiative hired three opinion research firms to gauge public understanding of the connections between population, environment and consumption so as to "mobilize Americans" on these issues. The researchers found that the public generally did not feel strongly about population growth or see it as a "personal threat." Their conclusion: An "emotional component" is needed to kindle population fears. Those interviewed complained that they had already been overexposed to "images of stark misery, such as starving children." Although the study notes that these images may in fact "work," it recommends finding "more current, targeted visual devices." One strategy is to build on people's pessimism about the future: "For women, particularly, relating the problems of excess population growth to children's future offers possibilities."

SACRIFICED RIGHTS

Whatever nods the new "consensus" makes towards women's broader rights and needs, family planning is its highest priority. USAID views family planning as "the single most effective means" of reducing population growth; it intends to provide "birth control to every woman in the developing world who wants it by the end of the decade."

The promotion of female contraception as the technical fix for the "population problem" ignores male responsibility for birth-control and undermines the quality of health and family planning services. The overriding objective is to drive down the birth rate as quickly and cheaply as possible, rather than to address people's broader health needs.

In Bangladesh, for example, at least one-third of the health budget is devoted to population control. The principal means is poor-quality female sterilization with incentives for those who undergo the procedure, including cash payments for "wages lost" and transportation costs, as well as a piece of clothing (justified as "surgical apparel"). The World Bank and population specialists are now heralding Bangladesh as a great family planning success story. But at what human cost? Because of the health system's nearly exclusive emphasis on population control, most Bangladeshis have little or no access to primary health care, and infant and maternal death rates remain at tragically high levels.

Lowering the birth rate by itself has hardly solved the country's problems. Poverty in Bangladesh has much more to do with inequitable land ownership and the urban elite's stranglehold over external resources, including foreign aid, than it does with numbers of people. The great irony is that many people in Bangladesh wanted birth control well before the aggressive and often coercive sterilization campaign launched by the government with the help of the World Bank and AID. A truly voluntary family planning program, as part of more comprehensive health services, would have yielded similar demographic results, without deepening human suffering.

The prejudice against basic health care is also reflected in the UN's first draft of the "Program of Action" for the Cairo conference. It asks the international community to spend $10.2 billion on population and family planning by the year 2000, and only $1.2 billion on broader reproductive health services such as maternity care. After pressure from women's groups and more progressive governments, the UN raised this figure to $5 billion, but family planning still has a two-to-one advantage. Meanwhile, the Vatican is attacking women's rights by bracketing for further negotiation any language in the Cairo document which refers to abortion, contraception or sexuality. Women are caught between a rock and a hard place, bracketed by the Vatican, and targeted by the population establishment.

The current focus of population programs is on the introduction of long-acting, provider-dependent contraceptive technologies. The hormonal implant Norplant, for example, which is inserted in a woman's arm, is effective for five years and can only be removed by trained medical personnel. But often, these methods are administered in health systems that are ill-equipped to distribute them safely or ethically; In population programs in Indonesia, Bangladesh and Egypt, researchers have documented many instances of women being denied access to Norplant removal, as well as receiving inadequate counselling, screening, and follow-up care.

A number of new contraceptives in the pipeline pose even more serious problems, in terms of both health risks and the potential for abuse at the hands of zealous population control officials. The non-surgical quinacrine sterilization pellet, which drug specialists suspect may be linked to cancer, can be administered surreptitiously (it was given to Vietnamese women during IUD checks without their knowledge in 1993). Also potentially dangerous are vaccines which immunize women against reproductive hormones. Their long-term reversibility has not yet been tested, and the World Health Organization has expressed some concern about the drugs' interaction with the immune system, especially in people infected with the AIDS virus. Simpler barrier methods, such as condoms and diaphragms, which also protect against sexually transmitted diseases, continue to receive considerably less attention and resources in population programs since they are viewed as less effective in preventing births.

Recently, a network of women formed a caucus on gender issues in order to pressure USAID to live up to its rhetoric about meeting women's broader reproductive health needs. The caucus emerged in the wake of a controversial USAID decision to award a $9 million contract for studying the impact of family planning on women's lives to Family Health International, a North-Carolina-based population agency, rather than to women's organizations with more diverse and critical perspectives.

Progressive environmentalists also intend to monitor USAID's planned initiative to involve Third World environmental groups in building "grass roots awareness around the issue of population and family planning." They fear that USAID funds will be used to steer these groups away from addressing the politically sensitive root causes of environmental degradation—such as land concentration, and corporate logging and ranching—toward a narrow population control agenda.

TROUBLE AT HOME

Within the United States, the toughest battle will be challenging the multimillion dollar public opinion "consensus" manufactured by Pew, the State Department, and CNN. Not only does this consensus promote heightened U.S. involvement in population control overseas, but by targeting women's fertility, it helps lay the ground, intentionally or not, for similar domestic efforts.

The Clinton administration is considering whether to endorse state policies that deny additional cash benefits to women who have babies while on welfare. (This despite the fact that women on welfare have only two children on average.) A number of population and environment groups are also fomenting dangerous resentment against immigrant women. The Washington-based Carrying Capacity Network, for example, states that the United States has every right to impose stricter immigration controls "as increasing numbers of women from Mexico, China and other areas of the world come to the United States for the purpose of giving birth on U.S. soil." And in many circles, Norplant is touted as the wonder drug which will cure the epidemic of crime and poverty allegedly caused by illegitimacy.

Such simple solutions to complex social problems not only don't work, they often breed misogyny and racism, and they prevent positive public action on finding real solutions. Curbing industrial and military pollution, for example, will do far more to solve the environmental crisis than controlling the wombs of poor women who, after all, exert the least pressure on global resources.

The real problem is not human *numbers* but undemocratic human systems of labor and resource exploitation, often backed by military repression. We need to rethink the whole notion of "carrying capacity"—are we really pressing up against the earth's limits because there are too many of us? It would make more sense to talk about "political carrying capacity," defined as the limited capacity of the environment and economy to sustain inequality and injustice. Viewed this way, the solution to environmental degradation and economic decline lies in greater democratic control over resources, not in a narrow population control agenda.

POSTSCRIPT

Is Limiting Population Growth a Key Factor in Protecting the Global Environment?

Harrison extols the virtues of Thailand's population-control program, which he claims has achieved success in significantly reducing birthrates without coercion while promoting women's health care and female education. He implies that this policy has contributed to a growth in average income and the ability to "compete in the modern high-tech world." He does not, however, respond to Hartmann's argument that such policies alone do not ensure a reduction in environmental degradation.

Anyone with a serious interest in environmental issues should certainly read Paul Ehrlich's *The Population Bomb* (Ballantine Books, 1968) and Barry Commoner's *The Closing Circle* (Alfred A. Knopf, 1971). Ehrlich was so distressed by the arguments contained in Commoner's popular book that he coauthored a detailed critique with environmental scientist John P. Holden, which Commoner answered with a lengthy response. These two no-holds-barred pieces were published as a "Dialogue" in the May 1972 issue of the *Bulletin of the Atomic Scientists*. They are interesting reading not only for their technical content but as a rare example of respected scientists airing their professional and personal antagonisms in public.

Another frequently cited, controversial essay in support of the neo-Malthusian analysis is "The Tragedy of the Commons," by Garrett Hardin, which first appeared in the December 13, 1968, issue of *Science*. For a thorough attempt to justify his authoritarian response to the world population problem, see Hardin's book *Exploring New Ethics for Survival* (Viking Press, 1972).

An economic and political analyst who is concerned about the connections among population growth, resource depletion, and pollution—but who rejects Hardin's proposed solutions—is Lester Brown, director of the Worldwatch Institute. His worldview is detailed in *The Twenty-Ninth Day* (W. W. Norton, 1978).

Anyone willing to entertain the propositions that pollution has not been increasing, natural resources are not becoming scarce, the world food situation is improving, and population growth is actually beneficial might find economist Julian Simon's *The Ultimate Resource* (Princeton University Press, 1982) amusing, if not convincing.

For an assessment of needs and strategies to control population growth by several international authorities, including Commoner, see "A Forum: How Big Is the Population Factor?" in the July/August issue of *EPA Jour-*

nal. Paul Ehrlich's present views, which have been somewhat modified in response to criticism by feminists and Third World peoples, are presented in an article that he coauthored with Anne Ehrlich and Gretchen Daily in the September/October 1995 issue of *Mother Jones*. A series of articles on the connections among population, development, and environmental degradation are included in the February 1992 issue of *Ambio*.

Harrison's essay is part of a special section entitled "Population, Consumption and Environment" in the Winter 1994 issue of *The Amicus Journal*, which includes other articles focusing on the needs and concerns of Third World people, along with brief statements representing the views of people from all over the world about the issues that were to be debated at the 1994 Cairo population conference. The Spring 1994 issue of that journal includes an essay by Jodi L. Jacobson that addresses some of the same concerns raised by Hartmann. Distinguished environmentalist Michael Brower addresses the population debate in the Fall 1994 issue of *Nucleus*, the magazine of the Union of Concerned Scientists. A provocative response to the Cairo meeting is the article by Norway's prime minister and sustainable development advocate Gro Harlem Brundtland in the December 1994 issue of *Environment*. Gita Sen, in "The World Programme of Action: A New Paradigm for Population Policy," *Environment* (January/February 1995), describes and analyzes the World Programme of Action, which is the main working document emanating from the Cairo conference. Robin Morgan, in "Dispatch from Beijing," *Ms.* (January/February 1996), reports on the follow-up UN Fourth World Conference on Women, which was held in Beijing in 1995.

In her book *Reproductive Rights and Wrongs: The Global Politics of Population Control*, rev. ed (South End Press, 1995), Betsy Hartmann offers a radical critique of the extent to which the women's rights movement has accepted the politics and rhetoric of what she refers to as the "population establishment."

Finally, for an Internet site related to this issue, see http://www.ucsusa.org/global/population.html. This Union of Concerned Scientists Net site is an excellent source of information for understanding the population/environment connection.

ISSUE 6

Should Property Owners Be Compensated When Environmental Restrictions Limit Development?

YES: Ed Carson, from "Property Frights," *Reason* (May 1996)

NO: Doug Harbrecht, from "A Question of Property Rights and Wrongs," *National Wildlife* (October/November 1994)

ISSUE SUMMARY

YES: Ed Carson, a reporter for *Reason* magazine, bemoans the fact that property rights activists have thus far been unsuccessful in convincing voters that owners should be compensated when the state restricts the uses of their land.

NO: *Business Week's* Washington correspondent Doug Harbrecht claims that it is absurd to have to pay owners of private property for obeying environmental regulations.

The question of possible conflicts between the public interest and a private landowner's development plans for his or her property is not a new issue. It has, however, taken on new meaning over the past decade as a result of a growing U.S. property rights movement that has been attempting, with some success, to prevent local, federal, and state governments from imposing environmentally motivated restrictions on the use of private property without due compensation for any resulting loss of value to the landholder.

Those who defend the absolute development rights of landowners frequently justify their position by quoting from the writings of seventeenth-century political philosopher John Locke. They further cite as a legal basis for their position the eminent domain clause of the Fifth Amendment, which prohibits the government from "taking" private property for public use without just compensation.

Opponents of the property rights activists maintain that Locke based his position on the abundant availability of land that prevailed in his day and that he considered undeveloped land to be of no value, a position that would find few supporters today. They argue further that the environmental problems that have resulted from population pressures coupled with inappropriate development could hardly have been foreseen by a seventeenth-century philosopher. In their view the language of the Fifth Amendment was meant to preclude actual seizure of property by the government, not loss of value resulting from regulatory restrictions.

The courts have historically supported this latter interpretation. However, in a few recent cases, court rulings have interpreted the "taking" of property as possible, including those cases where the regulatory restriction was such as to render the property totally worthless or where the public benefits resulting from the restriction could not be shown to be at least commensurate with the loss of value suffered by the property owner.

Only the most extreme property rights advocates argue that all regulations require compensation to a landowner for the potential value of activities they preclude. Few would support the rights of a landowner to profit from a project that results in a serious pollution problem that is not confined to the owner's property. It is also generally recognized that investment in property is a speculative activity and that the purchaser should be aware that potential actions by governments or private parties can result in either the enhancement or the diminution of the worth or value of the property.

Despite the legislative and judicial progress that has been made, the property rights movement has not had much success at the ballot box. Well-publicized property rights initiatives were soundly defeated by the voters in Arizona in 1994 and again in the state of Washington in 1995.

Ed Carson is a reporter for *Reason*, a magazine that supports the libertarian political perspective, which includes almost unqualified support for the rights of private property owners. In the following selection, he exhorts rural landowners to find some way of convincing urban and suburban voters of the primacy of property rights if they are to prevail in future statewide initiatives. Doug Harbrecht is a Washington-based correspondent for *Business Week*. In his view environmental laws do more to protect than to reduce property rights. He fears that legislative proposals that would require compensation to property owners for decreases in value resulting from such laws will make it economically impossible for the government to require an ecologically sound development policy.

YES   Ed Carson

PROPERTY FRIGHTS

When Phil Marble went door to door in Bellevue and Seattle, Washington, last fall soliciting support for Referendum 48, a sweeping statewide property rights initiative, he used his own experience to get people's attention.

A Washington native, Marble had worked as a reforestation contractor and landscaper in the '70s and '80s. Then in 1990 he decided to start a nursery that would specialize in native plants. He bought 16 acres in a rural area of Whatcom County, which butts up against the Canadian border.

Six months later, the nearby Nooksack River flooded and scoured topsoil off of much of his property, leaving one-third to one-half useless for nursery purposes. The state Soil Conservation Department quickly approved Marble's plan to replace the topsoil. But several of his neighbors were major players in the local and county governments, and they wanted to direct future flood waters from their land onto his. Naturally, they didn't want to pay for it.

"I was the fall guy. I was new on the block, and I guess they figured I could be a pushover," Marble says.

Just as Marble was finally ready to begin replacing 40,000 yards of soil, the country suddenly issued a stop-work order in September 1993. The order didn't list any specific violations; it just stated that he was exceeding the approved restoration plan. Later county officials told Marble he was filling in a floodway and ordered him to create a channel seven feet deep, 200 feet wide, and 1,200 feet long. But according to Marble, no such floodway had ever existed in the past—and he has an engineering study and 50 years of aerial photographs to prove it. Gene Aarstol, one of Marble's neighbors and head of the Deming Diking Association, wrote in a February 12, 1996, letter to Whatcom County Executive Peter Kramen that "there has been a floodway and overflow channel through Mr. Marble's property ever since my 94-year-old father and I can remember."

County officials didn't back down, so Marble filed suit against the county on Fifth and 14th Amendment due process grounds. His case has been in federal court for nearly two years, and chances are it will drag on for years to come.

Marble estimates he's racked up $300,000 in engineering studies and lawyers' fees, and that's not counting the cost of keeping nearly half his land idle. To get by, he's been freelancing as a landscaper. Though he doesn't want to dwell on his predicament, it's clear he's very concerned about the future.

"Look, I'm 49, It's taken five years of my life, and it takes years to get any plants on line. What am I going to do?"

Even if he wins, he could lose.

"We're talking about so much money that the county would have to pony up. I could end up winning, but still owe large amounts to my lawyer," says Marble.

When Marble finished telling his story, people would shake his hand, tell him how much they sympathized with his situation—and say they were going to vote against Referendum 48.

"It was very disheartening," he says.

Disheartening not only to Marble but to property rights supporters in Washington and across the country. Referendum 48 was a high-profile showcase for the movement, and it lost by a resounding 3–2 margin. The measure was pounded in urban and suburban areas. And it wasn't the first time voters had rejected a property rights measure. In 1994, Arizona voters overturned a 1992 takings bill by the same ratio.

In many respects 1995 was a banner year for the property rights movement. Protecting property rights was a key component of the Contract with America, and dozens of states considered takings legislation. But for all their successes, property rights supporters have yet to show that they can win at the ballot box. They have not demonstrated that they can convince the broad majority of citizens that protecting property rights —and compensating people for their losses—is a matter of good government and simple justice. And they've made political and drafting mistakes that have further hampered their cause.

* * *

Future political historians may look at these setbacks as rookie errors. It's easy to forget, but the modern property rights movement is less than 10 years old. "When we founded our organization in July 1990, you probably could have counted the state and local organizations on one hand," says Peggy Riegle, chairman of Fairness to Landowners Committee, a national property rights organization.

In the mid-1980s, University of Chicago law professor Richard Epstein provided the intellectual framework for the property rights movement. Historically, property owners have received compensation only when the state takes outright possession of their land. Epstein argued that regulations that diminish the use and value of property are no different from any other kind of taking. Public interest law firms, such as the Institute for Justice, Pacific Legal Foundation, and Northwest Legal Foundation, used Epstein's work to launch a property rights renaissance in the courts. Disgruntled ranchers, farmers, and foresters began to coalesce and form grassroots organizations across the country.

In many parts of the country property rights groups focus their attention on federal laws: on the Endangered Species Act, the Environmental Protection Agency, and wetlands regulations. But the federal government isn't the only threat. Washington state groups direct much of their attention on the State Environmental Policy Act and state buffer zones, wetland ordinances, and fish and wildlife habitat regulations.

"Most of the buffer zones and designated wetlands come from the state," says John Carlson, chairman of the Washington Institute for Policy Studies and host of a local conservative radio talk show. Hence the movement to do something about takings at the state level.

The Washington property rights movement expanded and broadened its base following passage of the Growth Management Act in 1990 and 1991, which implemented comprehensive statewide land-use planning standards for the first time. The GMA created urban growth boundaries, sharply limiting the permissible uses of property outside them. "Thousands of property owners were wiped out at the stroke of a pen," says Jim Klauser, executive director of the Northwest Legal Foundation.

But though the property rights movement in Washington and elsewhere grew rapidly, activists spent most of those early years in rural areas out of the limelight and without political influence. Like the Congressional Black Caucus today, property rights supporters were a minority faction in the minority party. In Washington state, they spent five years at the legislature just trying to get committee hearings for their bills. Frustrated by inaction, Dan Wood of the Washington State Farm Bureau organized a petition drive for an "initiative to the legislature" in 1994. As the name suggests, this type of initiative goes to the legislature, which must pass the measure within two years without any changes or it goes to the ballot. If the initiative passes, it becomes law without the governor's signature.

Activists didn't have high expectations that the legislature would pass any property rights bill, so they went for the brass ring. Unlike most takings legislation, Initiative 164, as Referendum 48 was known then, had no threshold for compensation—compensation was due for *any* regulatory taking, no matter how small—and was not limited to environmental regulations. The measure would have required state and local agencies to prepare an economic impact statement before adding new land-use regulations for public benefit and to choose the option with the least impact on private property. Then those agencies would compensate property owners for any resulting loss in value.

The initiative languished, but then the 1994 elections changed the political environment. Republicans took control of the state House and narrowed the gap in the Senate. Suddenly Initiative 164 had a chance—if it qualified. Developers poured money into the campaign and gathered the necessary signatures. The House passed the initiative 69–27. It was bottled up in the Senate for some time, but Republicans and rural Democrats forced a floor vote and it passed 27–20. Supporters didn't have much time to savor the victory, however, because opponents quickly gathered signatures to place the measure on the ballot that November as Referendum 48. They figured that property rights protections couldn't survive a showdown at the ballot box.

Something similar happened in Arizona. There, property rights supporters had an easier time winning their initial legislative victory because the state legislature and governor were pro–property rights. The 1992 bill would have required every state agency to determine the impact of new regulations and decide how to compensate landowners for any loss in property value. Before the bill could become law, however, green groups put the measure before the voters as a referendum.

* * *

Used to being a minority in the minority, property rights activists in both states previously had little incentive or opportunity to go beyond their circle or true believers and those who were well-versed in property rights. Suddenly they had to take their case to voters who knew little or nothing about the issue and find a way to convince them in 15- and 30-second soundbites.

Bob Robb, an Arizona political consultant, says the campaigns made the mistake of assuming that most voters already understood and embraced their viewpoint. "Most Americans are not taught that private property is essential to our freedoms. They are taught that property rights are inferior," he says.

Robb says another problem that proponents of the Arizona campaign had was showing "clear-cut abuses that this law would prevent," because most of the egregious takings cases in that state are committed by the federal government. Dan Jansen, counsel to Arizona Speaker Mark Killian, who led the legislative effort to pass the property rights bill, concedes that may be true but says, "If you're in the state legislature, you do what you can. You can't pass a law that reins in the EPA."

Activists in Washington didn't have that problem because they could target SEPA, the Growth Management Act, and other state and local laws resulting in regulatory takings. The Referendum 48 campaign highlighted the experiences of Phil Marble and other property owners, hoping to convince voters that the state was unfairly imposing the cost of regulations on real people. These horror stories had played well among people in rural areas, who were legitimately afraid that regulations could devastate their livelihoods. But a family living in the suburbs isn't worried about bureaucrats declaring their backyard a protected habitat for the spotted owl or their swimming pool a wetland.

"Proponents never did go to the average person who rents or has a single-family home and say this situation is intolerable and is hurting the average person," says Skip Richards, founder of the Committee for Land Use Education (CLUE) in Whatcom County. He says the campaign should have stressed how government restrictions on property hurt average voters by increasing the cost of housing and limiting job growth. But that is a hard case to make. The only direct experience that most people have with land-use regulation is with zoning ordinances. Even though people may understand intellectually that zoning raises the price of housing, those costs are hidden and indirect. If people can't see the cost, it doesn't make them upset.

And the truth is that most people like zoning. They believe it preserves the property values and character of the neighborhood. As with the school choice issue, voters in the suburbs see stronger property rights as something that would help *other* people, but would raise *their* taxes and threaten *their* neighborhoods. And if suburban voters won't give inner-city kids educational alternatives, they aren't going to vote to pay rural landowners and developers to comply with environmental regulations.

"If there is even the slightest risk that something could raise their taxes, they'll vote no," says CLUE's Richards.

That's what Marble discovered going door to door.

"People didn't want to pay for it. I heard that so many times from people I talked to," he says.

Environmental concerns also helped the opposition. Opponents in Washington and Arizona said the referenda were "pay the polluter" measures that would eviscerate environmental regulations. That charge fueled voters' already negative perception of Republicans and conservatives on environmental issues. Republican pollster Linda DiVall found in a recent nationwide survey that voters prefer Democrats 2–1 over Republicans on the environment. More damning was her finding that *Republican* voters, particularly those in the suburbs, have more confidence in the Democratic Party to protect the environment. Washington and Arizona voters are no exception.

But for the most part the opposition campaigns soft-pedaled green concerns and concentrated on a pocketbook message: This measure will raise taxes and increase bureaucracy. Late in the Referendum 48 campaign a study by the University of Washington's Institute for Public Policy and Management estimated that the initiative's cost could run as high as $12 billion. Many observers say it was a fatal blow to the pro side. "After that [study was released], most people stopped listening," says Richards.

Proponents tried to discredit the study, pointing out that it was funded by environmental foundations with connections to the opposition campaign and used data collected from local governments, which opposed 48. They argued that the study's estimates were way off, in large part because it assumed that government agencies would continue business as usual.

"I'm convinced that if [Referendum 48] had passed, it would have changed the government's behavior. We wanted government to think twice before imposing new regulations, and make sure it was worth the cost," says Tom McCabe, executive vice president of the Building Association of Washington and one of the leaders of the "yes on 48" campaign.

But they hadn't convinced voters that government behavior needed to be radically changed—certainly not at the price of higher taxes. A *Seattle Times* poll found that people who thought their taxes would go up voted no by a 3–1 margin. Even worse, Referendum 48 even lost in rural eastern Washington by 6,000 votes.

"They used a conservative argument to defeat a conservative idea," says McCabe.

* * *

Many people who supported Referendum 48 say the initiative was its own worst enemy, however. "Referendum 48 was recklessly written. Even those who defended it had to add caveats as to how the legislature could fine-tune it," says radio host Carlson, who led a successful initiative campaign in Washington to pass the nation's first "three strikes" law. "They had all the right ideas and all the right principles, but [Referendum 48's] vagaries allowed critics to make worst-case scenarios."

Wallace Rudolph, a professor of constitutional and administrative law at Seattle University, says he voted for Referendum 48, but its ambiguous wording left several important components open to interpretation: The measure would certainly apply to relevant regulations that were passed after the measure became law. But would it trigger compensation for new enforcement of old regulations (probably), or current enforcement of old regulations (very unlikely)?

Property restrictions for the public benefit—Referendum 48 listed regulations protecting wetlands, buffer zones, fish and wildlife habitat as examples—would have required compensation. Regulations that curtail public nuisances, which represent a harm to the entire community, would not. But there is no comprehensive list or standard to apply.

The public-nuisance standard probably would apply to some zoning regulations, such as prohibiting sewer plants in residential neighborhoods—though House Majority Leader Dale Foreman suggested that a ban on spraying pesticides near a school might require compensation. But most zoning laws would seem to fall under the public benefit heading because they protect and preserve the "essential characteristics" of neighborhoods.

However, John Groen, staff attorney for the Bellevue, Washington, office of the Pacific Legal Foundation, says that Referendum 48 would have required compensation only for regulations similar to the wetland, buffer zone, and habitat restrictions cited in the initiative—which usually leave a portion of the land completely idle. This interpretation would exclude popular zoning ordinances. But it also would mean that government agencies would have been obligated to compensate landowners when *part* of the property is rendered *completely* idle, yet could have imposed regulation that sharply *limited* the use of *all* of the property without compensation.

Even Dan Wood, the measure's original sponsor, wrote in a memo to Referendum 48 supporters shortly after the defeat that "our opponents have identified 'problem areas' with 164/48. Zoning, Retroactivity, and the Economic Impact Statement were identified as problem areas, as well as some technical language."

How could property rights supporters have drafted an initiative that Carlson says "became a millstone around the necks of its supporters"? Rudolph, who helped write the state's term limits initiative that passed in 1992, says that too often "when people get together to draft an initiative they only see the virtue of their side and no one tries to pick it apart." In the legislative process, confusing or unpopular provisions in a bill can be clarified, modified, or removed at any point until it's signed into law. But an initiative's language is frozen once it's filed, and that includes initiatives to the legislature. By the time Initiative 164/Referendum 48's "problem areas" were identified, it was too late to change anything.

Because of the 1994 elections, property rights had far more supporters in the legislature than Initiative 164's backers had anticipated. Legislators could have drafted a narrower and less-ambiguous bill, but ironically it would have had less chance of becoming law than the flawed 164. A property rights bill, unlike the initiative to the legislature, would have required Democratic Gov. Mike Lowry's signature, and he would have vetoed it. So legislators passed 164, but not before Majority Leader Foreman and Rep. Mike Padden engaged in a colloquy—a scripted exchange—intended to clarify what the legislature believed the initiative would and would not do. The legislators hoped the courts would consider that interpretation when they determined the measure's scope.

But arguing that the scope of Referendum 48 *probably* wouldn't wipe out zoning and *probably* wasn't retroactive—after all, no one could know for sure until it became law—didn't play well with the voters. "I believe the courts would have handled it and come up with the correct interpretation, but that's not going to cut it in an initiative campaign," says law professor Rudolph.

* * *

Property rights supporters looking at the results from Washington should be careful not to blame their defeat entirely on bad drafting, however. The Arizona bill was technically sound, and it was trounced by the same margin and lost in many rural areas of the state. Working on a more modest scale, however, activists have made gains even in those states. Arizona enacted a limited bill in 1995 that codifies the 1994 *Dolan* Supreme Court decision, which ruled that governments cannot force individuals to give up property rights in exchange for other rights without compensation.

In Washington state, Richard Sanders, a veteran property rights lawyer, was elected to the state Supreme Court Jeanette Burrage, former executive director of the Northwest Legal Foundation, was elected to the King County Superior Court. Voters in Whatcom County approved a "mini 48" backed by CLUE, adding property rights language to the county charter. The state House has passed a bill this session known as "48 lite" or "48 done right," but no one gives the bill any chance of becoming law this year. Supporters are hoping a new, pro-property rights governor will be elected this fall.

Nationally, federal takings legislation remains stalled and congressional Republicans are rethinking their strategy for the entire environmental reform agenda. Referendum 48's defeat has dampened enthusiasm for property rights initiatives in other states. However, 17 states passed some takings legislation in 1995. Florida, Louisiana, Mississippi, and Texas enacted laws with compensation provisions, though none as sweeping as Washington's would have been.

Fairness to Landowners' Riegle says activists will continue to focus on legislative efforts. But property rights organizations are strongest in the West, where virtually all of the states have an initiative and referendum process. After their victories in Arizona and Washington, property rights opponents in those other states are sure to challenge any major takings measure. So in the end property rights forces will have to face voters directly in many cases.

"They say conservatives are liberals who get mugged. Maybe more rural people need for it to happen to them to be convinced," Riegle says. That might help in rural areas, but property rights activists cannot win any statewide initiative without significant support from urban and suburban areas. Until they can solve this electoral question, they aren't going to like the voters' answer.

NO

Doug Harbrecht

A QUESTION OF PROPERTY RIGHTS AND WRONGS

Ralph Seidel's livelihood depends on the clean waters of Natrona Creek in rural Pratt County, Kansas, where he owns a golf course, a private fishing resort and a trailer park. But for more than two decades, starting in the late 1960s, neighboring cattle outfit Pratt Feeders dumped livestock wastes into the creek, causing repeated fish kills, according to state environmental officials. When the company's pollution-control permits came up for renewal a few years ago, Seidel organized a public uprising that led to state changes in Pratt Feeders' permits requiring more stringent treatment of its waste water.

Seidel's property rights, not Pratt's, were the issue. "That's what 'property rights' has always meant for conservationists: protections for average Americans and their property," says National Wildlife Federation [NWF] attorney Glenn Sugameli. But a new property-rights movement is afoot, one that could lead polluters like Pratt Feeders—to claim loss of *their* property rights through regulations. All over the country, ranchers, developers, mining companies and others are charging that property owners should be "compensated" if obeying the law lowers the value of private property or results in less-than-anticipated corporate profit.

The notion may seem absurd. "The whole idea that the government needs to pay people not to do bad things is ridiculous," says John Humbach, a property-rights expert at Pace University. "The reason the government exists in the first place is to define what is for the common good and what's not."

Absurd or not, the movement has become a political force to be reckoned with, linked as it is to the powerful notion that landowners should be allowed to do what they want with their property. "People better start taking this movement seriously," says Robert Meltz, a property-law expert at the Congressional Research Service. "This isn't just some fringe element anymore." The proof can be found in Congress, where proposed property-rights amendments are delaying nearly all major environmental legislation.

The new movement has the potential to disrupt a delicate balance between private greed and public need forged over two centuries of U.S. property law, legal experts say. The outcome will affect the survival of endangered wildlife, and it threatens not only environmental protections like pollution laws, but also zoning regulations and even obscenity laws. "Extremists are trying to take away the ability of Americans to act through their government to protect neighboring private-property owners and the public welfare," says NWF's Sugameli.

In Congress, property-rights debates have held up renewal of the Endangered Species Act, originally slated for 1993, and reauthorization of the Clean Water Act. Property-rights issues have also helped hold up bills to reform the Mining Law of 1872, elevate the Environmental Protection Agency to Cabinet status and reauthorize the Safe Drinking Water Act. The delays are due in large part to property-rights lobbying for amendments such as a ban on volunteers collecting data on private land for the National Biological Survey or a requirement that the government do "loss-of-value" assessments when regulations "could" cause a change in the worth of private property ranging from land to stocks and bonds.

At the state level, "takings" bills similar to those in Congress have been introduced in 37 state legislatures in the past two years; nearly all have been defeated. Many of the bills would require taxpayers to "compensate" landowners, including corporations, for property values diminished because of regulation. Such payments could be extremely costly, and the measures could erode state authority to protect public health and safety—as well as wreak havoc on long-established planning tools such as zoning.

For the most part, the new movement is not faring well in the courts either but it has scored some wins. In one case directly affecting wildlife, last March the U.S. Court of Appeals for the

District of Columbia struck down a U.S. Fish and Wildlife Service regulation that prevented private landowners from destroying habitat of federally listed species.

The court declared the provision as "neither clearly authorized by Congress nor a 'reasonable interpretation'" of the Endangered Species Act. The Clinton Administration has asked the court to reconsider the decision. If it stands, the ruling would allow landowners to take actions such as chopping down a tree containing the nest of an endangered red-cockaded woodpecker or bulldozing a beach where threatened sea turtles lay their eggs—*as long as the animals are not around.* No matter that the animals later would return to their habitat; no protections would exist in their absence.

While that case raises the issue of how much conservation laws apply to private land, it is technically a question of the intent of Congress in passing the Endangered Species Act. In contrast, the heart of most of the property-rights debate lies in a Fifth Amendment clause in the Constitution's Bill of Rights: " ... nor shall private property be taken for public use, without just compensation." Legal historians interpret the original intent as requiring that landowners be paid when the government seizes property for public conveniences like roads and dams.

No one disagrees that if the government takes all of a person's property for public use, then just compensation is required. But the new movement pushes the argument a big step further, contending that regulation of landowners' ability to do as they wish with their property is a "taking" as well. The movement was sparked by the 1987 book *Takings,* by University of Chicago professor Richard Epstein. Epstein argued that the broad definition of a taking "invalidates much of the 20th-century legislation."

Such arguments mask the myriad ways governments increase the value of public property. Partly for this reason, editorial boards at newspapers across the country have condemned property-rights legislation. In one April 1994 editorial, *The Atlanta Constitution* called the demands of property rights forces "pure hypocrisy." As an example, it cited Arizona, "one of the fastest-growing states in the country and a hotbed of property-rights legislation. But its cities and suburbs would still be worthless desert if not for water brought from hundreds of miles away, at huge expense to the federal government."

Other examples: Developers in coastal areas that depend on taxpayer-subsidized insurance and agri-businesses that thrive with federal price support and crop insurance. Property values often exist only because of sewers, roads and other government-paid amenities.

The takings argument has quickly reached the level of the absurd. "Compensation" has been asked for costs incurred in widening restroom doors to allow wheelchair access required by law, losses due to limits on the sale and import of assault rifles—and even losses due to restrictions on "dial-a-porn" services.

In Mississippi and Georgia, religious groups have joined environmentalists in opposing proposed property-rights legislation. The bills would require taxpayers to compensate pornography dealers prevented from locating next to schools and churches. "Where this leads is to the end of government's role as protector of the little guy and provider of amenities the market alone cannot provide," says Jessica Mathews, a se-

nior fellow at the Council on Foreign Relations. "Things like public health, worker safety, civil rights, environment, planning, historic preservation and anti-discrimination measures."

The rule of law in the United States has long been that landowners must not use their land in any way that creates a public or private nuisance (in other words, harms the public or neighbors). "(A)ll property in this country is held under the implied obligation that the owner's use of it shall not be injurious to the community," the Supreme Court ruled 100 years ago. In a string of cases since then, the high court has consistently reaffirmed that bedrock principle.

In 1992, the Supreme Court did rule conditionally in favor of South Carolina developer David Lucas, who had been denied permission to build on two ocean-front lots after the state adopted a coastal-zone management plan. Lucas owned two lots appraised at $1 million. The Court ruled he was entitled to compensation in part *if* the action deprived him of "all economically viable use" of his land. The case then went back to the state courts, where it was eventually settled. Justice Antonin Scalia, who wrote the Supreme Court's majority opinion, warned that anyone who purchases property always takes a risk that government regulation will diminish its value. He wrote that a lakebed owner "would not be entitled to compensation when he is denied the requisite permit to engage in a landfilling operation that would have the effect of flooding others' land." In other words, says NWF attorney Sugameli, "Property ownership does not include the right to flood your neighbors."

Even permits for livestock grazing on public land, claim "takings" advocates, are property. In Nevada, rancher Wayne

Hage is suing the U.S. government for $28 million in damages for diminishing the value of his property (his permit) in a number of ways. But the range that Hage's cattle roamed is not his. It's yours: 700,000 acres of the Toiyabe National Forest in Nevada he leased from the federal government. In 1990, the Forest Service warned Hage he was letting his cattle overgraze. The animals were devouring vegetation along clear-running streams among the mountain meadows and piñon pine, birch and aspen trees—and in the process destroying key habitat for fish, birds, elk and other wildlife.

After Hage didn't respond to repeated warnings, in July 1991 contract cowboys protected by armed Forest Service rangers rounded up 73 of Hage's scofflaw bovines. Later, 31 more were taken in. Hage sold off the remainder of his herd of 2,000 and has taken his grievances to court. Among them are his claims that the government ruined his business by introducing elk, which competed with his cattle for grass; allowing backpackers and elk to drink from springs used by his livestock; and restricting how heavily his cattle could graze streamside vegetation. Federal officials say that by ignoring grazing regulations, Hage has only himself to blame for his troubles. On behalf of several environmental groups and the state of Nevada, the National Wildlife Federation is actively participating in the case as a friend of the court.

So-called property-rights advocates like to portray themselves as average Janes and Joes fighting the daunting power of federal bureaucrats and tree-hugging elites. Says J. T. "Jake" Commins, executive vice president of the antiregulation Montana Farm Bureau, "Walt Whitman was speaking to the universal aspiration of humanity throughout history when he said, 'A man is not whole and complete unless he owns a house and the ground it stands on.'"

But loss of regulations often benefits big landowners most. Charles Geisler, a sociologist at Cornell University, has found that the nation's land is concentrated in the hands of the wealthy few. According to the Department of Agriculture, almost three quarters of all the privately owned land in the country is owned by less than 5 percent of the landowning population. "This is important to keep in mind when the property-rights people talk about fighting for the little guy," says Geisler.

Who are the nation's largest private landowners? Timber and mining companies, agri-businesses, developers and energy conglomerates, says Geisler. These owners appear to be prime movers behind the property-rights movement.

One example: When M & J Coal Company of Marion County, West Virginia, was ordered by federal officials not to mine portions of coal deposits because a gas line ruptured and huge cracks opened on the land of homeowners living over the underground mine, the company sued. Though it earned a 34.5 percent annual profit on the mine, the company claimed the restrictions were a "regulatory taking" for which it was entitled to $580,000 in lost profits. The court rejected the claim earlier this year; the company has appealed.

In Wyoming, the Clajon Corporation recently challenged in court state limits on the number of hunting licenses issued to large landowners. As owner of a large ranch, Clajon contended that it owned the right to hunt wildlife on its land and that the state's hunting-license limit was a taking of the company's property rights. The Wyoming Wildlife Federation and NWF's Rocky Mountain Natural Resource Center were leaders in fighting the claims, which were thrown out by Wyoming's federal district court in June.

Despite such cases, legal experts do not dismiss the takings movement in general. Even Humbach of Pace University maintains environmentalists have two decades of their own success partly to blame for the current backlash. "People concerned about the wise use of land should be equally concerned about misapplied and heavy-handed government rules that turn average Americans into poster children for the property-rights movement," he says.

Environmentalists might even agree with that notion—at least up to the mention of poster children. "I am convinced there is no actual case of an 'American poster child' for the property-rights movement," says NWF's Sugameli. NWF has examined hundreds of such purported cases. "And every single case either falls apart or doesn't exist at all," he says.

One example: the well-publicized 1988 jailing of Hungarian immigrant John Pozsgai for filling in a small wetland next to his Pennsylvania diesel mechanic shop. Property-rights advocates portray Pozsgai as a hapless victim who only meant to make his own land useful. But according to the Environmental Protection Agency, engineers told Pozsgai before he bought the property that there were wetlands on it; he even used that information to negotiate a $20,000 reduction in the land's purchase price. He then refused to obtain the required federal permit to fill his wetlands, filled them without the permit and ignored repeated official notification to stop doing so. Said the judge during Pozsgai's sentencing, "It is hard to visualize a more stubborn violator of the laws that were designed to protect the environment."

Such cases aside, environmentalists say they do recognize a need for collaboration. "The whole environmental community should be advancing the view that environmental laws are vital to protecting property rights, not taking them away, says Michael Bean, chairman of the Wildlife Program of the nonprofit Environmental Defense Fund. To that end, the group is exploring a plan to help save the endangered red-cockaded woodpecker in the pine forests of North Carolina, where private landowners own most of the prime habitat. The idea involves "land-use credits" for leaving large stands of trees untouched. The credits could take the form of lower taxes, regulatory relief from parts of the Endangered Species Act or some other tangible asset.

And in Kern County, California, conservationists have long supported a plan aimed at allowing developers to build near habitat of the endangered kit fox in return for undisturbed parcel setasides and a developer-funded conservation program, both of which would aid the fox.

That sort of thinking may be the best hope for habitat and wildlife in the future. "In recent years, proponents of various private property-rights amendments have come to view the protection of private-property rights and government regulation as mutually exclusive goals," says Senator John Chafee (R-Rhode Island). "That view is wrong." In the end, property rights are as much an issue for Ralph Seidel and the elk in Toiyabe National Forest as for Wayne Hage. The framers of the Constitution wouldn't have had it any other way.

POSTSCRIPT

Should Property Owners Be Compensated When Environmental Restrictions Limit Development?

Harbrecht takes comfort in the fact that the legislative program of the property rights movement has not been very successful thus far. Even in the Republican-dominated 104th Congress, efforts to undermine the Endangered Species Act and the Clean Water Act by imposing the requirement for costly compensation to affected landowners was unsuccessful. However, reenactment of these acts remains stalled, and it seems likely that the Clinton administration may be forced to accept at least some of the proposed property compensation amendments to win approval from the legislature for either of these major environmental laws.

University of Chicago law professor Richard Epstein's book *Takings: Private Property and the Power of Eminent Domain* (Harvard University Press, 1985) is credited with providing the property rights movement with legal arguments, which have been used in courtroom challenges, to regulations that have invoked the Fifth Amendment. For a concise debate between Epstein and John Echeverria about the legal aspects of the issue, see the May/June 1992 issue of the *Cato Policy Report*, published by the Cato Institute in Washington, D.C. Another dialogue, specifically on the issue of the environment versus property rights, appears on the op-ed page of the March 15, 1995, issue of *The New York Times*.

For another slant by an environmentalist who opposes the property rights position, see Carl Pope's article in the March 1994 issue of *Sierra*. In a cover story in the November 1995 issue of *The Progressive*, Erik Ness argues that the private property movement is carving up America. For the perspective of those who see environmental restrictions on property rights as part of a leftist-inspired government conspiracy to control all aspects of our lives, see William Norman Rigg's article in the August 9, 1993, issue of *New American*.

Chapter 2 of *Foundations of Environmental Ethics* by Eugene C. Hargrove (Prentice Hall, 1989) is a review of philosophical attitudes toward land use and property rights.

For an Internet site related to this issue, see http://www.publiceye.org/pra/privprop.html, which contains a detailed discussion of the principles and politics involved in the regulatory takings and private property rights controversy.

PART 2

The Environment and Technology

Most of the environmental concerns that are the focus of current regulatory debates are directly related to modern industrial development—the pace of which has been accelerating dramatically since World War II. Thousands of new synthetic chemicals have been introduced into manufacturing processes and agricultural pursuits. New technology, its byproducts, and the exponential increases in the production and use of energy have all contributed to the release of environmental pollutants. How to continue to improve the standard of living for the world's people without increasing ecological stress and exposure to toxins is the key question that underlies the issues debated in this section.

- Should the Industrial Use of Chlorine Be Phased Out?

- Do Environmental Estrogens Pose a Potentially Serious Health Threat?

- Should the New Clean Water Act Aim at "Zero Discharge"?

- Is Rapid Introduction of Electric Cars a Good Strategy for Reducing Air Pollution?

- Does Feeding People and Preserving Wildlands Require Chemical-Based Agriculture?

ISSUE 7

Should the Industrial Use of Chlorine Be Phased Out?

YES: Joe Thornton, from "Chlorine: Can't Live With It, Can Live Without It," Speech Prepared for the Chlorine-Free Debate Held in Conjunction With the International Joint Commission Seventh Biennial Meeting, Windsor, Ontario, Canada (October 1993)

NO: Ivan Amato, from "The Crusade to Ban Chlorine," *Garbage: The Independent Environmental Quarterly* (Summer 1994)

ISSUE SUMMARY

YES: Greenpeace research coordinator Joe Thornton presents the case for a systematic phaseout of chlorinated organic compounds as the only effective means of protecting humans and animals from the toxic effects of these chemicals.

NO: Science writer Ivan Amato emphasizes the industry's argument that only a few chlorinated compounds are proven health threats, and he states that Greenpeace's claims that substitutes exist are misleading.

In 1991 Greenpeace, the largest international grassroots environmental organization, launched a campaign to phase out most industrial uses of chlorine and chlorinated organic compounds. The basis for this strategy is the growing evidence that a wide variety of chlorinated compounds—such as dioxins, PCBs, chlorinated pesticides, vinyl chloride, carbon tetrachloride, and chloroform—are highly toxic or carcinogenic and that chlorine-containing compounds are destroying the protective ozone layer.

Prior to the 1970s the legislative restriction on the production, sale, or use of industrial chemicals in both capitalist and socialist economies was limited to a very small number of substances that were either clear and obvious threats to public health, such as the use of mercury- or arsenic-containing agricultural chemicals or radioactive isotopes. The growing environmental consciousness about the potential human health and ecological impacts due to the enormous number of synthetic chemicals introduced into industrial use following World War II has resulted in the enactment of numerous laws. These laws have been designed to reduce environmental pollution or public exposure to a rapidly growing list of proven, or suspected, hazardous substances. These laws attempt to limit air emissions, water contamination, land contamination, food contamination, and industrial exposure.

Efforts to find a scientifically valid, economically and politically feasible strategy for protecting the public and the ecosphere from the deleterious effects of hazardous substances have proven to be problematic and controversial. Lack of adequate data for valid risk assessments, inability to do direct, controlled tests on human subjects, questions about the validity of deducing human health concerns from animal test data, the difficulty of interpreting the results of epidemiological studies, lack of access to industrial data that is considered proprietary, and the complications due to possible synergistic effects among different pollutants are among the factors that have plagued regulatory agencies.

With few exceptions the practice has been to consider each suspected toxic chemical individually. This expensive and time-consuming approach has resulted in a growing backlog of untested industrial chemicals being introduced into processes or products that result in exposure to workers and consumers. Citizen's groups concerned about hazardous chemicals have unsuccessfully lobbied for a change in the regulatory philosophy that generally considers a new industrial chemical innocent as a potential health hazard until proven guilty.

The chemical industry was caught off guard by the rapidity with which the proposal to phase out nonessential uses of chlorine compounds led to endorsements and action. Chlorine gas has been eliminated as a bleach for pulp and paper in Europe. Norway has commissioned research on the policy effects of a total chlorine ban, and the International Joint Commission on the Great Lakes has recommended a broad organochlorine phaseout. Nations within the European Union are evaluating proposals to reduce the use of polyvinyl chloride and other chlorine-containing products. The UN Economic Commission for Europe is negotiating an agreement with 50 countries that would restrict the use of many persistent chlorinated compounds, including PCBs and DDT. The American Public Health Association issued a resolution in 1993 supporting a reduction in industrial uses of chlorine. Although the new drinking water and pesticide regulations adopted by the 104th Congress do not ban the use of chlorine or chlorinated compounds, they do require screening for the presence of those chlorine-containing chemicals that act as endocrine disrupters. New processes that eliminate the use of perchlorethylene are becoming popular in the U.S. dry cleaning industry.

A counterattack has recently been launched in the form of a well-financed lobbying effort by the chemical industry to convince government officials and the public that the benefits of chlorine compounds outweigh the risks. This campaign appears to be succeeding in slowing the antichlorine bandwagon.

Pros and cons of the issue are discussed in detail in the following articles by Greenpeace research coordinator Joe Thornton and science writer Ivan Amato.

YES   Joe Thornton

CHLORINE: CAN'T LIVE WITH IT, CAN LIVE WITHOUT IT

In medicine, an ounce of prevention is worth a pound of cure. When it comes to the global environment, however, an ounce of prevention is priceless, for serious damage to the biosphere cannot be repaired before the health of millions of humans and other species has been affected. Already, toxic chlorine-based organic chemicals—called organochlorines—have contaminated the global environment and caused widespread damage to human health and the ecosystem; these chemicals cannot be removed from the tissues of the human population, the food chain or the general environment. It is time for society to adopt a precautionary strategy to prevent further damage by organochlorines.

My purpose here is three-fold: first, to show that organochlorines are a major hazard to health and the global environment; second, to show that for the purpose of environmental policy these thousands of related chemicals should be treated as a class, and that a planned phase-out of the industrial production and use of chlorine and organochlorines is necessary to prevent further injury to health and the environment; and third, to show that a phase-out of chlorine is technologically and economically feasible.

Already, numerous international institutions have called for a chlorine phase-out. For instance, the International Joint Commission on the Great Lakes (IJC)—a binational advisory body to the governments of the U.S. and Canada—concluded in 1992 and reiterated in 1994 that chlorine-based organic chemicals are a primary hazard to human health and the environment. On the IJC's list of the eleven pollutants requiring the most urgent action, eight are organochlorines; of the 362 on the "secondary track," more than half are chlorinated. The IJC argued that these chemicals should be treated as a class and subject to a policy of Zero Discharge, and recommended that the governments of the U.S. and Canada should, "in consultation with industry and other affected interests, develop timetables to sunset the use of chlorine and chlorine-containing compounds as industrial feedstocks."

Such diverse organizations as the Paris Commission on the Northeast Atlantic—a ministerial convention of 15 European governments—the

From Joe Thornton, "Chlorine: Can't Live With It, Can Live Without It," from a speech prepared for the Chlorine-Free Debate held in conjunction with the International Joint Commission Seventh Biennial Meeting, Windsor, Ontario, Canada (October 1993). Copyright © 1993 by Joe Thornton. Reprinted by permission.

International Whaling Commission, the Arctic Wildlife Congress, and the 21-nation Barcelona Convention on the Mediterranean have all concluded that discharges of persistent, bioaccumulative substances—particularly organochlorines—should be eliminated entirely.

In late 1993, the American Public Health Association, the nation's premier organization of public health scientists and professionals, resolved that "chlorinated organic chemicals are found to pose public health risks involving the workplace, consumer products, and the general environment," and recognized that "elimination of chlorine and/or chlorinated organic compounds from certain manufacturing processes, products, and uses may be the most cost-effective and health protective way to reduce health and environmental exposures to chlorinated organic compounds." The APHA concluded that organochlorines should be treated as a class, presumed harmful unless shown otherwise, and phased-out, with exceptions made only if a given use or substance can be proven safe or essential.

And in early 1994, the Clinton White House announced as part of its proposal for the Clean Water Act that the Environmental Protection Agency (EPA) be authorized to conduct a study and develop a strategy to "substitute, reduce, or prohibit the use of chlorine and chlorine-containing compounds." The White House specifically sited growing evidence that links contamination of the environment by these persistent toxic substances "not only to cancer but also to neurological, reproductive, developmental, and immunological adverse effects."

WHAT ARE ORGANOCHLORINES?

Organochlorines are the products and by-products of industrial chlorine chemistry. In nature, chlorine exists almost solely in its stable ionic form, called chloride. Chloride ions circulate constantly through our bodies and the ecosystem, primarily in the familiar form of sea salt (sodium chloride, NaCl); these ions do not react or combine with the carbon-based organic matter that is the basis of living things.

The chemical industry takes this sea salt and subjects it to a powerful electric current, transforming ionic chloride into elemental chlorine gas (Cl_2), along with the co-product sodium hydroxide. The energy input in this "chlor-alkali process" fundamentally changes the chemical character of the chlorine atom. Unlike natural chloride, chlorine gas is a toxic, greenish gas that is highly unstable, combining quickly and randomly with organic matter to produce a new class of chemicals called organochlorines.

Since World War II, the chlorine industry has grown very rapidly, reaching production of 40 million tons of chlorine each year. Of this, about 80 percent is used within the chemical industry to manufacture 11,000 different organochlorine products, including plastics, pesticides, and solvents. The remainder is sold to other industries—most of it to the pulp and paper industry—for uses such as bleaching and disinfection. In addition to the many organochlorines produced on purpose, thousands more—including dioxin—are formed as accidental by-products in all uses of chlorine, and whenever organochlorines are used or disposed in reactive environments, such as incinerators.

Chlorine is useful in industry for the same reasons it is a hazard to health and the environment. Its reactivity makes it a powerful bleach and disinfectant—and an effective reactant in chemical synthesis —but this quality results in the formation of unintended by-products. Organochlorines tend to be very stable, resisting natural breakdown processes, so they are useful as plastics, refrigerants, di-electric fluids, pesticides, and other chemicals, but this same quality makes them long-lived in the environment and in the bodies of living organisms. Further, organochlorines tend to be oil-soluble, so they work well as degreasing solvents, but this causes them to concentrate in the tissues of living things. And organochlorines tend to be toxic, so they are powerful pesticides and drugs; the negative impacts of this characteristic are obvious.

In contrast to the now large-scale industrial production of these chemicals, organochlorines are largely foreign to living systems. Only one organochlorine is produced naturally in significant amounts—chloromethane, the simplest organochlorine, which serves in the natural regulation of the stratospheric ozone layer. Several hundred organochlorines are produced in trace amounts, primarily by lower organisms such as algae and fungi; none are known to occur naturally in the tissues of mammals or terrestrial vertebrates, and none circulate freely and ubiquitously throughout the general environment. Moreover, the organisms that produce organochlorines do so precisely because of their toxicity or other biological activity: organochlorines serve in nature not in the mainstream of biochemistry but as chemical defenses against predators and parasites, as pesticides, and as signalling molecules (i.e., pheromones). The limited role of organochlorines in nature confirms the view that this class of compounds is hazardous to complex living organisms.

GLOBAL CHLORINE POLLUTION

After only about fifty years of large-scale industrial chlorine production, the entire planet is now blanketed with a cocktail of hundreds or thousands of toxic, long-lived organochlorines. This is because of the huge quantities of these chemicals produced by the chemical industry, and because organochlorines tend to persist in the environment and build up in the food chain. Even those organochlorines that do break down almost always degrade into other organochlorines— which are often more toxic and/or persistent than the original substance— compounding the problem further.

In the Great Lakes, for instance, 168 organochlorines have been unequivocally identified in the water, sediments or food chain—making up about half of all the pollutants that have been found in that ecosystem. The list includes the most infamous organochlorines—PCBs, dioxins, and pesticides like DDT and aldrin— but it also contains scores of lesser known organochlorines. Great Lakes contaminants span the entire spectrum of the class of these substances—including simple chlorinated solvents and refrigerants, a host of chlorinated benzenes, phenols and toluenes, a selection of exotic chlorinated by-products, alcohols, acids, and the newer chlorinated pesticides like atrazine and alachlor.

The problem, of course, is not just in North America but is truly global. Because organochlorines tend to be so persistent in the environment, they can travel thousands of miles on currents of wind and water, resulting in a distribution that affects everyone on the planet. In the Arctic circle, for instance, far from any known sources of these compounds, some of the world's highest concentrations of organochlorines can be found in the tissues of polar bears, people, and other species.

And because many organochlorines are more soluble in fat than in water, they bioaccumulate, concentrating in the fatty tissues of living things and multiplying in concentration as they move up the food chain. Concentrations of these chemicals in the bodies of predator species may be millions of times greater than the levels found in the ambient environment. Thus, the bulk of the general population's exposure to many of these compounds occur through the food supply—particularly foods high in fat such as fish, meats, and dairy products.

Since humans are inextricably connected with our environment—though we often forget it—we too are contaminated. Because we are at the top of the foodchain, we bear some of the highest exposures of all. 177 organochlorines have been identified in the fat, blood, mother's milk, semen, and breath of the general population of the U.S. and Canada. These chemicals are in absolutely everyone's body, not just people living near pulp mills and chemical plants.... Organochlorines accumulated in the body are also passed from one generation to the next through the placenta and through mothers' milk.

Worst of all, these 177 organochlorines that have been identified are just the tip of the iceberg: they represent only a fraction of the thousands of contaminants that are known present in our bodies but have not yet been specifically identified....

HEALTH AND ENVIRONMENTAL IMPACTS

The health damage that organochlorines can cause has been well-established, though the existing data may only hint at the full-scale of the problem. Organochlorines are known to disrupt the body's hormones, to cause genetic mutations and metabolic changes, to cause or promote cancer, to reduce fertility, impair childhood development, cause neurological damage, and suppress the function of the immune system. The International Agency for Research on Cancer has identified 117 organochlorines or groups of organochlorines that are known or suspected carcinogens.

Some organochlorines are among the most potent poisons ever studied, though the potency and specific effects vary from one chemical to another. A recent study for the U.S. and Canadian pulp and paper industry admitted that adding chlorine to an organic chemical almost always increases its toxicity, persistence, and tendency to bioaccumulate.

As the America Public Health Association concluded, "virtually all organochlorines that have been studied exhibit at least one of a wide range of serious toxic effects..., often at extremely low doses, and many chlorinated organic compounds... are recognized as significant workplace hazards." A large body of scientific literature shows that people exposed in the workplace to a wide variety of organochlorines—pesticides, PCBs, dioxins, solvents, vinyl chloride, chemical intermediates, and so on—have elevated rates of cancer, infertility, hormonal abnormalities, nervous system damage, and other effects.

By itself, this information is enough to justify a phase-out of these chemicals.

Common sense tells us that we should not be exposing ourselves and other species to chemicals that can cause such a wide range of severe health effects. If they persist or bioaccumulate—making the impacts long-lived and virtually irreversible —the folly of dumping these compounds into the environment becomes even more obvious....

Because these chemicals are persistent and ubiquitous, we confront a threat to our health unlike most hazards associated with toxic chemicals: a global hazard to the health of the entire population, not simply a local set of exposures and health risks.... Although it is so difficult for epidemiologists and environmental scientists to catalogue long-term, large-scale damage and trace it back to its causes, a large body of scientific information that has emerged over the last few years indicates that organochlorines are causing a global epidemic of serious health effects among people and wildlife.

Some of the best information comes from the Great Lakes—one of the best-studied large ecosystems in the world. Here, scientists have documented severe chemically-induced epidemics among 14 species—virtually every predator species in the ecosystem, from bald eagles to salmon, mink to snapping turtles, herring gulls to humans. In each case, the consumption of Great Lakes fish contaminated with organochlorine mixtures appears to be the cause. These epidemics primarily affect reproduction and development, with effects including population declines, inability to reproduce, physical and behavioral feminization of males, birth defects, embryonic mortality, wasting syndrome and other developmental effects, behavioral changes and learning impairment, and immune system suppression. Most alarming, the ef-fects are most severe not in the exposed generation but in its offspring, and they are often not apparent until the offspring reach adulthood.

The problem is not getting any better. Some of the pesticides and PCBs that were restricted in the 1970s declined somewhat by the mid-1980s, but those chemicals have now stabilized at levels that are still unsafe. Others, such as the chlorinated dibenzofurans, are actually increasing. This summer, four newborn eaglets were discovered with life-threatening birth defects, including crossed bills and clubbed feet, that are consistent with organochlorine exposure. Finding one deformed eagle in a single year would be cause for concern; finding four, especially in a population that is bearing few young anyway, is truly alarming.

Similar effects are occurring worldwide. Epidemics of infertility, reproductive problems, hormonal disruptions and population declines have been documented among seals, fish and birds in the Baltic, the North Sea, the Wadden Sea, the Mediterranean, and the Pacific coast of North America. And organochlorines have been implicated in the mass die-offs of dolphins in recent years, as immune suppression caused by these chemicals appears to have made the animals more susceptible to infectious diseases.

What does this evidence mean for humans? Because they tend to have shorter generation times and more consistent feeding habits than people, wildlife are canaries in the coal mine for effects that can be expected in humans....

In fact, the evidence suggests that the impacts on human health are starting to occur already. In Michigan, a series of studies has found that children born to mothers who had eaten just two to three meals per month of organochlorine-contaminated Great Lakes fish were born sooner, weighed less, and had smaller heads. As they developed, these children suffered an impaired ability to learn, with measurable impacts on short-term memory. These impacts lasted for years, and the severity correlated with the concentrations of organochlorines in the mother's blood. The results from Michigan are consistent with other studies from Wisconsin, North Carolina, Taiwan, and New York state that have found similar behavioral and neurological effects among the offspring of women and animals exposed to PCB, dioxin, or contaminated Great Lakes fish. Based on the severity of the effects and the low doses at which they occur, scientists have concluded that a substantial number of children from the general population may be suffering from this "diminished potential" due to chemical exposures.

Since World War II, average sperm density among men worldwide has declined by about half, and the proportion of men who are infertile has increased accordingly. Dioxin, PCBs, pesticides and other organochlorines that disrupt the body's hormones are known to cause male reproductive impairment, including low sperm counts, feminization, smaller gonad size, and reduced sex drive—even when only a tiny dose is fed to the mother on a single critical day of pregnancy. Several studies have found a relationship between low sperm count and high concentrations of certain organochlorines in a man's semen or blood. Recent articles in the scientific literature have argued that organochlorine exposure of the male fetus before birth may be an important factor in the worldwide decline in male fertility. This body of evidence also suggests that organochlorines may also be factors in testicular cancer and other defects of the male reproductive tracts, both of which can be caused by hormone-disruptors and have increased by 2- to 4-fold in recent decades.

Organochlorines have also been linked in a number of excellent studies to the worldwide epidemic of breast cancer that now strikes about one in nine women in most industrialized nations. Chlorinated solvents and the by-products of chlorination in drinking water have been linked to leukemia, bladder cancer, and colorectal cancer. And a recent large study by the New Jersey Department of Health links these same chemicals in drinking water to increased risk of spontaneous abortion, low birth weight, and a number of types of birth defects, particularly those —such as malformations of the cardiovascular system—that have been rising at an alarming rate among the general population.

In 1994, U.S. EPA released its long-awaited reassessment of the toxicity of dioxin. This three-year effort concluded that dioxin has severe effects upon a wide range of organ systems in humans and animals, that the evidence from studies of people suggests that dioxin has caused cancer, hormonal changes, and an array of biochemical effects in groups of people exposed to dioxin in the workplace or in their community, and that the most severe effects of dioxin are impairment of reproduction, development, and immune system function. Particularly sobering is EPA's conclusion that the current "background" body burden of dioxin and related chemicals in the tissues of the general U.S. population is already in the range at which these effects are known to occur in laboratory animals. There is no margin of safety remaining.

Finally, a few words about the impacts of the destruction of the stratospheric ozone layer, which has been caused primarily by chlorine-containing refrigerants and solvents. The United Nations Environment Programme has estimated that current ozone depletion trends will result in an additional 300,000 cases of skin cancer every year, plus at least 1.6 million cases of cataracts‚ and an unknown but probably very large number of cases of immune suppression. Also expected are worldwide decreases in the productivity of agriculture and the marine foodchain, possibly leading to serious consequences for both humans and the global ecosystem.

... I will stop with these examples, and make two points about all the effects that have been linked to organochlorines. First, none were predicted before the chemicals went into commerce, and all required a lag time of decades before they were discovered. Once the evidence was in, the damage was irreversible. Second, in no study have scientists been able to pinpoint individual chemicals that are responsible for these health and ecological impacts, because it is the mixture of hundreds of organochlorines—along with other factors—that is causing the injury.

POLICY APPROACHES TO ORGANOCHLORINE POLLUTION

... The chemical industry would have us regulate organochlorines one by one. Risk assessments can be used, the industry argues, to determine exposure levels that are safe and environmental concentrations that do not exceed the ecosystem's "assimilative capacity." From these assessments, "acceptable discharges" can be calculated, and the industry proposes using pollution control and disposal de-

vices—filters, incinerators, and the like—to keep releases within those limits.

But this is precisely the current regulatory system, which is primarily reactive: it attempts to control chemicals after they have been produced, and these actions are taken only after the chemicals have been shown to cause harm. The industry's suggestion represents no change from the status quo, really.... This may explain part of why the industry advocates it.

... We need a fundamental shift to a precautionary, public health-based approach. Such a policy seeks to *prevent* damage to our health and the environment before it happens; it accepts the irreversibility of harm and the limits of our scientific knowledge and technological control over toxic chemicals. This new approach is based upon three central ideas: the precautionary principle, zero discharge, and clean production processes.

First, the precautionary principle. Our current system is reactive: it takes action only after harm has already occurred. DDT, PCBs, and CFCs were phased-out, but only after overwhelming evidence linked them to severe impacts on health and the environment. The precautionary principle, which has already been adopted by the UN and other international fora, says that chemicals that *may* cause harm should not be discharged into the environment. In the face of scientific uncertainty, we should err on the side of caution. This idea is analogous to the first laws of medicine and public health practice: first do no harm, with prevention the goal.

Second, zero discharge. Approving "acceptable" discharges of persistent toxic chemicals is a recipe for disaster, because these chemicals—even when released in small amounts—build up in the environment over time, eventually reaching levels that cause health effects. The assumption that the environment has an "assimilable capacity" for pollution may be appropriate for conventional pollutants like oil and grease, which break down in the environment. But for persistent toxic substances, as the IJC has said, the ecosystem's assimilative capacity is zero....

Finally, clean production. We know that "back-end" solutions—pollution control and disposal measures that deal with chemicals and wastes after they are produced—have failed utterly to prevent toxic discharges, because they merely move chemicals from one environmental medium to another. Only front-end solutions—eliminating the production and use of toxic substances and feedstocks—truly prevent environmental contamination. As Barry Commoner has shown, the history of environmental regulations for the last two decades supports the view that pollution control has been marginally effective at best, while bans and phase-outs—on leaded gasoline, PCBs, and certain pesticides, for example—are responsible for all of our major success stories.

... [W]e need to eliminate the use of chlorine and chlorinated compounds by installing chlorine free alternative production processes. As discussed below, chlorine-free technologies are available for all major uses of chlorine—including plastics, pesticides, paper bleaching, solvents, and other chemical uses.

TREATING ORGANOCHLORINES AS A CLASS

The current system, which regulates each compound one-by-one, considers chemicals "innocent until proven guilty."

There are 80,000 chemicals in commerce—11,000 of them organochlorines—plus thousands more formed as accidental by-products. Only a handful have been subject to thorough hazard assessments, and many have not even been identified. Although virtually all organochlorines that have been tested have turned out to cause one or more adverse effects, we continue to presume that the untested ones are safe.

Chemicals do not have constitutional or human rights. The current system mistakenly grants chemicals the right to be considered innocent until proven guilty, while treating people as if we were guinea pigs who should be experimentally exposed to untested chemicals.... It is people who are innocent until proven guilty, and it is people who have the right not be exposed to chemicals that may harm their health.

... The precautionary principle tells us that synthetic chemicals—and the industrial processes that generate them—should be presumed harmful until demonstrated safe and compatible with the basic processes of the ecosystem....

Reversing the burden of proof also allows us to leave behind the cumbersome focus on individual organochlorines numbering in the thousands, and in the impossible bureaucracy that approach creates. Instead, we can target the far smaller set of processes and feedstocks that produce these diverse mixtures. For instance, dioxin and related compounds appear to be formed in virtually all uses of elemental chlorine (including the manufacture of a full range of organochlorine products, including pesticides, solvents, PVC feedstocks, and chemical intermediates), in many uses of organochlorines (especially those that take place in reactive or high-temperature environments) and whenever organochlorines are burned in incinerators, recycling facilities, or in accidental fires. Dioxin is even produced when chlorine gas is produced from salt. Even if our goal is simply to eliminate pollution by dioxin—the single most hazardous organochlorine known—we would have to restrict the use of chlorine in dozens of processes, along with the myriad of individual organochlorine products that are associated with dioxin at some point in their lifecycle.

We do know that all these organochlorines share a common root: the chlorine feedstock. That fact presents the opportunity for a clear and focused chemical policy: we should seek to replace chlorine-based processes with clean alternatives. With a single program, we can eliminate the largest and most hazardous group of toxic pollutants on the planet—a goal that the regulatory bureaucracy now in place has not even been able to consider.

IMPLEMENTING A CHLORINE PHASE-OUT

A chlorine phase-out does not mean that all chlorine-based processes are banned overnight. The process of conversion should be well-planned in order to set priorities, minimize costs, maximize benefits, and insure that both are equitably distributed. The program should begin with a reversal of the burden of proof: organochlorines and the processes that produce them will be presumed to be phased-out unless industry can provide convincing evidence of their safety.

Second, priorities should be set so that the largest, most polluting processes for which alternatives are available now are addressed first. PVC, pulp and paper, solvents, pesticides, other major chem-

ical manufacturing processes, incineration of chlorine-containing waste, and in-plant water disinfection are logical priorities. Of course, products that serve a compelling social need for which alternatives are not yet available—such as certain pharmaceuticals, which account for well under one percent of all chlorine use —could be exempted.

Finally, a transition fund should be established to insure that workers and communities do not bear the economic burden of the transformation to a non-toxic economy. This fund, financed with revenues from a tax on chlorine and related products, should be used for two purposes. First, the fund should be used [for] local new investment and to create new jobs in clean production processes in the same communities in which dislocation is most likely, thus placing priority on keeping people employed. Second, workers whose jobs are eliminated should be offered meaningful assistance, protection, and new opportunities: one proposal is the GI Bill for Workers, advocated by the Oil, Chemical and Atomic Workers International Union, would provide full income, up to four years of higher education, and health care coverage to all workers whose jobs are lost because of phase-outs of industries that are incompatible with environmental concerns. Governance of the transition planning fund should include full participation by all interested parties— particularly workers and communities.

CHLORINE ALTERNATIVES AND ECONOMICS

The chemical industry has responded to the calls for a chlorine phase-out by arguing that such a program will result in exorbitant costs (about $100 billion per year) and massive job losses in the U.S. and Canada. The industry's scenario, however, is based upon invalid assumptions that drastically overestimate the costs and underestimate the benefits of a well-planned transition from chlorine-based process to clean production.

In fact, society can realize significant economic gains in this transition, provided that the process is guided by careful planning to use the best alternatives, set sensible priorities, minimize costs, maximize benefits, and insure that both are equitably distributed. Safe, effective alternatives are available now for all major uses of chlorine, preserving or even increasing employment. Further, a prevention-based approach would eliminate the gargantuan social costs and economic drag caused by expenditures on pollution control ($90–$150 billion per year in the U.S.) and contaminated site remediation (up to $750 billion to remediate the current legacy of toxic sites). Further, the International Joint Commission's Virtual Elimination Task Force has estimated that health care costs associated with the effects of persistent toxic substances range from $100 to $200 billion per year. The net contribution of polluting industries to our economy does not appear to be positive.

By prioritizing major chlorine use-sectors, the cost of the phase-out can be substantially reduced. The industry's alarming figures assume that the chlorine phase-out will be implemented all at once, without thought or prioritization and without any attempt to use the most effective and least expensive alternatives. Even based on the industry's own inflated estimates, 97 percent of all chlorine use could be phased out for just $22 billion per year—one-fifth of the assumed cost of a total phase-out and only a fraction of the amount spent annually on toxics-related health care.

The industry has also drastically inflated its estimates of job loss by assuming that all jobs that involve chlorinated chemicals in some way will be lost when chlorine is restricted. But alternative processes will be used instead of chlorine, a chlorine phase-out does not mean that all productive economic activity once associated with chlorinated chemicals will stop.... In many cases, these alternatives create jobs because they are more labor-intensive than the current chemical-intensive processes.

For instance, traditional materials or chlorine-free plastics can substitute for all major uses of PVC plastic—the largest single chlorine use sector. There are dozens of communities, several hospitals and numerous manufacturers of autos, furniture, flooring, and packaged products—mostly in Europe—that have entirely or virtually eliminated the use of PVC. For instance, Tarkett AG—one of the world's largest flooring manufacturers—recently announced it will phase-out all PVC products from its line in favor of chlorine-free plastics and other materials. Tarkett workers will still be employed; they will simply use a different material to produce flooring.

Pulp and paper mills use chlorine to bleach wood pulp bright white, releasing huge quantities of organochlorine discharges in the process. But oxygen-based bleaching processes (using ozone, hydrogen peroxide, oxygen gas, enzymes, and improved control over production conditions) are capable of producing top-quality chlorine-free paper. Already, there are 55 mills around the world producing totally-chlorine-free (TCF) paper for the most demanding uses, including the large-circulation high-profile newsweeklies Der Spiegel and Stern in Germany. TCF production is rapidly coming to dominate paper production and consumption in Western Europe, and the North American industry risks being left behind in the global marketplace if it does not adopt these technologies. In fact, chlorine-free pulp production—following an initial investment—is less expensive than chlorine bleaching because of reduced costs for chemicals, pollution control and disposal, and energy consumption; by switching to chlorine-free bleaching, the North American industry could reduce its operating costs by over $500 million per year.

Chlorinated solvents—used primarily for cleaning and coating in manufacturing industries—are the next largest chlorine use sectors. But in the last 5 years, dozens of manufacturers of electronics, autos, and other types of equipment—including IBM and GE—have begun to eliminate chlorinated solvents in favor of process changes, such as aqueous or mechanical cleaning and coating. According to the U.S. Office of Technology Assessment, these changes result in net savings due to reduced costs for chemical procurement, waste disposal, and liability. For example, U.S. EPA concluded last year that clothing dry cleaners can replace chlorinated solvents with a water-based process that is just as effective but requires a 42 percent lower capital investment and provides a 78 percent better return on investment, a 5 percent increase in profits, a 21 percent increase in jobs and a 38 percent increase in total wages.

As for chlorinated pesticides, the U.S. National Academy of Sciences has found that farmers who eliminate their use of pesticides in favor of organic agriculture lower their costs and increase their yields. Farmers now spend close to $8 billion per year on synthetic pesticides, of which 99 percent are dispersed into the environment without ever reaching their target crop....

Wastewater treatment accounts for about 4 percent of chlorine use, while drinking water treatment uses less than 1 percent of the chlorine in the U.S. Alternatives are available in [this] sector, as well. Hundreds of wastewater treatment plants in the U.S. and Canada are already using ultraviolet light for disinfection prior to discharge, with operating costs lower than those associated with chlorine. Several hundred drinking water systems—mostly in Europe, including those in Berlin and Amsterdam—use UV, ozone, or modern filtration methods to provide safe, chlorine-free water to their communities.

There is no doubt that phasing out chlorine will require substantial technological conversion. Based on industry estimates, the investment in new technology would itself stimulate the creation of about 925,000 job-years of employment. But while we expect the net economic effect to be positive, there will be real disruption for some sectors—specifically those involved in the production of chlorine and chlorinated chemicals. Some chemical firms will have to establish a new production line or go out of business. There are already signs that the largest chemical manufacturers—including Dow, DuPont, Monsanto, and Bayer—are introducing chlorine-free products and seeking to eliminate chlorine from their own processes to anticipate the trend away from chlorine. But who is thinking about the chemical industry workers and communities whose jobs may be moved or lost in the transition? The transition planning fund described above can help preserve jobs, pre-

vent dislocation, and provide meaningful protection for workers and communities, who should not bear the burden of the conversion to a non-toxic economy.

CONCLUSION

Chlorine pollution is not a fact of life. It is the result of decisions made by industry in the last five decades to produce and use toxic synthetic chemicals for convenience, efficiency, or profit. And it is our society that has decided to permit industry to make such choices. We as citizens have the right not to be contaminated by toxic chemicals. We have the right not to worry that our grandchildren will be denied the opportunity to live full and healthy lives because their world has been contaminated by long-lived poisons. We have the right to decide —based on current scientific evidence and our commitment to an ethical public policy on health and the environment— that chlorine chemistry should no longer play a role in our society's production processes.

NO
Ivan Amato

THE CRUSADE TO BAN CHLORINE

Only in the past year or two did the chemical industry realize a meteor was coming its way: a dead-serious proposal to eliminate or drastically curtail the industrial use of chlorine, skillfully brought to legislators and the public by Greenpeace and other environmentalists known for anti-technology positions. "This is the most significant threat to chemistry that has ever been posed," says Brad Lienhart, a longtime industry executive who heads the Chemical Manufacturers Association's new $5 million campaign to counter as much of that threat as possible, for as long as possible.

At issue is the industry's previously unquestioned right to use massive amounts of chlorine, number 17 on the Periodic Table of Elements. Since the end of World War II, chlorine, a pale green gas in its elemental form, has become central to the chemical industry, and thus to thousands of processes and consumer products. "It is the single most important ingredient in modern [industrial] chemistry," says W. Joseph Stearns, director of chlorine issues for Dow Chemical Company, one of the largest producers and users of chlorine.

"It is such a valuable and useful molecule because it does so many things and is involved in so many end products," remarks John Sesody, vice president and general manager of Elf Atochem North America's basic chemical business. Chemists and chemical engineers acknowledge that chlorine is dangerous to use and handle, but argue that industry can manage these dangers well enough for society to safely enjoy chlorine's many benefits.

In fact, many in the chemical industry are passionate about the overall good they say chlorine chemistry does for society (as passionate as the anti-chlorine forces are about its potential for damage). With uses ranging from making pesticides to commodity polymers to synthesizing pharmaceuticals and disinfecting 98% of the nation's water supply, say defenders, chlorine is a substance society cannot do without.

Detractors couldn't disagree more. Polarizing the issue perfectly, "There are no uses, of chlorine that we regard as safe," remarks Joe Thornton, a Greenpeace research analyst who in 1991 authored Greenpeace's case for a chlorine phaseout in a document titled "The Product is the Poison."

From Ivan Amato, "The Crusade to Ban Chlorine," *Garbage: The Independent Environmental Quarterly* (Summer 1994). Copyright © 1994 by *Garbage: The Independent Environmental Quarterly*, 2 Main St., Gloucester, MA 01930. Reprinted by permission.

Among the documented "criminal actions" of some chlorine-containing chemicals: contaminating riverbeds and lush aquatic habitats such as the Great Lakes water basin; accumulating in the tissue of birds and other wildlife, where they contribute to reproductive disorders and increased incidence of disease; and causing a rare form of liver cancer in some plastics workers who were exposed to high amounts of vinyl chloride monomer (the building block of polyvinylchloride [PVC]) during the 1960s, before the Occupational Safety and Health Administration imposed stringent exposure regulations.

Chlorinated organic molecules have been found in human tissues, and anti-chlorine advocates assert they may be responsible for some of the increase in breast-cancer rates over the past few decades. *No one can claim a causal link* between chlorine-containing chemicals and breast cancer, but the mere suggestion alarms the anti-chlorine camp enough for them to call for its phaseout. As alternatives are available for at least some chlorine-containing products and processes, activists conclude it's better to play it safe and simply banish the element from industry. For example, activists have claimed in all sincerity, we could return to metal piping instead of PVC.

SCIENCE ISN'T THE NAME OF THE PLAYING FIELD

When asked what they think of the call to eliminate industrial use of chlorine, most chemists throw back a "yeah, right" look. Then they denounce it. "The idea of banning chlorine is patently ridiculous and scientifically indefensible," says Steven Safe, a Texas A&M toxicologist who for 20

years has studied such chlorinated compounds as dioxins and PCBs [polychlorinated biphenyls]. Mario Molina, the atmospheric chemist now at M.I.T. who, with Sherwood Rowland, first identified the link between CFCs [chlorofluorocarbons] and ozone depletion, agrees. He told *Science* magazine last summer that banning chlorine "isn't taken seriously from a scientific point of view."

Industry may have been counting on science to throw out this challenge. Yet many participants and observers of the debate doubt that standard scientific study will play a decisive role in determining the fate of chlorine chemistry. Each side of the chlorine debate has corralled vast amounts of data (quite often the same data) to support their diametrically opposed arguments. But public perception can change much more quickly than science can unambiguously determine the real impact of chlorine on the environment and on human health.

That point hit industry in the solar plexus this past February when EPA [Environmental Protection Agency] Administrator Carol Browner was quoted in the *New York Times*, the *Washington Post*, and other national media as saying that the agency's proposals for reauthorizing the Clean Water Act would include a "national strategy for substituting, reducing, or prohibiting the use of chlorine and chlorinated compounds." Ms. Browner's bombshell drew 2,000 angry letters from citizens and elected officials, and an additional 300 letters from industry, says an EPA source who asked not to be identified. "We quickly answered the ones from Congress, and now we are getting into the boxes [of letters.]"

The EPA's reply, which its public-affairs office has been busy delivering to reporters, is more in line with what most scientists would suggest. The Agency's prepared statement says it "will study chlorine and chlorinated compounds to determine whether actions may be necessary to protect aquatic resources from discharges of these compounds, and it is premature to draw any conclusions about EPA's final actions before the study is completed." Even if the study becomes part of a reauthorized Clean Water Act, it is extremely unlikely that any action would be in the form of a blanket ban on chlorine, say EPA insiders.

Despite that clarification, the potential fact of industrial life without elemental chlorine, which the coverage of Ms. Browner's statements displayed in neon, puts raw fear into the heart of chlorine's defenders.

The chemical industry has never been known as a master of public relations. Greenpeace, on the other hand, the most aggressive member of the anti-chlorine consortium, could have written the book. With their "Chlorine Free" campaign, Greenpeace and allies have used every outlet to make their case.

Realizing the court of public relations will likely adjudicate the chlorine debate, the Chemical Manufacturer's Association established and bankrolled the Chlorine Coordinating Council (since renamed the Chlorine Chemistry Council [CCC]), with Brad Lienhart as its managing director. The group hopes to counter what it views as anti-chlorine prejudice fueled more by environmentalist hysteria than hard science and sober risk assessment. Chlorine compounds, they say, ought to be regulated like other compounds—based on determinations of their individual risks and benefits, not on the mere presence of chlorine atoms in their molecular anatomies.

As its first order of business, the CCC commissioned reports on chlorine which included a massive analysis—totaling 10 volumes and 4,000 pages—of the toxicological literature on chlorinated organic compounds. The Chlorine Institute, an older industry group devoted "to the safe production, handling, and use of chlorine," has even prepared packaged school lessons and a video that takes students on a tour of chlorine's role in everyday products. Big chemical companies including Dow have created new full-time positions such as Director of Chlorine Issues. The aim of this emerging infrastructure, says Lienhart, is to offer the public a different view of chlorine chemistry than the one anti-chlorine forces have been purveying unchallenged for years.

Industry remains the underdog. Last October 15, the anti-chlorine lobby got the likes of Bella Abzug, the fiery former New York congresswoman and a cancer survivor, to publicly endorse a Greenpeace document linking the rise of chlorine chemistry over the past few decades to rising rates of breast cancer. The Associated Press reported the event and sent the story over the wires. That sort of lachrymose (and toxicologically meaningless) coverage just isn't available to the CCC.

ELEMENTAL CHLORINE IS A CORNERSTONE OF INDUSTRIAL CHEMISTRY

To the community of manufacturers, chlorine remains a cornerstone of chemistry, playing a role in virtually every nook and cranny of modern society. By volume, chlorine is one of the largest chemical feedstocks, rivaling even petroleum. Global chlorine production now hovers around 38 million tons a year.

In the United States, the number is more like 11 million tons of chlorine.

The Chlorine Institute reports that about 28% of the chlorine supply goes into making plastics, mostly polyvinyl-chloride (PVC), from which thousands of products are derived, among them wall coverings, floor tiles, siding, pipes, shoe soles, electrical insulation, automobile components, and medical equipment. Saran Wrap is made from another major chlorine-containing polymer —polyvinylidene chloride. Just over one-third of the chlorine supply is used for synthesizing an estimated 11,000 commercial chemicals. Among the lengthy list of chlorine-dependent products are most herbicides and pesticides, dyes, chlorosilanes for making semiconductor materials, carbon tetrachloride for making nonstick cookware and refrigerants, dichlorophenyl sulfone for making computer components and power-tool housings, propylene chlorohydrin that is used first to make propylene oxide, which in turn is used to make a range of products including lubricants, coatings, brake fluids, cleaners, adhesives, pharmaceuticals, and soft-drink syrups.

Just under one-fifth of the chlorine supply is consumed by chlorinated solvents such as methylene chloride, a degreaser and paint stripper, although demand for such solvents is declining as manufacturers switch to water-based and otherwise less environmentally troublesome materials and methods. Approximately 14% of the chlorine supply is used for bleaching pulp and paper; the pulp and paper industry is likewise undergoing a transition toward bleaching processes that use less chlorine or no chlorine at all. The remaining few percent of the chlorine supply goes mostly into agents for purifying drinking and waste water, and for manufacturing pharmaceuticals.

Although undisputed estimates are hard to come by, in one way or another chlorine use amounts to at least tens of billions of dollars of commerce each year in the United States alone. It employs directly or indirectly at least hundreds of thousands of people. The highest estimates, from a widely cited and much disputed economic analysis conducted for the Chlorine Institute by the Charles River Associates consulting firm in Boston, contends that chlorine accounts for $91 billion of economic input in the U.S. and, directly and indirectly, over 1.3 million jobs.

THE SEEDS OF CONTROVERSY WERE PLANTED IN THE 1960s

The controversy began well before Greenpeace focused its worldwide campaign on chlorine chemistry in the mid-1980s, following the lead of Germany's Green Party. Never mind the once undisputed public-health successes of chlorine use in disinfecting water, controlling insect-borne diseases, and manufacturing pharmaceuticals. Such benefits to society can easily be forgotten once the anti-chlorine alliance unleashes its ordnance.

Consider DDT, an insecticide so effective against malaria that the World Health Organization once considered shortages as threats to public health. DDT, which stands for dichlorodiphenyl-trichloro-ethane and includes five chlorine atoms in its molecular structure, became the rallying point of the then-nascent environmental movement when Rachel Carson documented its unanticipated effects on the environment and wildlife in her 1962 book *Silent Spring*. (Although DDT has never been proved to be a significant human hazard, it was banned from use in the U.S. because it was known to bioaccumulate or be deposited in body fat at relatively low levels of exposure.)

Add the notoriety of chlorovillain PCBs, or polychlorinated biphenyls, a family of about 180 compounds that have anywhere from two to ten chlorine atoms in their molecular anatomies. PCBs' stability, low flammability; and insulating properties made them favorites for electrical and hydraulic equipment, but those same properties (along with their solubility in fat) likewise enabled them to accumulate to levels of concern in the cells and fat tissue of animals and people.

DDT and PCBs are not the only so-called organochlorine compounds that have a place among chemicals non grata. Even inorganic chlorine compounds that do not themselves persist in the environment, and presumably pose little long-term risk on their own, can break down into harmful molecules that do stick around. When the elemental chlorine used to bleach paper and the volatile chemicals used to make PVC plastic break down in the environment, they can spawn polychlorinated dibenzodioxins (PCDDs) and polychlorinated dibenzofurans (PCDFs). Both are suspected human carcinogens and both have documented adverse affects on wildlife in the Great Lakes region and elsewhere.

CFCs, or chlorofluorocarbons, whose nontoxicity, low cost, and physical and chemical properties had for decades made them just about perfect for large-scale cleaning and refrigeration uses, have become perhaps the best known and most vilified chlorinated compounds of all. CFCs' probable ozone-depleting properties, which never occurred to their originators in the 1930s, now overshadow all that's good about them. By the end of 1995, industry will halt the manufacture of CFCs in accordance with the international Montreal Protocol, a global response that anti-chlorine advocates view as an important precedent for their more ambitious goal of banning the industrial use of chlorine entirely.

The above-noted "chemical black list" represents a tiny fraction of the chlorinated compounds in use. Even so, activists in Germany's Green Party and then at Greenpeace began, as Brad Lienhart puts it, "connecting the dots" between those few notorious chlorovillains and all chlorine-containing compounds. Even though the majority of chlorinated compounds have never been studied for their toxicological effects, Greenpeace views them as a single class of chemicals that should be considered unfit for commercial use until proven safe—a virtual impossibility, both scientifically and economically.

If Greenpeace were alone in its fight against chlorine, the Dows, Monsantos, and Du Ponts of the world might not have much to worry about. But the chemical industry decided that the call for a ban was more than environmentalist bravado when a normally conservative United States/Canadian commission, the International Joint Commission [IJC], officially announced comprehensive anti-chlorine recommendations, to their respective governments in their biannual report of 1992.

The IJC's scientific panels and advisors convinced its six commissioners that chlorinated compounds are persistent enough in the Great Lakes region that a recommendation to phase them out is prudent. Although the Commission concedes that many of the synthetic chlorinated organic substances identified in the water, sediment, and biota of the region have not been identified as individually toxic, it concludes that many of these chemicals—because of their shared chemical characteristics—will be identified as persistent toxicants.

The IJC recommended in 1992 that the U.S. and Canada "develop timetables to sunset [phase out] the use of chlorine and chlorine-containing compounds as industrial feedstocks, and the means of reducing or eliminating other uses [such as water treatment and paper bleaching] be examined." Moreover, other treaty organizations that oversee the use of international waters have articulated similar antichlorine positions.

"The IJC lit up our lives," says Rick Hinds, legislative director of Greenpeace's toxics campaign.

Despite rigorous lobbying by the CCC to stop lumping the entire menagerie of chlorine-containing compounds into one huge regulatory class, the IJC is standing firm. Its 1994 biannual report, issued following its most recent gathering in Windsor, Ontario, redoubled calls for sunsetting chlorine. Brad Lienhart, who participated in the IJC meeting, thinks that some gains were made despite the anti-chlorine message. The IJC's Virtual Elimination Task Force, which develops strategies to eventually eliminate all toxic inputs to the Great Lakes, agreed there is a need for "a thorough and complete analysis of chlorine chemistry before any schedule for sunsetting chlorine is implemented," Mr. Lienhart says. He believes such an analysis will vindicate much of chlorine chemistry as a sensible, environmentally responsible choice for manufacturers.

Following that mild concession by the IJC, though, another voice joined the anti-chlorine chorus. In early November,

the American Public Health Association, which represents 50,000 public-health workers, registered some of the strongest anti-chlorine positions yet heard. A final draft of the APHA's position states "the only feasible and prudent approach to eliminating the release and discharge of chlorinated organic chemicals and consequent exposure is to avoid the use of chlorine and its compounds in manufacturing processes." The resolution concedes that not *all* uses of chlorine, especially such public-health uses as disinfecting drinking water and pharmaceutical production, have feasible alternatives—thereby implying that those uses of chlorine ought to be continued. But APHA calls for provisions to retrain workers displaced from a shrinking chlorine industry.

THE CASES FOR AND AGAINST MAY REST ON RISK OR BENEFIT TO SOCIETY

Like looking at clouds, both sides can see what they want in existing data, or commission hand-picked scientists to do studies that lend credence to their respective interpretations.

In lieu of objective scientific debate, methodological and philosophical issues are at the fore. One of the largest gulfs between the two camps centers on the unprecedented call to consider all chlorinated compounds in use as a single class subject to regulatory action. The case for banning all industrial uses of chlorine is easier to explain, which gives it a decided advantage over the more complicated argument of chlorine's defenders. The basic argument starts with reference to DDT, PCBS, dioxins, CFCs and a few other compounds that have documented effects. Next the argument points out that all of these compounds have one thing in common, namely, the presence of chlorine atoms in their molecular structures.

Finally, the argument takes an inferential step—and this is the precise point of contention. It concludes that, because of this commonality, all other chlorine compounds are suspected environmental and biological hazards. The concept of "reverse onus" would be applied to all chlorinated compounds: an assumption that they produce toxicity unless otherwise proved by the seller. Since chlorine detractors admit that most chlorine-dependent compounds have never been shown to have hazardous effects and have never even been studied, they refer to this conclusion as "the precautionary principle."

Another key component of the argument points to correlations between the presence of chlorinated organics in sediments, water basins, and tissues of animals and humans, on the one hand, and, on the other, incidences of wildlife population declines, reproductive and developmental anomalies in animals and people, and various diseases, including cancer. Theo Colborn, a Fellow at the World Wildlife Fund who chaired an often-cited gathering of toxicologists, ecologists, immunologists, and other scientists three years ago, said in an interview that "we have reached a point [of loading toxic synthetic chemicals in the environment and living tissue] that we ought to be concerned about releasing more."

The so-called "precautionary principle" is seductively simple. There are simply too many chlorinated compounds to study on a one-by-one basis to assess their safety. "There aren't enough rats in the world to assess individual compounds and what their combined effects might be," says Tufts University biologist Ana Soto, who is studying how compounds including PCBs can mimic the hormonal effects of estrogen.

Nevertheless, the pro-chlorine advocates assert that the only scientifically defensible way to ascertain chlorine's health and environmental effects is to do toxicological, epidemiological, and other studies of specific organochlorine chemicals. They point out that the scientific data simply does not exist to implicate any but a very few organochlorine compounds, such as DDT and PCBs—which have been studied for many years. Brad Lienhart tirelessly points out that the many thousands of organochlorine compounds in use cannot legitimately be thought of as a single class because they are chemically, physically, and biologically heterogeneous. Adds W. Joseph Stearns, Dow's director of chlorine issues: "The substantive part of this issue is that *some* organochlorines are persistent toxics, not that all organochlorines contain chlorine."

Indeed, many organochlorine compounds have short lifespans in the natural world. Mr. Stearns argues that to condemn any compound because it contains chlorine in its molecular structure will lead to a whole host of environmental regulations that the actual risks do not call for. And depriving society of thousands of useful, chlorine-based products without ascertaining if the risks are unacceptable, says the pro-chlorine camp, is a misguided formula that will greatly damage the nation's economic strength and standard of living.

GREENPEACE'S INSISTENCE THAT "SUBSTITUTES EXIST" IS MISLEADING

Chlorine's defenders can point out the importance of its use in modern industrial chemistry, and try to explain the complex toxicological reasons why tens of thousands of compounds having nothing in common but chlorine should not be treated as a single class of chemicals. But their strongest argument may be that, while substitutes for chlorine and chlorinated compounds may exist in many cases, the costs to switch are prohibitive and the substitutes not necessarily any less risky.

Susan Sieber, a toxicologist and Deputy Director of the Division of Cancer Etiology at the National Cancer Institute, warns that hasty blanket bans can have the unwanted effect of pushing alternatives that are worse. "You need to assess the risks and benefits," she says.

Attempts at sober assessment that would fall between the two camps have begun in earnest. One example is a 180-page report that the M.I.T. Program in Technology, Business and Environment prepared for the Norwegian government and European industry groups. The report begins the daunting task of assessing the economic, social, and environmental costs and gains of non-chlorine substitutes, focusing on several areas including cleaning solvents in the electronics industry, polyvinylchloride (PVC) plastic, chlorinated pesticides, and chlorine-based bleaching agents.

The report notes that a trend toward chlorine-free bleaching technologies in the paper industry shows that major categories of chlorine use are not absolutely necessary for the industries that have been heavy chlorine users. "This suggests that concerns over the unavailability of such alternatives in other cases of chlorine use may be overblown," concludes the summary of the report's findings.

Availability of substitutes, however, is only part of the story. Among the big caveats:

• Substitutes carry their own environmental and health effects. For example, water-based substitutes for CFCs in the electronics industry add a new source of water pollution. The return of hydrocarbon coolants and insulating fluids for electrical transformers has brought back the fire hazards that PCBs had virtually eliminated.

• Chlorine-based technologies themselves may have been less hazardous replacements for nastier technologies. A chlorine-dependent route to titanium dioxide, a widely used pigment in white paint, replaced the dangerous lead-based pigments that contributed to a public-health calamity. The chlorine-dependent process produces one-sixth the hazardous waste of an alternative process that relies on sulfuric acid.

• Affordable alternatives that can perform as well as the chlorine-dependent product may not exist. In these cases, technological innovation and development can take a long time, at great cost. The report cites the absence of any drop-in replacements for CFCs that automakers could use for air conditioning systems of cars after the CFC ban goes into effect.

FEW SEE THE WHOLE PICTURE, BUT LEGISLATORS AND USER GROUPS HAVE BEGUN TO REACT

Greenpeace believes it has industry on the run. "The writing is on the wall," says Jay Palter, Toronto director of the group's Chlorine Free campaign. "A chlorine phaseout is inevitable and industry is just stalling for time."

Industry representatives don't see it that way. "Greenpeace is not fundamentally changing the way we do business," says Michael W. Berezo, director of environmental strategy for Monsanto. At the moment, neither EPA nor its Canadian counterpart, Environment Canada, has accepted the notion that all chlorine compounds ought to be regulated or phased out as a class. Berezo does concede that the ascent of the chlorine issue is pushing Monsanto and other companies to look more aggressively at alternatives to chlorine-containing chemicals. But industry's dilemmas lack easy answers.

Specific user groups have begun to wrestle with the chlorine issue as it affects them. The Jan/Feb '94 issue of the newsletter *Environment Building News* ran a 10-page article titled "Should We Phase Out PVC?" The report makes a Herculean effort to integrate the available information on PVC's benefits and the dangers stemming from its manufacture into a picture that might guide its readers. After concluding that its account left more questions than answers, the article counseled the 1,200 builders and architects who subscribe to the newsletter to "seek out better, safer, and more environmentally responsible alternatives" to polyvinylchloride—without actually suggesting that readers completely avoid vinyl materials. PVC accounts for more than a quarter of worldwide chlorine use,

so such recommendations can have far-reaching effects.

Perhaps the most newsworthy feature of the chlorine controversy is that it has progressed to the point where a ban is being taken seriously by governments and industry. And even if the meteor of a ban is deflected by pragmatic concerns, chlorine chemistry may be forever changed by an asteroid shower of legislation. In October, Rep. Bill Richardson (D-NM) delighted environmentalists by reintroducing a bill that would legislate chlorine out of the pulp and paper industry within five years. In October, the Clinton administration nearly issued an executive order that would have mandated government to buy paper made without chlorine. (The requirement didn't make it into the final order.)

Even a year ago, engineering professor David Marks, who is coordinating M.I.T.'s $1.8 million cross-disciplinary study of chlorine, thought the anti-chlorine movement couldn't box its way out of an unbleached paper bag. Now he wonders. "The chlorine industry could wake up one day and see many anti-chlorine bills on the table in Congress," he warns. "Things are moving so fast, it's hard to tell how it will end up."

Industry is well aware how quickly a few Bella Abzugs can alter public perception. Despite the difficulties in switching to chlorine-free production, progressive companies are eyeing such strategies as pollution prevention and substitution to preempt future, more costly adjustments. Truly farsighted companies aim to turn anti-chlorine sentiment into a market. Dow has created a new business entity called Advanced Cleaning Systems, which provides water-based cleaning technology and support services for green industrial niches. And Louisiana

Pacific, one of the country's largest paper manufacturers, is trumpeting its new chlorine-free bleaching process at a plant in Samoa, California.

Should there be a chlorine phaseout, it would probably occur in a piecemeal fashion, hopping from product category to product category. Both sides will continue to debate the data on what effects chlorinated compounds have on the environment and human health. But it seems quite possible that even without government-imposed limits, public perception and the market forces that follow from it will dictate the future of chlorine's role in industry and society.

POSTSCRIPT

Should the Industrial Use of Chlorine Be Phased Out?

Industry claims that the cost of eliminating those chlorinated organics that are either not essential or for which there are available substitutes would be prohibitive, as well as suspect, without an independent assessment by an agency that does not have a vested interest in maintaining the status quo. Similar claims, which greeted the initial demands to phase out most uses of asbestos and chlorofluorocarbons, proved to be vastly overstated. Omitted from the chlorine industry's economic analysis of the issue is the savings that would accrue to the general public from a general restriction on chlorinated compounds, due to the fact that regulatory agencies would be relieved of the financial burden of assessing the hazards of individual compounds and enforcing regulations for each one that required restriction. On the other hand, Thornton's claim that "97% of all chlorine use could be phased out for just $22 billion per year" would likely not stand up to the scrutiny of an unbiased analysis.

Transition Planning for the Chlorine Phaseout and *Chlorine, Human Health and the Environment: The Breast Cancer Report* are publications available from Greenpeace. The technical arguments used by the chlorine industry in their opposition to the phaseout are contained in the April 1993 *Assessment of the Economic Benefits of Chlor-Alkali Chemicals to the United States and Canadian Economies,* prepared by Charles River Associates, Inc., for the chlorine industry. A more even-handed analysis is "The Crusade Against Chlorine," by Ivan Amato, in the July 9, 1994, issue of *Science.* An article that strongly condemns the antichlorine initiative as a "campaign against modern industrial society" is "Chemical Warfare," by Michael Fumento, *Reason* (June 1994).

In the July 11, 1994, issue of *Chemical and Engineering News,* Elisabeth Kirschner reports on a rebuttal by a panel of Michigan scientists of the U.S.–Canadian International Joint Commission's recommendation to phase out chlorine-containing compounds as industrial feedstocks. Gordon Graff's article "The Chlorine Controversy," *Technology Review* (January 1995) is an analysis that presents the Greenpeace campaign in a generally favorable light.

For a recent review of the activities and strategies of both the antichlorine environmental crusaders and their industrial opponents, as well as changes that are occurring due to international regulatory activity, public pressure, and market forces, see "The Changing Landscape of the Chlorine Debate," by Terry F. Yosie, in the November 1996 issue of *Environmental Science and Technology*.

For an Internet site related to this issue, see `http://www.ecotopia.be/epe/sourcebook/2.7.html`, where responding to the chlorine controversy is presented as an example of how industry will need restructuring to meet the goals of sustainable development.

ISSUE 8

Do Environmental Estrogens Pose a Potentially Serious Health Threat?

YES: Jon R. Luoma, from "Havoc in the Hormones," *Audubon* (July–August 1995)

NO: Stephen H. Safe, from "Environmental and Dietary Estrogens and Human Health: Is There a Problem?" *Environmental Health Perspectives* (April 1995)

ISSUE SUMMARY

YES: Environmental journalist Jon R. Luoma asserts that pollutants that mimic estrogens have caused reproductive problems in wildlife and are considered by many researchers to threaten humans as well.

NO: Toxicologist Stephen H. Safe argues that the suggestion that industrial estrogenic compounds contribute to increased cancer incidence and reproductive problems in humans is not plausible.

Following World War II there was an exponential growth in the industrial use and marketing of synthetic chemicals. These chemicals, known as "xenobiotics," were used in numerous products, including solvents, pesticides, refrigerants, coolants, and raw materials for plastics. This resulted in increasing environmental contamination. Many of these chemicals, such as DDT, PCBs, and dioxins, proved to be highly resistant to degradation in the environment; they accumulated in wildlife and were serious contaminants of lakes and estuaries. Carried by winds and ocean currents, these chemicals were soon detected in samples taken from the most remote regions of the planet, far from their points of introduction into the ecosphere.

Until very recently most efforts to assess the potential toxicity of synthetic chemicals to bio-organisms, including human beings, focused almost exclusively on their possible role as carcinogens. This was because of legitimate public concern about rising cancer rates and the belief that cancer causation was the most likely outcome of exposure to low levels of synthetic chemicals.

Some environmental scientists urged public health officials to give serious consideration to other possible health effects of xenobiotics. They were generally ignored because of limited funding and the common belief that toxic effects other than cancer required larger exposures than usually resulted from environmental contamination.

In the late 1980s, Theo Colborn, a research scientist for the World Wildlife Fund who was then working on a study of pollution in the Great Lakes, began the process of linking together the results of a growing series of isolated studies. Researchers in the Great Lakes region, as well as in Florida, the U.S. West Coast, and Northern Europe, had observed widespread evidence of serious and frequently lethal physiological problems involving abnormal reproductive development, unusual sexual behavior, and neurological problems exhibited by a diverse group of animal species, including fish, reptiles, amphibians, birds, and marine mammals. Through Colborn's insights, communications among these researchers, and further studies, a hypothesis was developed that all of these wildlife problems were manifestations of abnormal estrogenic activity. The causative agents were identified as more than 50 synthetic chemical compounds that have been shown in laboratory studies to either mimic the action, or disrupt the normal function, of the powerful estrogenic hormones responsible for female sexual development and many other biological functions.

Concern that human exposure to these ubiquitous environmental contaminants may have serious health repurcussions was heightened by a widely publicized European research study, which concluded that male sperm counts had decreased by 50 percent over the past several decades (a result that is disputed by other researchers) and that testicular cancer rates have tripled. Some scientists have also proposed a link between breast cancer and estrogen disrupters. A recent significant finding is the powerful synergistic effect by which synthetic chemicals acting together have been shown to have estrogenic potencies more than a thousand times greater than the sum of the effects of the individual compounds.

In response to the mounting scientific evidence that environmental estrogens may be a serious health threat, the U.S. Congress passed two acts during the summer of 1996. This legislation requires that all pesticides be screened for estrogenic activity and that by 1998 the Environmental Protection Agency (EPA) develop procedures for detecting environmental estrogenic contaminants in drinking water supplies.

The following article by Jon R. Luoma is a concise summary of the history of the research that has resulted in the growing concern about environmental compounds with hormonal properties. Steven H. Safe's opposing article was chosen even though it includes technical arguments that presume a background in biochemistry that few readers of this book are likely to possess. It is, however, the most often-cited denunciation of the likelihood of a causative relationship between environmental estrogens and human health problems. Safe's principal arguments concern the relatively low dietary intake of synthetic chemicals as compared to food chemicals that have estrogenic activity, and he cites evidence countering the correlations between either breast cancer incidence or sperm count decreases and exposure to synthetic estrogen mimics. This evidence can be understood independently of the more technical information and arguments that Safe presents.

YES

Jon R. Luoma

HAVOC IN THE HORMONES

Louis Guillette, a University of Florida wildlife endocrinologist with salt-and-pepper hair and matching beard, is stalking an alligator, one of dozens with which we presently share a large cage.

This is not high adventure. The alligators are babies—the young of the year, a foot or so long. They scramble away from Guillette, scurrying among potted plants or diving and swimming furiously across the shallow pool in the center of the cage's concrete floor. They are fast and nimble, but Guillette soon has one in his hand, a male about 14 inches long. He grips it like a sort of huge, green hypodermic, nestling its torso in his palm, its head between two crooked fingers.

"There is no way in the world, just looking at this little alligator, that you could tell there was anything wrong with him," says Guillette, stroking the animal. The little reptile certainly seems robust, pumping its stubby legs in the air and squeaking the curious distress call—a quasi-electronic chirp—of a baby alligator in the clutches of predatory danger. But beyond its present predicament, something is indeed very wrong with it.

Guillette turns the alligator upside down and opens a pinkish genital structure on its abdomen. The oddity of this strikes me for a moment: that I have traveled all the way to Gainesville to look at an alligator's penis.

There isn't much to a baby alligator's penis; it is small, almost threadlike. But although a layman wouldn't know it simply by looking, this one is smaller than it should be. And that's part of a larger story that perhaps should have us all sounding an alarm.

The upshot of the story is this: In the past decade, scientists like Guillette have been finding more and more evidence that molecules of some chemical pollutants—ranging from pesticides to polychlorinated biphenyls (PCBs) and from dioxins to additives in some plastics and industrial detergents—can behave like hormones in the bodies of both animals and humans. Mimicking natural hormones (or blocking, amplifying, or otherwise disrupting them), these pollutants have already created biological chaos in the bodies of some exposed animals, like this alligator. And since such pollutants abound in ecosystems, as well as in animal and human tissues, some scientists worry that the problems seen so far represent only the tip of an iceberg.

Hormones are the body's chemical messengers. Secreted in infinitesimal amounts into the bloodstream, they can trigger dramatic changes in the body, like the alert, hair-raising, heart-pounding sensation brought on by a surge of adrenaline, or the exquisite sequence of timing in the ovulation cycle. Hormones also exert enormous control over fetal development, enhancing the growth of skin, the nervous system, and some brain cells, and determining whether an embryo will develop the body of a male or a female.

A hormone molecule functions by docking onto a cell structure called a receptor, which has an affinity for the hormone's unique chemical design. Like a molecular key fitting into a specially designed keyhole, the hormone essentially flips a biochemical switch, which in turn can trigger a cascade of physical changes. But, says Guillette, "we now know for certain that some pesticides and other chemicals act like keys too—as fake messengers."

The alligator Guillette holds in the palm of his hand was born near Orlando on Lake Apopka. There, pesticide residues from agriculture as well as contaminants from a factory owned by the Tower Chemical Company continue to pollute the food chain even now, more than a decade after the plant was closed. As a bizarre consequence of that pollution, this alligator may not, in fact, be a male at all.

In terms of its hormonal chemistry, it seems to be closer to a female. Like other "males" born on the lake, its blood is high in estrogen and low in testosterone.

As it matures, its penis could grow to as little as one-fourth the normal size; the animal is likely to be, like many of the Apopka alligators, "reproductively incompetent," as Guillette puts it.

It took Guillette and a group of colleagues years to piece together the puzzle of Lake Apopka's alligators. Since the mid-1980s they had known that something had caused the population to crash and that the alligators had strange anomalies. For instance, when he examined the ovaries of young female alligators, Guillette found that they were producing abnormal eggs, with multiple nuclei, and more than the usual one egg per egg follicle. A critical puzzle piece fell into place in 1992, when fellow endocrinologist Howard Bern visited Guillette's lab.

Bern, of the University of California, Berkeley, is a well-known expert on the now-banned drug DES, a synthetic estrogen that was prescribed for millions of women in the 1940s, '50s, and '60s; years later, the daughters of DES-exposed mothers began to have severe gynecological problems. During his visit, Bern showed Guillette and his students slides of the ovaries of laboratory mice that had been exposed to DES.

"A chill went up my spine," says Guillette. "It was the same pattern that I'd seen in my female alligators. But DES is a synthetic estrogen. I wondered where in the world my alligators were getting estrogen."

As Guillette accumulated data, the picture became clear: Pesticides (including dicofol—a close relative of DDT—and some DDT that had been produced as a contaminant during dicofol manufacture) had moved into the food chain of the Lake Apopka ecosystem. Studies by other scientists working with birds and laboratory rodents had shown that these kinds of pesticides, from a class of chemicals known as organochlorines, were not only tenacious once they entered animal tissues but also could mimic, amplify, or block natural sex hormones like estrogen and testosterone. Indeed, Guillette has been able to duplicate the resultant gender-bending effects in his laboratory by infusing clean alligator eggs with similar pesticides.

Guillette's discovery was far from isolated. If this were a problem with one pesticide and one species, the story of the alligators would be little more than a scientific oddity. But Theo Colborn, a zoologist and senior scientist with the World Wildlife Fund, says the phenomenon is all too common: Chemicals that disrupt the endocrine system now abound in ecosystems and, at least in the most polluted areas, are causing obvious problems. "We're seeing this same pattern of anomalies linked to endocrine disrupters across a whole suite of animals and humans around the world," she says.

In fact, from Europe's North Sea to the Great Lakes to the California coast, scientists have been piecing together remarkably similar puzzles, from seals with immune-system disorders to gulls with vestiges of both male and female gonads to fish that fail to mature sexually —all carrying high burdens of synthetic chemicals, most notably organochlorines.

Further, some scientists believe that the ubiquitous synthetic pollutants that virtually all of us now carry in our own fatty tissues could explain, for instance, why rates of breast and testicular cancer have soared, and why male sperm counts in the industrialized world have plummeted by a startling 50 percent since the dawn of the "chemical revolution" that began after World War II.

Theo Colborn has often served as the synthesizer who, beginning in the late 1980s, has helped bring together researchers who had made largely isolated discoveries about pieces of this puzzle. Yet for her, the discovery that the puzzle existed at all was an accident. Hired in 1987 by the World Wildlife Fund to assemble a report on Great Lakes environmental problems, Colborn began to pore over articles that highlighted problems observed in wildlife in the Great Lakes ecosystem: terns and double-crested cormorants born without eyes or with twisted, crossed beaks; salmon in polluted waters that failed to mature; gulls that showed no interest in nesting. She was intrigued by what she sensed was a pattern, but, she says, "I just couldn't sort out how all these pieces fit together."

Eventually, after she began plugging the data into a chart, a clearer pattern began to emerge. Virtually all the affected species were top predators, mostly fish eaters. Although data showed that they had relatively high levels of compounds like PCBs, dioxins, and a wide range of pesticides, most of the problems were not showing up as defects in adults. Rather, the adults were either failing to reproduce or producing offspring that failed to thrive. Eagles, for instance, that had recently migrated to the shores of industrially contaminated bays bore healthy chicks. Yet those that had fed on contaminated fish for years were either failing to reproduce or were bearing chicks with defects like beaks so mangled they were unable to eat.

Colborn also ran into studies by developmental psychologists Joseph and Sandra Jacobson at Wayne State University, in Michigan, suggesting that children born of mothers who had regularly eaten contaminated fish weighed less than average at birth, had smaller heads, and, as they matured, began to show decreases in short-term memory and attention span. Once again, the mothers seemed healthy.

Since the adults were fine, Colborn concluded that something was happening at the embryonic or fetal level, that somehow pollutants accumulated by the mother were affecting the offspring. But how? Just as Guillette, an endocrinologist, was led into the world of toxicology, more digging led Colborn, who was trained in wildlife toxicology, into the world of hormones.

Studies by Michael Fry, an avian toxicologist at the University of California, Davis, helped provide the tip-off. By the early 1980s, Fry had managed to replicate in his laboratory a bizarre anomaly he'd found in the 1970s among western gulls off the California coast. According to his research, male gulls in one DDT-contaminated area were ignoring breeding colonies, and females were nesting with females. (DDT use was restricted in the United States in 1972, but residues remain in food chains.) Dissecting some birds, he found that some males were functional hermaphrodites, with at least partially formed female sex organs. He was later able to reproduce this effect in his lab by infusing clean gull eggs with DDT or estrogens.

Colborn also found studies showing that laboratory rodents exposed to either natural hormones or a range of environmental toxicants, including dioxin, could literally have their sexual orientation altered. In one study by University of Wisconsin toxicologist Dick Peterson, male rats whose mothers had been injected with dioxin not only were disin-

clined to mate with females but moved into a femalelike mating position when in the presence of normal males. Although adults exposed to the pollutants seemed unharmed except at high dosages, the rats exposed in utero produced only half the usual amount of sperm. Even tiny doses caused effects in offspring.

In a 1985 study at the Environmental Protection Agency's Health Effects Research Laboratory in North Carolina, female hamsters exposed to Xearalenone, a common fungicide, developed what EPA scientist Earl Gray calls masculine behaviors, including an inclination to mount another female in estrus. The scientists believe that exposure to the poison may have altered the organization of cells in the brain that control sexual behavior.

In 1991 Colborn brought together many of the scientists studying this issue for a conference in Racine, Wisconsin. Among other things, participants agreed that pollutants can mimic or otherwise disrupt hormones, that "many wildlife populations are already affected" by endocrine-disrupting pollutants, and that because the same pollutants are accumulating in human cells, "a major research initiative on humans must be undertaken."

Colborn says, "This scares us all enough that we'd be delighted if someone could prove we're wrong." But she believes there is already enough evidence of risk to human health that federal regulatory agencies should insist that chemicals be tested for hormone-like effects before allowing them to be loosed upon the world.

Experimental studies can't be performed on humans. But the artificial estrogen DES may have served as a sad and unwitting experiment. Just as with wildlife and experimental animals exposed to toxins, the drug appears to have had little effect on most mothers who took it. But when their daughters reached maturity, many suffered from infertility, had malformed reproductive tracts, or were afflicted with an otherwise exceedingly rare cancer, clear-cell vaginal adenocarcinoma. DES sons showed an increased rate of problems such as undescended testicles, testicular cancer, and reduced sperm counts.

At a January 1994 conference on "environmental estrogens" in Washington, D.C., Danish researcher Niels Skakkebaek and British reproductive biologist Richard Sharpe reported that similar problems among men have been rising since midcentury, including a tripling of testicular-cancer rates in the United States and Britain and a plummeting rate of sperm production across the industrialized world.

"Why should we be concerned about what's happened to wildlife?" asks Robert Kavlock, who directs the EPA's developmental-toxicology division. "One word: *canaries* [a reference to the old coal miners' practice of using a canary as a monitor for poison gas]. We know there are problems with reproductive health among humans. It's hard to know what the cause is. But we know that if the problem is the environment, it's going to show up first in species with shorter life cycles than ours. We know there are hot spots for wildlife where we've seen these kinds of problems. The issue we've got to address is whether there are problems in the general environment."

Stephen H. Safe, a Texas A&M chemist whose work is partially funded by the Chemical Manufacturers Association—a trade and lobbying group—is skeptical of the mounting research. In the April 1995 issue of the journal *Environmental Health*

Perspectives, he flatly stated that "the suggestion that industrial estrogenic chemicals contribute to an increased incidence of breast cancer in women and male reproductive problems is not plausible." Although he agrees that reductions in such compounds in the Great Lakes "correlates with the improved reproductive success of highly susceptible fish-eating water birds," he points to naturally occurring hormonelike chemicals in some foods, like soy, as an estrogen mimic; further, he suggests that human intake of industrial compounds is too low to cause serious health problems.

However, Guillette and other researchers note that the human body has most likely evolved to cope with natural hormone mimics in foods, and that food-based compounds do not build up in fat cells, as do many of the synthetic industrial compounds. Guillette cautions, "Tying all of this into effects on the general human population at lower exposures is theoretical. But there are enough data to be concerned. There's no question that we have laboratory data showing that quite a few of these substances are endocrine disrupters. It's clear that in contaminated animals in the wild we have the same kinds of abnormalities we've produced in the lab. It's also true that in humans we're seeing increasing rates of these same kinds of problems. We're jumping ahead of the data if we try to say 'X causes Y.' But we aren't jumping ahead if we hypothesize and then support it with data. And it seems like the more data we collect, the more support we have.... So far, we have found data that falsify the hypothesis.

"People love to think that we're different from other animals, and certainly different from insects. But at the cellular level, we are fundamentally the same. If we design a compound to be toxic to an insect cell, why does it surprise us when we find out that the same compound is toxic to a human cell? We've always thought the issue was mass—that these things could be toxic to an insect without having significant effects in a much larger human. But how big is an embryo?"

NO

Stephen H. Safe

ENVIRONMENTAL AND DIETARY ESTROGENS AND HUMAN HEALTH: IS THERE A PROBLEM?

Recent reports have suggested that background levels of industrial chemicals and other environmental pollutants may play a role in development of breast cancer in women and decreased male reproductive success as well as the reproductive failures of some wildlife species. These suggestions have been supported by articles in the popular and scientific press and by a television documentary which have described the perils of exposure to endocrine-disrupting chemicals such as estrogenic organochlorine pesticides and pollutants. During the past two decades, environmental regulations regarding the manufacture, use, and disposal of chemicals have resulted in significantly reduced emissions of most industrial compounds and their by-products. Levels of the more environmentally stable organochlorine pesticides and pollutants are decreasing in most ecosystems including the industrialized areas around the Great Lakes in North America. Decreased levels of organochlorine compounds correlates with the improved reproductive success of highly susceptible fish-eating water birds in the Great Lakes region. This article reviews key papers that have been used to support the hypotheses that environmental estrogens play a role in the increased incidence of breast cancer in women and decreased sperm counts in males. Environmental/dietary estrogens and antiestrogens are identified and intakes of "estrogen equivalents" are estimated to compare the relative dietary impacts of various classes of estrogenic chemicals.

ROLE OF ESTROGENS IN BREAST CANCER AND MALE REPRODUCTIVE PROBLEMS

Concerns regarding the role of environmental and dietary estrogens as possible contributors to the increased incidence of breast cancer were fueled by several reports that showed elevated levels of organochlorine com-

From Stephen H. Safe, "Environmental and Dietary Estrogens and Human Health: Is There a Problem?" *Environmental Health Perspectives*, vol. 103, no. 4 (April 1995). References omitted.

pounds in breast cancer patients.... Polychlorinated biphenyls (PCBs) and 1, 1-dichloro-2, 2-bis(p-chlorophenyl)ethylene (DDE) are the two most abundant oganochlorine pollutants identified in all human tissues with high frequencies. In one Scandinavian study, levels of DDE or PCBs in adipose tissue from breast samples were not significantly different in breast cancer patients compared to controls. In another study in Finland, β-hexachlorocyclohexane levels were elevated in breast cancer patients; however, this compound was not detected in adipose tissue of some individuals in the patient and control groups and has a relatively low frequency of detection in human tissue samples. Falck and coworkers reported that PCB levels were elevated in mammary adipose tissue samples from breast cancer patients in Connecticut. In contrast, serum levels of DDE (but not PCBs) were significantly elevated in breast cancer patients enrolled in the New York University Women's Health Study. DDE (but not PCB) levels were also elevated in estrogen receptor (ER)-positive but not ER-negative breast cancer patients from Quebec compared to levels in women with benign breast disease. It was initially concluded by Wolff and co-workers that "these findings suggest that environmental chemical contamination with organochlorine residues may be an important etiologic factor in breast cancer." The correlations reported in the two U.S. studies heightened public and scientific concern regarding the potential role of these compounds in development of breast cancer. These observations undoubtedly reinforced advocacy by some groups for a ban on the use of all chlorine-containing chemicals. However, the proposed linkage between PCBs and/or DDE and breast cancer is questionable for the following reasons:

- Most studies with PCBs indicate that these mixtures are not estrogenic, and the weak estrogenic activity observed for lower chlorinated PCB mixtures may be due to their derived hydroxylated metabolites;

- p,p'-DDE, the dominant persistent metabolite of 1, 1, 1-trichloro-2, 2-bis(p-chlorophenyl)ethane (p,p'-DDT), is not estrogenic, and levels of $o,p' = $DDT, the estrogenic member of the DDT family, are low to nondetectable in most environmental samples;

- Epidemiology studies of individuals occupationally exposed to relatively high levels of DDT or PCBs do not show a higher incidence of breast cancer; and

- No single class of organochlorine compounds was elevated in all studies, suggesting that other factors may be critical for development of breast cancer.

Krieger and co-workers recently reported results from a nested case–control study of women from the San Francisco area which showed that there were no differences in serum DDE or PCB levels between breast cancer patients and control subjects. The authors concluded that "the data do not support the hypothesis that exposure to DDE and PCBs increases risk of breast cancer." This was duly noted in *Time* magazine by a three-line statement in "The Good News" section. Moreover, combined analysis of the 6 studies which report PCB and DDE levels in 301 breast cancer patients and 412 control patients showed that there were no significant increases in either DDE or PCB levels in breast cancer patients versus controls.

The second major link between environmental/dietary estrogens and human disease was precipitated by an article published in the *Lancet*, in which Sharpe and Skakkebaek hypothesized that increased estrogen exposure may be responsible for falling sperm counts and disorders of the male reproductive tract. Unlike the proposed link between environmental estrogens and breast cancer, this hypothesis was not based on experimentally derived measurements of increased levels of any estrogenic compounds in males. Previous studies with diethylstilbestrol, a highly potent estrogenic drug, showed that *in utero* exposure results in adverse effects in male offspring, and the authors' hypothesized that *in utero* exposure to environmental/dietary estrogens may also result in adverse effects in male offspring. A critical experimental component supporting the authors' hypothesis was their analysis of data from several studies which indicated that male sperm counts had decreased by over 40% during the past 50 years. These observations, coupled with the hypothesis that environmental estrogens including organochlorine chemicals were possible etiologic agents, were reported with alarm in the popular and scientific press and in a BBC television program entitled "Assault on the Male: a Horizon Special." Subsequent and prior scientific studies have cast serious doubts on both the hypothesis and the observed decrease in male sperm counts. In 1979, Macleod and Wang reported that there had been no decline in sperm counts, and reanalysis of the data presented by Carlsen and co-workers showed that sperm counts had not decreased from 1960 to 1990. Thus, during the time in which environmental levels of organochlorine compounds were

maximal, there was not a corresponding decrease in sperm counts. Moreover, a reevaluation of the sperm concentration data was recently reported by Brownwich et al. in the *British Medical Journal*, and their analysis suggested that the decline in sperm values in males was a function of the choice of the normal or reference value for sperm concentrations. The authors contend that their analysis of the data does "not support the hypothesis that the sperm count declined significantly between 1940 and 1990."

These results suggest that the increasing incidence of human breast cancer is not related to organochlorine environmental contaminants and that decreases in sperm counts is highly debatable. Nevertheless, human populations are continually exposed to a wide variety of environmental and dietary estrogens, and these compounds clearly fit into the category of "endocrine disrupters." The remainder of this article briefly describes the different structural classes of both environmental and dietary estrogens and quantitates human exposures to these compounds.

SYNTHETIC INDUSTRIAL CHEMICALS WITH ESTROGENIC ACTIVITY

The estrogenic activities of different structural classes of industrial chemicals were reported by several research groups in the late 1960s and 1970s in which o,p'-DDT and other diphenylmethane analogs and the insecticide kepone were characterized as estrogens. Subsequent studies have confirmed the estrogenic activity of o,p'-DDT and related compounds whereas the p,p'-substituted analogs were relatively inactive. In addition, p,p'-methoxychlor and its hydroxylated metabolites elicit estrogenic responses. Ecobichon and Comeau investigated the estrogenic activities of commercial PCB mixtures (Aroclors) and individual congeners in the female rat uterus and reported estrogenic responses for some Aroclors and individual congeners. Studies in this laboratory showed that a number of commercial PCBs did not significantly increase secretion of procathepsin D, an estrogen-regulated gene product, in MCF-7 human breast cancer cells. It should be noted that several hydroxylated PCBs bind to the ER, and it is possible that *para*-hydroxylated PCB metabolites may be the active estrogenic compounds associated with lower chlorinated PCBs. A recent study reported that several additional organochlorine pesticides including endosulfan, toxaphene, and dieldrin exhibit estrogenlike activity and induce proliferation of MCF-7 human breast cancer cells.

Other industrial chemicals or intermediates that have been identified as estrogenic compounds include bisphenol-A, a chemical used in the manufacture of polycarbonate-derived products; phenol red, a pH indicator used in cell culture media; and alkyl phenols and their derivatives, which are extensively used for preparation of polyethoxylates in detergents.

NATURAL ESTROGENIC COMPOUNDS

Human exposure to estrogenic chemicals is not confined to xenoestrogens derived from industrial compounds. Several different structural classes of naturally occurring estrogens have been identified, including plant bioflavonoids and various mycotoxins including zearalenone and related compounds. The plant bioflavonoids include different structural classes of compounds which contain a flavonoid backbone: flavones, flavanones, flavonols, isoflavones, and related condensation products (e.g., coumesterol). The estrogenic activities of diverse phytoestrogenic bioflavonoids and mycotoxins have been extensively investigated in *in vivo* models, *in vitro* cell culture systems, and in ER binding assays, and most of these compounds elicit multiple estrogenic responses in these assays. In addition, a number of plant foodstuffs contain 17 β-estradiol (E_2) and estrone.

ENVIRONMENTAL AND DIETARY ANTIESTROGENS

Several different structural classes of chemicals found in the human diet also exhibit antiestrogenic activity. 2, 3, 7, 8-Tetrachlorodibenzo-*p*-dioxin (TCDD) and related halogenated aromatics including polychlorinated dibenzo-*p*-dioxins (PCDDs), dibenzofurans (PCDFs), and PCBs are also an important class of organochlorine pollutants that elicit a diverse spectrum of biochemical and toxic responses. These chemicals act through the aryl hydrocarbon receptor (AhR)-mediated signal transduction pathway, which is thought to play a role in most of the responses elicited by these compounds. AhR agonists such as TCDD have been characterized as antiestrogens using rodent and cell models similar to those used for determining the estrogenic activity of dietary and environmental chemicals. In the rodent model, TCDD and related compounds inhibit several estrogen-induced uterine responses including increased uterine wet weight, peroxidase activity, cytosolic and nuclear progesterone receptor (PR) and ER binding, epidermal growth factor (EGF) receptor binding, EGF receptor mRNA, and c-*fos* mRNA levels. In parallel studies, the antiestrogenic activities of TCDD and related compounds have also been investigated in several human breast cancer cell lines. For example, structurally diverse AhR agonists inhibit the following E_2-induced responses in MCF-7 human breast cancer cells: post-confluent focus production, secretion of tissue plasminogen activator activity, procathepsin D (52-kDa protein), cathepsin D (34-kDa protein), a 160-kDa protein, PR binding sites, glucose-to-lactate metabolism, pS2 protein levels, and PR, cathepsin D, ER, and pS2 gene expression. Moreover, TCDD inhibits formation and/or growth of mammary tumors in athymic nude mice and female Sprague-Dawley rats after long-term feeding studies or initiation with 7,12-dimethylbenzanthracene. A recent epidemiology study on women exposed to TCDD after an industrial accident in Seveso reported that breast cancer incidence was decreased in areas with high levels of TCDD contamination (particularly in the age class 45 to 74) and among women living longest in an area of low TCDD contamination. Endometrial cancer showed a remarkable decrease, particularly in areas with medium and low TCDD contamination. Thus, TCDD and related compounds exhibit a broad spectrum of antiestrogenic activities and, not surprisingly, so do other AhR agonists such as the polynuclear aromatic hydrocarbons (PAHs), indole-3-carbinol (IC), and related compounds found in relatively high levels in foodstuffs. PAHs are found in cooked foods and are ubiquitous environmental contaminants. IC is a major component of cruciferous vegetables (e.g., brussels sprouts, cauliflower) and

exhibits antiestrogenic and anticancer (mammary) activities.

Bioflavonoids have been extensively characterized as weak estrogens and therefore may also be active as antiestrogens at lower concentrations. The interaction between estrogenic bioflavonoids and E_2 depends on their relative doses or concentrations, the experimental model, and the specific estrogen-induced endpoint. Markaverich and co-workers reported that the estrogenic bioflavonoids quercetin and luteolin inhibited E_2-induced proliferation of MCF-7 human breast cancer cells and E_2-induced uterine wet weight increase in 21-day-old female rats. Similar results were also observed in this laboratory for quercetin, resperetin, and naringenin. For example, the bioflavonoid naringenin inhibited estrogen-induced uterine hyptertrophy in female rats and estrogen-induced luciferase activity in MCF-7 cells transfected with an E_2-responsive plasmid construct containing the 5'-promoter region of the pS2 gene and a luciferase reporter gene (unpublished results). In contrast, a recent study reported that coumestrol, genistein, and zearalenone were not antiestrogenic in human breast cancer cells. The antiestrogenic activities of weak dietary and environmental estrogens require further investigation; however, it is clear that at subestrogenic doses, some of these compounds exhibit antiestrogenic activities in both *in vivo* and *in vitro* models.

MASS/POTENCY BALANCE

The uptake of environmental or dietary chemicals that elicit common biochemical/toxic responses can be estimated by using an equivalency factor approach in which estrogen equivalents (EQs) in any mixture are equal to the sum of the concentration of the individual compounds (EC_i) times their potency (EP_i) relative to an assigned standard such as diethylstilbestrol (DES) or E_2. The total EQs in a mixture would be:

$$EQ = \Sigma \left([EC_i] \times EP_i\right)$$

A similar approach is being used to determine the TCDD equivalents (TEQs) of various mixtures containing halogenated hydrocarbons. Verdeal and Ryan have previously used this approach with DES equivalents assuming that the oral potency of E_2 is 15% that of DES. Winter has estimated the dietary intake of pesticides based on FDA's total diet study, which includes estimates of food intakes and pesticide residue levels in these foods. The results presented in Table 1 summarize the estimated exposure of different groups to estrogenic pesticides. For example, 14- to 16-year-old males were exposed to a total of 0.0416 [µ]g/kg/day of the estrogenic pesticides, DDT, dieldrin, endosulfan, and p,p'-methoxychlor (note: the DDT value represents p,p'-DDE and related metabolites, which are primarily nonestrogenic). Thus, the overall dietary intake of these compounds by this age group was 2.5[µ]g/day.

The relative potencies of dietary and xenoestrogens are highly variable. The results of *in vitro* cell culture studies suggest that estrogenic potencies of bioflavonoids relative to E_2 are 0.001 to 0.0001 whereas Soto and co-workers have assigned an estrogen potency factor of 0.000001 for the estrogenic pesticides. These relative estrogen potency factors for bioflavonoids and pesticides may be lower when derived from *in vivo* studies since pharmacokinetic factors and metabolism may decrease bioavailability. Thus, a more accurate assessment of

Table 1

Estimated Dietary Intake of Estrogenic Pesticides by Different Age Groups Based on Food Intakes and Pesticide Levels in These Foodstuffs

	Estimated exposure (µg/kg/day)		
	6–11	14–16[a]	60–65
Pesticide	months	years	years
DDT (total)	0.077	0.0260	0.0103
Dieldrin	0.0014	0.0016	0.0016
Endosulfan	0.0274	0.0135	0.0210
p,p'-Methoxychlor	0.0005	0.0005	0.0001

[a]Maximum exposure: 60 × 0.0416 = 2.5 µg/day.

dietary/environmental EQs requires further data from dietary feeding studies that evaluate these compounds using the same experimental protocols.

The results in Table 2 summarize human exposure to dietary and environmental estrogens and the estimated daily dose in terms of EQs. The relative estrogenic intakes for various hormonal drug therapies were previously estimated by Verdeal and Ryan; the average estimated daily intake of all flavonoids in food products was 1020 and 1070 mg/day, (winter and summer, respectively). The results show that the estimated dietary EQ levels of estrogenic pesticides are 0.0000025 [µ]g/day, whereas the corresponding dietary EQ levels for the bioflavonoids are 102 [µ]g/day. Thus, the EQ values for the dietary intake of flavonoids was 4 × 10 times higher than the daily EQ intake of estrogenic pesticides, illustrating the minimal potential of these industrial estrogens to cause an adverse endocrine-related response in humans.

Previous studies have also shown that AhR agonists, such as TCDD and related compounds, PAHs and IC and its most active derivative, indolo[3,2-b]carbazole (ICZ) all inhibit E_2-induced responses in MCF-7 cells. At a concentration of 10^{-9} M, TCDD inhibits 50–100% of most E_2-induced responses *in vitro* in which the concentration of E_2 is 10^{-9} M. Therefore, 1 TEQ is approximately equal to 1 EQ. The estimated daily intakes of TCDD and related compounds, PAHs, and ICZ (in 100 g brussels sprouts) are summarized in Table 2. The relative potencies of PAHs and ICZ as antiestrogens compared to TCDD are approximately 0.001 in MCF-7 cells. Thus, the TEQs or antiestrogen TEQs can be calculated for the dietary intakes of TCDD and related organochlorines and PAHs (in all foods). The antiestrogen TEQs for the three classes of dietary AhR agonists are orders of magnitude higher than the estimated dietary intakes of estrogenic pesticide EQs. Thus, the major human intake of endocrine disrupters associated with the estrogen-induced response pathways are naturally occurring estrogens found in foods. Relatively high serum levels of estrogenic bioflavonoids have also been detected in a Japanese male population, whereas lower levels were observed in a Finnish group, and this is consistent with their dietary intakes of these estrogenic compounds, p,p'-DDE is present in human serum; however, the estrogenic o,p'-DDE and o,p'-DDT analogs and other weakly estrogenic organochlorine compounds are not routinely detected in serum samples. A recent study identified several hydroxylated PCB congeners in human serum. All of the hydroxylated compounds were also substituted with chlorine groups at both adjacent meta positions. Based on results of previous structure-activity studies (43) for hydroxylated PCBs, these compounds would exhibit minimal estrogenic activity; however, further studies on the activity of hydroxylated PCBs are warranted.

SUMMARY

The hypothesized linkage between dietary/environmental estrogens and the increased incidence of breast cancer is unproven; there is a lack of correlation between higher organochlorine levels in breast cancer patients compared to controls and the low levels of organochlorine EQs in the diet (Table 2). Higher levels of bioflavonoids are unlikely to contribute to increased breast cancer incidence because these compounds and the foods they are associated with tend to exhibit anticarcinogenic activity. The hypothesis that male reproductive problems and decreased sperm counts are related to increased exposure to environmental and dietary estrogens is also unproven. As noted above, dietary exposure to xenoestrogens derived from industrial chemical residues in foods is minimal compared to the daily intake of EQs from naturally occurring bioflavonoids. Moreover, there are serious questions regarding the decreased sperm counts reported by Carlsen and co-workers. Reanalysis of Carlsen et al.'s data suggests that there has not been a decrease in sperm counts in males over the past 30 years and possibly over the past 50 years. Thus, in response to articles in the popular and scientific press such as "The Estrogen Complex" and "Ecocancers: Do Environmental Factors Underlie a Breast Cancer Epidemic?", the results would suggest that the linkage between dietary or environmental estrogenic compounds and breast cancer has

Table 2

Estimated Mass Balance of Human Exposures to Environmental and Dietary Estrogens and Antiestrogens

Source	Estrogen equivalents (μg/day)
Estrogens	
Morning after pill	333,500
Birth control pill	16,675
Post-menopausal therapy	3,350
Flavonoids in foods (1,020 mg/day × 0.0001)	102
Environmental organochlorine estrogens (2.5 × 0.000001)	0.0000025
Antiestrogens	TCDD antiestrogen equivalents (μg/day)
TCDD and organochlorines (80–120 pg/day)	0.000080–0.000120[a]
PAHs in food (1.2–5.0 × 106 pg/day; relative potency ~ 0.001)	0.001200–0.0050[b]
Indolo[3,2-b]carbazole in 100 g brussels sprouts (0.256–1.28 × 106 pg/day; relative potency ~ 0.001)	0.000250–0.00128[b]

[a]In most studies, 1 nM TCDD inhibits 50–100% of 1 nM E_2-induced responses in MCF-7 cells; therefore, 1 estrogen equivalent $\cong$ 1 antiestrogen equivalent.
[b]The antiestrogenic potencies of PAHs and indolo[3,2-b]carbazole compared to E_2 were approximately 0.001.

not been made, and further research is required to determine the factors associated with the increasing incidence of this disease.

Note Added in Proof: A recent study reported a 2.1% decrease in sperm concentrations in France from 1973 to 1979.

POSTSCRIPT

Do Environmental Estrogens Pose a Potentially Serious Health Threat?

The statement by Safe that is most often quoted by authors of popular articles about the environmental estrogen controversy is, "The suggestion that industrial estrogenic chemicals contribute to an increased incidence of breast cancer in women and male reproductive problems is not plausible." This quote is taken from the abstract that was published along with his article in *Environmental Health Perspectives*. Note that in the article he draws the much more cautious conclusion that a link between these consequences and estrogenic compounds is "unproven." Drawing conclusions about estrogenic potency based upon the average person's low dietary exposure to a few common pesticides is suspect for several reasons. Individuals living near highly contaminated bodies of water and consuming fish and other foods from them may take in far higher levels of synthetic estrogens. Furthermore, results reported by Steven F. Arnold et al. in *Science* (vol. 272, 1996), pp. 1489–1491, show that a very large synergistic factor makes certain combinations of these compounds far more potent than estimates based on the sum of individual exposures. The complex and variable manner by which different compounds with estrogenic properties affect organisms makes comparisons risky. As Luoma points out, some researchers have suggested that humans and other animals may have evolved tolerances to naturally occurring estrogenic compounds but not to the synthetics.

Although Theo Colborn says that she would like to be proven wrong, she is among those researchers who believe that there is already convincing evidence of extensive damage to wildlife caused by synthetic estrogenic chemicals and that the likelihood that humans are experiencing similar health problems due to these industrial pollutants is frighteningly high. This is made clear in the highly acclaimed book *Our Stolen Future* (Dutton, 1996), which she coauthored with environmental journalist Dianne Dumanoski and John Peterson Myers, director of the W. Alton Jones Foundation. For a review by Jeff Jonson, which, like the book's preface by Vice President Al Gore, compares its possible impact to that of Rachel Carson's *Silent Spring*, see the April 1996 issue of *Environmental Science and Technology*.

There have been numerous articles about the environmental endocrine issue in both popular and technical journals and magazines. For three different perspectives on the controversy, see "Hormone Mimics Pose Challenge," *Chemistry and Industry* (May 20, 1996); "Environmental Estrogens," by J. A. McLachlan and S. F. Arnold, *American Scientist* (September/October 1996); and "Hormone Hell," by C. Dold, *Discover* (September 1996).

The suspicion that hormone-mimicking chemicals in the environment may be one of the causes of breast cancer has been bolstered by the recent proposal of a biochemical mechanism by which these chemicals may act. This hypothesis is explained by its authors, Devra Lee Davis and H. Leon Bradlow, in the October 1995 issue of *Scientific American*. Margie Patlak presents a synopsis of the proposal along with some reactions to it from other researchers in her article in the May 1996 issue of *Environmental Science and Technology*.

The provisions in the Food Quality Protection Act of 1996 and the 1996 Safe Drinking Water Act amendments, requiring screening for endocrine disrupters, has focused the attention of EPA scientists on developing practical tests for chemicals with hormonal activity in time to meet the 1998 implementation date in this legislation. For an interesting discussion of the technical problems that need to be overcome to meet this challenge, see the article by Margie Patlak in the December 1996 issue of *Environmental Science and Technology*.

For an Internet site related to this issue, see http://www.mcl.tulane.edu/cbr/ECME/EEHome/default.html, which contains an excellent educational service and an interactive forum on all aspects of the environmental estrogen issue.

ISSUE 9

Should the New Clean Water Act Aim at "Zero Discharge"?

YES: Jeffery A. Foran and Robert W. Adler, from "Cleaner Water, But Not Clean Enough," *Issues in Science and Technology* (Winter 1993/1994)

NO: Robert W. Hahn, from "Clean Water Policy," *The American Enterprise* (November/December 1993)

ISSUE SUMMARY

YES: Environmental health and policy professor Jeffery A. Foran and Clean Water Project director Robert W. Adler argue that the goal of zero discharge of toxic pollutants can be achieved if the revisions to the Clean Water Act are designed to promote pollution prevention rather than control.

NO: American Enterprise Institute scholar Robert W. Hahn advocates a market-based approach based on cost-benefit analysis as a replacement for the present "command and control" approach to water regulation.

In 1621 Robert Burton wrote in *The Anatomy of Melancholy*, "They that use filthy, standing, ill-coloured, thick, muddy water [will] have muddy, ill-coloured, impure and infirm bodies. And because the body works upon the mind, they shall have grosser understandings, dull, foggy, melancholy spirits, and be really subject to all manner of infirmities." Although modern science has discredited this particular kind of causal analysis, one can nevertheless say that water pollution had long been recognized as a health hazard. The most important factor in increasing life expectancy in developed countries has been the prevention of contamination of public water supplies by human and animal wastes.

Recent concerns about water purity relate to the increasing contamination of both surface and groundwater by all manner of toxic and hazardous chemicals that are the by-products of our modern industrial societies. In the United States, the first comprehensive attempt to respond to this problem was the enactment of the 1972 Clean Water Act followed by the 1974 Safe Drinking Water Act. By limiting the permissible discharge of contaminants into bodies of water and establishing water quality standards, this legislation, along with strengthening amendments enacted in 1977 and 1987, has resulted in marked improvement in some of the most polluted lakes and rivers in the United States, such as Lake Erie and the Hudson River.

But industrial expansion and population increases have resulted in the need for new strategies to stem the spread of water pollution. The International Joint Commission on the Great Lakes has called for stringent measures to halt the accumulation of chemical toxins in the water and sediments of those commercially important bodies of water. Groundwater, previously considered a reliable source of pure water, is becoming increasingly polluted. Fish kills and algal blooms are becoming more frequent in the bays and estuaries that border areas of high population density. In the spring of 1993 more than 350,000 Milwaukee, Wisconsin, residents became ill due to contamination of their water supply, which derives from Lake Michigan, by the *Cryptosporidium* protozoan. This event, along with other recent episodes of infestation of public water supplies by toxic organisms, has alerted the public to the continued vulnerability of drinking water.

The Clean Water Act was among the major environmental laws that were scheduled for reauthorization when President Bill Clinton was elected in 1992. A major revision of the legislation that would both strengthen existing regulatory mandates as well as extend federal water protection to include previously neglected problems was anticipated early in his term of office. Several bills were introduced in Congress, but consideration of all of them has been stalled by major disputes that have developed over how to respond to such economically sensitive problems as the protection of wetlands.

One of the goals stated in the original 1972 Clean Water Act was to ultimately achieve zero discharge of pollutants into navigable bodies of water. In practice, the so-called end-of-the-pipe strategies that have been employed in the implementation of the legislation have abandoned this goal. In the following selection, Jeffery A. Foran, director of the Risk Science Institute in Washington, D.C., and attorney Robert W. Adler, who directs the Natural Resources Defense Council's Clean Water Project, suggest that by shifting strategy to encourage "pollution-prevention activities such as chemical substitution and process changes that reduce pollution at the source," the original zero-discharge goal may be achievable.

Robert W. Hahn, a resident scholar at the American Enterprise Institute, also advocates a major change in clean water strategies away from "command-and-control" regulation, but not with the aim of achieving zero discharge. He calls for a risk-benefit assessment of Clean Water Act goals, followed by the use of marketplace incentives—such as subsidies, pollution charges, and marketable permits—to achieve those goals that are economically justified.

YES

Jeffery A. Foran and
Robert W. Adler

CLEANER WATER, BUT NOT CLEAN ENOUGH

The Clean Water Act has undeniably helped control and reduce pollution of the nation's surface waters. Many gross pollution problems that existed a generation ago have been eliminated. Thirty years ago, Lake Erie had deteriorated so much that an article in *Science News* declared the lake dead. In 1969, the Cuyahoga River, which was heavily contaminated with flammable oils and grease, actually caught fire. These particular problems, of course, no longer exist. In addition, more subtle but no less important pollution problems have also improved since the 1960s. For example, levels of polychlorinated biphenyls (PCBs) have declined dramatically in fish and other aquatic biota in systems such as the Great Lakes.

The Clean Water Act, which was passed in 1972, has been a critical factor behind improving water quality. Major amendments enacted in 1977 and 1987 included provisions aimed at further improving the regulation of toxic substances. But despite its many successes, the Clean Water Act (CWA) and its amendments have failed to adequately control many sources of toxic pollutants.

For example, the act required that by 1983 all surface waters should have attained a quality that "provides for the protection and propagation of fish, shellfish, and wildlife and provides for recreation in and on the water." Surface waters that achieve this level of quality are classified under the act as fishable and swimmable. Yet, according to the Environmental Protection Agency's (EPA) most recent National Water Quality Inventory, at least a third of assessed rivers, half of assessed estuaries, and more than half of assessed lakes are not yet clean enough to merit this classification.

Continuing pollution problems in surface waters have also led the U.S./Canadian International Joint Commission (IJC), a quasi-governmental body that oversees quality issues in waters shared by the two nations, to designate 42 regions in the Great Lakes basin as highly contaminated. Also, nearly all states now declare that at least some fish taken by sport anglers from contaminated lakes and streams should not be consumed. And the cost of losses in recreational fishing, swimming, and boating opportunities caused by the discharge of toxic pollutants is estimated by the U.S. General Accounting Office (GAO) to be as high as $800 million per year.

The types of pollutants that continue to cause water quality impairments are widely varied. A total of 362 contaminants, including metals such as lead and mercury, an array of pesticides, and organic industrial chemicals such as PCBs and dioxin, have been found in the Great Lakes ecosystem. Eleven of these substances have been classified by the IJC as pollutants of "critical concern."

Research conducted by the IJC and others in the Great Lakes basin has provided specific information on the loads of some highly toxic pollutants that are discharged to surface waters. For example, Lake Superior receives nearly 500 pounds of PCBs (mainly from nonpoint sources) annually, and Lakes Michigan, Huron, Erie, and Ontario receive up to 5,000 pounds annually (mainly from nonpoint sources, although over 1,000 pounds are discharged to Lakes Erie and Ontario from point sources annually). Between 1,000 and 5,000 pounds of mercury are discharged to each of the Great Lakes annually mainly from nonpoint sources, although point sources appear to contribute the major portion of mercury in Lake Erie. Large loads of lead are also contributed to the Great Lakes, mainly from point sources. Over 1,000 pounds of lead are discharged annually to Lakes Superior and Huron, over 8,000 pounds are discharged to Lake Ontario, over 30,000 pounds are discharged to Lake Erie, and over 50,000 pounds are discharged to Lake Michigan annually.

Pollutants in water are responsible for damage to wildlife that includes eggshell thinning, reduced hatching success and infertility, immune system suppression, behavioral changes, physical impairments such as crossed beaks and clubfeet as well as adverse effects on populations and communities of organisms. Similarly, the health of human populations has been affected by toxic substances in surface waters. For example, cognitive and other deficits have been documented in children born of mothers who were exposed to PCBs through consumption of large quantities of contaminated fish.

Congress is expected to reauthorize and possibly amend the CWA again early in 1994. This presents an opportunity to correct the law's flaws, which have allowed some water-pollution problems to remain. In particular, we see a need to strengthen the provisions aimed at preventing pollution rather than relying on mechanisms to treat pollution at the point of discharge.

SOURCES OF FAILURE

The objective of the CWA is to restore and maintain the chemical, physical, and biological integrity of the nation's waters. In pursuit of that objective, the act explicitly states as one goal that "the discharge of pollutants into the navigable waters be eliminated." Congress designated 1985 as the date to achieve the zero-discharge goal. A 1992 IJC report found that the United States had yet to completely eliminate the discharge of any persistent toxic substance. Failure to achieve this goal and the act's other objectives, as well as continuing water-quality problems, are attributable to inadequacies in the existing water quality regulatory process.

To understand the reasons for our failure to achieve the act's goals, it is necessary to examine the two approaches that are used concurrently under the act to control toxic substances discharged to surface waters. The first approach is the mandated use of specific treatment technology for discharges from point sources of pollution, such as industry and waste treatment plants. For each category of industry, EPA issues industrywide effluent limitations defined as the "best available technology economically achievable." However, the designated technology may not be adequate to protect all surface waters from harm.

The second approach was developed for situations where technology-based controls do not protect water quality. This "water-quality-based" approach requires EPA and the states to set maximum allowable concentrations of toxic pollutants in surface waters without regard to economic impacts or technological achievability. The concentrations are supposed to be low enough so that they pose no threat to individual organisms (including humans) or to populations, species, communities, and ecosystems. Safe concentrations of toxic pollutants are defined under the CWA by chemical-specific, numeric Water Quality Criteria (WQC). In principle, WQCs could be set at zero where necessary to protect human health and the environment. In practice, however, WQCs are set well above zero, based on often-contentious concepts of risk assessment or implicit assumptions about technological and economic attainability.

States are required under the CWA to adopt WQCs and to use them in determining how much to control the discharge of toxic pollutants from point sources as well as from nonpoint sources (such as agricultural runoff and pollutants from the atmosphere). What the states do, though it is not necessarily sanctioned by the law, is to require that pollutant concentrations meet WQC in lakes or streams only after a discharge has been diluted by mixing with water in the receiving system. Thus an industry or waste-water treatment plant is allowed to discharge toxic pollutants in its effluent at concentrations higher than WQC for those pollutants, so long as pollutant concentrations are then diluted enough in the receiving water to meet WQC.

There are two problems with this approach. First, it does not force dischargers to comply with the CWA mandate of zero-discharge of pollutants to surface waters. In fact, the entire WQC system is based on the assumption that there is an acceptable level of pollutant discharge. Second, WQC and dilution capacity are used even where the ability of the environment to assimilate pollutants has been exceeded, or where adverse impacts have occurred, particularly in receiving systems far downstream from the point of discharge. Even though a lake has unacceptable levels of a pollutant, the pollutant can be discharged into a stream that empties into the lake so long as it is diluted to acceptable levels in the stream.

Under the 1972 act, technology-based effluent guidelines were supposed to require pollution-reduction technologies that not only became increasingly more stringent until zero-discharge was achieved, but that, in theory, would progress from end-of-pipe treatment approaches to changes in manufacturing processes and other strategies that would actually prevent pollution at its sources. This progression was expected to continue to reduce pollutants while also reducing the economic burden associated with installing increasingly costly treatment technology at the point of discharge. Unfortunately, EPA has been locked into a largely end-of-pipe treatment approach to pollutant control. The result has been only partial progress toward zero-discharge under the technology-based approach, along with ever-rising costs associated with more stringent forms of waste treatment.

The water-quality-based approach to toxicant control could also force technology toward increasingly strict pollution control requirements—and, ultimately, zero-discharge. But that will not happen as long as the operating assumption is that there are acceptable levels of pollution in surface waters and that we can count on receiving systems to dilute toxic effluents.

A POLLUTION-PREVENTION STRATEGY

The most effective way to reduce the discharge of a toxic pollutant into water is to reduce the use of the chemical or its precursors. Pollution prevention can be attained by reducing the use of a chemical through changes in industrial processes (including more efficient use of chemicals), substitute chemicals, and recycling. Or reduction (and in some cases elimination) may be accomplished by the phaseout of chemicals, product changes or bans, and behavior changes that affect consumption, use, or disposal of products that create pollutants.

Each prevention strategy should result in less waste production and toxic pollutant release, not just to surface waters but to other parts of the environment as well. Thus, prevention will reduce discharges of toxic pollutants below the levels possible with waste treatment alone. Ultimately, where a toxic chemical is eliminated via substitution, process change, or other mechanisms, or where environmental releases are eliminated, the discharge of that chemical will also be eliminated. The zero-discharge goal of the CWA can thus be met without risk-based arguments about acceptable pollutant levels, without the use of dilution to determine discharge limits, and without increasingly expensive treatment technologies applied at the point of discharge.

The difficulty of choosing chemical-specific pollution-prevention mechanisms and developing a schedule for their implementation is a potential obstacle to achieving pollution prevention. We therefore propose a scientific priority-setting process to determine a chemical's toxicity and assess the potential for exposure to it.

Exposure is assessed by evaluating a chemical's propensity to accumulate in the tissues of fish and other organisms, its persistence in the environment, and the amount that is released to the environment. Toxicity to aquatic plants and animals, as well as to terrestrial species (including birds and humans), is assessed by criteria that include death, impairment of growth and reproduction, and other adverse impacts, including cancer, from short- and long-term exposures.

Each toxicity and exposure component includes a set of triggers to determine whether a chemical can be classified as of high, moderate, or low concern relative to other chemicals. Once chemicals have been screened and classified, appropriate pollution-prevention activities and schedules for those activities (including the time it will take to reach zero-discharge) can be chosen.

Other factors may also influence the choice of pollution-prevention activities and the time it will take to implement them. For example, where it is determined that a hazardous chemical should be phased out of an industrial process, the pace of the phaseout may be influenced by whether there are safer substitutes, by the availability of different technologies that may not use toxic chemicals, and by the cost of developing these new chemicals or technologies. It should be generally recognized, however, that although such considerations may determine the length of time it takes to phase out a hazardous chemical, they should not affect the basic decision to phase it out.

MAKING IT LAW

Two different approaches should be taken to incorporate pollution-prevention measures into the CWA. First, the provisions of the law designed to implement technology-based and water-quality-based controls should be fine-tuned to point EPA back in the direction of zero-discharge. Fairly modest statutory changes might achieve the desired results. Second, broader changes and new requirements should be added to promote planning for pollution prevention by government and private parties.

Several requirements of the CWA should be modified to maximize the degree to which existing programs require or encourage prevention of pollution. First, the sections of the act that dictate the rules under which EPA writes categorical effluent limitations (and related pretreatment standards for dischargers to public sewers) could be modified to reinforce the original pollution-prevention philosophy, emphasizing technology-based requirements for the control of toxic pollutants.

Existing provisions require EPA to "take into account" such factors as "process changes" and "non-water-quality environmental effects." The former is designed to take EPA beyond treatment applied at the discharge point and the latter to prevent impacts on other parts of the environment besides surface water. Nothing, however, forces EPA to select such options over traditional treatment methods. The act should be modified to include a hierarchy of options, under which pollution-prevention activities such as chemical substitution and process changes that reduce pollution at the source must be exhausted before point-of-discharge treatment is considered. In addition, limitations on the concentration of a toxic pollutant in a discharge could be expressed in terms of the efficiency of particular industrial processes (as efficiency relates to chemical usage), as well as the amount of reduction of the chemical in the effluent that can be achieved by pollution prevention.

Closing loopholes in the water-quality-based approach also would stimulate pollution prevention. Dischargers should be induced to adopt prevention methods through discharge permits that require the application of WQC at the point of discharge rather than allowing dilution of the effluent in the receiving water. Elimination of the dilution allowance would require reductions in the concentration and mass of pollutants that could be discharged. Industries and waste-water treatment plants could achieve these reductions by employing more expensive treatment technologies or by potentially cheaper pollution-prevention techniques.

The act should also be modified to achieve consistency among state WQC for toxicants and in the procedures used to translate criteria into discharge limits. At present, states may set their own criteria and develop their own implementation procedures, albeit with EPA guidance and authority to approve criteria and procedures. This creates an opportunity for states to use lax standards to attract business. EPA's water-quality criteria should apply nationwide, unless a state's criteria are stricter. With this change, industries and waste-water treatment plants would be forced to find ways to meet national criteria through pollution prevention. They could no longer exert pressure for lower standards by threatening to move their factories and jobs to another state.

SPURRING INNOVATION

Although amendments to existing requirements may enhance the degree to which programs encourage pollution prevention, they will not necessarily encourage or require industries and waste-water treatment plants to alter their fundamental operations to prevent pollution. We suggest two principal strategies to encourage industrial innovation. One is based on traditional "technology-forcing" for the most dangerous pollutants, and the other is designed to promote more comprehensive pollution-prevention planning by all dischargers of toxic substances.

The first approach is to identify and then ban or phase out the use and release of the most toxic, persistent, and bioaccumulative pollutants. Specific substances would be identified by the criteria discussed earlier in this article. Several hurdles must be overcome to achieve this result. The law must include a clear definition of the standards for identifying the specific toxicants subject to a ban or phaseout. A simple approach is to include a list of chemicals that warrant elimination. A specific set of criteria that EPA must use to expand the list should also be included.

Once a chemical is listed, it will be necessary to determine who decides the schedule and mechanism for phaseout. One possibility is simply to set a date and wait for technological innovation by industry, an approach that appears to have succeeded to phase out ozone-destroying chlorofluorocarbons. Another is to convene broadly representative panels that can evaluate replacements for each chemical and set reasonable deadlines for making substitutions. The least satisfactory option is to ask EPA to dictate the date and means by which processes and chemicals should change. Whatever approach is taken should be spelled out clearly in the act.

The second principal strategy is to require comprehensive pollution-prevention planning at the company, site, and production levels. At the company level, this might entail strategic decisions about how products are manufactured and sold. For example, a pesticide manufacturer might decide to phase out production of chlorinated pesticides in favor of new compounds that are less toxic to humans or that are less persistent in the environment. Or chemical pesticides might be eliminated entirely in favor of biological pest controls. At the site or plant level, pollution prevention could include covering storage areas to reduce runoff of spilled or open materials, or reuse of residues from one product or process as input into a related product or process.

At the production level, engineers are learning to substitute less-toxic input chemicals and to change the sequence, tuning, temperature, or other production conditions in ways that reduce residual toxic substances. One example of production-level pollution prevention is the replacement of elemental chlorine with chlorine dioxide or oxygen to bleach paper products. This substitution decreases chlorinated dioxins and furans as well as other highly toxic chlorinated organic compounds.

The major hook on which to hang this approach is the existing program that requires permits for all facilities that wish to discharge pollutants from point sources into surface waters. The original philosophy of this permit requirement is that no one has the right to discharge pollutants unless there is a need to do so—that is, unless it can be shown that eliminating the discharge is, for technological or economic reasons, not feasible. Over the years, this legal presumption has been implicitly reversed. Permittees can discharge until the government limits the amount and nature of the effluent. Pollution-prevention planning would help turn this presumption around.

The *Water Quality 2000* report, prepared by representatives from industry, environmental groups, academia, and government, recommended that pollution-prevention planning be conducted at all industrial facilities but that the facilities themselves decide on pollution-reduction goals and methods. Facilities would have to disclose the results of their planning to the public, stating their goals for reducing pollution and reporting on their success in achieving those goals. Such an approach could readily be included by requiring pollution-prevention plans as a condition for receiving a permit. This would take an important step back toward the direction of the original law because facilities would have to evaluate all alternatives to pollution creation and discharge as part of the permit process.

NONPOINT SOURCES

Preventing pollution may be particularly important for dealing with runoff and other nonpoint sources of toxicants, such as atmospheric deposition and contaminated sediments. The problem is extensive and in many ways more difficult to control than point sources. Furthermore, the time may be right to push for pollution prevention for nonpoint sources because this approach does not carry the political baggage of the established (and inadequate) regulatory process that governs point sources of toxic pollutants.

The 1987 amendments to the CWA require states to identify which waters are impaired by polluted runoff and other nonpoint sources and to describe measures to control these sources. Most states have met these requirements, and many have recommended voluntary implementation of "best management practices," which include approaches to pollution prevention. Therefore, there may be less resistance to mandatory implementation of newer prevention-based strategies, particularly when pollution prevention is cheaper—as it can be, for example, with the substitution of biological pest control for the use of expensive pesticides in farming.

Although we have yet to make significant progress in reducing nonpoint-source pollution from agriculture, numerous opportunities to do so exist.

These include changes in crop rotation patterns, which result in more efficient use of chemicals; substitution of less hazardous for more hazardous pesticides, along with phaseout of particularly hazardous chemicals; product changes, such as selection of disease- and pest-resistant crops that require smaller quantities of pesticides; and persuading consumers to change their behavior—by, for example, being more willing to buy cosmetically imperfect (but perfectly nutritious) produce. We do not have quantitative estimates of their pollution-prevention potential, but there is widespread agreement that concurrent implementation of a mix of them will reduce polluted runoff. And at least some of them—especially reduced use of pesticides—will probably also save money.

One promising approach that might encourage use of pollution-prevention techniques in agriculture and other land uses is site-specific planning, as incorporated in the 1990 amendments to the Coastal Zone Management Act (CZMA). This legislation requires EPA and the National Oceanic and Atmospheric Administration to publish detailed guidance on pollution-prevention measures for nonpoint sources. Each coastal state must, as a condition of its programs under both the CWA and the CZMA, develop enforceable mechanisms to ensure that such practices are employed on a site-specific basis by all major sources of polluted runoff affecting water quality in coastal areas. The *Water Quality 2000* report recommended a similar strategy for agriculture. Under this proposal, the CWA would be amended to require major landowners in impaired watersheds to develop, with EPA and state guidance, site-specific pollution-prevention plans designed to help restore the health of disturbed watersheds. This could provide the incentive for farmers to implement available pollution-prevention techniques.

CAN WE AFFORD IT?

No one has conducted a comprehensive analysis of the costs of implementing pollution prevention. Some preventive strategies may indeed entail high upfront costs. However, at least in some cases, pollution prevention can also be profitable. According to a recent GAO report, the installation of a $50,000 system to recover waste at a Clairol hair-care products plant resulted in savings of about $240,000 a year. The report also describes how a campaign in Palo Alto, California, to encourage industrial users of silver to deliver their wastes to a silver reclaimer and to urge hobbyists to dispose of their silver solutions at hazardous waste-collection sites made it possible to avoid a $20 million per year expenditure for installing and operating new equipment to remove silver from the waste stream of its waste-water treatment plant.

Uncertainty about the economics of various pollution-prevention strategies is only one of the complexities with which the CWA must deal. The large number of toxic pollutants that are entering the nation's surface waters, the wide array of point and nonpoint sources of these pollutants, and the broad diversity of possible pollution-prevention activities are challenges for lawmakers considering reauthorization of the CWA. We believe that our proposals incorporate the flexibility and the scientific rigor necessary to continue the critical work of protecting our rivers, lakes, and streams.

NO
Robert W. Hahn

CLEAN WATER POLICY

The first major piece of environmental legislation to reach President
Clinton's desk is likely to be the reauthorization of the Clean Water
Act, last amended in 1987. Over the past two decades, water pollution regulation has been aimed at cleaning up municipal waste and
reducing industrial water pollution. This effort has successfully reduced pollution and improved water quality in some circumstances.
For example, between 1972 and 1988, there was a 69 percent increase
in the population being served by technically sophisticated sewage
treatment plants. The overall trends in water quality are less clear,
however. Between 1978 and 1987 no significant progress was made
in traditional measures of quality such as the levels of dissolved
oxygen and bacteria in the water. Water in many parts of the country, moreover, is still priced well below its economic value, leading
to excessive consumption and, in some cases, to lower levels of
water quality. In addition, agricultural and other sources of water
pollution such as runoff from urban areas (called nonpoint sources
because of their diffuse nature) remain largely unregulated.

Three bills are presently circulating in Congress to strengthen clean water
regulation, all of which focus primarily on water quality. Senators Max Bau-
cus (D-Mont.) and John Chafee (R-R.I.) have recommended expanding the
bureaucracy that enforces current laws, increasing the funding for sewage
treatment, and adding toxic substances and nonpoint sources to existing regulations. Congressman Jim Oberstar's (D-Minn.) bill focuses on the regulation
of nonpoint sources of pollution. Finally, a bill introduced by Congressman
Gerry Studds (D-Mass.) calls for a system of user fees on toxic discharges and
products known to contribute to water pollution, and for an excise tax on
ingredients in pesticides and fertilizers. The revenue from these taxes would
be invested in clean water infrastructure such as stormwater controls.

All of these bills would increase regulation with little regard for the
economic consequences. Moreover, none of them promotes innovative approaches to regulation that could achieve better water quality at a cost lower
than traditional methods of regulation.

From Robert W. Hahn, "Clean Water Policy," *The American Enterprise* (November/December
1993). Copyright © 1993 by The American Enterprise Institute. Reprinted by permission.

There is an alternative to traditional water quality regulation. We now can achieve improved levels of water quality at lower cost to the public, provided that Congress is willing to embark on a new approach.

DIRECTIONS FOR REFORM

The great British economist Joan Robinson once asked: "Why is there litter in the public park, but no litter in my back garden?" The answer, of course, involves incentives—we have clear incentives to keep our backyards clean. And while each of us would like to see the park kept clean, we would prefer that other people do it.

The same problem arises in managing water resources. Because we collectively own most of our major water bodies, none of us has an incentive to take care of these resources the way we would our own homes and yards. Congress should therefore change the incentive structure so that individual consumers, governments, and businesses have a direct stake in taking better care of our precious water resources.

There are basically two ways to change the incentive structure and achieve better management of water resources. The first is to sell off major public waterways, including rivers, lakes, and streams. Putting these assets into private hands would improve water quality and quantity, provided that property rights for water quality and quantity were well defined and enforceable. The new owners of these assets would have a very strong incentive to manage these water resources as well as they take care of their own backyards. Acting rationally, they would keep the water clean and allow people to use it only if they paid a price that reflected the water's value. But this approach, however meritorious, simply isn't realistic in many situations. Privatizing the nation's water resources would start a political firestorm, if not a revolution.

A less radical way to manage water resources is to apply basic economic analysis to the public management of them. This involves two steps: first, identifying appropriate goals for water quality and water use; and second, choosing appropriate methods for achieving these goals.

The level of water quality we aim for will be determined, among other things, by the economic benefits associated with consuming or using the water resource and the economic costs of providing that resource. High water quality can help preserve species habitat; allow both commercial and recreational uses of water bodies including fishing, swimming, and boating; and provide a safe drinking water supply and the satisfaction that comes from knowing waterways are clean.

INTRODUCING COST-BENEFIT ANALYSIS

According to conventional methods of cost-benefit analysis, standards should be set so that the incremental benefit of cleaning up the water just equals the incremental cost. The costs and benefits of water improvement, however, are difficult to quantify, particularly the benefits. Nonetheless, it is absolutely imperative to try to quantify them if clean water policy is to be developed in a way that leads to improvements in our standard of living.

The Environmental Protection Agency (EPA) has not devoted significant resources to developing analyses that pinpoint the areas where regulatory efforts should be best focused under the Clean Water Act. The most comprehensive analysis of the costs and benefits of current plans to achieve the objectives of the Clean Water Act was performed by economists Randy Lyon, then at Georgetown University, and Scott Farrow of Carnegie Mellon. They argue that in many current implementation plans the incremental costs of improving water quality exceed the incremental benefits. This means that many existing EPA standards and regulatory approaches are wasteful. At the same time, there are certainly heavily polluted and/or heavily used water bodies where significant improvements in water quality are well worth the cost.

Results from studies by these authors and from other studies suggest that more cost-benefit analyses should be done so that Congress and the states can concentrate on the right water problems in the right water bodies. Specifically, EPA should commission a state-of-the-art cost-benefit analysis of the current Clean Water Act so that the political debate on reauthorization can be better informed. This analysis should attempt to point out where standards should be tightened and where they should be relaxed.

The analysis should also identify key areas of uncertainty in the estimation of benefits so that more informed decisions about appropriate standards can be made. At present, relatively little is known about the relationship between the level of pollution and human health for many water contaminants, or the extent to which people value clean water that they themselves do not use.

EPA should also develop a database that permits a more accurate assessment of the benefits and costs of the Clean Water Act, and the agency should be re-quired to submit a report to Congress every two years that addresses the benefits and costs of controlling different pollutants in different waterways. (A provision in the Clean Air Act Amendments of 1990 mandates that a cost-benefit analysis be used for selected statutes in the act.) Without such information, Congress will not be in a position to make informed decisions about the economic consequences of proposed statutes.

ECONOMIC INCENTIVES

Once a standard has been chosen, the government must determine how that standard should be achieved. One way is to prescribe a technology that each company in an industry must use. This is sometimes referred to as "command-and-control" regulation. Command-and-control regulation has been criticized by economists because it does not give businesses and individuals much choice in how they achieve an environmental goal. For example, a law may require that a power plant use a scrubber to reduce air pollution, even though another technology or group of technologies might be more effective in achieving the same level of air quality. Because this approach does not take into account differing circumstances and costs, society ends up paying more.

There is a better way to meet the government's standard. The introduction of economic incentives can address many pollution problems effectively. The idea behind using economic incentives is to save resources while achieving a particular environmental goal. For example, in 1990, Congress adopted an economic incentive approach for reducing acid rain that could save as much as $1 billion annually when compared to a conventional command-and-control approach that required the largest polluters to install scrubbers.

There are, moreover, many different kinds of economic incentives. They include subsidies, taxes, deposit-refund schemes, pollution charges, marketable permits, and the removal of institutional barriers that lead to price distortions. In the interest of brevity, I will discuss only pollution charges and marketable permits.

Charge systems impose a fee or tax on pollution. For example, a chemical manufacturer would be charged for every unit of a pollutant that it discharged into a river. Several European nations, including France, the Netherlands, and Germany, currently use water pollution charge systems.

Pollution charges by themselves do not restrict the amount of pollutants that may be emitted; rather, they tax emissions. Such taxes ensure that a firm will internalize the previously external pollution costs. A firm can choose to pay the full tax or to reduce its emissions partially or completely—whichever option best fits its interests.

The advantage of the system is that all businesses face the same incentive to limit pollution at the margin. A firm will control pollution up to the point where the marginal cost of control just equals the tax it must pay. The result is that the total costs of pollution control are minimized, unlike other methods of allocating the pollution control burden across businesses. Pollution charges, like other market-based mechanisms, also provide ongoing incentives for businesses to develop and adopt better pollution control technologies.

MARKETABLE PERMIT SYSTEMS

Marketable or tradable permits can achieve the same cost-minimizing allocation of the pollution control burden as the pollution charges do, while achieving a particular environmental target. Under a tradable permit system, an overall allowable level of pollution is established for the affected area, portions of which are then allotted to businesses and government entities in the form of permits. A business that keeps its emission levels below its allotted level may sell or lease its surplus permits to others.

As with a charge system, the marginal cost of control is identical across businesses and thus the total cost of control is minimized for any given level of total pollution control. In the case of local water pollution control, for example, this approach could be substantially more efficient than current regulatory methods, both because its inherent flexibility takes advantage of differences in control costs and because it allows individual businesses to decide where and how to make desired reductions in pollution.

In the event that overall environmental targets are viewed as too strict, the government may choose to increase the supply of permits. Likewise, regulators could take the opposite stance and reduce the supply of permits in order to reduce allowable emissions.

Permit systems have been used primarily in the United States. Examples include the Environmental Protection Agency's Emissions Trading Program for reducing air pollution; the nationwide lead phasedown program for gasoline, which allowed fuel refiners to trade reductions in lead content; and the gradual phaseout of chlorofluorocarbons, where businesses are allowed to trade the right to produce or import limited quantities of these chemicals. In addition, several Western states have implemented water quantity trading in limited forms. Some states are also considering trading programs to control discharges from farms and municipal wastewater treatment plants in the least costly way.

BETTER WATER MANAGEMENT

Congress could encourage EPA to implement both pollution charge systems and marketable permit approaches. But because charges are likely to encounter political resistance, Congress should promote more widespread use of marketable permits by requiring EPA to use them as the tool of choice for improving water quality or to justify in writing why it has not chosen this alternative.

This would move the agency away from the command-and-control approach it has used for the last 20 years. A system of marketable permits could promote trading of environmental credits among a variety of sources.

Municipal treatment plants and private companies, such as chemical plants and pulp and paper plants, that can measure the amount of pollution they produce at specific points within their plants (so-called point sources) can trade permits among themselves. This approach will be effective in areas where current requirements have not succeeded in achieving water quality goals as well as in areas where load-based requirements are used, which specify a target level of pollution for a waterway. Those entities that treat their own waste and can easily reduce pollution will do so, and they will be able to make money by selling surplus permits to those who cannot cheaply reduce their own effluent. Polluters whose efflu-

ent is treated at a sewage plant can also trade permits among themselves.

Nonpoint sources—farms with fertilizer or pesticide runoff, for example—can trade both among themselves and with point sources. Many current problems with water quality have arisen because nonpoint sources, such as agricultural runoff, are typically unregulated or minimally regulated. Over 18,000 water bodies will not attain water quality standards even if all point sources meet their technical requirements due to pollution from nonpoint sources. While EPA has acknowledged that nonpoint sources are a major problem, little has been done to cope with the problem.

Potentially, great cost savings can be achieved if nonpoint sources can be brought into the system. One way to do this is for EPA to develop guidelines for trading with nonpoint sources. Even if nonpoint sources remain largely unregulated, heavily regulated point sources should have the ability to trade antipollution permits with nonpoint sources provided they can show that water quality will improve as a result.

Technical uncertainties make it hard to judge how pollution levels from nonpoint sources affect water quality; there is no smokestack, for example, that can be easily fitted with a measuring device. These difficulties may initially lead to problems in determining acceptable emissions levels. Where monitoring can only be done at great cost, experts may need to rely on their practical judgment to ensure that water quality will improve. One promising application for controlling nonpoint source pollution involves the farms just north of Florida's Everglades. I have proposed a marketable permit system to limit phosphorous entering the Everglades by restricting the amount of phosphorous leaving the Everglades Agricultural Area. If a marketable permit system is not practical, it may be possible to tax a pollutant, such as phosphates in detergent, to limit its use.

Markets and permit trading can play an important role in reducing nonlocalized contaminants such as phosphorus in a cost-effective way. For example, I am working with the government in Sydney, Australia, to establish trading rules for farmers along the Hawkesbury-Nepean river system; the new rules will encourage the cost-effective phosphorus reductions needed to limit the growth of the blue-green algae that sometimes clogs parts of the river system.

The technical challenges of regulating nonpoint sources are not unique to a market-based approach, but apply to all regulatory systems including command-and-control ones. A key advantage of trading with nonpoint sources is that it will provide environmental benefits while lowering the overall cost of regulation. If regulation remains largely voluntary, a market-based approach will provide a positive incentive to limit water pollution. ·

Congress should also direct EPA to develop and implement rules for trading among different kinds of wetlands. Wetlands trading would provide property owners with appropriate incentives for preserving wetlands, while giving owners greater flexibility in deciding how they can develop their property. For example, Disney World agreed to restore and maintain a wetland in exchange for the right to develop its site. Because artificial wetlands can be constructed and wetlands can be restored, there is latitude for trading among wetlands. Establishing the rules for trading will be a challenge, but EPA should provide guidance on this issue.

Congress should also encourage EPA and the states to establish total maximum pollution levels for water bodies that do not meet water quality standards. The focus on environmental outcomes is likely to lead to better environmental quality at lower cost. Where there are unacceptable damages associated with pollution from specific sites, some command-and-control regulation may be necessary to set the maximum ceilings on pollution from these sites. Nonetheless, the goal of regulation should be to provide the maximum improvement in environmental quality per dollar spent. This is best achieved through making greater use of market-based approaches.

Most, if not all, of the preceding recommendations could be implemented under the existing Clean Water Act, but explicit congressional support for marketable permits will spur their use. Congress should make it clear that it is primarily concerned with making necessary improvements in water quality in a timely manner. The precise method of achieving these environmental improvements should be left to the business and government entities responsible for making the needed reductions.

WHITHER WATER REGULATION?

Integrating water quantity and water quality concerns will be a fundamental aim of the 1990s. The recommendations here have focused primarily on quality issues, but the two issues are inextricably linked. Just as water quality can be improved through the introduction of markets, so too can water quantity. Moreover, markets for water quantity can improve water quality by encouraging water conservation. While water quantity issues are generally subject to state law, the federal government could help by endorsing the use of water markets and allowing the transfer of water contracts for federal reclamation water supply projects.

We have the technical know-how to apply market-based economic methods that will improve water quality and allocation. The question is whether we have the political will. I am optimistic that more markets for improving water management will be introduced. The only question is whether Washington will lead the charge or follow. The reauthorization of the Clean Water Act provides Congress with a unique opportunity to demonstrate leadership in a way that benefits the health and welfare of the American people.

POSTSCRIPT

Should the New Clean Water Act Aim at "Zero Discharge"?

Although Hahn includes the preservation of species habitats among the goals of water quality protection, the cost-benefit approach that he advocates typically ignores such ecological benefits whose economic value is difficult to assess. Environmentalists who opposed the incorporation of pollution permit trading into the Clean Air Act amendments, on the grounds that treating the right to pollute as a commodity is unethical, will surely react the same way to Hahn's marketplace strategy. Requiring comprehensive pollution-prevention planning, as Foran and Adler propose, may prove difficult to write into law in a way that will ensure its effectiveness in achieving toxic pollutant control.

One of the water quality problems that most experts agree needs more attention is pollution caused by runoff. For a critique of the provisions to deal with this problem that were first introduced in the 1987 amendments to the Clean Water Act, see "Runoff Runs Amok," by Julie St. Onge, *Sierra* (November/December 1988). For a thorough critique of the entire federal program to regulate water pollution and a set of recommendations for a strategy that differs from both the proposals of Hahn and those of Foran and Adler, read "Turning the Tide on Water Quality," by William F. Pedersen, Jr., *Ecology Law Quarterly* (vol. 15, no. 1, 1988).

The complexities that prevent scientists from reliably answering many basic questions about water quality is the theme of a review and analysis of the 20-year history of the Clean Water Act written by Debra S. Knopman and Richard A. Smith in the January/February 1993 issue of *Environment*. A more detailed treatment of the same theme is Robert Adler's book *The Clean Water Act: 20 Years Later* (Island Press, 1993). Adler's book is excerpted in the Summer 1994 issue of *EPA Journal*, which is entirely devoted to analyzing approaches to water protection legislation.

For a review of the status of the effort to revise the Clean Water Act and arguments by members of Congress for and against proposed amendments, see the December 1995 issue of *Congressional Digest*.

For an Internet site related to this issue, see http://www.cnie.org/ nle/h2o-2.html, which contains a Congressional Research Service report for Congress on the Clean Water Act reauthorization.

ISSUE 10

Is Rapid Introduction of Electric Cars a Good Strategy for Reducing Air Pollution?

YES: Daniel Sperling, from "The Case for Electric Vehicles," *Scientific American* (November 1996)

NO: Richard de Neufville et al., from "The Electric Car Unplugged," *Technology Review* (January 1996)

ISSUE SUMMARY

YES: Environmental engineering professor Daniel Sperling argues in favor of policies that would speed the introduction of electric vehicles as the most effective way of combating air pollution and reducing greenhouse gas emissions.

NO: Technology and Policy Program chair Richard de Neufville and several of his MIT colleagues oppose electric vehicle mandates, claiming that current electric cars are technically inadequate and expensive, and that they will not significantly improve air quality.

The fouling of air due to the burning of fuels has long plagued the inhabitants of populated areas. After the industrial revolution, the emissions from factory smokestacks were added to the pollution resulting from cooking and household heating. The increased use of coal combined with local meteorological conditions in London produced the dense, smoky, foggy condition first referred to as "smog" by Dr. H. A. Des Vouex in the early 1900s.

Dr. Des Vouex organized British smoke abatement societies. Despite the efforts of these organizations, the problem grew worse and spread to other industrial centers during the first half of the twentieth century. In December 1930, a dense smog in Belgium's Meuse Valley resulted in 60 deaths and an estimated 6,000 illnesses due to the combined effect of the dust and sulfur oxides from coal combustion. This event, and a similar one in Donora, Pennsylvania, received public attention but little response. Serious smog control efforts did not begin until a disastrous "killer smog" in London in December 1952 resulted in approximately 4,000 deaths.

The first major air pollution control victory was the regulation of high-sulfur coal burning in populated areas. The last life-threatening London smog incidents were recorded in the mid-1960s. Unfortunately, a new smog problem, linked to the rush hour traffic in large cities such as Los Angeles, was fast developing. This highly irritating, smelly, smoky haze—now referred to as photochemical smog—is caused by sunlight acting on air laden with nitrogen oxides, unburned hydrocarbons from automotive exhausts, and other sources. The resulting chemical reactions produce ozone and a variety of more exotic chemicals that are very irritating to lungs and nasal passages—even at very low levels.

The Clean Air Act of 1963 was the first comprehensive U.S. legislation aimed at controlling air pollution from both stationary sources (factories and power plants) and mobile sources (cars and trucks). Under this law and its early amendments, regulations have been issued to establish maximum levels for both ambient air concentrations and emissions from tailpipes and smokestacks for common pollutants such as sulfur dioxide, suspended particulates (dust), carbon monoxide, nitrogen dioxide, ozone, and airborne lead. Although these standards, coupled with required state plans to reduce air pollution, have had a significant impact, the exponential growth in the number of motor vehicles has resulted in only a modest average reduction in pollutant levels. Many urban areas in the United States still exceed the limit for one or more pollutants. Satellite photographs reveal chronic pollution over vast areas, such as the entire U.S. northeastern coast. Even more severe air pollution plagues other industrialized urban centers around the globe, such as Mexico City.

After years of debate Congress finally passed the 1990 Clean Air Act amendments. This complex piece of legislation includes significantly more stringent standards and extends controls to many additional sources of air emissions. It is designed to produce a marked improvement in air quality by the end of the century, as well as to reduce the incidence of acid precipitation that occurs when nitrogen- and sulfur-oxide emissions return to earth hundreds of miles from their sources in the form of rain, snow, or fog laden with sulfuric and nitric acids.

The amendments prescribe a special program for California, requiring that zero-emission vehicles (ZEVs) constitute 2 percent of all car sales by 1998, 5 percent by 2001, and 10 percent by 2003. New York and Massachusetts have also chosen to abide by these requirements. This ZEV mandate was strongly opposed by the automobile industry, and in March 1996 California agreed to eliminate the 1998 and 2001 quotas, retaining only the goal for 2003.

Daniel Sperling is a civil engineering professor and director of the Institute of Transportation Studies at the University of California, Davis. In the following selection, Sperling argues that the introduction of electric vehicles is the only sustainable transportation option that will reduce air pollution and greenhouse gas emissions. Professor Richard de Neufville, a transportation system analyst, chairs MIT's Technology and Policy Program. In the opposing selection, he and his coauthors from MIT engineering programs use a variety of technical and economic arguments to explain why they oppose the mandated introduction of electric vehicles.

YES   Daniel Sperling

THE CASE FOR ELECTRIC VEHICLES

Cars account for half the oil consumed in the U.S., about half the urban pollution and one fourth the greenhouse gases. They take a similar toll of resources in other industrial nations and in the cities of the developing world. As vehicle use continues to increase in the coming decade, the U.S. and other countries will have to address these issues or else face unacceptable economic, health-related and political costs. It is unlikely that oil prices will remain at their current low level or that other nations will accept a large and growing U.S. contribution to global climatic change.

Policymakers and industry have four options: reduce vehicle use, increase the efficiency and reduce the emissions of conventional gasoline-powered vehicles, switch to less noxious fuels, or find less polluting propulsion systems. The last of these—in particular the introduction of vehicles powered by electricity—is ultimately the only sustainable option. The other alternatives are attractive in theory but in practice are either impractical or offer only marginal improvements. For example, reduced vehicle use could solve congestion woes and a host of social and environmental problems, but evidence from around the world suggests that it is very difficult to make people give up their cars to any significant extent. In the U.S., mass-transit ridership and carpooling have declined since World War II. Even in western Europe, with fuel prices averaging more than $1 a liter (about $4 a gallon) and with pervasive mass transit and dense populations, cars still account for 80 percent of all passenger travel.

Improved energy efficiency is also appealing, but automotive fuel economy has barely budged in 10 years. Alternative fuels such as methanol or natural gas, burned in internal-combustion engines, could be introduced at relatively low cost, but they would lead to only marginal reductions in pollution and greenhouse emissions (especially because oil companies are already spending billions of dollars every year to develop less polluting formulations of gasoline).

Electric-drive vehicles (those whose wheels are turned by electric motors rather than by a mechanical gasoline-powered drivetrain) could reduce urban pollution and greenhouse emissions significantly over the coming decade.

And they could lay a foundation for a transportation system that would ultimately be almost pollution-free. Although electrically driven vehicles have a history as old as that of the internal-combustion engine, a number of recent technological developments—including by-products of both the computer revolution and the Strategic Defense Initiative (SDI) in the 1980s—promise to make this form of transportation efficient and inexpensive enough to compete with gasoline. Overcoming the entrenched advantages of gas-powered cars, however, will require a concerted effort on the parts of industry and government to make sure that the environmental benefits accruing from electric cars return to consumers as concrete incentives for purchase.

EFFICIENCY IMPROVES

The term "electric-drive vehicle" includes not only those cars powered by batteries charged with household current but also vehicles that generate electricity on board or store it in devices other than batteries. Their common denominator is an efficient electric motor that drives the wheels and extracts energy from the car's motion when it slows down. Internal-combustion vehicles, in contrast, employ a constantly running engine whose power is diverted through a series of gears and clutches to drive the wheels and to turn a generator for the various electrically powered accessories in the car.

Electric vehicles are more efficient —and thus generally less polluting— than internal-combustion vehicles for a variety of reasons. First, because the electric motor is directly connected to the wheels, it consumes no energy while the car is at rest or coasting, increasing the

effective efficiency by roughly one fifth. Regenerative braking schemes—which employ the motor as a generator when the car is slowing down—can return as much as half an electric vehicle's kinetic energy to the storage cells, giving it a major advantage in stop-and-go urban traffic.

Furthermore, the motor converts more than 90 percent of the energy in its storage cells to motive force, whereas internal-combustion drives utilize less than 25 percent of the energy in a liter of gasoline. Although the storage cells are typically charged by an electricity-generating system, the efficiency of which averages only 33 percent, an electric drive still has a significant 5 percent net advantage over internal combustion. Innovations such as combined-cycle generation (which extracts additional energy from the exhaust heat of a conventional power plant) will soon make it possible for the utility power plants from which the storage cells are charged to raise their efficiency to as much as 50 percent. This boost would increase proportionately the fraction of energy ultimately delivered to the wheels of an electric vehicle. Fuel cells, which "burn" hydrogen to generate electricity directly onboard an electric car, are even more efficient.

Further air-quality benefits derive from electric drives because they shift the location from which pollutants disperse. Conventional cars emit carbon monoxide and other pollutants from their tailpipes wherever they travel, whereas pollution associated with electric power generation is generally located at a few coal- or oil-burning plants at a distance from urban centers.

Battery-powered electric vehicles would practically eliminate emissions of carbon monoxide and volatile unburned hydrocarbons and would greatly diminish nitrogen oxide emissions. In areas served by dirty coal-fired power plants, they might marginally increase the emissions of sulfur oxides and particulate matter. Pollution associated with the modern manufacture of batteries and electric motors is negligible, however.

Hybrid vehicles (those combining small internal-combustion engines with electric motors and electricity storage devices) will reduce emissions almost as much as battery-powered electric vehicles; indeed, in regions where most electricity is generated with coal, hybrids may prove preferable. The impact of electric vehicles on air pollution would be most beneficial, of course, where electricity is derived from nonpolluting solar, nuclear, wind or hydroelectric power. Among the chief beneficiaries would be California, where most electricity comes from tightly controlled natural gas plants and zero-emission hydroelectric and nuclear plants, and France, where most electricity comes from nuclear power.

These environmental benefits could be very important. Many metropolitan areas in the U.S. have air significantly more polluted than allowed by health-based air-quality standards, and most will continue to be in violation of the law in the year 2000. Pollution in Los Angeles is so severe that even if every vehicle were to disappear from its streets, the city would have no chance of meeting the standards. Many other regions in this country have little prospect of meeting their legal mandates, even with much cleaner-burning gasoline and improved internal-combustion engines. And elsewhere in the world, in cities such as Bangkok, Kathmandu and Mexico City, air pollution is more severe than in Los Angeles.

ENERGY STORAGE IS THE KEY

Electric vehicles now on the market rely on lead-acid batteries charged from a standard wall plug. They are unlikely ever to take the market by storm. Not only are lead-acid batteries expensive and bulky, they can drive a car little more than 150 kilometers between charges. This problem, however, is often overstated. First, there appears to be a significant market for short-range vehicles; second, new energy storage devices are even now making the transition from laboratory to production line.

A regional survey that my colleagues at the University of California at Davis and I conducted suggests that about half of all households owning more than one car—the majority of U.S. households, accounting for more than 70 percent of new car purchases—could easily adapt their driving patterns to make use of a second car with a range of less than 180 kilometers. Many respondents indicated a willingness to accept even much shorter ranges. Environmental benefits and the advantage of home recharging (many people actively dislike refueling at gasoline stations) compensate for the limited range.

Batteries are likely to play a diminishing role in electric vehicles. Among the replacements now being developed are ultracapacitors, which store large amounts of electricity and can charge and discharge quickly; flywheels, which store energy in a spinning rotor; and fuel cells, which convert chemical fuel into electricity, emitting water vapor.

Ultracapacitors owe much of their early development to the SDI's ballistic-missile defense program. Advanced manufacturing techniques can eliminate the tiny imperfections in a conventional capacitor's insulating film that allow charge to leak away. New materials make it possible to interleave a capacitor's carbon and liquid electrolyte much more finely than before. As a result, ultracapacitors can store about 15 watt-hours (enough energy to run a one-horsepower motor for about a minute) in a one-liter volume, and a one-liter device can discharge at a rate of three kilowatts. Ultracapacitors are already available in small units for calculators, watches and electric razors.

Flywheels first saw use in transportation in the 1950s. Flywheel-powered buses traveled the streets of Yverdon, Switzerland, revving up their rotors at every stop. Since then, designs have changed substantially: now composite rotors spin at up to 100,000 revolutions per second, a speed limited only by the tensile strength of their rims. Magnetic bearings have reduced friction so that a rotor can maintain 90 percent of its energy for four days. The first high-powered ultracapacitors and flywheels are likely to appear in commercial vehicles around the year 2000. Because they can provide power very rapidly, they will be paired with batteries—the batteries will supply basic driving needs, and the capacitors or flywheels will handle peak requirements when the car accelerates or climbs a hill. This combination will allow the use of smaller battery packs and extend their service life.

Even the most optimistic projections for advanced energy storage technologies still do not compare with the 2,100 kilojoules stored in a 38-liter (10-gallon) tank of gasoline; for this reason, many researchers have predicted that the most popular electric-drive vehicles will be hybrids—propelled by electric motors but ultimately powered by small internal-combustion engines that charge batteries, capacitors or other power sources. The average power required for highway driving is only about 10 kilowatts for a typical passenger car, so the engine can be quite small; the storage cells charge during periods of minimal output and discharge rapidly for acceleration. Internal-combustion engines can reach efficiencies as high as 40 percent if operated at a constant speed, and so the overall efficiency of a hybrid vehicle can be even better than that of a pure electric drive.

Perhaps the most promising option involves fuel cells. Many researchers see them as the most likely successor to the internal-combustion engine, and they are a centerpiece of the ongoing Partnership for a New Generation of Vehicles, a collaboration between the federal government and the Big Three automakers. Fuel cells burn hydrogen to produce water vapor and carbon dioxide, emitting essentially no other effluents as they generate electricity. (Modified versions may also use other fuels, including natural gas, methane or gasoline, at a cost in increased emissions and reduced efficiency.) Although the devices are best known as power sources for spacecraft, an early fuel cell found its way into an experimental farm tractor in 1959. Prototype fuel-cell buses built in the mid-1990s have demonstrated that the technology is workable, but cost is still the most critical issue. Proton-exchange membrane (PEM) fuel cells, currently the most attractive for vehicular use, cost more than $100,000 per kilowatt only a few years ago but are expected to cost only a few thousand dollars after the turn of the century and perhaps $100 a kilowatt or less—competitive with the cost of internal-combustion engines—in full-production volumes. Daimler-Benz announced in July that it could start selling fuel cell–equipped Mercedes cars as soon as 2006.

SUSTAINABLE TRANSPORTATION

Fuel cells will generally be the least polluting of any method for producing motive power for vehicles. Furthermore, the ideal fuel for fuel cells, from both a technical and environmental perspective, is hydrogen. Hydrogen can be made from many different sources, but when fossil fuels become more scarce and expensive, hydrogen will most likely be made from water using solar cells. If solar hydrogen were widely adopted, the entire transportation-energy system would be nearly benign environmentally, and the energy would be fully renewable. The price of such renewable hydrogen fuel should not exceed even a dollar for the equivalent of a liter of gasoline.

In addition to the power source, progress in aspects of electric vehicle technology has accelerated in recent years. A technological revolution —in electricity storage and conversion devices, electronic controls, software and materials—is opening up many new opportunities. For example, advances in power electronics have led to drivetrains that weigh and cost only 40 percent of what their counterparts did a decade ago. Until the early 1990s, virtually all electric vehicles depended on direct-current motors because those were easiest to run from batteries. But the development of small, lightweight inverters (devices that convert direct current from a battery to the alternating current that is most efficient for running a motor) makes it possible to abandon DC. AC motors are more reliable, easier to maintain and more ef-ficient than their DC counterparts; they are also easier to adapt to regenerative braking. Indeed, the electric-vehicle motor and power electronics together are now smaller, lighter and cheaper to manufacture than a comparable internal-combustion engine.

Every major automaker in the world is now investing in electric vehicle development as well as improvements in less critical technologies such as those underlying car heaters and tires. The resulting advanced components will be the building blocks for very clean and efficient vehicles of the future, but in the meantime many of them are finding their way into internal-combustion vehicles.

Although automakers worldwide have spent perhaps $1 billion on electric vehicles during the 1990s, in the context of the industry as a whole this investment is relatively small. The auto industry spends more than $5 billion a year in the U.S. alone on advertising and more than that on research and development. And oil companies are spending about $10 billion in the U.S. this decade just to upgrade refineries to produce reformulated low-emission gasoline.

Much of the investment made so far has been in response to governmental pressure. In 1990 California adopted a zero-emission vehicle (ZEV) mandate requiring that major automakers make at least 2 percent of their vehicles emission-free by 1998, 5 percent by 2001 and 10 percent by 2003. (These percentages correspond to the production of about 20,000 vehicles a year by 1998.) Failure to meet the quota would lead to a penalty of $5,000 for every ZEV not available for sale. New York State and Massachusetts enacted similar rules shortly thereafter.

The major automakers aggressively opposed the ZEV mandate but rapidly

expanded their electric-vehicle R&D programs to guard against the possibility
that their regulatory counterattack might
fail—and that markets for electric cars
might actually emerge either in the U.S.
or abroad. Their loudest complaint was
that the rules forced industry to supply
an expensive product without providing consumers with an incentive to buy
them—even though local, state and federal governments were enacting precisely
such incentives.

This past March California regulators
gave in to pressure from both the automobile and oil industries and eliminated
the quotas for 1998 and 2001, leaving only
a commitment to begin selling electric vehicles and the final goal for 2003. Industry
analysts expect that U.S. sales will be no
more than 5,000 vehicles total until after
the turn of the century.

One crucial factor in determining the
success of electric vehicles is their price
—a figure that is still highly uncertain.
General Motors's newly introduced EV1
is nominally priced at $33,000; Solectria
sells its low-volume-production electric
vehicles for between $30,000 and $75,000,
depending on the battery configuration.
(Nickel-metal hydride batteries capable
of carrying the car more than 320
kilometers add nearly $40,000 to the price
of a lead-battery vehicle.) The adversarial
nature of the regulatory process has
encouraged opponents and proponents
to make unrealistically high or low
estimates, so it will be impossible to
tell just how much the vehicles will
cost until they are in mass production.
Comparisons with the price history of
other products, including conventional
automobiles, however, suggest that full-
scale production could reduce prices to
significantly less than half their present
level.

AN UNCERTAIN ROAD

Faced with the inevitability of electric
vehicle production, automakers are de-
vising strategies to produce them inex-
pensively. Many (including Peugeot in
Europe) are simply removing engines,
gas tanks and transmissions from the
bodies of existing gasoline vehicles and
inserting batteries, controllers and electric motors with minimal modification.
Others, including Ford, are selling "glid-
ers" (car bodies with no installed drive
components) to smaller conversion companies that then fit them with an electric drive. A third strategy is to build
very small vehicles, such as the Mercedes
Smart—known popularly as the Swatch-
mobile—targeted at the emerging market
niche for limited-range urban vehicles. Of
all the major manufacturers, only General
Motors has thus far committed to mass
production of an ordinary car designed
from the ground up for electric drive.

The cost of batteries (and fuel cells)
will probably always render electric
vehicles more expensive to purchase than
comparable gasoline vehicles. On a per-
kilometer basis, however, the cost of an
electric and internal-combustion vehicle
should eventually be about the same.
Fuel for electric vehicles is inexpensive,
maintenance is minimal, and it appears
that electric motors last significantly
longer than gasoline engines. Taking
into account the cost of air pollution,
greenhouse gases and other market
externalities (that is, factors that society
at large must now pay for) would tip the
scale in favor of electric vehicles in many
circumstances.

The challenge for policymakers and
marketers is to assure that consumers
take into account these full costs, a goal
that has thus far been difficult to pur-

sue. In California, where powerful air-quality regulators have led the way toward electric vehicles, progress has been slowed by opposition from both auto manufacturers and oil companies. On a national level, early hopes for the Partnership for a New Generation of Vehicles have foundered on inadequate funding, political infighting and excessive caution. As a result of this internal conflict, vehicles to be built in 2004 will ostensibly have their designs set in 1997, making it likely that the partnership will embrace only the smallest of incremental improvements rather than spearheading the introduction of fuel cells and other radically new technologies.

Nevertheless, it seems certain that electric-drive technology will eventually supplant internal-combustion engines—perhaps not quickly, uniformly nor entirely—but inevitably. The question is when, in what form and how to manage the transition. Perhaps the most important lesson learned from the current state of affairs is that government should do what it does best: provide broad market incentives that bring external costs such as pollution back into the economic calculations of consumers and corporations, and target money at innovative, leading-edge technologies rather than fund work that private companies would be doing in any case.

The emergence of electric vehicles has important economic implications. Whoever pioneers the commercialization of cost-competitive electric vehicle technologies will find inviting export markets around the world. Electric vehicles will be attractive where pollution is severe and intractable, peak vehicle performance is less highly valued than reliability and low maintenance, cheap electricity is available off-peak, and investments in oil distribution are small. Indeed, if the U.S. and other major industrial nations do not act, it is quite possible that the next generation of corporate automotive giants may arise in developing countries, where cars are relatively scarce today.

NO
Richard de Neufville et al.

THE ELECTRIC CAR UNPLUGGED

To comply with the federal Clean Air Act of 1990, the California Air Resources Board has ruled that, by 1998, 2 percent of all vehicles offered for sale in the state must be so-called zero-emission vehicles. As a practical matter, California has mandated electric vehicles—the only available technology meeting the requirement that the power train produce no emissions. Two other states have followed suit. By 2003, roughly 10 percent of all new personal vehicles sold in California, Massachusetts, and New York must be electric.

The aim of these programs—to combat the smog that engulfs Los Angeles and other cities—is worthy. Even the programs' focus on cars is appropriate because there is little question that auto emissions contribute greatly to urban air pollution. Unfortunately, however, the electric vehicle is not yet ready for large-scale commercial use. No such vehicle now sold meets the demands of a consumer market for road transport.

Highway-worthy electric vehicles for mass consumption have neither been produced nor tested in significant volumes over the range of likely driving conditions. Their reliability over a standard warranty period, such as 3 years and 50,000 miles, is unknown. Electric vehicles for actual road use are still highly experimental.

The mandate to produce and sell a significant number of electric vehicles thus needs careful scrutiny. The measure is unprecedented. Previous environmental mandates, such as the Clean Water Act, required the public to adopt the best available technology—whatever that turned out to be in different cases—for reducing pollution. The California rules, however, require a specific experimental technology, and mandate a tight schedule.

The effort to pursue electric vehicles on a large scale is also uniquely American. Britain uses electric vehicles for milk delivery, France has proposed pilot production of special urban vehicles, and the German Post Office wants to operate about a hundred delivery vans in the years ahead. In addition, Volkswagen has recently started to produce electric-powered Golf sedans at the rate of about one per day. But despite this interest in electric vehicles, the existing programs in other countries are orders of magnitude smaller than what is required by the California rules, which aim for manufacturers to sell

From Richard de Neufville, Stephen R. Connors, Frank R. Field III, David Marks, Donald R. Sadoway, and Richard D. Tabors, "The Electric Car Unplugged," *Technology Review,* vol. 99, no. 1 (January 1996). Copyright © 1996 by *Technology Review.* Reprinted by permission.

some 18,000 electric vehicles in 1998 (some 2 percent of the 906,000 new cars registered in California in 1994).

Meanwhile, in the United States, the program to develop electric vehicles has already proved expensive. Ford and General Motors alone have reportedly spent hundreds of millions of dollars on R&D, and federal and state agencies have sponsored a wide range of demonstration programs. The budget for the U.S. Advanced Battery Consortium alone (an alliance of the U. S. Department of Energy, the Big Three automobile manufacturers, the Electric Power Research Institute, Southern California Edison, and others to develop batteries for the vehicles) is $260 million. In fact, the cumulative cost of research on electric vehicles in the United States is approaching $1 billion, roughly equal to half of the National Science Foundation's entire research budget.

By any measure then, the commitment to manufacture and sell electric vehicles in large volume is a major piece of national industrial policy that aims to substantially reduce the nation's transportation and pollution problems. One supposes that such a mandate would have been preceded by a comprehensive analysis. Yet no investigation of the overall performance or effectiveness of electric vehicles—either by themselves or compared with alternatives—has been undertaken. Our research group found that available material either deals with just one element of the system, such as batteries, or is obviously partisan, coming from enthusiasts—such as electric vehicle makers, battery suppliers, or electric utilities—with a stake in the outcome.

To address this gap, our team assessed the total environmental and economic effects of the manufacture and use of electric vehicles made with different materials and powered by many types of batteries. We also attempted to compare the electric-car mandate to alternative systems for reducing air pollution.

In our judgment, the electric vehicle policy defined by the California Air Resources Board is neither cost-effective nor practical. Electric vehicles will not contribute meaningfully to cleaner air if they are introduced as now proposed; over the next decade their effect will be imperceptible compared with other major improvements in automotive and other combustion technologies. Furthermore, even if it could be justified on environmental grounds, the technology of electric vehicles is still far from meeting the needs of a mass consumer market and it is unclear when, if ever, it will do so. Finally, the projected costs of implementing the California electric vehicle policy are enormous, requiring subsidies as high as $10,000 to $20,000 per vehicle.

DISPLACING EMISSIONS

Because conventional cars and trucks create significant emissions, the use of electric vehicles sounds like a good way to combat air pollution. But because producing electricity also creates pollution, electric vehicles do not eliminate emissions—they simply move them elsewhere. Unless this electricity comes from nuclear power plants (neither environmentally acceptable nor economically feasible right now) or renewable sources (unlikely to be sufficient), the power to propel electric vehicles will come from burning fossil fuels. But using fossil fuels to power electric vehicles is doubly pernicious. The fuel loses up to 65 percent of its energy when it is burned to produce electricity; 5 to 10 percent of what is left is lost in transmitting and distributing the electricity before it even gets to the electric car.

Of course, moving pollutant emissions elsewhere could arguably be worthwhile, but such a policy needs to be considered carefully. For regions upwind of power plants, electric vehicles would obviously reduce local pollution. Los Angeles, for instance, obtains part of its electric power from coal plants in the Four Corners region (where Arizona, Colorado, New Mexico, and Utah meet). Adopting electric vehicles in Los Angeles therefore simply increases pollution over large expanses of the Southwest.

Meanwhile, regions downwind of fossil fuel-burning power plants, such as Boston and the Northeast seaboard generally, will not escape the pollution produced by generating electricity for electric vehicles, which may be substantial. What's more, many discussions of electric vehicles have supposed that the plants used to create the extra power would be clean and inexpensive, since the electric cars would mostly be recharged "off peak." But this is unlikely to be the case. Much of the power from the cleanest and least expensive plants is already in use today even during off-peak hours; supplying the additional loads will inevitably require using older, dirtier, and less efficient facilities.

Even in areas where electric cars may lower urban air pollution, the great effort to get them on the road may not perceptibly improve the environment. For the past decade, new vehicles have met more stringent pollution standards, and the upgrading of the fleet has cut total U.S. automotive emissions dramatically. Even without electric vehicles, the fleet of cars now on the road will be almost completely renewed in this decade and thus the average emissions from cars will be almost halved. Ironically, the environmental benefit of each electric vehicle would be particularly small in the years ahead because it would substitute for another brand-new vehicle that will be far cleaner than the current average.

The schedule for the introduction of new electric vehicles implies that only about 4 percent of the total fleet in California, Massachusetts, and New York will be electric by the year 2005, and about 10 percent by the year 2015, some 20 years from now. And improvement will not be immediate: since only about 10 percent of the automotive fleet is renewed each year in the United States, it takes about a decade for the percentage of electric vehicles on the road to match the percentage of those sold each year. Thus given the small percentages involved and the long delays, electric vehicles will have only a modest effect on overall automotive pollution. This is true of any policy that imposes marginal improvements on a small fraction of the cars on the road. The important effects result from changes to the entire fleet. Thus the requirement that all cars use catalytic converters to limit carbon monoxide emissions improved air quality significantly, but the California mandate to introduce electric vehicles will not. Many developers have demonstrated electric vehicles with adequate power and speed. Ford and General Motors each have a version that accelerates easily into freeway traffic and can cruise comfortably at the speed limit. The trouble is that these vehicles cannot sustain this performance for very long.

Range of travel is the major concern for electric vehicles. The technological question is whether it will be possible, at reasonable cost, to design vehicles that can reliably travel some 100 to 150 miles, in normal traffic, before their batteries must be recharged. This design range represents a round-trip distance from home to work plus an allowance for errands and safety. The implied commuting distance of 30 to 50 miles is high but appropriate for Los Angeles, New York, and Boston, the prime target areas today.

The desirable range is difficult to achieve in practice. A recent test of available models of electric vehicles conducted by the Environmental Protection Agency found actual driving ranges between 30 and 50 miles per battery charge. Driving on city streets involves stopping, waiting in traffic jams, starting, and constant changes in acceleration to cope with hills and variations in the speed of traffic—all factors that reduce the range that can be attained. Driving to work must also be done in cold weather when batteries tend to perform poorly. And in winter in Massachusetts and New York, as much energy will be needed to heat a car while it is being operated as to drive it—effectively cutting the electric vehicle's range in half. (This is vividly illustrated by the fact that Ford's electric "zero pollution" vehicle actually includes a diesel heater complete with tailpipe!) Of course, driving also requires lights and windshield wipers which use energy and further reduce the maximum practical range. Thus, record-breaking results occasionally reported in the press do not fairly represent what everyday drivers of electric vehicles may experience. What a professional test driver can achieve operating under optimal conditions on a flat track with no passengers or loads in no way compares with the range an ordinary commuter could hope to attain in the rain at rush hour.

Users of laptop computers will recognize the problem. The performance of rechargeable batteries is often half their rated capacity because performance relates to the way they have previously been discharged and the amount of power required for specific tasks. The net result is that similar batteries, nominally capable of supporting a computer the same number of hours, perform quite differently in practice.

The problem of providing electric vehicles with enough range is rooted in a fundamental physical reality: the batteries required to power electric vehicles are enormously heavy. Batteries store very little energy per unit of weight. The energy density of lead-acid batteries—the kind used in conventional cars—is about 35 watt-hours per kilogram, less than one-three-hundredth that of gasoline, which is about 12,000 watt-hours per kilogram. As a rule of thumb, 1 gallon of gasoline, weighing about 6 pounds, has the same energy content as 400 pounds of lead-acid batteries.

Golf carts are the prototype feasible electric vehicles at this stage. Their low range and speed require only about 1 percent of the power required of electric vehicles for highways. They can thus be powered by about 50 pounds of batteries. But because of their added demands, commuter cars could easily require batteries that account for one-third of the total weight of the vehicle. Thus, roadworthy electric vehicles developed so far are essentially battery packs on wheels.

The problem is a basic conflict between good performance per unit of weight and durability. For example, the ABB sodium batteries used by Ford produce good peak power but last only about a year and a half (some 600 cycles). The long-lasting nickel-iron batteries, on the other hand, have far less peak power as well as lower energy density.

Government and industry are spending considerable sums on developing better batteries for electric vehicles, efforts coordinated since 1993 by the Advanced Battery Consortium. Nevertheless, progress in electrochemistry has not been rapid. Materials scientists simply do not yet know how to make reliable long-life batteries even in the laboratory. Progress has been made primarily in engineering developments that push existing capabilities to their limits. And, in part because of the tight timetable required by the California mandate, money for batteries is going into engineering rather than into the basic research from which needed progress must come.

Even promising leads produced by this focus have tended to lose their appeal. The recent experience with sodium-sulfur batteries, which Ford chose to power its prototype electric vehicles, illustrates the point. Unfortunately, this technology has had major practical difficulties: in a German laboratory, sodium-sulfur batteries caught fire after one was overcharged, and a test vehicle caught fire in the parking lot of the California-based Electric Power Research Institute (whose employees were knowledgeable enough, fortunately, to alert firefighters to the battery's makeup so they could avoid the dangers of mixing sodium with water).

Of course, we can only speculate on the future of battery technology. Breakthroughs are possible, and should be sought. Advances cannot be guaranteed, however. It is entirely possible that the kind of cost-effective batteries needed to achieve the desired range for electric vehicles in the United States may simply not be available in our genera-

tion. An attempt to legislate the results of the research and development process is therefore unrealistic and unworkable. It is one thing to goad manufacturers to stretch their capabilities within the framework of an existing technology, as was done for catalytic converters and air bags. It is quite another to force them into new technologies whose possibilities are not known. Both airbags and catalytic converters were demonstrably capable of meeting the required technical performance requirements when they were mandated. The situation is very different for electric vehicles.

HIGHER COST, POORER PERFORMANCE

For the foreseeable future, electric vehicles manufactured for a broad consumer market will cost about twice as much as comparably sized conventional automobiles, even though the electric vehicles will have only about half the range. This conclusion is based on models of automobile manufacturing developed by the MIT Materials Systems Laboratory over many years and validated by comparisons with actual practice in the United States and Europe.

Some entrepreneurs making prototype electric vehicles report costs competitive with those of ordinary cars, but their experience cannot be extrapolated to full-scale production. Unlike prototypes, industrial production of automobiles must take into account the costs of marketing, distribution, and service; of extensive testing (to reduce product liability); and long-term relationships with labor (including health and pension benefits). These inescapable additional costs roughly equal the costs of manufacturing.

Moreover, the opportunities for reducing the costs of manufacturing electric vehicles through economies of scale or learning curves are limited. To take one example, the lightweight bodies required by electric vehicles are likely to be made of plastic that, on a per pound basis, is roughly three times as expensive as sheet steel. Because the lightweight plastic is also much less stiff than steel, considerably more material is needed to achieve comparable performance, offsetting the weight advantage. These two factors alone greatly increase the manufacturers' cost of producing the bodies of electric vehicles. And as automakers already know from using plastics in car bodies of specialty cars such as the Corvette, and in components of GM's Saturn line, plastics take an order of magnitude more time to fabricate than their steel counterparts. This limitation, which makes little difference in producing small numbers of cars, will require costly machinery for large-scale production and prevent the expected economies of scale.

The batteries for electric vehicles will also raise the lifetime costs of owning the car. Batteries wear out after roughly 1.5 to 2 years, or some 500 cycles of daily discharge and recharge. The cost of a set of batteries for an electric vehicle will drop as manufacturers produce them on a regular basis, but the replacement batteries are still projected to be in the range of several thousand dollars. Buyers will have to pay this cost at the time of purchase and every few years thereafter.

It seems clear that rational buyers will not spend twice as much for a car that has worse performance than competing vehicles. Even though electric vehicles may cost as much to produce as conventional luxury sedans, they will have to compete with the significantly cheaper compact and subcompact cars they resemble in appearance. To sell electric vehicles in the required quantities, then, manufacturers will have to discount them as much as $10,000 to $20,000 per car—far below their cost to produce and market. In effect, this means the public will pay handsomely to get electric vehicles on the road since car manufacturers will naturally pass these losses along to buyers of conventional cars. Manufacturers have done this before. To meet the Car Average Fuel Economy regulations spawned as part of the Clean Air Act, which stipulate that automakers sell cars whose average gas mileage meets certain stiffening goals each year, manufacturers sell their smallest cars at a loss and raise the prices on the others. The cost of a similar subsidy to implement the electric vehicle policy could average out to about $200 to $400 per new internal combustion car sold where California rules on electric vehicles prevail.

We estimate the total annual cost of the subsidy required to implement the electric vehicle policy in California alone will be somewhere between a quarter and half a billion dollars. Since the electric vehicle policy appears to yield imperceptible overall environmental benefits, the added cost is extremely hard to justify.

DRIVING FORWARD

Unfortunately, because today's policy fixates prematurely on a specific technological solution, it has diverted attention from the basic issue: How should we improve air quality in polluted urban areas? To obtain a practical result, we need to consider both the instrument of the problem—that is, the technology—and the cause of the problem, the users. We need to adopt a flexible strategy that permits us to choose the most effective options as they develop. We must also define approaches that can command the support of all the important participants.

Rather than mandate development of the electric vehicle on a short timetable, we should promote research and development over a broad front on a range of alternative vehicles. These should certainly include refined versions of currently accessible technologies such as ultra-low-emission vehicles that use catalytic converters and microelectronics to control combustion precisely; and so-called hybrid vehicles, which combine constant-speed (and therefore highly efficient) gasoline or diesel engines with electric generators to extend the range and power of batteries stored on board. Fuel-cell vehicles are a technological possibility that also requires investigation.

Development could also be divided into three phases. The first might focus on creating prototypes, culminating in a competition between technologies. The second phase could then concentrate on large-scale development and testing of finalist systems, leading to a final choice for implementing in the third phase. In light of all the uncertainties, it is unlikely that a particular schedule for such implementation, set a decade in advance, can work.

Organizational changes should also complement, or even replace, technological solutions. Perhaps the real issue is that communities such as Los Angeles are too dependent on the use of personal automobiles. Because the total level of pollution is of course the product of two factors—the dirtiness of the vehicle and the distance it travels—targeting the level of emissions produced per vehicle-mile addresses only half the problem. The fact is that the number of vehicle-miles traveled is growing steadily in the United States, particularly in the Los Angeles area. More people live farther away from jobs and travel more. If this trend continues, the resulting increase in pollution will counteract any reduction achieved by introducing electric vehicles. An effective policy to reduce total automotive pollution should thus include encouraging collective transport through the use of car pools and buses, reducing driving through disincentives such as higher parking fees and gas taxes, and facilitating alternatives to driving such as telecommuting.

In the first phase of any such plan, decision makers should identify actions that can produce immediate results cheaply—in essence, picking the low-hanging fruit. They should, for example, consider a program of buying up the most severely polluting vehicles—those among the 7 to 10 percent of vehicles that produce 50 percent of on-road generation of carbon monoxide and hydrocarbons. Because one of these mostly older, severely polluting vehicles produces roughly 10 time the pollution of an average vehicle, and because one electric vehicle will only reduce pollution equal to one-half of an average car, such a program would have 20 times the effect per vehicle and would be far more cost effective.

Such a multifaceted and dynamic strategy would surely improve air quality more quickly than a proposed mandate that will have no perceptible effect on pollution for many years, if ever.

POSTSCRIPT

Is Rapid Introduction of Electric Cars a Good Strategy for Reducing Air Pollution?

The analysis of the options available for reducing the air pollution resulting from the transportation of people and goods is complex and, like most tech nological problems related to environmental protection, it requires the use of many unprovable assumptions For this reason, even those highly trained ex perts with no vested interest in the result come to very different conclusions about the best path to follow

Many alternative strategies were evaluated by the Environmental Protec tion Agency (EPA) and its consultants during the decade of political struggle that preceded the enactment of the 1990 Clean Air Act amendments The January/February issue of *EPA Journal* is devoted to a discussion of the new law. In this issue, the agency presents technical details about the amendments and a justification of the regulatory strategy that they embody. For another critical evaluation of the likely impact of several of the motor vehicle emission standards in the new law, see Achieving Acceptable Air Quality Some Re flections on Controlling Vehicle Emissions, by J G Calvert, J B. Heywood R. F. Sawyer, and H. H Seinfeld, in the July 2, 1993, issue of *Science* For a dif ferent analysis about the future of personal transportation and how various scenarios concerning the automobile are likely to affect the environment, see the article by Stephen Wilkinson in the May/June 1993 issue of *Audubon*

Another environmental issue related to electric vehicles not focused on by either Sperling or de Neufville et al is the potential for lead pollution asso ciated with the large numbers of lead-acid batteries that would be required by the currently available models of such vehicles An analysis of this issue in 'Environmental Implications of Electric Cars,' by Lester B Lave, Chris T Hendrickson, and Francis Clay McMichael, *Science* (May 19, 1995) indicates that the hazard due to the increased release of lead into the environment from electric vehicles would outweigh the benefits resulting from urban air pollution reduction This article stimulated an unusual number of letters to the editor, which were published in the August 11, 1995, issue of *Science* The authors of these letters took issue with the facts, assumptions, and analytical methods, as well as the conclusions of Lave et al

The EPA announced in late November 1996 that it plans to seek more strin gent regulations to control fine particulates and ozone levels, which are two types of urban air pollution that have been found to cause health problems in susceptible individuals at currently acceptable levels The background to this plan, which is certain to run into serious congressional opposition, is discussed in a feature article by Catherine M. Cooney in the July 30, 1996, issue of *Environmental Science and Technology.*

For an Internet site related to this issue, see http://www.cnie.org/nle/air-9.html, which contains a 1995 Congressional Research Service report for Congress entitled *Implementing the Clean Air Act Amendments of 1990: Where Are We Now?*

ISSUE 11

Does Feeding People and Preserving Wildlands Require Chemical-Based Agriculture?

YES: Ronald Bailey, from "Once and Future Farming," *Garbage: The Independent Environmental Quarterly* (Fall 1994)

NO: Katherine R. Smith, from "Time to 'Green' U.S. Farm Policy," *Issues in Science and Technology* (Spring 1995)

ISSUE SUMMARY

YES: Environmental journalist Ronald Bailey asserts that intensive farming, relying on pesticides and fertilizers, is needed to feed the world's people without requiring increased land use, which would destroy wildlife.

NO: Katherine R. Smith, policy studies director at the Henry A. Wallace Institute for Alternative Agriculture, asserts that use of chemicals causing serious environmental problems that could be solved through the promotion of "green" alternatives.

The use of naturally occurring chemicals in agriculture goes back many centuries. After World War II, however, the application of synthetic chemical toxins to croplands became sufficiently intensive to cause widespread environmental problems. DDT, used during the war to control malaria and other insect-borne diseases, was promoted by agribusiness as the choice solution for a wide variety of agricultural pest problems. As insects' resistance to DDT increased, other chlorinated organic toxins—such as heptachlor, aldrin, dieldrin, mirex, and chlordane—were introduced by the burgeoning chemical pesticide industry. Environmental scientists became concerned about the effects of these fat-soluble, persistent toxins whose concentrations became magnified in carnivorous species at the top of the ecological food chain. The first serious problem to be documented was reproductive failure resulting from DDT ingestion in such birds of prey as falcons, pelicans, osprey, and eagles. Chlorinated pesticides were also found to be poisoning marine life. Marine scientist Rachel Carson's best-seller *Silent Spring* (Houghton Mifflin, 1962) raised public and scientific consciousness about the potential devastating effects of continued, uncontrolled use of chemical pesticides.

In 1966 a group of scientists and lawyers organized the Environmental Defense Fund in an effort to seek legal action against the use of DDT. After a prolonged struggle, they finally won a court ruling in 1972 ending nearly all uses of DDT in the United States. In that same year amendments to the Federal Insecticide, Fungicide, and Rodenticide Act gave the Environmental Protection Agency authority to develop a comprehensive program to regulate the use of pesticides. By 1978 many other chlorinated organic pesticides had been banned in the United States because of evidence linking them to health and environmental problems. Pesticide manufacturers switched to more biodegradable organophosphate and carbamate pesticides. However, the acute human toxicity of many of these chemicals has caused a rise in pesticide-related deaths and illnesses among agricultural field workers. Pesticide manufacture has also resulted in the poisoning of many workers and in serious environmental problems such as the contamination of Virginia's James River. The 1984 Bhopal disaster, which caused 3,500 deaths and 200,000 injuries, was due to the release of a chemical precursor being used by Union Carbide to manufacture a pesticide.

Since 1975 the sale and use of insecticides has leveled off, but use of herbicides (weed killers) has continued to increase worldwide. These plant poisons also pose environmental and human health threats. Five million acres of Vietnamese countryside were decimated by Agent Orange (a mixture of two potent herbicides), 12 million gallons of which were sprayed on that country by the U.S. Air Force during the Vietnam War. The dioxin contaminant in Agent Orange is a proven, potent carcinogen and an immune system poison —and the resulting exposure to this toxin of Vietnamese people and U.S. soldiers has resulted in claims that they have suffered from its effects.

The role of pesticides in world agriculture is hotly contested. Many high-yield varieties of grains have been developed that are dependent on the intensive use of both pesticides and fertilizers. Increased crop yields in developed countries have been accompanied by significant environmental degradation. The greatly increased cost of this type of farming has limited the value of this high-technology agriculture in solving local food problems in Third World countries, where the principal effect has often been to increase the fraction of acreage used to grow export crops.

In the following selections, Ronald Bailey contends that only by using chemically intensive agriculture will we be able to feed the world's growing population without decimating most of the remaining wilderness that nurtures the flora and fauna needed to maintain biodiversity. Katherine R. Smith argues that current agricultural practices, including the heavy reliance on pesticides and fertilizers, cause serious environmental pollution. Rather than trying to impose specific regulatory controls, which would be impractical, she proposes that agricultural subsidy programs be redesigned to provide solutions for agroenvironmental problems.

YES   Ronald Bailey

ONCE AND FUTURE FARMING

For those of us who wish to preserve the planet s diversity of species, high tech, chemically-assisted agriculture is an environmentalist's best friend.

That's right. Soaring growth in human population threatens to destroy most of the world's remaining rainforests, wetlands, and montane ecosystems drastically reducing species diversity. Despite advances in organic farming techniques, such as integrated pest management and fertilizing with "green" manures, overly relying on these practices will result in the plow down of forests to feed a population that is estimated to nearly double by 2050.

Environmentalists must face up to the fact that unless high-yield crop varieties, pesticides, and fertilizer are widely adopted in developing nations, the world's food supply will be outstripped by spiraling demand. Inadequate crop yields translate directly into more forests falling under the plow.

Many of the environmental community resist this conclusion. They tend to be very skeptical of high-tech, chemically-assisted farming.[1] Some pine for a smaller scale, more communitarian type of agricultural system. They dismiss modern agriculture as a form of "industrialization," or demonize it for its "chemicalization." Some activists badly assert that the "drive to industrialize agriculture and increase output has also led to major ecological disasters because of the artificial nature of all agricultural systems."[2]

Much of the environmental community's disenchantment with modern, high-intensity agriculture can be traced to Rachel Carson's 1962 book, *Silent Spring*. She was certainly right to warn of the dangers of excessive pesticide use. But ironically, the real threat to birds, mammals, and even insects comes not from modern farming methods and agricultural chemicals, but from what would happen if they were eliminated.

AS DEATH RATE SLOWS, POPULATION SOARS

The central ecological fact of our time is that the world's human population is going to increase substantially for at least another generation. No matter what urgent steps we take now, another 2 billion people—at minimum—will join us during the first part of the next century. The more likely scenario, according to United Nations' projections, is that the world's population will probably double in the next 50 years.

It is a popular misconception that skyrocketing birth rates are causing the increase in human population. That is simply not true. Such rapid growth is a result of a dramatic reduction in the death rate during the 20th century. Human life spans have increased dramatically, from a global average of 30 years in 1900 to more than 65 years by 1990.[3]

"Rapid population growth commenced not because human beings suddenly started breeding like rabbits, but rather because they finally stopped dying like flies," says Nick Eberstadt, a demographer at Harvard University.[4]

Despite all the hype that you heard from September's United Nations' Population Conference in Cairo about reducing population growth, the plain fact is that billions more people need to be fed. "Just to keep pace with population growth and rising incomes, the world will need to produce an extra 32 million tons of grain (principally rice, what, and corn) every year," predicts agronomist and Nobel Peace Laureate Norman Borlaug.[5]

The methods we employ for feeding such a vast population will make all the difference to the kind of world we will live in. Will humanity inhabit a planet still rich with millions of wild species, or will we need to farm countless acres of wildlife habitat to feed our vast numbers?

BOOSTING CROP YIELDS PRESERVES LAND

Biologists such as Harvard University's E. O. Wilson fear that thousands of irreplaceable plant and animal species may soon go extinct, as farmers redouble their efforts to sustain the world's expanding population. In his book *The Third Revolution: Environment, Population and a Sustainable World* (Penguin, 1992), Paul Harrison estimates that "loss of habitat to humans menaces two-thirds of threatened vertebrate species." But modern, high-yield farming, if not derailed by bad environmental and economic policies, will guarantee that this won't happen, say a growing number of agricultural researchers.[6]

By dramatically increasing the amount of food grown on land already under cultivation, humankind has already managed to save millions of square miles of natural landscapes from being plowed under. Higher yields were achieved by substituting more productive crop varieties, pesticides, and fertilizers for extra acreage.

Before the 20th century, the world increased its food supply chiefly by expanding the amount of land cleared and planted in crops. Yields of wheat, rice, and other staples were not much higher than in the Middle Ages. Only with the advent of science-based agriculture did crop productivity take off.[7] While world population has doubled over the past 40 years, agricultural productivity has tripled.[8] Much of that increased productivity resulted from the "Green Revolution" of the late 1960s and early 1970s. International teams of agricultural scientists led by Norman Borlaug developed highly productive dwarf varieties of staple grains such as wheat and rice. These fertilizer-responsive hybrids were adopted throughout the world, dramatically boosting crop yields and forestalling the massive famines forecast by famous population doomsters like Paul Ehrlich, who in 1968 predicted that during the

1970s, "due to famines—hundreds of millions of people are going to starve "

In fact, food is cheaper and more abundant than at any other time in modern history. Since 1980, according to the World Resources Institute, the global average price of food has plummeted by an astonishing 57%. And yet, worldwide, crops are grown on just slightly more land than in the 1960s—nearly 6 million square miles—an area equal to that of South America.[9]

Norman Borlaug recently told Congress that "by sustaining adequate levels of output on land already being farmed in environments suitable for agriculture, we restrain and even reverse the drive to open more fragile lands to cultivation."

U.S. Department of the Interior analyst Indur Goklany calculates that without the dramatic productivity increases that high-tech farming achieved since 1950, globally "an additional [910 million] hectares would have been converted from forest, wood, pasture, and grasslands—an amount equivalent to the net global loss of forest and wood lands between 1850 and 1980."[10] In other words, adopting chemical-based agriculture saved more than 3.5 million square miles of rainforests, wetlands, and mountain terrain from the farmer's plow.

Dennis Avery, who worked for many years on international food issues at the U.S. Department of Agriculture and who now heads the Hudson Institute's Center for Global Food Issues, thinks that Mr. Goklany's numbers for the amount of land spared through modern farming are too low. He figures roughly that tripling yields translates directly into preserving as much as 10 million square miles of wilderness from the plow—more than the total area of North America.

High-yield farming has already enjoyed marked success in India, reports agricultural researcher Paul Waggoner of the Connecticut Agriculture Experiment Station. In a paper titled "How Much Land Can 10 Billion People Spare for Nature?", Dr. Waggoner calculates that if India's wheat yields had remained at 1960s levels, local farmers would have been forced to clear an additional 42 million hectares (162,000 square miles) to grow the food they supply today.

"Environmentalists are guilty of bad ecological accounting," says Mr. Avery. "Today's typical environmentalist worries about how many spiders and pigweeds survive in an acre of monoculture corn without giving credit [to] the millions of organisms thriving on the two acres that didn't have to be plowed because we tripled crop yields."

PESTICIDES KEY TO HIGH-YIELD FARMING

Even if modern agriculture is responsible for saving millions of square miles of natural ecosystems, can yields increase enough to prevent future losses?

Lester Brown, head of the Worldwatch Institute, doesn't think so. Earlier this year, he declared in a Worldwatch press release that there is a "diminishing backlog of agricultural technology"; he further warned, in *State of the World 1994* (Norton), that there are "no new technologies that could lead to quantum leaps in world food output."

Dr. Brown's views are increasingly in the minority. The growing consensus among researchers is that scientific agriculture is nowhere near the limits for improving crop yields. And the biggest gains in yields will continue to come from breeding more productive, pest- and drought-resistant crop varieties.

Donald Plucknett, the recently retired senior scientific advisor of the Consultative Group on International Agricultural Research (CGIAR is the international network of agricultural research institutes which nurtured the Green Revolution), attributes 50% of the increase in today's yields to genetic improvements in modern cultivars.[11] For example, hybridization has already boosted top yields in corn by more than six-fold. The growing season for rice has been shortened from 180 to 110 days, allowing for double and triple cropping. And Dr. Plucknett believes farmers can increase rice productivity by 60% in the early 21st century.

Some of the credit for boosting yields must also go to pesticides and fertilizers. In 1962, Rachel Carson wrote in her classic *Silent Spring* that using pesticides was a "smooth superhighway" to disaster. She urged farmers to take "another road," free of "poisonous chemicals." In apocalyptic tones, she warned that turning away from pesticides was "our only chance to reach a destination that assures the preservation of the Earth."[12]

Ms. Carson argued that instead of relying on synthetic pesticides to control pests, we should develop and employ "biological solutions" (e.g., using pest predators and sterile males of insect pests, and applying organic pesticides). More than 30 years later, we now know that her hopes for biological pest controls were too optimistic. Many of the "solutions" she recommended are still little more than glimmers in the eyes of laboratory scientists. Those that are available for field application are relevant just for a few niche crops. In a very real sense, survival of the world's wildlands is due directly to continued use of the "poisonous chemicals" that Ms. Carson opposed.

High-yield agriculture, now and for the foreseeable future, will be impossible to sustain without herbicides, insecticides, and fungicides. Of course, we should reduce chemical residue and their adverse health effects on consumers and workers where practicable. But if pesticide use were significantly curtailed, crop yields here and abroad would fall dramatically. Which is worse for wildlife and biodiversity—millions of square miles of habitat cleared and planted in low-yield corn and wheat, or the relatively transient harm caused by pesticide residues?

Consider what's really at stake. A 1992 task force on pesticides for the Council for Agricultural Science and Technology estimated that "all crop production in the [world] would decline 30% and food costs would increase by 50% or more without the use of agricultural pesticides." Millions of acres of wildlife habitat would be destroyed to make up for the shortfall in crop production that would result from the total elimination of pesticides. This is not only true for farmers in the U.S. In the Philippines, "long-term trials on rice show that without pesticides, losses amount to more than 30% of the crop."[13] If yields were reduced to anywhere near these levels, clearly much more land would be converted to crop production to make up for the losses.[14]

Some environmentalists, hungering for a chemical-free utopia, point to "Integrated Pest Management" [IPM] or "organic" agricultural techniques. IPM can reduce pesticide use, but it is certainly not the royal road to completely chemical-free farming. IPM is very knowledge intensive, relying on a suite of nonchemical techniques to control pests. Such methods include, according to the World Resources Institute, "crop rotation, planting more than one crop, early or delayed planting to protect a crop during the most vulnerable stages of growth, manipulation of water and fertilizer, field sanitation (such as plowing under harvest stubble to remove pest hideaways), and the use of 'trap crops' to lure pests away from the main crop." IPM seeks to establish a threshold of "acceptable damage" to a crop, after which farmers will often need to resort to pesticides to protect their crops. "[IPM] is not a panacea, it is unlikely to eliminate the need for chemical pesticide use entirely," conclude International Food Policy Research Institute analysts Peter Oram and Behjat Hojjati

Researchers have made advances in developing more environmentally benign pesticides such as glyphosate and the sulfanylureas, which are replacing longlasting organochlorides. Leonard Gianessi, a senior research associate at the National Center for Food and Agricultural Policy, points out that "many new herbicides are used at rates as low as 0.02 pounds per acre in comparison to 2 pounds per acre for older herbicides "[15] He adds that for many modern pesticides, the "active ingredients are present in amounts so small that their presence in the environment cannot be measured "

Some environmentalists herald new biological pesticides as a way to avoid synthetics. The problem is that many are very specifically targeted. This sounds good, but farmers often need wide-spectrum herbicides to control the huge variety of weeds they find in their fields at any one time. Dr. Gianessi predicts that for the foreseeable future, wide-spectrum pesticides of all types will be necessary to keep crop yields high

The choice that environmentalists face is between saving the world's biodiversity by forestalling the plow-down of wildlife habitat through the continued use of farm chemicals, or protecting themselves from the minuscule health risks posed by pesticides And the health risks *are* minuscule

University of California at Berkeley biochemist Bruce Ames calculates that "about 99.99% of all pesticides in the human diet are natural pesticides from plants. All plants produce toxins to protect themselves against fungi, insects, and animal predators such as humans."[16] Plants are packed with potent natural rodent carcinogens such as caffeic acid in lettuce and hydrazines in mushrooms Dr Ames estimates the average person ingests daily about 1,500 milligrams of natural pesticides and just 0.09 milligrams of synthetic pesticide residues. Of the pesticides we consume, just one-ten thousandth are synthetic

Dr. Ames, who developed the chief method used by laboratories worldwide for detecting carcinogens, estimates that far less than 1% of all human cancers are due to exposure to synthetic chemicals (including pesticides) or pollution. Toxicologist Robert Scheuplein of the Food and Drug Administration's Center for Food Safety agrees "Ordinary food contains an abundance of cancer initiators which in total dwarf all of the synthetic sources," writes Dr. Scheuplein in an essay for *Global Food Progress* 1991 (Hudson Institute). "The total risk from all pesticides and contaminants is a thousand times less than the estimates of cancer risk due to naturally occurring carcinogens

CAN FARMING WITH CHEMICALS SAVE WILDLIFE?

The greatest threat to biodiversity remains the burgeoning populations in developing nations, particularly in the tropics, where many farmers continue to practice low-input, low-yield agriculture. Dr. Borlaug noted the unsustainability of "low-input" farming in recent testimony before the Agriculture Committee of the House of Representatives. He told Congress that "slash and burn agriculture [is] a practice that presently causes the annual loss of more than 25 million acres of tropical rainforest. As an aside, it is worth mentioning that slash and burn techniques supported agriculture in traditional societies for millennia. It was not until population pressures accelerated the demands on this system that it became unsustainable."

Interior Department analyst Indur Goklany also criticizes low-input farming: "One consequence of low-input sustainable agriculture (LISA) is that more land would be devoted to crops than would be otherwise. This extra land used for agriculture will mean that much less is available to other species. What we need is not LISA, but HOSA—high-output sustainable agriculture."

Can the agricultural productivity of developing nations be raised in time to save the world's biodiversity? Yes, according to a recent report by Donald Plucknett, the former chief scientist of the authoritative Consultative Group on International Agricultural Research. He concludes that worldwide harvests could be boosted by 50%, just by making existing improved crop varieties and agricultural know-how more widely available. For instance, corn yields in West Africa currently are a meager eight-tenths of a ton per hectare. By switching to hybrid seeds and using fertilizer, African farmers could boost production nine-fold, to seven tons per hectare. The Hudson Institute's Dennis Avery estimates that for every hectare converted to high-yield farming, as many as eight hectares could be allowed to return to their natural state.

Dr. Plucknett argues that until farmers in developing countries adopt high-yield techniques, they "tend to move more and more onto marginal lands to meet food and production needs, destroying natural ecosystems in the process." Once yields per hectare begin to increase, expansion of the agricultural frontier onto marginal lands slows dramatically. Thus, high-yield farming is "land-saving agriculture" and is very "environmentally friendly," says Dr. Plucknett.

Ironically, many environmentalists refuse to believe the good news. In *State of the World 1994*, Lester Brown warns that world grain production per capita peaked in the 1980s, and that the "bottom line is the world's farmers can no longer be counted on to feed the projected additions to our numbers."

It is true that world grain production has slowed, but that's because the U.S. and Europe, which are drowning in surpluses, are paying their farmers to cut production. "More is not produced because it is not needed," writes Nikos Alexandratos of the Food and Agriculture Organization of the United Nations, in a paper titled "The Outlook for World Food and Agriculture to the Year 2010."

Throughout the 1980s, grain production in developing nations rose at the spectacular rate of 5% per year, easily outpacing the Third World's population growth of 1.9% annually, according to the Hudson Institute. In the 1980s, China's agricultural output soared by an unprecedented 50%, while Indonesia increased its rice productivity by more than one-third. Looking to the future, Dr. Alexandratos predicts that once "satisfactory" levels of per capita food consumption have been achieved, extraordinary gains in productivity will no longer be necessary. More cautious than many analysts, Dr. Alexandratos expects that world food production could slow to a 1.8% increase per year—but adds that "it will continue to outpace a 1.5% growth rate in world population."

To show clearly how chemical-based agriculture slows land clearing, Douglas Southgate, an associate professor of agricultural economics at Ohio State University, contrasts the experiences of Chile and Ecuador. Ecuadorian farmers have not increased their yields and are clearing land at a blindingly fast pace—crop and pasture land is increasing 2% annually, the second highest rate in Latin America. Meanwhile, Chile has invested in high-tech agriculture, including higher applications of pesticides and fertilizers and increased irrigation. Consequently, Chile's agricultural frontier has hardly expanded at all—land cleared for crops has increased by just 0.1% annually.

"My statistical analysis pretty clearly shows that countries that boosted their agricultural yields are the same countries where land clearing is very, very slow," says Dr. Southgate. "By contrast, countries where yields are flat are the same countries that are losing tropical forests and other natural ecosystems at a rapid rate."

Abundant evidence suggests that environmentalists who want to preserve the world's diminishing biodiversity must become advocates of modern, high-yield agriculture Those who refuse should attempt to honestly answer Dennis Avery's pointed question: "How many millions of square miles of wildlife habitat are [you] willing to give up in order to have chemical-free farming?" He adds, "This is a strange way to save wildlife." Indeed it is

NOTES

1. See Carson, Rachel, *Silent Spring*, (Houghton Mifflin, 1962); Goering, Peter et al., *From the Ground Up: Rethinking Industrial Agriculture*, (Zed Books, 1993); Bender, Jim, *Future Harvest: Pesticide Free Farming*, (University of Nebraska Press, 1994); and Conford, Philip, ed., *A Future for the Land: Organic Practice From a Global Perspective*, (Green Books, 1992).

2. Conford, 1992, p. x.

3. Eberstadt, Nicholas, "Population, Food and Income: Global Trends in the Twentieth Century," July, 1994, manuscript, p. 25.

4. Eberstadt, p. 26.

5. Borlaug, Norman. Testimony of the Former General Director of the International Maize and Wheat Improvement Center before the House Agriculture Committee. Subcommittee on Foreign Agriculture and Hunger. March 1, 1994. Federal Document Clearinghouse, Inc.

6. See Waggoner, Paul, "How Much Land Can Ten Billion People Spare for Nature?", Task Force Report No. 121, Council for Agricultural Science and Technology & The Rockefeller University (February, 1994); Plucknett, Donald, Senior Scientific Advisor, Consultative Group on International Agricultural Research, Paper: "Prospects of Meeting Future Food Needs Through New Technology," prepared for the Roundtable on Population and Food in the Early 21st Century (February 14–16, 1994, Washington, D.C.); Oram, Peter & Behjat Hojjati, Paper: "The Growth Potential of Existing Agricultural Technology," prepared for the Roundtable on Population and Food in the Early 21st Century (February 14–16, 1994, Washington, D.C.); Goklany, Indur & Merritt Sprague, "An Alternative Approach to Sustainable Development: Conserving Forests, Habitat, and Biological Diversity by Increasing the Efficiency and Productivity of Land Utilization," Office of Program Analysis, U.S. Department of the Interior (Washington, D.C., April 4, 1994); Avery, Dennis, Director of the Center for Global Food Issues at the Hudson Institute, *Biodiversity: Saving Species with Biotechnology* (Hudson Institute, 1993); Avery, Dennis, "Saving the Planet with Pesticides and Plastics," unpublished manuscript, 1994

7. Waggoner, Paul, 1994, pp. 24–30; Plucknett, Donald, 1994, pp. 7–18.

8. U.N. Long-Range World Population Projections, p. 14; *World Resources 1994–1995*, (Oxford University Press, 1994), pp. 27–42, 107–28, 262. Lester Brown et al. *State of the World 1994*, (Norton, 1994), p. 182; Avery, Dennis, *Biodiversity: Saving Species with Biotechnology*, p. 36.

9. Goklany, Indur. Paper 'Is It Premature to Take Measures to Adapt to the Impacts of Climate Change on Natural Resources?" Office of Policy Analysis, U.S. Department of Interior, 1994, Table 1, p. 3; Avery, interview, October 1993.

10. Goklany, 1994, p. 2.

11. Plucknett, Donald. "Science and Agricultural Tansformation," International Food Policy Research Institute Lecture No. 1, September, 1993.

12. Carson, 1962, p. 244.

13. Oram et al., 1994, p. 34.

14. Pickett, John. Chemistry and Industry, Safer Insecticides: Development and Use." January 6 1992, p. 25.

15. Gianessi, Leonard. 'The Quixotic Quest for Chemical-Free Farming," *Issues In Science and Technology*, Fall 1993, p. 32.

16. Ames, Bruce and Lois Gold. "Environmental Pollution and Cancer: Some Misconceptions," In *Phantom Risk: Scientific Inference and the Law*, edited by Foster et al. (MIT Press, 1993), p. 153; see also Gold, Lois et al., *Science*, "Rodent Carcingens' Setting Priorities," (October 9, 1992), p. 261; see also, Ames, Bruce et al., Proceedings of the National Academy of Science (Vol. 87 1990), pp. 7772–7776

NO

Katherine R. Smith

TIME TO "GREEN" U.S. FARM POLICY

During the past decade, taxpayers have footed the bill for farm-subsidy programs to the tune of close to $15 billion per year, and they have little to show for it. Farm subsidies are no longer needed to guarantee the nation's food security. They do provide essential income support for some farmers; nonetheless, two-thirds of the payments go to relatively wealthy farmers. If the U.S. public is going to continue to support the income of the nation's farmers, taxpayers ought to be able to expect some kind of return on their investment.

Indeed, there is really only one valid justification for continuing high levels of farm subsidies: as a tool for dealing with the serious and varied environmental problems caused by agriculture, including water pollution, soil degradation, the loss of biodiversity, and the destruction of wildlife habitat. The current agricultural commodity programs, however, perversely discourage farmers from adopting environmentally sound practices. And supplemental conservation and environmental programs have largely been ineffective in dealing with the problems.

This year's congressional debate on renewing farm programs provides an important opportunity to improve these programs and possibly go beyond them, ideally to a system in which farm subsidies are replaced by "green payments"—income incentives to farmers to encourage them to operate in an environmentally sound manner. "Greening" the farm bill could help to secure farmers' livelihoods, prevent the degradation or depletion of natural resources, and stabilize, if no cut, the cost of farm programs.

ENVIRONMENTAL EFFECTS

As industrial and municipal sources of pollution have come under more stringent regulatory control, agriculture has emerged as one of the most intransigent contributors to environmental damage. One of the highest agroenvironmental priorities is water quality. According to the Environmental Protection Agency (EPA), agriculture is now the leading source of surface water pollution. Unlike industrial pollution, which enters the water at specific points,

From Katherine R. Smith, "Time to 'Green' U.S. Farm Policy," *Issues in Science and Technology* (Spring 1995), pp. 71–78. Copyright © 1995 by The University of Texas at Dallas, Richardson, TX. Reprinted by permission.

agricultural pollution usually occurs when sediments, salts, chemicals, and excess nutrients, such as nitrogen and phosphorus, drain into lakes and rivers from agricultural lands. Although many lakes and rivers suffering from point-source pollution have been cleaned up as a result of federal regulations, many of those affected by nonpoint agricultural pollution have not.

Nutrient and pesticide runoff can cause serious environmental problems. When excess nutrients enter lakes and rivers, they can cause algae populations to multiply, depleting oxygen in the water and killing many species of fish. Pesticides can be toxic to plant and fish life as well. These materials can threaten the viability of environmentally essential ecosystems, including estuaries such as the Chesapeake Bay, which host a wide variety of species, protect inland areas from flooding, and filter sediments and pollutants before they enter marine waters. They also severely damage commercial fishing in these areas. For example, oyster populations in the Chesapeake Bay have declined 96 percent during the past century as a result of the influx of excess nutrients.

Nutrient runoff is common throughout the entire southeastern coastal plain. It is also concentrated along the Michigan peninsula, in central Wisconsin and Minnesota, in the claypan soils of eastern Texas, and on the tablelands of central Nebraska. In some areas of the western United States, surface waters have become toxic to a range of plant and animal life due to the high concentration of salts and heavy metals drained off from irrigated cropland.

Sediment washed off farmland silts up waterways, canals, water-storage facilities, and drainage ditches, requiring $3 billion to $5 billion in dredging and cleanup costs every year and damaging fish and wildlife populations. This problem is concentrated along the Appalachian regions southward from Pennsylvania, in the Corn Belt states, along the Missouri and Mississippi Rivers, and in southern Wisconsin and western Illinois.

Groundwater, an important source of drinking water, is also contaminated by agricultural activity. In its 1988–1990 national well-water survey, EPA found nitrates in more than half of the wells it sampled; it detected residues of at least one pesticide in 10 percent of the nation's community water-system wells. The potential for pesticide and nitrate leaching is highest in the Southern coastal plain, along the Mississippi Valley, in central Nebraska, and in California's Central Valley. Although it is uncertain whether current concentrations pose a significant public health problem, pesticides and nitrates continue to accumulate in otherwise undisturbed aquifers and may pose a more serious threat in the future.

Another area of special concern is the effect of agricultural practices on soil quality. A 1993 National Research Council report indicated that soil compaction, salinization, loss of organic matter, and declining biological activity may be affecting the productivity of large areas of farmland. This decrease in productivity may force farmers to apply greater amounts of fertilizer; at the same time, declining biological activity in the soil may make fertilizer less and less effective. Eventually, crop yields could dwindle.

Finally, agricultural expansion has aggravated the destruction of wetlands, which are among the most productive ecosystems in the world. In the Great Plains prairie pothole regions, for instance, seasonal wetlands provide important wildlife habitat and also help to regulate the supply and flow of water. Historically, farming has been the major cause of wetlands conversion. It accounted for 87 percent of all losses between the mid-1950s and the mid-1970s. In recent decades, other factors, such as urban growth and industrial development, have begun to contribute to this problem as well. Although various regulations and incentive programs have substantially slowed wetlands losses, agriculture continues to pose a threat to wetlands.

WHY NOT REGULATE?

Compared to sectors such as mining, manufacturing, construction, and energy, agriculture is subject to little federal environmental regulation. Existing regulations focus largely on the use of pesticides; even the Clean Water Act contains no provisions regulating farm activities. The question arises, then, why not address agriculture's environmental consequences with standard environmental regulations?

Besides the obvious constraint posed by the antiregulatory mood of the 104th Congress, there are several reasons for avoiding regulation. First, there is more uncertainty about identifying nonpoint sources of pollution than there is about readily observable point sources. For example, if leaching and runoff from multiple lands are contributing to the degradation of a single watershed, it is very difficult to trace pollutants back to each source or to determine which farmers in the area are contributing to the problem.

On the other hand, it is equally useless to develop technology-based regulations that specify uniform environmental practices. Farming practices vary tremendously with climate, soil quality, type of crop, and specific characteristics of the landscape. As a result, effective management strategies for both commodity production and pollution prevention are highly site-specific. A regulatory approach is simply impractical.

In addition, it is difficult to regulate decisions involving the use of private rather than public resources. In other industries, environmental concerns focus on the private use of public goods, such as air and water, for discharge of wastes. But agricultural regulations intended to protect resources such as soil, wetlands, wildlife habitat, or biodiversity raise complicated property rights issues because they involve farmers' right to use the land they own; restricting those uses might diminish the market value of the land, imposing a special burden on the farmer.

Finally, regulation could place severe strains on small farms and family farms, which are regarded with special reverence in this country. Opinion polls conducted during the past 10 years show that Americans strongly favor government support of small and family farmers. Although the biggest farms—those generating annual sales of more than $100,000 a year—receive the bulk of farm subsidies, a recent report by the U.S. Department of Agriculture's (USDA) Economic Research Service shows that the smaller farms are more heavily dependent on government assistance. These smaller farmers are less likely than their larger counterparts to be able to invest in the types of environmental technologies that standards-based regulation might require. So far, the public and EPA have been reluctant to enact environmental regulations that would impose major costs of farmers or to replace subsidies with regulations.

Given the difficulties in regulating agricultural pollution and the special place of small and family farms in American life, national farm policy is the logical vehicle for federal agroenvironmental protection. Through farm policy, the public interest in maintaining a stable, reasonable priced food supply and a healthy farm economy can be reconciled with the goals of conserving resources and improving environmental quality—goals that might otherwise conflict.

ENVIRONMENTAL DISINCENTIVES

Unfortunately, the farm bill, the nation's quintennially revisited omnibus legislation for food and agricultural matters, has so far done a poor job of balancing food, farm, and environmental priorities. For one thing, its outdated commodity program provisions continue to discourage farmers from adopting environmentally sustainable practices.

The commodity programs are intended to ensure an adequate supply of domestically produced food while stabilizing the prices of specific commodities, including corn, sorghum, wheat, small grains, cotton, and rice. Without income supports, farm prices and farmers' incomes would crash in times of surplus, potentially driving farmers out of business, reducing the domestic food supply in following years, and boosting prices.

Farmers who participate in commodity programs receive a guaranteed price for their crops. If the market price falls below the price guaranteed by the government, the government makes up the difference in a subsidy called a deficiency payment. The price guarantee applies only to a government-set proportion of the producer's "base" acres, the land on which the supported commodity is grown In

exchange for this subsidy, participating farmers must agree to set aside a portion of their base acres and keep them out of production in years when oversupply is likely to drive market prices down. Although only one-third of the nation's farmers participate in commodity programs, the programs cover the majority of U.S. cropland and affect the management of most of the acreage devoted to each of the subsidized crops.

Commodity programs affect the environmental performance of agriculture in several ways. First, they give participants an incentive to maximize their base acreage, because the number of base acres is directly related to the income provided by deficiency payments. As a result, farmers grow the covered crop on as many acres as possible, year after year (If the land is planted with a different crop, it is subtracted from the farmer's base acreage.) This creates ecological instability: Pests that feed on that particular crop multiply while soil nutrients are de pleted. Instead of rotating crops to keep pest populations under control and restore nutrients to the soil, farmers rely more heavily on chemical fertilizers and pesticides.

Many farmers manage pesticide and nutrient use to minimize environmental damage. But there are regions where farmers could substantially reduce pesticide and fertilizer requirements simply by using highly diversified crop rotations. A study by Washington State University researchers Walter Goldstein and Douglas Young of the Palouse region of Washington state found that wheat farmers could maintain their profitability and cut chemical inputs in half by rotating wheat with other crops. The study also showed, however, that farmers enrolled in the commodity program would earn greater profits by planting wheat continuously and applying pesticides and fertilizers at conventional rates. As a result, it concluded, the subsidies discourage farmers from making economically viable, ecologically beneficial choices.

A second problem with the commodity program is that it gives participants an incentive to farm their land intensively. Because farmers are periodically required to set aside a fixed proportion of their acreage from production, they try to make up for it by increasing their harvest from the remaining land. In addition, enrolling land in the program increases its value because crops grown on it can earn a guaranteed price. Naturally, farmers try to maximize the return on these expensive acres by enhancing their productivity. As a result, they are likely to apply larger amounts of chemicals or to uproot trees or hedgerows that shelter birds or animals that prey on crop pests. In the absence of commodity programs, farmers could use less-intensive land-management systems that profitably maintain soil quality and reduce dependence on chemicals.

CONGRESSIONAL ACTIONS

Recognizing agriculture's role in environmental quality, Congress added a number of conservation and environmental provisions to the 1985 and 1990 farm bills. By 1994, USDA administered 19 separate, farm bill-authorized federal land-use, conservation, and environmental-incentive programs at an annual cost of $3.5 billion. But these provisions fail to provide an adequate framework for offsetting the environmental disincentives entailed in the commodity programs.

Most of these provisions call for purely voluntary programs in which farmers are given education, technical assistance, and/or financial assistance to adopt environmentally sound land-management practices. The largest of these is the Conservation Reserve Program (CRP), which costs $1.8 billion per year. The CRP was established in 1985 to reduce erosion and improve water quality while controlling the supply of certain commodities. Under the original program, owners or operators of highly eroding cropland could opt to take the land out of production over a 10-year contract period and plant it with grasses or trees. In exchange, they would receive annual rental payments from the government. Later, the program was expanded to include lands whose cultivation poses a threat to water quality—for instance, those that lie along the banks of lakes or rivers or that leach directly into groundwater through sandy soil.

A total of 36 million acres of cropland, most of it qualifying on the basis of its erodibility, is now enrolled in the CRP. The program has reaped tremendous benefits in terms of reducing soil erosion (by and estimated 700 million tons per year) and, incidentally, providing wildlife habitat. For example, ring-necked pheasant populations have more than doubled in several states, duck populations have dramatically increased, and declines in a range of grassland wildlife species have been reversed. But a land-retirement program is a very expensive way to achieve these benefits; in most cases, farmers could probably have achieved adequate results simply by adopting better land-use practices while continuing to farm. The number of acres that need to be retired in order to protect adjoining surface waters or provide wildlife habitat is much smaller (estimated at 8 million to 10 million acres) and more geographically concentrated than the number currently enrolled in the CRP.

In 1996, the program's initial 10-year contracts will begin to expire. Whether and in what form they will be extended are major farm policy issues. If the CRP is not reauthorized in 1995, agricultural analysts estimate that 20 million acres of reserved land will go back into production by the year 2000. There is no guarantee that these will be the acres that are responsive to environmentally sensitive management....

OPTIONS FOR REFORM

There are three general approaches to greening the 1995 farm bill without increasing the burden on taxpayers. One is to reform the commodity program and other traditional provisions of farm policy; the second is to improve the efficiency and effectiveness of current conservation and environmental provisions of farm policy. The third option is to merge farm support and environmental protection provisions into a single, multiple-objective farm policy that would give farmers income incentives (so-called green payments) to operate in an environmentally sound manner.

One particularly promising option for commodity program reform is to give participants greater flexibility in choosing which crops to grow. At present, farmers can use up to 25 percent of their base acreage to grow crops other than the supported commodity. However, they receive no deficiency payments for the alternative crops. A new study from the World Resources Institute concludes that if technical information on profitable, sustainable agriculture systems were accessible to farmers, simply increasing the proportion of "flex

acres" to 50 percent could encourage farmers to diversify their crops, achieving significant soil quality, water quality, and energy efficiency gains as well as reductions in greenhouse gas emissions. Aggregate farm income would remain about the same, while the cost of the farm program would be cut in half, according to the study.

However, it is not clear whether farmers would be willing to risk the potential loss of income entailed in growing non-supported crops on their base acreage. Moreover, farmers have more flexibility in some regions than in others: In the Great Plains, for instance, few crops can be grown as profitably as wheat.

Another option for greening farm policy in the context of existing commodity programs is to use environmental criteria to designate set-aside acreage. At present, each farmer sets aside the same percentage of his or her base acreage. But some farmers have better land than others; as a result, some farmers must set aside land that is highly productive and poses no unusual environmental threat, whereas others continue to farm more fragile land. Under an environmentally based set-aside program, USDA officials could pool the base acreage in a given region and designate specific sites as potential set-aside land. Although the same number of acres would be set aside in any given year, different farmers might set aside different proportions of their lands. Those with a higher proportion of set-aside acreage could be compensated by receiving a higher guaranteed price and therefore higher deficiency payments than those who could continue to farm most or all of their land.

A market-based alternative would be to allow commodity program participants to trade the right to set aside acreage. If the market worked properly, farmers with the most productive land would buy the right to cultivate more base acres from participants whose land is less productive. Both would be better off. To the extent that marginally productive land is also more environmentally sensitive (and we know the correlation is not perfect), the market-based solution should reallocate commodity program production and reduce potential environmental damage.

A more direct and efficient approach to enhancing agroenvironmental quality is to make existing agricultural conservation and environmental programs more effective. For instance, Congress could consolidate the funding for the 19 separate environmental programs included in the farm bill and create a smaller number of programs targeted at one of more high-priority problems. One example would be water quality, perhaps the most serious environmental problem associated with modern agriculture. If water quality were designated as the number one priority, the federal government could purchase easements to retire permanently the 3 million to 5 million acres whose cultivation poses a direct threat to surface or groundwater resources. At the same time, the government could create financial incentives for farmers to adopt better management strategies on cultivated or grazed land so as to reduce threats to water quality. The total cost —$300 million per year to $500 million over 10 years for the easement program (easements cost about $1,000 per acre) and another $1.5 billion to $2 billion per year in incentives —would save $1 billion to $1.7 billion per year—while achieving concentrated rather than diffuse results.

This strategy would succeed only if it focused on a single environmental priority rather than using the shotgun approach characteristic of the current provisions. Moreover, because specific high-priority problems are more likely to be concentrated geographically, the distribution of incentives would not cover as many different farmers as are eligible for incentive programs today. Finally, without concurrent change in commodity programs, the effectiveness of even a consolidated, carefully targeted set of agricultural resource and environmen tal programs will be limited by the counterincentives posed by commodity programs.

GREEN PAYMENTS

Green payment programs, by contrast, would combine the goals of protecting farm income and environmental quality. Unlike existing incentive programs, green payments would provide a new basis for farm income support. A De cember 1994 poll by Peter D. Hart Associates indicated broad public support for green payments: 64 percent of the respondents agreed with the statement that "the government should use existing financial subsidies to reward those farmers who take steps to keep chemical pesticides from polluting food and water because these chemicals can be harmful to people, especially children."

Green payments could exist alongside existing commodity subsidies or be coupled with these subsidies to marginally redirect farm income support away from exclusive dependence on commodity supply and price control, or they could even replace commodity programs altogether. Interested parties are discussing options that fit into each of these categories as part of the upcoming farm bill debate

One particularly complex aspect of designing a green payment program is balancing the goal of supporting the income of some specified group of farmers, such as small and family farmers, and that of addressing one or more environmental problems. Because the geographic distribution of agroenvironmental problems does not perfectly match the current distribution of government payments for income support, particularly among farmers dependent on government subsidies, no green payments program can be expected to simultaneously retain current income support patterns and optimize environmental results.

But the beauty of green payment schemes is that they can be targeted. For instance, a green payment scheme could be specially designed to help small and family farms address one or more high-priority agroenvironmental problems, such as water pollution or habitat destruction....

Regardless of the approach taken to reform federal commodity and/or conservation and environment programs, an important supplement to a truly green farm bill would be some greening of the farm bill-authorized research and education programs that fund the discovery, development, and extension of new agricultural technologies. Legislators should earmark an expanded portion of the $2.5 billion per year currently devoted to agricultural research and education efforts and target it to fundamental agroecological research, development, testing, and broad extension of knowledge on environmentally sustainable farm practices and systems, as well as to the development of new cost-effective technologies for farm-level resource conservation and environmental protection. This essential investment in U.S. agroenvironmental quality should be recouped through reduced environmental and agricultural costs in future years

A WIN-WIN SOLUTION

... Rather than simply eliminating current farm programs, Congress should design new programs that can deliver valued public goods. Because environmental protection and support for small and family farmers are among the goods that the American public expects the federal government to provide, a change in the basis of farm income support, from market-distorting commodity price supports to stewardship incentives achieved through green payments, makes a great deal of sense. It can also be done at a lower and more stable cost than current programs.

In addition, Congress should give USDA more flexibility in carrying out conservation and environmental programs by abolishing the patchwork of current programs and consolidating their funding. USDA must then bite the bullet and set specific agroenvironmental priorities, targeting remaining funds to their resolution.

Farmers and the U.S. public will be better off with a green farm bill than with no farm programs or with the continuation of current farm programs. Making the change may not be easy and some current program participants are sure to lose out. Nonetheless, this solution is likely to be far less onerous than either coping with the high costs of agricultural source pollution or watching farmers struggle to meet the environmental regulations which, ultimately, states, localities, and eventually the federal government will put in place to prevent further degradation.

POSTSCRIPT

Does Feeding People and Preserving Wildlands Require Chemical-Based Agriculture?

Bailey asserts that his perspective on how to feed the world's people while preserving biodiversity is supported by a growing consensus of agricultural experts. In fact, it is primarily those researchers and analysts affiliated with the agricultural establishment in the United States and other developed nations who continue to advocate chemically intensive agriculture. Many independent agronomists and entomologists would agree with Smith that the practices Bailey advocates result in extensive environmental pollution and are not sustainable. In *Food First* (Houghton Mifflin, 1977), Frances Moore Lappe and Joseph Collins popularized the results of their research on the effects of the use of pesticide- and fertilizer-intensive agriculture in the developing world. They found, contrary to Bailey's claims, that pesticide use exacerbated local food shortages due to the shift to producing export crops while often poisoning poor agricultural laborers.

A report frequently quoted by pesticide advocates is "Benefits and Costs of Pesticide Use in U.S. Food Production," by David Pimentel et al., *Bioscience* (December 1978). The conclusion reached by noted agricultural scientists Pimentel and his coworkers is that ending all U.S. pesticide use—a more extreme restriction than that advocated by integrated pest management (IPM) proponents—would cause an immediate increased annual crop loss worth $8.7 billion, whereas the cost of chemical controls is $2.2 billion. Those who cite these conclusions usually fail to mention that the authors admit they have not included the ecological and social costs of pesticide use and that much of the crop loss may be eliminated once pest predators reestablish a natural balance.

Another problem concerning pesticides that have been banned in wealthier countries, which tend to have stricter environmental and health regulations, results when these chemicals contaminate food that is imported into these wealthier nations from developing countries in which there are few restrictions on agricultural toxins. For details about this widespread practice, see *Circle of Poisons* by D. Weir and M. Shapiro (Institute for Food and Development Policy, 1981).

The means by which farmers get trapped into the environmentally damaging reliance on chemical poisons is frequently referred to as "the pesticide treadmill." For a detailed explanation of this problem, see Michael Dover's article in the November/December 1985 issue of *Technology Review*. Omar Sattaur's article in the July 14, 1988, issue of *New Scientist* describes the successful use of IPM strategies in Third World countries. A much less optimistic assessment of the potential of IPM programs is contained in Leonard Gianessi's article in the Fall 1993 issue of *Issues in Science and Technology*.

Bailey implies that the new generation of insecticides and herbicides are relatively safe. This view is refuted by Ted Williams in his article in the March/April 1993 issue of *Audubon*. In the September/October 1993 issue of the same magazine, John Grossman discusses another growing concern about pesticides and herbicides: the pollution caused by their highly intensive use on golf courses throughout the world.

Several biotechnology companies are using genetic engineering techniques to produce herbicide-resistant crops. The fear that this practice may be a threat to sustainable agriculture is the subject of *Biotechnology's Bitter Harvest*, a research report available from the Environmental Defense Fund. This issue is discussed by Roger Wrubel in the May/June 1994 issue of *Technology Review*.

For two articles that focus on the need to develop sustainable agricultural practices that will allow developing countries to increase food production while also protecting the environment, see Donald L. Plucknett and Donald L. Winkelmann, "Technology for Sustainable Agriculture," *Scientific American* (September 1995) and Mark W. Rosegrant and Robert Livernash, "Growing More Food, Doing Less Damage," *Environment* (September 1996).

For an Internet site related to this issue, see http://www.bcca.org/services/lists/noble-creation/wsaa.html, which contains the goals and activities of the World Sustainable Agriculture Association.

PART 3

Disposing of Wastes

Modern industrial societies generate many types of waste. Manufacturing and construction activities yield hazardous liquid and solid residues; treatment of raw sewage produces sludge; mining operations generate mountains of tailings; radioactive waste results from the use of nuclear isotopes in medicine and in the nuclear power and nuclear weapons industries. Each of these forms of waste, as well as ordinary household garbage, contains toxins and pathogens that are potentially serious sources of air and water pollution if they are not disposed of properly. We must now deal with the legacy of waste contamination problems that have resulted from years of neglect and inappropriate waste disposal methods. This section exposes some of the major controversies concerning proposed solutions to three important waste categories.

- Hazardous Waste: Should the "Polluter Pays" Provision of Superfund Be Weakened?

- Municipal Waste: Should Recycling Efforts Be Expanded?

- Nuclear Waste: Should Plans for Underground Storage Be Put on Hold?

ISSUE 12

Hazardous Waste: Should the "Polluter Pays" Provision of Superfund Be Weakened?

YES: Bernard J. Reilly, from "Stop Superfund Waste," *Issues in Science and Technology* (Spring 1993)

NO: Ted Williams, from "The Sabotage of Superfund," *Audubon* (July/August 1993)

ISSUE SUMMARY

YES: DuPont corporate counsel Bernard J. Reilly argues that in both defining standards and assigning costs related to waste cleanup, "Congress should focus the program on reducing real risk, not on seeking unattainable purity."

NO: *Audubon* contributing editor Ted Williams claims that insurers and polluters are lobbying to change the financial liability provisions of Superfund, and he warns against turning it into a public welfare program.

The potentially disastrous consequences of improper hazardous waste disposal burst upon the consciousness of the American public in the late 1970s. The problem was dramatized by the evacuation of dozens of residents of Niagara Falls, New York, whose health was being threatened by chemicals leaking from the abandoned Love Canal, which was used for many years as an industrial waste dump. Awakened to the dangers posed by chemical dumping, numerous communities bordering on industrial manufacturing areas across the country began to discover and report local sites where chemicals had been disposed of in open lagoons or were leaking from disintegrating steel drums. Such esoteric chemical names as dioxins and PCBs have become part of the common lexicon, and numerous local citizens' groups have been mobilized to prevent human exposure to these and other toxins.

The expansion of the industrial use of synthetic chemicals following World War II resulted in the need to dispose of vast quantities of wastes laden with organic and inorganic chemical toxins. For the most part, industry adopted a casual attitude toward this problem and, in the absence of regulatory restraint, chose the least expensive means available. Little attention was paid to the ultimate fate of chemicals that could seep into surface water or groundwater. Scientists have estimated that less than 10 percent of the waste was disposed of in an environmentally sound manner.

The magnitude of the problem is truly mind-boggling: Over 275 million tons of hazardous waste is produced in the United States each year; as many as 10,000 dump sites may pose a serious threat to public health, according to the federal Office of Technology Assessment; and other government estimates indicate that more than 350,000 waste sites may ultimately require corrective action at a cost that could easily exceed $500 billion.

Congressional response to the hazardous waste threat is embodied in two complex legislative initiatives. The Resource Conservation and Recovery Act (RCRA) of 1976 mandated action by the Environmental Protection Agency (EPA) to create "cradle to grave" oversight of newly generated waste, and the Comprehensive Environmental Response, Compensation, and Liability Act, commonly called "Superfund," gave the EPA broad authority to clean up existing hazardous waste sites. The implementation of this legislation has been severely criticized by environmental organizations, citizens' groups, and members of Congress who have accused the EPA of foot-dragging and a variety of politically motivated improprieties. Less than 20 percent of the original $1.6 billion Superfund allocation was actually spent on waste cleanup.

Amendments designed to close RCRA loopholes were enacted in 1984, and the Superfund Amendments and Reauthorization Act (SARA) added $8.6 billion to a strengthened cleanup effort in 1986 and an additional $5.1 billion in 1990. While acknowledging some improvement, both environmental and industrial policy analysts remain very critical about the way that both RCRA and Superfund/SARA are being implemented. Once again both of these hazardous waste laws are up for reauthorization, and proposals for major changes are stimulating heated debate.

In the following selections, Bernard J. Reilly, who manages the legal aspects of DuPont's Superfund program, argues that the legislation has turned into an "unjustifiable waste of the nation's resources at the expense of other critical society needs." He calls for major changes, which would "focus the program on practical risk reduction." One specific change he advocates is in the "polluter pays" provision of the law, which he argues holds companies liable for more than their fair share of the costs. Ted Williams, a contributing editor to *Audubon*, acknowledges that the Superfund program has been very costly and has cleaned up little waste. But he blames this on sabotage of the law by the Bush and Reagan administrations. He specifically warns against recommendations to abandon the policy of holding polluters strictly liable for the damage they have caused, which he fears would "turn it into a public works program" whereby "citizens will pay twice, once with their environment and once with their tax money."

YES

Bernard J. Reilly

STOP SUPERFUND WASTE

President Clinton's economic plan is a clear attempt to reorder federal spending priorities by putting more money into "investments" that will spur economic growth and increase national wealth, while cutting unproductive activities. One important way he could further his agenda would be to push for reform of one of today's most misguided efforts: the Superfund hazardous waste cleanup program. The President has already paid lip service to this goal, telling business leaders in a February 11 speech at the White House that, "We all know it doesn't work—the Superfund has been a disaster."

Superfund, created by the Comprehensive Environmental Response, Compensation, and Liability Act of 1980 (CERCLA) in the wake of the emergency at the Love Canal landfill in Niagara Falls, New York, was designed as a $1.6-billion program to contain the damage from and eventually clean up a limited number of the nation's most dangerous abandoned toxic waste sites. But in short order it has evolved into an open-ended and costly crusade to return potentially thousands of sites to a near-pristine condition. The result is a large and unjustifiable waste of our nation's resources at the expense of other critical societal needs.

No one questions that the nation has a major responsibility to deal with hazardous waste sites that pose a serious risk to public health and the environment. It is the manner and means by which the federal government has pursued this task, however, that are wasteful. Superfund legislation has given the U.S. Environmental Protection Agency powerful incentives and great clout to seek the most comprehensive, "permanent" cleanup remedies possible—without regard to cost or even the degree to which public health is at risk. Although the EPA does not always choose the most expensive remedial solution, there is strong evidence that, in many cases, waste sites can be cleaned up or sufficiently contained or isolated for a fraction of the cost, while still protecting the public and the environment. Further, EPA's selection of "priority" cleanup sites has been haphazard at best. Indeed, it has no system in place for determining which of those sites—or the many potential sites it has not yet characterized—pose the greatest dangers.

From Bernard J. Reilly, "Stop Superfund Waste," *Issues in Science and Technology* (Spring 1993), pp. 57–60, 62–64. Copyright © 1993 by The University of Texas at Dallas, Richardson, TX. Reprinted by permission.

A 180-degree turn in policy is needed. When the Superfund program comes up for reauthorization next year, Congress should direct the EPA to abandon its pursuit of idealistic cleanup solutions and focus the program on practical risk reduction, targeting those sites that pose the greatest health risks and tying the level and cost of cleanup to the degree of actual risk. Only by making such a fundamental change can the nation maximize the benefits of its increasingly huge investment in the remediation of hazardous waste sites.

COSTS ARE ESCALATING

Estimates for cleaning up, under current practice, the more than 1,200 sites on the EPA's "national priority list" (NPL) range from $32 billion by EPA (based on a $27 million per-site cost) to $60 billion by researchers at the University of Tennessee (based on a $50 million per-site cleanup cost). These estimates are likely to be well below the ultimate cost, since EPA can add an unlimited number of sites to the list. The agency plans to add about 100 sites a year, bringing the total by the year 2000 to more than 2,100. But more than 30,000 inactive waste sites are being considered for cleanup and the universe of potential sites has been estimated at about 75,000. Most experts believe that far fewer—from 2,000 to 10,000—will eventually be cleaned up. The University of Tennessee researchers make a best guess of 3,000 sites, which would put the cost at $150 billion (in 1990 dollars) over 30 years, not including legal fees.

This $150 billion might be acceptable if the U.S. economy were buoyant and limitless funds existed for other needs. It most certainly would be justified if many sites posed unacceptable dangers to the public. But neither of these situations exists.

SKEWED PRIORITIES

A key flaw in Superfund is that most of its effort and money are directed to a relatively small number of "priority" sites, while thousands of others are ignored and, in most cases, not even sampled or studied. For this reason, it is doubtful that the NPL includes all the worst sites.

"Deadly" chemical landfills buried under residential neighborhoods have hardly been typical of the sites EPA has placed on the NPL. Indeed, EPA's efforts to create a system for ranking hazards have not been geared to actually finding the riskiest sites but to satisfying the letter of the CERCLA law. In the first ranking scheme, sites were evaluated for various threats and a score of 28.5 (on a scale of 100) was determined to be sufficient for an NPL listing. However, the listings were not necessarily based on an actual determination of the degree to which they posed threats to public health or the environment. Rather, the sites were included because Congress had determined that 400 sites must be on the NPL, and a score of 28.5 resulted in 413 listings.

Several years ago, the ranking scheme was made much more elaborate, with threats from contaminants in the air, water, and soil weighed differently. The same maximum score of 100 and listing score of 28.5 were used. Why? EPA said that it was "not because of any determination that the cutoff represented a threshold of unacceptable risk presented by the sites" but because the 28.5 score was "a convenient management tool." So much for the rigors of a system designed to cull the Love Canals from town dumps.

A 1991 report by a committee of the National Research Council (NRC) strongly faulted EPA's methods of selecting sites and setting priorities. The report said that EPA has no comprehensive inventory of waste sites, no program for discovering new sites, insufficient data for determining safe exposure levels, and an inadequate system for identifying sites that require immediate action to protect public health.

In a perfect world, every "dirty" site would be cleaned, regardless of the degree of risk it presented. In practice, this is impossible, so we should be spending more to prioritize in order to focus our limited resources on real risks.

EXTREME REMEDIES

However it is accomplished, once a site makes the NPL, money is no object in the remediation process. This was not necessarily the case under the original 1980 Superfund law. CERCLA left some ambiguity about how extensive the cleanups had to be—whether only reasonable risks needed to be eliminated or whether the site had [to] be returned to a preindustrial condition. When it enacted the Superfund Amendments and Reauthorization Act (SARA) in 1986, however, Congress, motivated by a deep distrust of the Reagan-era EPA, took a hard-line stance. SARA, which increased funding for the program to $8.5 billion and ordered action to begin at ever more sites, directed EPA to give preference to cleanup remedies that "to the maximum extent practicable" lead to "permanent solutions." The emphasis on permanence was further reinforced by a requirement that cleanups must comply with any

"applicable or relevant and appropriate requirement" (ARAR) in any other state or federal law relating to protection of public health and the environment.

SARA was deeply flawed. For one thing, it effectively forced EPA to continue remedial action even after all realistic risks at a site had been eliminated. One example is the Swope Superfund site, a former solvent reclamation facility in Pennsauken, New Jersey. Although all major sources of contamination had been removed from the site, EPA ordered the installation of a $5-million vapor extraction system to remove more contaminants. The purpose was to protect groundwater in case any private wells were sunk in the future. But EPA neglected to consider the fact that private wells had been banned in the area.

SARA's requirements also serve to exclude the use of other far less costly remedies that would give the public the same or at least acceptable protection from harm. For example, at the Bridgeport Rental and Oil Services Superfund site in Logan Township, New Jersey, EPA ordered the construction of an onsite, $100-million incinerator after PCBs were found in several sludge samples. In making its decision, EPA used the ARAR requirement to retroactively apply the federal Toxic Substances Control Act (TSCA), which requires incineration of currently generated wastes if samples indicate that PCBs in the soil exceed 500 parts per million.

The absurdity of the plan became apparent when EPA decided to create an on-site landfill to dispose of the heavy metal residues from the incineration. Given that a landfill was to be created anyway and that PCBs at the site were so scarce that EPA had to import them for trial burns of the incinerator, the agency could have opted to contain the sludge on site in the first place —using existing proven technologies— while more than adequately protecting the public at an estimated one-fifth of the cost of incineration.

A similar tale is unfolding at another Superfund site in Carlstadt, New Jersey, which is contaminated with solvents, PCBs, and heavy metals. A trench has been cut around the site to an underlying impervious soil layer and then filled with clay to prevent any migration of the contaminants. The site has also been pumped dry to protect groundwater and capped to keep out rain. Remediation work has cost about $7 million, and DuPont as well as other responsible parties have pledged to maintain these containment systems for as long as necessary. However, despite the absence of any current or reasonably foreseeable public exposures, EPA may decide to require incineration of the top 10 feet of soil at an estimated cost of several hundred million dollars. This would be a foolish waste of money.

EPA must also consider that extreme, costly remediation solutions often are not without costs of their own. Incineration, for instance, cannot destroy metals. Does the public really benefit when lead is released into the air as a byproduct? By the same token, when contaminated soil is ordered excavated and carted elsewhere, one neighborhood gets a "permanent" solution, whereas another gets a landfill with toxic residues.

RISKS EXAGGERATED

Superfund legislation is not the only force driving EPA to seek "permanent" solutions. EPA decides on a remedy only after assessing the risks at a site. However, EPA often uses unrealistic assumptions that exaggerate the risks and lead to excessive actions. For example, according to the Hazardous Waste Cleanup Project, an industry group in which DuPont has been involved, EPA may make estimates of exposure based on a scenario in which an individual is assumed to reside near a site for 70 years, to consume two liters of water every day during those 70 years, and to obtain all of that water from groundwater at the site. It has even made exposure estimates based on the length of time a child will play (and eat dirt) on a site in the middle of an industrial location surrounded by a security fence. Each of these scenarios is highly improbable.

Questions involving risk assessment are, of course, going to be contentious ones for some time to come. Clouding the Superfund debate is the fact that there is no scientific consensus as to the precise magnitude of the dangers posed by chemicals typically found at Superfund sites.

The existence of toxic wastes at a site does not necessarily mean that they pose a threat to nearby residents. Epidemiologic studies of waste sites have severe technical limitations, and it is difficult at best to determine whether exposure to hazardous wastes can be blamed for medical problems when a long gap exists between exposure and disease. Even at such a well-known site as Times Beach, Missouri, where the entire community was evacuated, research in recent years has shown that the potential health risks were relatively small or even nonexistent.

The most comprehensive assessment of the risks from Superfund sites came in the 1991 NRC report, which concluded that "current health burdens from hazardous-waste sites appear to be small," but added that "until better evidence is developed, prudent public policy demands that a margin of safety be provided regarding public health risks from exposures to hazardous-waste sites."

No one can argue with a margin of safety. However, that is not the focus of the current Superfund program, which, far more than any other environmental program, makes no rational attempt to link costs with benefits. EPA's own Science Advisory Board, in a 1990 report that attempted to rank the environmental problems for which the agency is responsible, concluded that old toxic waste sites appeared to be "low to medium risk." Other hazards, such as radon gas in homes and cigarette smoke, were considered to pose much larger risks.

THE LIABILITY MESS

The bulk of the Superfund tab will be picked up by industry, through taxes imposed under CERCLA, out-of-pocket cleanup costs, or settlements with insurance companies. Industry recognizes that it must assume its fair share of the financial and operating burden of the cleanup effort, and it acknowledges that Superfund has compelled it to become exceptionally vigilant not only in disposing of toxic wastes but also in minimizing their generation in the first place. But it objects to a system in which EPA seemingly has put a higher priority on pinning the blame and the bill on companies than on ensuring the protection of public health.

CERCLA dictated a "polluter-pays" philosophy to deal with what had largely been lawful disposal of wastes. CERLCA and court interpretations of it also have created an extremely broad liability scheme. Virtually any company remotely involved in a site-waste generators, haulers, site owners or operators, and even, in some cases, the companies' bankers—could be held responsible. One or a few companies could be forced to pay the entire bill, even though they were only minor participants and other parties were involved—a provision called joint-and-several liability. No limits were imposed on the amount of money that could be extracted from "guilty" parties.

One problem with this liability system is that it completely lacks cost accountability. With industry paying for most of the cleanup, the funds are not in EPA's budget and thus do not have to compete in budget battles with other cash-starved federal programs. And given the strictness of the law, why should EPA regulators subject themselves to possible congressional criticism by selecting a less-than-perfect solution, especially if money is no object? But let us not kid ourselves. Although this money may seem "free" to Congress, EPA, and the public, companies must make up the difference by raising prices, cutting investment and jobs, or taking other undesirable actions

An even more damning problem is that the liability provisions have spawned countless legal brouhahas that are consuming a large and increasing share of Superfund resources—even as the cleanup process itself has languished. (The average length of a site cleanup is 8 years, and fewer than 100 sites have been "permanently" remediated.) In the approximately 70 percent of Superfund sites that involve multiple parties, companies must fight with the EPA, among themselves, and with their insurance companies over who dumped what, when, and how much—questions extremely difficult to answer many years after the alleged "dumping" is thought to have occurred. Some experts believe that these "transaction costs" will eventually account for more than 20 percent of all Superfund expenditures. This is a boon for lawyers but a waste for the nation.

Legal costs—as well as burdensome technical and administrative expenses—could potentially be greatly reduced if Congress would allow EPA to take a more practical approach to risk reduction. Unlike other environmental laws, such as the Clean Air Act and Clean Water Act, which have sought to deal with problems in successive stages, Superfund's emphasis on finding a one-time, complete, and permanent solution magnifies the stakes to all parties, prolonging disputes and greatly increasing the costs. If companies could count on a more realistic remediation approach, they might be more willing to compromise, which could lead to faster cleanups.

The liability mess could get completely out of hand if Congress goes along with a patently unfair proposal to exempt municipalities from liability at closed municipal landfills, which account for about 20 percent of NPL sites. Municipal governments argue that most of these landfills largely contain household wastes not covered by Superfund and thus they should not be billed for the cleanup. But in many cases this is not true. For example, at the Kramer Superfund site in Mantua, New Jersey, municipal governments contributed the greatest share of hazardous substances. Despite this, EPA is no longer even naming municipalities in cost-recovery suits. (EPA's tendency to selectively enforce the law has been increasing. At Kramer, EPA sued 25 parties even though hundreds were potentially responsible.)

Industry recognizes that many municipal governments are severely strapped for revenues. Yet companies, which provide jobs and help create the tax base needed to support municipal services, should not be milked to pay for Superfund shares properly owed by others.

One last concern with the liability provisions is that they may be having a chilling effect on new investment at sites in older urban areas—areas that sorely need such investment. The reason is that any party that buys such a property would be caught in Superfund's liability web. For example, investors seeking to build a coal-fired power plant in an area with a projected need for such a use recently approached DuPont about buying a property that had been used for manufacturing for more than 100 years and clearly contains some contaminated soil. Virgin land is not needed for a site to burn coal, and risk assessments indicated that workers could be protected with commonsense steps such as paving. But efforts to get reasonable compromises from regulators on containing the site proved fruitless, and now the investment will not be made, at least in this area.

STEPS TO REFORM

It is time for a major redirection of the Superfund program. Congress should tell EPA to abandon its focus on idealistic cleanup remedies and emphasize practical risk reduction. Instead of continuing its haphazard site selection and unjustifiably costly cleanup remedies, EPA should first define the universe of sites that may present real health risks and then take steps to deal with the most immediate dangers, taking costs into consideration. Once a national inventory has been established, extensive site evaluations can be undertaken, with the purpose of setting priorities for cleanup. Only after these actions are taken will we be able to make non-hysterical decisions as to how much we should invest in cleaning these sites, balancing such factors as risks, costs, and other societal needs.

It is particularly crucial that remedy decisions be based on the expected future use of the land and the costs and practicality of the proposed solution. If residential development is planned near the site, the cleanup may need to be extensive. In many cases, however, especially when another industrial use is planned on or near an old waste site, use of containment technologies may be sufficient to protect against risk of exposure. In the most troublesome cases, where major remediation is necessary, costs are high, and existing technology has limitations, it makes much more sense to isolate the site until more cost-effective treatment techniques are developed or increased land values justify a large investment.

In making these decisions, it would be helpful if EPA had much better information on the benefits and costs of different levels of cleanup. Currently, less than 1 percent of EPA's Superfund budget goes for research on the scientific basis for evaluating Superfund sites. Much more should be spent. EPA also should increase its research on the environmental consequences of different types of remedial actions, such as whether incineration actually increases risk by transferring hazardous substances from the ground or water into the air.

The liability provisions of the Superfund program also need to be changed. DuPont and companies in the chemical, petroleum, and other industries favor replacing the very unfair joint-and-several liability provision (making one or a few companies liable for all the costs, even though many others, often defunct, were also responsible) with proportional liability. In other words, responsible parties would pay only in proportion to the share of the cleanup costs associated with the wastes that they contributed at a site. EPA would then be forced to either find and sue all responsible parties or pay for the remainder of the cleanup costs itself. EPA is already authorized to pay for cleanup costs in cases where parties cannot be found or cannot afford to pay—shares which are often sizable. But in practice it has sought to recoup all cleanup costs under the joint-and-several provision. Proportional liability would inject more fairness into the process, and since the polluter-pays principle would be retained, it would continue to encourage responsible parties to pressure EPA to pursue the most cost-effective cleanup remedy. Most important, proportional liability would impose much-needed financial discipline on EPA, since it would be forced to pay for more of the cleanups out of its own budget. For the first time, EPA would have to consider whether the benefits were worth the costs.

Proportional liability would not, of course, solve the problem of how to divide up responsibility in the first place. One possible way out of this morass is to formalize in the law an alternative dispute resolution process in which any or all potentially responsible parties could participate. It would be chaired by neutral parties satisfactory to all. Its findings on shares could be appealed to the courts, but any party that concurred with the decision would be authorized to pay its share and exit the process. This solution would help cut site contention, reward cooperative parties, and leave messy litigation to those unwilling to pay their fair shares. It would also diminish Superfund's luster as a federally mandated entitlements program for lawyers.

More extensive reform of the liability provisions has been proposed by the insurance industry, which wants to eliminate all liability at sites in which more than one party is involved and in which waste disposal occurred prior to enactment of either CERCLA in 1980 or SARA in 1986. Site cleanup would then be paid out of the Superfund budget, financed by increased taxes on industry, including insurers. Although this proposal would eliminate contentious fights over specific site responsibility, substantially cut transaction costs, and possibly speed up site cleanups, it would be unacceptable to DuPont and other parties at Superfund sites if the new taxes were unfairly levied on the same companies already paying disproportionately large shares of the current Superfund cleanups.

Finally, the liability scheme must be changed so that prospective owners of older urban sites are not deterred from making new investments in them. New owners should certainly not be held responsible for contamination that they did not cause. One approach would be for current owners to demonstrate, before sale, that their sites, while not pristine, are adequately contained and do not pose unacceptable risks to the public. The new owner would be expected to maintain or monitor whatever containment system was developed. If EPA later did a more extensive site evaluation and determined that greater threats existed, the new owner would not have to pay. In addition, current owners should be able to make new investments in their property if they demonstrate that the sites are adequately contained.

* * *

The limits of our national wealth have not been so obvious since the 1930s. More than ever, we must make choices among competing, compelling demands for scarce resources. We recognize that a dollar spent on defense cannot be spent on health care. We must also recognize that a dollar spent on hazardous waste cleanup is similarly unavailable. As with other federal programs, Superfund spending must be balanced and managed. This can be done if we refocus our Superfund investment on real risks, give EPA a stake in doing its job cost-effectively, and bring more fairness into the process.

NO   Ted Williams

THE SABOTAGE OF SUPERFUND

The setting was perfect: Cold rain and gull-filled mist blowing in from Buzzards Bay. Litter clinging to the bare ribs of dead brush like shards of rotten umbrella silk. Derelict, graffiti-streaked trailers stuffed to overflowing with bald truck tires. Ratty mattresses and broken easy chairs strewn about the cratered parking lot. Glass from the abandoned mill crunching under my boots and snatches of Eliot's *The Waste Land* resounding in my brain as I trudged along Wet Weather Sewage Discharge Outfall No. 022: "Sweet Thames run softly, till I end my song..."

Until this day, March 28, 1993, I had avoided Superfund sites. So this was my first visit to the waterfront of New Bedford—an impoverished, predominantly Hispanic seaport in southern Massachusetts, now as famous for the polychlorinated biphenyls (PCBs) on the bottom of its harbor as for its whaling history. PCBs, widely used in the manufacture of electrical components until banned in 1978, do hideous things to creatures that come in contact with them—such as causing their cells to proliferate wildly and warping their embryos. I wasn't about to touch anything without my rubber ice-fishing gloves.

Where the sewage dribbled into the dark Acushnet River I jumped down onto gray silt and, breathing through my teeth, scooped up five handfuls of muck. The Environmental Protection Agency's guideline for protecting marine life from chronic toxic effects of PCBs is 30 parts per trillion. I cannot accurately report the PCB content of my amateur sample (taken illegally, the EPA later informed me), but the greasy globules that floated up through the surface scum were likely very rich. Had I been able to get out into the river and upstream to the old Aerovox Inc. discharge pipe, I could have found concentrations of at least 200,000 parts per *million*, or 20 percent, among the highest ever recorded. That means that with a similar test dredging I'd have retrieved one handful of pure PCBs, along with a tangle of wriggling sludge worms, about the only creatures that can live in such habitat.

I was rinsing my gloves and boots in a rain-filled pothole when *The Waste Land's* Fisher King materialized through the gloom—a wispy, gray-haired figure in a red plaid jacket, toting a stout spinning rod. He had parked next to a sign that read in Spanish, Portuguese, and English: "Warning. Hazardous

Waste. No wading, fishing, shellfishing. Per order of U.S. EPA." His name, which he printed with his forefinger on the wet trunk of his car, was Robin Rivera; he knew only enough English to make me understand that he and his family eat the fish he catches here.

Not until 1978 did the nation get angry about the indiscriminate disposal of poisonous chemicals. In that year people who lived near Hooker Chemical Company's Love Canal dump in Niagara Falls, New York, were distressed to smell vile chemical odors in their basements and observe a malevolent secretion bubbling out of the ground at a local school yard. County health officials and Hooker reps tried vainly to contain the alarm, but their assurances that all was well sounded as wrong as the uncontained leachate looked and smelled.

Eventually the citizens took their case to the young commissioner of the state Department of Environmental Conservation—Peter A. A. Berle, now president of the National Audubon Society. Although Berle had no authority to act on public health issues, he sent his people out to test houses on the strength of his environmental mandate. The benzene levels they found were, in his words, "right off the chart." Eventually 600 homes were abandoned and 2,500 residents relocated.

In response to the Love Canal horror show Congress enacted the Comprehensive Environmental Response, Compensation, and Liability Act of 1980, better known as Superfund. Amended in 1986, the law uses taxes on crude oil and 42 commercial chemicals to maintain a fund with which the EPA may, as it likes to say, "remediate" hazardous-waste sites. If perpetrators can be found and are still in business, the EPA may require one or all to clean up the entire site. This essential principle of Superfund is called joint and several liability.

For an idea of the pace at which cleanup proceeds, consider that the EPA and its contractors have been studying and planning what to do about New Bedford's harbor ever since it was declared a "National Priority" Superfund site 11 years ago. Nationwide, the EPA has spent $7.5 billion on its Superfund program, with pitiful results. In some cases remediation has created more problems than it has solved by stirring up contaminants that had been dormant. In other cases vast sums have been squandered at sites that posed little threat to the public, while deadly brews seethed nearby. Superfund contractors have consistently ripped off the EPA, billing it for everything from office parties to work they were supposed to do and didn't.

At this writing only 163 of 1,204 sites have been remediated, and in many cases polluters have been granted what the EPA calls the "containment" option—a feline approach to toxic-waste management in which they just cover their messes and walk away. The average cleanup has cost about $25 million and taken 7 to 10 years to complete.

No one remotely connected with Superfund is happy about the way it has functioned. Polluters identified by the EPA have been madly rummaging through dumps, trying to identify other polluters by their trash and so spread liability. In the process small towns, businesses, and individuals that contributed legally and insignificantly to landfills have been intimidated and assessed for cleanup costs in a fashion utterly inconsistent with the intent of Congress. Environmentalists are at the throats of insurance companies who want to do away with the polluter-pay tenet. The insurance companies are warring in court with industries to whom they have rashly sold pollution-liability policies. People who live atop and beside toxic waste claim—often correctly—that they have been ignored and lied to by the EPA, and as a result, they sometimes oppose well-advised cleanup plans.

Hearings for Superfund's 1994 reauthorization are already under way. "We all know it doesn't work," says President Bill Clinton. "Superfund has been a disaster."

* * *

Even as I wished the Fisher King good luck, I found myself greeting the first of 94 demonstrators from the New Bedford–area citizen's group Hands Across the River. We stood in the rain, listening to fiery speeches amplified by bullhorn about the EPA's plan to dredge the five acres that contain roughly 45 percent of the PCBs extant in the 28-square-mile site, then cleanse the spoil by fire in portable incinerators set up on the downstream side of Sewage Outfall 022.

"You and I will be breathing their mistakes," bellowed rally leader Richard Wickenden. "They made their decision to incinerate behind closed doors with a total disregard for the local citizenry."

He spoke the truth. The New Bedford City Council had found out about the plan not from the EPA but from Hands Across the River, which had found out about it from federal documents at the library. "State-of-the-art incinerators" have a long history of malfunction, even when run by the most conscientious contractors. This one will be operated by Roy F. Weston, a large environmental-

consulting firm based in West Chester, Pennsylvania, which in 1990 agreed to pay $750,000 to settle charges that it had defrauded the EPA by backdating data and submitting a bill for work it never did. Finally, people downwind—mostly people like Robin Rivera—are likely to be breathing mistakes, along with all manner of toxic PICs (products of incomplete combustion) that won't be monitored or even identified.

In attempting to clean up one point of pollution the EPA and its contractors will be creating others, asserted New Bedford City Councilman George Rogers. They'll be unleashing PCBs and heavy metals on moving seawater, hauling them onto the bank, then casting them to the four winds during dewatering and combustion. "They're doing this because New Bedford is a poor community; we don't have clout. They wouldn't do it in Miami Beach." He, too, spoke the truth. A study released last September by *The National Law Journal* reveals that the EPA is lenient in penalizing polluters of minority and low-income communities and that cleanups in such areas are slower and less thorough. Toxic racism, activists call it.

Equally veracious were the allegations of David Hammond, president and founder of Hands Across the River, that polluters love incineration because their liability goes up the stack along with the toxic PICs and that the EPA has undermined Superfund's effectiveness and its own credibility by ordering remediation studies from companies that make their money remediating. In particular, Hammond is upset that Weston was hired to do the New Bedford Remedial Action Master Plan, then wound up with the $19.4 million incineration contract.

Both the city council and Hands Across the River hasten to point out that they are not against remediation. But instead of incineration they favor the "Eco Logic" process—a relatively contained heat treatment developed in Rockwood, Ontario, which combines hydrogen with PCBs to form methane and hydrogen chloride and which has been getting rave reviews in the press. "Stunning New Method Zaps Toxic Chemicals Efficiently," shouted a headline in *The Toronto Star* on January 30, 1993.

After the New Bedford speechmaking the congregation marched back and forth over the Acushnet River bridge, waving placards, obstructing traffic (much of which honked in sympathy), and chanting, "No way, EPA," and "Hey, Carol [Browner], if you please, don't you burn those PCBs. Not New Bedford, not the nation. We don't want incineration."

The citizens could scarcely have done a better, more honest job of drawing public attention to the perils of dredging and incinerating PCBs. But this doesn't mean that the EPA ought not to press ahead with its plan for New Bedford. When PCB concentrations are this high, the perils of doing something else or nothing at all are probably greater. One day the Eco Logic process may indeed be a "stunning method" of remediation. Now, despite the effusions of *The Toronto Star*, it's largely an experimental technology and therefore fraught with risk. Meanwhile, the PCBs are spreading out into the Atlantic with every tide and every storm. Humans and marine ecosystems —including half the North American population of endangered roseate terns, which nests on a single island in Buzzards Bay—don't have another decade to wait while the EPA collects data and shuffles papers.

* * *

In other contract deals the EPA has paid the New England office of Roy F. Weston, which it has criticized for poor performance, $635,000 to administer fieldwork that cost $340,000. But Weston looks like a model contractor when compared with some of the others.

Take, for example, consulting-engineering colossus CH2M Hill, which has worked on 275 major sites, including Love Canal, and which holds $1.4 billion worth of Superfund contracts. An inquiry by the House Subcommittee on Oversight and Investigations revealed that as part of alleged Superfund work, CH2M Hill billed the EPA $4,100 for tickets to basketball, baseball, and football games; $167,900 for employee parties and picnics, including the cost of reindeer suits, magicians, and a rent-a-clown; $15,000 for an office bash at a place called His Lordship; "thousands of dollars' worth" of chocolates stamped with the company logo; $63,000 for general advertising; $10,000 for a catered lobbying cruise on the Potomac; and $100 for a Christmas-party dance instructor. "I am all for rocking around the Christmas tree," commented Congressman Thomas J. Bliley Jr. (D-VA) at the hearing, "but does it have to be at the taxpayers' expense?"

Apparently yes, according to the testimony of CH2M Hill's president, Lyle Hassebroek. "No matter what differences of opinion exist on the manner in which we allocate costs," he explained, "CH2M Hill's charges to the government are fair to the taxpayer."

By no means is CH2M Hill aberrant. Last summer EPA investigators found that 23 companies hired for hazardous-waste cleanup in 1988 and 1989 spent 28 percent of their $265 million budget on wasteful administrative costs. Such inefficiency is cited by polluters and their insurance companies as a reason to "overhaul" Superfund—i.e., turn it into a public-works program whereby Uncle Sam would bail them out by picking up toxic litter (provided the offense preceded some stipulated date —1987, according to one proposal) and citizens will pay twice, once with their environment and once with their tax money.

Major polluters further foment discontent with Superfund by attempting to squeeze alleged shares of cleanup costs from everyone who might ever have sent a can of shoe polish to a landfill. The EPA and the courts don't want a nickel a day for 1,000 years and so avoid going after mom-and-pop polluters. But Mom and Pop don't know this, and technically they are liable. The real motive, charge environmental leaders, is not so much to collect money as to contrive broad support for Superfund "reform."

When Ford, Chrysler, General Motors, BASF Corporation, and Sea Ray Boats were fingered by the EPA for fouling the Metamora, Michigan, landfill with arsenic, lead, vinyl chloride, and the like, they proclaimed that 382 towns, businesses, and individuals were copolluters and tried to assess them $50 million to settle alleged liability quickly, including any unforeseen costs. Even the local Girl Scout troop was assessed $100,000. "That's a lot of cookies," declared a troop spokesperson.

In another case Doreen Merlino, the 25-year-old proprietor of a two-table pizzeria in Chadwicks, New York, offered the court officer the following plea when he served her with a two-inch-thick lawsuit in October 1990: "Aren't you at least gonna buy a pizza?" He kindly complied, but she didn't feel much better. In fact, she felt terrified. Cosmetics giant Chesebrough-Pond's and Special Metals Corporation were trying to extract $3,000 from her for helping them poison the local landfill. They weren't sure just what the trashman might have collected from her during the seven months she'd been in business—maybe pesticide containers or empty cleanser cans, they opined. But Merlino tells me she's never used pesticides and that she has always rinsed out her cleanser containers. A cover letter advised her that if she settled fast, she'd only have to pay $1,500. As it turned out, she had to pay no one save her lawyer, and none of her anger is directed at Superfund. Not all the 603 defendants were so philosophical.

When the EPA hits up polluters for toxic-waste-cleanup costs, polluters, naturally enough, hit up the insurance companies from which they have purchased pollution-liability coverage. Now the insurance companies would like to hit up the public—that is, rewrite Superfund so bygones can be bygones and taxpayers can spring for cleaning up old sites.

"Superfund's mission should be protecting human health and the environment, not fund-raising," contends the American International Group, an insurance company marshaling support for what it calls a National Environmental Trust Fund, by which Superfund money could be raised "from all economic sectors without regard to site-specific liability" via a surcharge on commercial- and industrial-insurance premiums.

Generating pity for the insurance industry requires a greater heart than beats in the breast of environmental consultant Curtis Moore. As an aide to former Republican senator Robert Stafford of Vermont, Moore was instrumental in writing both the original Superfund law and the amended 1986 version. Insurance companies, he points out, tend not to cover purposeful acts by anyone, including God; so the policies were restricted to "sudden and accidental" pollution. "You dump crude oil on the ground for fifteen years," he says, "and over a twenty-five-year period it migrates to the water table. Would you consider that sudden? Accidental? No? Well, I got news for you: The courts do. There was a string of decisions that construed the terms *sudden* and *accidental* as covering groundwater contamination. This trend started a long time ago—in the 1970s or earlier. It was clearly discernible. Any insurance lawyer with manure for brains could see it happening. Notwithstanding, the insurance industry continued to use the terms *sudden* and *accidental* in its policies.

"So here comes Superfund, and the chemical companies start casting around, trying to figure out how they can get someone else to pick up the tab. They file suits against their insurance companies and win. Well, there's only one way to fix the insurance industry's problem. You can either shift liability or, failing that, repeal Superfund."

Presuming to speak for the insurance industry, the American International Group complains that Superfund is "bogged down in a morass of legal warfare that delays cleanup and wastes enormous financial and human resources." True enough, but what it doesn't mention is that the insurance industry has been responsible for a great deal of this legal warfare. A Rand Corporation study reveals that between 1986 and 1989 insurers spent $1.3 billion on Superfund. Of this, $1 billion went to defending themselves against their policyholders or defending their policyholders against the EPA. One

leading attorney for the policyholders—Eugene Anderson, of the New York City firm of Anderson, Kill, Olick & Oshinsky—has gone so far as to suggest publicly that refusing all large claims is now seen as smart business procedure by insurers: Half the policyholders get scared away, and most of the others will settle out of court for less than full coverage.

* * *

Superfund has bombed, as the President, environmentalists, inhabitants of toxic neighborhoods, brewers of toxic waste, and especially the insurance industry have observed. But it is essential to remember the difference between Superfund the law and Superfund the program.

"The law was a creation of people like Bob Stafford, Ed Muskie, Jennings Randolph, John Chafee, Jim Florio," remarks Moore. "The program was the creation of Ronald Reagan; the people who were put in charge of implementing the law six weeks after it was enacted were people who six weeks earlier had been lobbying against it. They set out with the intent of making it unworkable, and they succeeded."

There is nothing in the statute that directs the EPA's contractors to dress up like reindeer or distribute customized confections at government expense. They engage in such excess because the EPA lacks the personnel to keep them honest. Nor is there anything in the statute that mandates stonewalling and procrastination on the part of polluters. But they have learned that endless negotiation is profitable because the EPA lacks the personnel to haul more than a few of them into court. Mr. Clinton, who proposes to trim $76 million from Superfund the program, appears not to understand this.

Certainly, the statute could stand repair. It needs to define how clean is clean, provide a better, more flexible means of selecting remedies, ensure state and local participation, create incentives for companies to take voluntary action instead of suing everyone in sight. But the fact is that Superfund the law isn't broken.

Even Superfund the program, disastrous though it has been, has produced some splendid if accidental results. "Joint and several liability," says Peter Berle, "has put the fear of God into everybody, which means they are careful in ways they never were before in what they do with their waste. I also think the cost risk of inappropriate toxic-waste disposal has been the major impetus toward waste minimization. When it gets too expensive to deal with it, then you make less."

Rick Hind, toxics director for Greenpeace, agrees. "It doesn't cost you and me anything if a big company wants to spend ten million dollars on lawyers to avoid an eleven-million-dollar cleanup," he offers. "That costs the company. Good! So it costs them twice what it should. That will teach them a lesson. When a Colombian drug cartel is in court nobody cares what their legal expenses are. Nor should we care about polluters."

Insurers and polluters—not environmentalists—are the ones driving for major surgery on Superfund the law. If they are permitted to degrade it from a dedicated fund to a public-works program whereby big government passes around public-generated revenues, the hemorrhage of federal pork will make the EPA nostalgic for the days when it used taxes on crude oil and chemicals to rent clowns for CH2M Hill. If they are permitted to do away with Superfund's liability provisions and weaken its polluter-pay principle, the United States will be poisoned on a scale unimagined even in New Bedford, Massachusetts.

It may be that Superfund is mortally wounded from a dozen years of sabotage. But it also may be that it can be salvaged and made to work. We need to try. Vendors of insurance and chemicals will shriek and sob, but the law wasn't written for them. It was written for Love Canal couples forced to watch as bulldozers razed their homes, for Robin Rivera and his family, for roseate terns, for sick and deformed children, for children yet unborn.

POSTSCRIPT

Hazardous Waste: Should the "Polluter Pays" Provision of Superfund Be Weakened?

Note that although Reilly does not question the need to "deal with hazardous waste sites that pose a serious risk to public health and the environment," he later qualifies this responsibility by claiming that "the existence of toxic waste at a site does not necessarily mean that they pose a threat to nearby residents." As citizens' groups, such as the New Bedford activists, whose concerns are described by Williams, have made clear, "nearby residents" reject Reilly's qualification and invariably demand remediation of toxic waste that has been identified in their neighborhoods. The "joint-and-several liability" provision of Superfund that Reilly thinks is unfair is a common provision of tort law that is considered necessary by many legal experts to enable courts to aportion penalties when there are several disputing liable parties.

A slightly more positive assessment of the accomplishments of the Superfund is presented by Karen Schmidt in her article in the April/May 1994 issue of *National Wildlife*. W. Kip Viscusi and James T. Hamilton share many of Reilly's views. In their essay in the summer 1996 issue of *The Public Interest*, they argue that accurate risk assessment, determining the extent of exposed populations, and appropriately balancing benefits and costs are the principles that should be used in reforming the Superfund.

The National Commission on the Superfund—established in 1992 as a joint project of the Environmental Law Center, Vermont Law School, and the Keystone Center—has recently issued its comprehensive *Final Consensus Report* (March 1, 1994). For a copy of this panel's report and recommendations, contact the Keystone Center, P.O. Box 8606, Keystone, Colorado 80435.

One controversial response to hazardous waste problems is the practice of buying out neighboring communities by the companies responsible for the problem. The pros and cons of this practice are discussed in "A Town Called Morrisonville," by John Bowermaster, *Audubon* (July/August 1993).

Another serious dimension of the hazardous waste problem is the growing use of developing nations as the dumping grounds for waste from the United States and other wealthier nations. "The Basel Convention: A Global Approach for the Management of Hazardous Wastes," by Iwonna Rummel-Bulska, *Environmental Policy and Law* (vol. 24, no. 1, 1994) is an assessment of the international treaty designed to prevent such waste dumping.

For an Internet site related to this issue, see http://www.epa.gov/superfund/, which is the EPA Superfund home page.

ISSUE 13

Municipal Waste: Should Recycling Efforts Be Expanded?

YES: John E. Young, from "The Sudden New Strength of Recycling," *World Watch* (July/August 1995)

NO: Chris Hendrickson, Lester Lave, and Francis McMichael, from "Time to Dump Recycling?" *Issues in Science and Technology* (Spring 1995)

ISSUE SUMMARY

YES: John E. Young, senior researcher at the Worldwatch Institute, argues that recycling has matured from an environmentally motivated "do good" activity to an economically viable waste management option.

NO: Engineering and economics researchers Chris Hendrickson, Lester Lave, and Francis McMichael assert that ambitious recycling programs are often too costly and are of dubious environmental value.

Since prehistoric times, the predominant method of dealing with refuse has been to simply dump it in some out-of-the-way spot. Worldwide, land disposal still accommodates the overwhelming majority of domestic waste. In the United States roughly 90 percent of residential and commercial waste is disposed of in some type of landfill, ranging from a simple open pit to so-called sanitary landfills where the waste is compacted and covered with a layer of clean soil. In a small, but increasing, percentage of cases, landfills may have clay or plastic liners to reduce leaching of toxins into groundwater.

By the last quarter of the nineteenth century, odoriferous, vermin-infested garbage dumps in increasingly congested urban areas were identified as a public health threat. Large-scale incineration of municipal waste was introduced at that time in both Europe and the United States as an alternative disposal method. By 1970 more than 300 such central garbage incinerators existed in U.S. cities, in addition to the thousands of waste incinerators that had been built into large apartment buildings.

Virtually all of these early garbage furnaces were built without devices to control air pollution. During the period of heightened consciousness about urban air quality following World War II, restrictions began to be imposed on garbage burning. By 1980 the new national and local air pollution regulations had reduced the number of large U.S. municipal waste incinerators to fewer than 80. Better designed and more efficiently operated landfills took up the slack.

During the past two decades, an increasing number of U.S. cities have been unable to find suitable, accessible locations to build new landfills. This has coincided with growing concern about the threat to both groundwater and surface water from toxic chemicals in leachate and runoff from dump sites. Legislative restrictions in many parts of the country now mandate costly design and testing criteria for landfills. In many cases, communities have been forced to shut down their local landfills (some of which had grown into small mountains) and to ship their wastes tens or even hundreds of miles to disposal sites.

The lack of long-range planning coupled with skyrocketing disposal costs created a crisis situation in municipal waste management in the 1980s. Energetic entrepreneurs seized upon this situation to promote European-developed incineration technology with improved air pollution controls as the panacea for the garbage problem. Ironically, the proliferation of these new waste incinerators in the United States coincided with increasing concern in Europe about their efficiency in containing the toxic air pollutants produced by burning modern waste. Citizen groups became aware of this concern and organized opposition to incinerator construction. The industry countered with more sophisticated air pollution controls, but these trapped the toxins in the incinerator ash, which presents a troublesome and expensive disposal problem. The result has been a rapid decrease in the number of municipalities that are choosing to rely on modern incineration to solve their waste diposal problems.

Recycling, which until recently has been dismissed as a minor waste disposal alternative, is being encouraged as a major option. The Environmental Protection Agency (EPA) and several states have established hierarchies of waste disposal technologies with the goal of using waste reduction and recycling for as much as 50 percent of the material in the waste stream. Several environmental groups are urging even greater reliance on recycling, citing studies that show that more than 90 percent of municipal waste can theoretically be put to productive use if large-scale composting is included as a component of recycling.

John E. Young was a senior researcher at the Worldwatch Institute when he wrote the following article. In it he describes the maturation of recycling from a waste management option—which, despite its poor economic prospects, was reluctantly adopted to satisfy environmental concerns—to a booming industry, which solid waste officials increasingly find to be cheaper than using landfills or incineration. Chris Hendrickson, a civil engineer, Lester Lave, an economist, and Francis McMichael, an environmental engineer, are all professors at Carnegie Mellon University in Pittsburgh, Pennsylvania. Generalizing from an analysis of the recycling program of their home city, they conclude that recycling is neither cost-effective nor environmentally advantageous.

YES

John E. Young

THE SUDDEN NEW STRENGTH
OF RECYCLING

Recycling, one of the key strategies for alleviating the pressures of the human presence on natural systems, has finally—and dramatically—arrived as a mainstream industrial activity in North America.

It's ironic that the breakthrough took so long. North America—or at least the U.S. and Canadian part of it—is where materials consumption is most profligate, and where the impacts of that consumption (in pollution from landfills and incinerators, energy production for manufacturing, and the spreading damage left by extractive industries) are therefore most troublesome. Yet, for a quarter-century after the first Earth Day, recycling advocates were forced to spend much of their energy trying to make their case to skeptical decisionmakers.

In the 1980s, recycling was still seen largely as a "do-good" activity. It was of little interest to fast-track business investors, who in those days were too busy pursuing "high-tech" ventures. The idea of founding a profitable business on old newspapers and empty bottles did not fit well with the ascendant lifestyles of the era. Local governments, many of which had to cope with rising landfill costs, were a bit more responsive, but still tended to regard their new recycling programs as burdens.

But now, suddenly, what was seen as a burden has become a major asset, and those communities that had the foresight to set up solid recycling programs a few years ago are beginning to reap real rewards. Since early 1994, prices for nearly all commonly collected recyclables have skyrocketed. In San Francisco, for example, recycling director Sharon Maves reports that the used paper, plastic, and metals the city picks up from curbs is bringing in "unprecedented revenue"—allowing the city to actually reduce household assessments for waste collection and recycling.

The story is the same across the continent. New York City, which [a few] years ago was paying $6 million per year to get rid of its newsprint, expect[ed] to *earn* $20–25 million from selling the same material [in 1996], says recycling chief Bob Lange. Early in 1994, Madison, Wisconsin was paying $13 per ton to the processors who took its recyclables; by the end of the year it was receiving nearly $23 per ton. Madison recycling coordinator George Dreckman calls his city's program a "cash cow" that yielded the city $240,000 in net revenue (after processing costs, but not including collection costs) in the first four months of 1994.

Such numbers are making recycling increasingly attractive to many city waste administrators. While every city's economics are different—and some still have cheap municipal landfills with years of remaining capacity—many well-run programs are collecting and marketing materials at costs well below those of landfilling or burning waste. Madison now saves $40 for every ton of material it keeps out of its landfill by recycling. In Seattle, the city's total cost of collecting and processing recyclables fell from an average of $89 per ton in 1993 to $28 per ton by April 1995—about $77 per ton less than what the city pays for disposal of what it can't recycle. In Canada, a number of communities in the province of Ontario are now earning profits of Cdn $50 per ton or more on recycling, including collection, processing, and capital costs, according to Atul Nanda, a senior official in Metro Toronto's recycling program.

Where recycling is not succeeding, a close look often reveals poor management. In Washington, D.C., for example, where city officials moved in late April to halt residential collection of recyclables, municipal administrators did not take into account the costs of landfilling and incineration that the city avoided by recycling. They tied funding for the recycling program to revenue from dumping by commercial waste haulers at the city landfill, which meant that the more trash was recycled, the less funding it received. And finally, they failed to renegotiate materials marketing contracts to take advantage of rising prices.

Even some communities with a history of successful recycling, such as Metro Toronto, have not been in a position to benefit from improved markets, because they locked themselves into long-term, fixed-rate contracts before materials prices soared. William Ferretti, director of the New York state Office of Recycling Market Development, says municipal officials and waste haulers alike need to "stop acting like garbagemen" and realize that they are now in the business of selling commodities.

As recently as 1993, North American markets for many recovered materials were unreliable, prices were low, and many communities were unsure about their long-term ability to sell the materials they collected. Now some cities are moving to expand their collection programs to take advantage of high prices for recyclables. San Francisco, for instance, is doing extensive public outreach in an attempt to recover more recyclables, and is expanding its program to cover previously uncollected materials. The high demand for recycled materials is allowing the city to market even lower-grade materials that in previous years might have been hard to sell.

THE BIG TURNAROUND

The most dramatic growth has occurred in prices for used paper products. Between January 1994 and March 1995, the average U.S. price of old newsprint —which had hovered near or below zero since mid-1991—rose 22-fold, according to *Recycling Times*. The price of old corrugated cardboard—used cardboard boxes—jumped five-fold. In early May 1995, a ton of baled corrugated cardboard that sold for $45 to $50 in 1991 or 1992 was commanding $230 to $250.

Other grades of paper saw smaller, but still substantial, price increases.

Over the same period, used aluminum beverage can prices doubled, and recycled glass prices rose 80 percent. Prices of HDPE and PET—the two plastics most commonly collected for recycling—went up by 260 percent and 160 percent, respectively.

What happened to cause these jumps? To some degree, they are a result of international economic developments. Simultaneous economic upturns in Japan, North America, and Western Europe have driven up demand and prices for many commodities, both primary and recycled. Increased aluminum prices, for example, are largely the result of a January 1994 international agreement between the major aluminum-producing nations to reduce their production. Prices for both primary and recycled aluminum had been depressed since 1991, when Russian smelters—which formerly sold nearly all of their output within the Soviet bloc—began selling large amounts of the metal on already-slack Western markets. Higher prices for some plastics are related to poor crops of cotton in several major growing regions, which have driven prices for the natural fiber to all-time highs and sent clothing manufacturers hunting for substitutes. China has been importing used plastic soft-drink bottles and turning the polymer they contain into new synthetic fibers for jackets and other garments.

But other factors are more basic and likely to last. Demand for products with recycled content has increased substantially with the rise of government and private procurement programs that give them preference, and experience with recycled-content products has removed much consumer apprehension about their suitability for a variety of uses. Most important, large capital investments have resulted in a dramatic expansion of industrial capacity for recycling. North American industry is "buying in" to recycling.

STRUCTURAL CHANGE

The paper industry is at the leading edge of this change. Paper accounts for a larger share (38 percent) of U.S. municipal solid waste than any other material, and has received more market-development attention from governments than other materials. Such efforts are now bearing fruit. The Environmental Protection Agency estimates that the amount of paper recovered from U.S. municipal waste grew from 13 million tons in 1985 to 26 million tons in 1993. During much of this period, wastepaper prices lagged, as the amount collected grew faster than the overall capacity of paper recycling plants. In 1994, however, the tables turned dramatically. Recovered paper consumption is growing more than twice as fast as total fiber consumption, and mills are scrambling for used paper supplies.

Behind this situation, say many in the paper industry, is a major change in the industry's structure. Heavy investment by papermakers in building new recycled-paper mills and retooling old plants to take in recycled fiber has created a much more mature, stable market for used paper. While prices will eventually decline again—as is to be expected to some degree with any commodity in response to normal business fluctuations—observers believe that the tremendous paper price crashes seen in previous years are unlikely to recur. Dan

Cotter, of Pacific Forest, a major broker of both used paper and new paper products, argues that recycled fiber has become a "primary" input for many paper manufacturers, rather than a last-resort substitute for virgin pulp. As a result, recycled fiber should experience future price swings no worse than those experienced in virgin pulp markets, whereas until recently, recycled-paper markets were far more volatile.

Recycling is revolutionizing the paper industry. The industry is actively moving to site its plants in areas with untapped reserves of wastepaper, and new paper mills are now being built in and near cities, rather than in more remote areas near large forests. Weyerhaeuser, for example, is a major partner in a large mill in Iowa—a state better-known for corn than for forests—to take advantage of the substantial amounts of wastepaper available from midwestern cities. The industry is also moving to recycle not just relatively low grades of paper—such as newsprint and old corrugated cardboard —but also office and coated papers, and is also making higher-grade products from recycled fiber.

The North American paper industry is pouring money into a resource it once resisted stubbornly. The American Forest & Paper Association (AFPA), its main trade group, estimates that its members will invest a total of $10 billion in recycling by the end of the 1990s. They have set a goal of recycling or reusing half of all U.S. paper production by the year 2000. AFPA estimates that the United States recycled 40.5 percent of the paper it used in 1994. More than 80 percent of this was paper recovered from the post-consumer waste stream, while the remainder was scrap from paper mills and printing plants.

So much new paper recycling capacity has come on-line that existing collection programs are barely providing enough fiber to meet the demand. And more is on the way: new plants with several million tons of paper-recycling capacity are scheduled to open in 1995. As a result, recycled-paper makers are becoming vocal supporters of paper collection programs. One paper broker describes the industry as "panicked" about future supplies of recycled fiber for the mills they have spent billions to build. Weyerhaeuser—a Fortune 500 company best-known for its timber production— has invested so much in recycling capacity that it is now offering cities 20-year, guaranteed market-rate contracts to purchase all the wastepaper they can collect. The company took in 2 million tons of wastepaper in 1994, and expects to consume 3 million tons in 1995.

The paper-recycling situation has completely reversed in just a few years. Before, paper companies were reluctant to invest in recycling, because they saw limited markets for recycled paper, and because they feared that large-scale municipal paper collection programs would not survive. Now, some industry officials are voicing caution about further investment in recycling capacity for the opposite reason—because markets have grown so fast that they are worried about obtaining adequate supplies of secondary fiber. Ironically, governments now need to reassure the companies not about the survival of the collection programs, but about their commitment to *expand* those programs over the long term.

THE GLUT THAT WAS

The reason that many governments embarked on the market-development programs for recycled materials is that for much of the late 1980s and early 1990s, collection of recyclables grew far faster than industrial capacity to absorb them. Thousands of recycling collection programs were initiated in North American communities in the last decade. According to *BioCycle* magazine's annual waste management survey, the number of U.S. curbside pickup programs for recyclables grew from 1,042 in 1988 to 6,678 in 1993. This growth, and similar growth in drop-off and commercial-waste recycling programs, led to an extraordinary increase in the overall tonnage of recycled materials collected, from some 16 million tons in the United States in 1985 to 45 million tons in 1993.

Not surprisingly, such rapid growth created a glut of materials. The hundreds of communities all starting up recycling programs at the same time created a structural problem in the recycling economy. Collection programs can be implemented almost as quickly as trucks can be purchased. The capacity to turn the materials collected into new products, however, can take years—and billions of dollars in capital investment—to build. Few communities devoted the same energy to developing recycling industries that they applied to their collection programs. But the market-development efforts of a few influential cities and states —and more recent actions by the U.S. federal government—set the stage for 1994's market turnaround.

The most obvious way to develop markets is to ensure that a guaranteed minimum quantity of goods with recycled content will be purchased. Governments are among the largest buyers of many goods, and among the first prominent market-development efforts were state laws requiring or encouraging govern-ment procurement of products with recy-cled content. Nearly all states now have such laws, with widely varying degrees of stringency. In 1993, the U.S. federal government joined in with an executive order requiring that the paper it pur-chases have 20 percent recycled content by 1995 and 25 percent by 2000. The ac-tion immediately guaranteed a huge mar-ket for recycled paper, since the federal government, at 300,000 tons per year, is the world's largest buyer of paper.

States have also moved to ensure that large private buyers of some commodi-ties buy a minimum of recycled mate-rial. The newsprint market has been most notably affected by such measures. Thir-teen states now have standards for mini-mum recycled content of newsprint; 15 more have negotiated voluntary agree-ments with newspaper publishers to in-crease their purchasing of recycled con-tent. According to New York's William Ferretti, the recycled-content standards for newsprint some states enacted in the late 1980s—and the threat of standards in other states—were the primary factors in the newsprint market's shift toward secondary fiber. Then, as publishers got accustomed to using recycled newsprint, they found that it could perform as well as virgin paper, and resistance to its use fell away.

FROM ENVIRONMENTAL PROTECTION TO ECONOMIC DEVELOPMENT

As municipal solid waste officials have realized that recycling can be a cheaper disposal method than landfilling or incin-eration, collection programs have taken off. Faced with market problems, pro-curement and recycled-content require-ments have been governments' first answer. But a few states are now beginning to make a crucial transition from viewing recycling simply as an environmental measure—a waste-disposal strategy—to seeing it simultaneously as an economic development opportunity. The most notable successes have come when economic development offices begin to promote recycling.

New York state took the lead in this area in 1988 when it created the Office of Recycling Market Development within its Department of Economic Development. The office offers financing, technical assistance, and market information—and a helping hand through the regulatory thickets—to companies that use recycled materials. Similar efforts are now underway in at least 18 other states, according to a 1994 *BioCycle* survey.

Bringing in state, regional, and local economic development officials to help promote recycling helps such businesses get access to a wide variety of proven tools: Industrial Development Bonds and other financing mechanisms, special property-tax treatment, siting assistance, and expedited regulatory action on permits, zoning, and related matters. Twenty-seven states now offer some form of tax incentive for recycling. The Environmental Protection Agency has supported these efforts by establishing a "Jobs Through Recycling" project, which offers grants for hiring Recycling Economic Development Advocates in state economic development offices, and has also helped establish Recycling Business Assistance Centers in four states.

California has become the laboratory for what is probably the most extensive effort in North America to develop recycling industries. The state has created 40 Recycling Market Development Zones, which are, in effect, enterprise zones specifically targeted toward recycling-based businesses. The state's Integrated Waste Management Board offers technical assistance with financing and marketing, and local governments also offer strong incentive packages designed to meet their communities' needs. The Board has approved some $12 million in loans for such enterprises, and is currently considering $3 million more. Board officials—who see the state financing as a bridge to much greater amounts of commercial capital—estimate that the zones have created 1,000 new jobs since the program was established in 1989.

During the long market slump—when cities were offering a few dollars per ton to anyone who would haul away their newsprint—extraordinarily cheap secondary materials helped lure entrepreneurs into recycling-related businesses. In the long run, however, businesses don't need cheap raw materials so much as they need predictable prices for what they buy and what they sell. In an effort to alleviate the uncertainty and unpredictability of recycled-materials markets, the Recycling Advisory Council (a program of the National Recycling Coalition) has been working with the Chicago Board of Trade, one of the world's premier commodities markets, to develop a formal trading system for recycled materials.

Among the project's elements are the development of product specifications that materials will have to meet to be traded, the design of an electronic trading system, development of dispute-resolution procedures, and an effort to inform and involve potential participants. The system initially will be only a cash market, but the feasibility of future markets will be investigated. The system

[was] being tested [in the summer of 1995], and trading in glass and some types of plastic was expected to begin in September.

DOING GOOD... AND MAKING MONEY

... [I]t has become clear that the recycling industry is maturing. And while recycling is worth doing for environmental reasons, its success will eventually be measured in dollars as well. Recycling is a business. Whether that business thrives will eventually determine the success or failure of community recycling programs.

The broad environmental benefits of recycling—especially, savings in natural resources and energy—will only be realized if manufacturers substitute used materials for a major share of the virgin wood, metals, and plastics they now consume. For this to happen, there must be a large, vigorous industrial sector devoted to taking used materials, processing them, and turning them into salable commodities. In North America, that sector is clearly now developing on a large scale, at least for some materials—and

the environmental benefits, though hidden, are substantial. The United States and Canada are now substituting generally less-polluting recycling facilities for virgin materials industries that are often among the greatest offenders in air and water pollution, energy use, and damage to ecosystems. The United States alone is now saving about 1 exajoule of energy—about 1 percent of total U.S. energy use —each year by recycling municipal solid waste.

With recycling beginning to fall into place, it is time for the next step. Within the limited universe of municipal solid waste (which is only a fraction of total U.S. waste production), growth in recycling appears to be stabilizing the amount of garbage going to landfills and incinerators, which had been growing for decades. Yet, U.S. waste generation is still increasing. In the long run, market mechanisms need to be developed not just to increase recycling, but to reduce the quantity of waste that we generate in the first place. Only then will a truly sustainable materials economy—one that consumes a minimum of virgin products and recycles most of what it takes in—be achieved.

NO

Chris Hendrickson, Lester Lave, and Francis McMichael

TIME TO DUMP RECYCLING?

After decades of lobbying by environmentalists and extensive experience with voluntary programs, municipal solid waste recycling has recently received widespread official acceptance. The U.S. Environmental Protection Agency (EPA) has set a national goal that 25 percent of municipal solid waste (MSW) be recycled. Forty-one states plus the District of Columbia have set recycling goals that range up to 70 percent. Twenty-nine states require municipalities or counties to enact recycling ordinances or develop recycling programs. Before celebrating this achievement, however, we need to take a hard look at the price of victory and the value of the spoils.

No one seeing the overflowing trash containers in front of each house on collection day can deny that MSW is a serious concern. Valuable resources are apparently being squandered with potentially serious environmental consequences. The popular media have carried numerous warnings that landfills are close to capacity, and we expect to find vehement local opposition to the siting of any new landfills. At first glance, recycling seems to be the perfect antidote, and it does have widespread public support.

Because it seemed to be the right thing to do, we have tolerated numerous glitches in establishing recycling programs. The supply of recycled material has grown much faster than the capacity for converting them to useful products. Prices for materials have fluctuated wildly, making planning difficult. It takes time to develop efficient collection and processing systems. But the public and policymakers have been willing to be patient as the kinks in the system are worked out. The self-evident wisdom of recycling reassured everyone that all these problems could be solved.

But as these difficulties are being resolved, we are developing a much clearer picture of the economics of recycling. Beneath the debates about markets and infrastructure lurk two fundamental questions: Is it cost effective? Does it actually preserve resources and benefit the environment? What "obviously" makes sense sometimes does not stand up to careful scrutiny.

From Chris Hendrickson, Lester Lave, and Francis McMichael, "Time to Dump Recycling?" *Issues in Science and Technology* (Spring 1995). Copyright © 1995 by The University of Texas at Dallas, Richardson, TX. Reprinted by permission.

UNDERSTANDING THE PROBLEM

The U.S. gross domestic product (GDP) of $6 trillion entails a lot of "getting and spending." From short-lived items such as food and newspapers to clothing, computers, cars, household furnishings, and the buildings we live and work in, everything eventually becomes municipal solid waste. The average U.S. citizen produces 1,600 pounds of solid waste a year.

For most of our history, waste was carted to an open site outside of town and dumped there. When the public became unhappy with the smell, the appearance, and the threat to public health of these traditional dumps, EPA ruled that waste would have to be placed in engineered landfills. These sophisticated capital-intensive facilities must have liners to keep the leachate from spreading, collection and treatment systems for leachate, and covers to keep away pests and to inhibit blowing dust and debris. EPA's regulations resulted in the closure of most dumps and the elimination of the most serious environmental problems caused by MSW. Still, most people objected if their neighborhood was picked as the site of a landfill. Some analysts erred in interpreting the closure of dumps and siting difficulties as signs that the country was running short of landfills. Although a few cities, notably New York and Philadelphia, are indeed having trouble finding nearby landfills, there is no national shortage of landfills. Thus, lack of space for disposing of waste is not a rationale for recycling.

But even without a pressing need to find a new way to manage MSW, many people would promote recycling as an economically and environmentally superior strategy. Recycling is portrayed as a public-spirited activity that will generate income and conserve valuable resources. These claims need to be examined critically.

THE PITTSBURGH STORY

To get a detailed picture of how current recycling programs work, we focus on Pittsburgh—an example of an older Northeastern city where one would expect waste disposal to be an expensive problem. In response to a state mandate, Pittsburgh introduced MSW recycling in selected districts in 1990 and gradually increased coverage of the municipality and the number of products accepted for recycling.

After studying numerous alternatives, Pittsburgh implemented a system by which recyclable trash was commingled in distinctive blue bags, separately collected at curbside, and delivered to a privately operated municipal recovery facility (MRF) for separation and eventual marketing to recyclers. The contract for operating the facility is awarded on the basis of competitive bidding. Recyclable trash is collected weekly by municipal employees using standard MSW trucks and equipment owned by the city. In addition, special leaf collections are made in the fall for composting purposes.

In 1991, the last year for which complete data are available, Pittsburgh collected 167,000 tons of curbside MSW. This represents roughly two-thirds of the city's total MSW; the other third included retail, industrial, office, and park wastes. Curbside pickup of glass, plastic, and metal produced 5,100 tons (3.1 percent of curbside MSW) for recycling. In 1993, newsprint collection was added, and the total curbside pickup of recyclable material was 6,700 tons of newsprint and 5,300 tons of glass, plastic, and metal.

When Pittsburgh started its recycling program in 1989, it sought bids from MRF operators. The best bid was an offer to pay the city $2.18 per ton of glass, metal, and plastic delivered to the MRF facility and to charge the city $8.39 per ton to take the material if newsprint was included. The tipping fee at the landfill at the time was $24 per ton. Either option was therefore less expensive than landfilling if—and as we will see, this is a very big "if"—one does not take collection costs into account.

In the second round of bidding in 1992, the city was committed to recycling newsprint, so it solicited only bids that included newsprint. The best bid was a cost to the city of $31.60 per ton. Meanwhile, the fee for landfilling had fallen to $16.15 per ton. The city therefore had to pay almost twice as much per ton to get rid of its recyclable MSW—again, without accounting for collection costs.

The increased tipping fees for recyclable materials reflects recognition of the sorting costs associated with the Pittsburgh blue bags and the difficulties of marketing MSW recyclables. A study by Waste Management, Inc. found that the price of a typical set of recyclable MSW materials had fallen from $107 per ton (in 1992 dollars) in 1988 to $44 per ton in 1992. Prices have continued to fluctuate widely since then. Although they are high at the moment, there is no guarantee about the future.

COLLECTOR'S ITEM

The price instability of recycled material has darkened the economic prospects for recycling and received extensive public attention. But an even more troubling problem—the cost of collecting recyclable material—has been largely overlooked.

Pittsburgh's experience is particularly eye-opening. The city uses the same employees and type of equipment as it uses for regular MSW, but the trucks on the recycling collection routes use a crew of two instead of three. Using the city's own accounting figures and dividing the costs between recycling and regular collection in proportion to employee hours worked and time of truck use, we calculated total collection costs. In 1991, it cost Pittsburgh $94 per ton to collect regular MSW and $470 per ton to collect recyclable MSW. With tipping fees for recyclables now higher than those for regular MSW, the total cost of disposing of recyclable MSW is more than four times the cost for regular MSW.

Several factors account for the very large difference. First is the lower density of recyclables; a full truck will hold fewer tons of recyclables. A second reason is that the amount of material picked up at each house is much smaller (recyclable material is less than 10 percent of the total MSW in Pittsburgh) so that the truck has to travel farther and make more stops to collect each ton of recyclable MSW. Because the purpose of recycling is to preserve resources and protect the environment, it should be noted that collecting recyclable MSW results in a significant increase in fuel use and combustion emissions.

Care must be taken in generalizing from Pittsburgh, where the narrow streets and hilly terrain make collection difficult, to other cities. The cost of collecting recyclable MSW is not that high in most cities. Waste Management, Inc., reports an average collection and sorting cost of $175 per ton for recycled material, based on its experience with 5.2 million households in more than 600 communities. However, the cost of collecting regular MSW is also significantly lower elsewhere, so that the difference in the costs of collecting recyclable and regular MSW is very large everywhere. Data available for other municipalities suggests that Pittsburgh's experience is not atypical. For example, San Jose reports costs of $28 per ton to landfill versus $147 per ton to recycle.

Although the cost estimates cited above are a very rough estimate of actual costs, the difference between landfilling and recycling is so large that we are convinced that more finely tuned financial data would not have any significant effect on the bottom-line conclusion that most recycling is too expensive. City officials are apparently beginning to reach the same conclusion. After some years of experience, Pennsylvania's cities have begun to scale back their recycling program as a result of the unforeseen additional costs.

DISAPPOINTING ALTERNATIVES

Because collection accounts for such a large share of the cost of recycling, we need to look at alternatives to Pittsburgh's system of separate curbside pickup. One option would be to improve the efficiency of the current pickup system. In Pittsburgh, collection routes are determined by tradition, with little attention paid to minimizing cost. However, research by graduate students at Carnegie Mellon found that savings from improved routing and other improvements in the current collections system would be small. Although any reduction in cost would be desirable, the savings are available to regular as well as recyclable MSW collection so there should be no change in the relative costs.

A related strategy would be to decrease the frequency of collection. For exam-

ple, under pressure from the city council to reduce costs, Pittsburgh adopted in mid-1994 a biweekly schedule for collecting recyclable MSW. By increasing the amount of recyclables at each residence, the density of collection has increased somewhat, but it still does not approach the density of regular MSW. Also, residences now have to store recyclable materials longer, which could weaken their willingness to participate. This might explain why Pittsburgh's 1994 collection of recyclables was 25 percent less by weight than it had been in 1993.

A second alternative for cost savings is to use a private firm for collection. This might result in marginal savings but could hardly be expected to make a significant difference. A third possibility is to use the same truck for collecting MSW and recyclables. The efficiency of this system depends on how much additional time is lost in collecting the recyclables and then dropping them off at the MRF on the way to emptying the MSW at a landfill. A few cities have adopted this approach, but no reliable economic evaluation has been done. For Pittsburgh, we estimate that combined collection would actually increase costs by 10 percent.

Fourth, collection of recycled MSW might be abandoned in favor of disturbed dropoff stations. Households would reap the benefits of lower taxes at the expense of dropping off their recyclables. The efficiency of this system depends on the amount of recyclables to be dropped off and the number of additional miles driven. To obtain a rough estimate, assume that each household drives three extra miles (30 percent of an average shopping trip) every two weeks. The household generates 150 pounds of MSW every two weeks, of which 8 percent (12 pounds) is recyclable. Thus, the $0.90 additional driving cost amounts to $0.075 per pound or $150 per ton. Costs of dropoff center implementation and maintenance should also be added. In Wellesley, Massachusetts, the operating cost of a dropoff center is reported as $16 per ton of recycled material in 1988–1989 or roughly $18 in 1992 dollars. Thus, an estimate of the total direct cost of recycling in dropoff stations is $168 per ton. This does not include the value of volunteer labor such as sorting recyclable material and driving to the dropoff center. At $5 per hour, the labor cost is more than the vehicle costs, with a total of about $400 per ton. Having more dropoff centers would lower driving costs but add a neighborhood nuisance and increase center costs. Another consideration is that the total volume of recycled material might be much smaller because people would not want to do the extra work. Smaller volume would make it more difficult to establish a market for the recycled material and to benefit from economies of scale in processing the material.

Because the value of recycled material varies so much, efficiency might be increased by limiting collection to the most valuable materials. For example, assuming that typical MRF processing costs $150 per ton, that collecting recyclable MSW costs $75 per ton more than collecting regular MSW, and that tipping fees are about $35 per ton, the recyclable material would have to sell for at least $190 per ton to be worth separating from MSW. Only aluminum, which was selling for about $750 per ton in 1993, qualifies on this criteria. At that time, plastic was $100–$130 per ton, steel and bimetal from cans was $80 per ton, clear glass was $50 per ton, and newsprint was $30 per ton. By limiting collection to aluminum and

other metal cans, plastic, and plastic containers, one could lower the separation costs at the MRF, but the unit collection cost would increase so much that it would probably dwarf the savings at the MRF. In addition, collecting only high-value materials contradicts the EPA goal of recycling 25 percent of all MSW.

A major problem with recycling is the low demand for recycled materials. For example, Germany instituted a packaging recycling program that collected essentially all used packaging, but now Europe is swamped with inexpensive (and subsidized) recycled plastic. One possible policy prescription for reducing the imposed costs of recycling is to stimulate the demand for recycled materials. For example, the federal government has changed its procurement policy to insure that 20 percent of paper purchases are of recycled pulp. In some cases, there is needless discrimination against recycled materials. However, at our estimated cost of $190 per ton for additional collection and separation costs, not many materials would be worth recycling even if demand for them surged.

Finally, we could move to a completely different arrangement such as the "takeback" system being tried in Germany in which the manufacturer is responsible for getting packaging material back from the consumer and recycling it. Germany is even considering legislation that would require manufacturers to take back and recycle their own products. In this system, firms would be required to arrange "reverse logistics" systems for collecting and eventually recycling their discarded products. For example, newspaper delivery services would have to collect used newspapers. The United States already has take-back regulation for a few particularly hazardous products such as the lead acid batteries used in automobiles. Although this approach creates strong incentives for manufacturers to reduce waste, the costs are likely to be much higher than those of the present system, because it will almost certainly require numerous collection systems.

WHAT ABOUT THE ENVIRONMENT?

Our analysis convinces us that recycling is substantially more expensive than landfilling MSW. But the primary motivation for recycling laws is not to save money; it is to save the environment. As it happens, saving the environment is not so different from saving money in this case. The greater costs stem from additional trucks, fuel, and sorting facilities. Every truck mile adds carcinogenic diesel particles, carbon monoxide, organic compounds, oxides of nitrogen, and rubber particles to the environment, just as building and maintaining each truck does. Collection in urban areas also increases traffic congestion and noise. Constructing, heating, and lighting for an MRF similarly use energy and other scarce resources. The variety of activities associated with the two- to four-fold increase in costs associated with recycling is almost certain to result in a net increase in resource use and environmental discharges.

For Pittsburgh and similar cities, the social cost of MSW recycling is far greater than the cost of placing the waste in landfills. No minor modifications in collection programs or prices of recycled materials are likely to change this conclusion. Approaches such as dropoff stations that attempt to hide the cost by removing it from the city ledger are likely to have the highest social cost.

Although many people object to landfill disposal, modern landfills are designed and operated to have minimal discharges to the environment. Current regulations are sufficient to minimize the environmental impacts of landfills for several decades. Nevertheless, landfills are unlikely to be the optimum long-term solutions.

The fundamental problem remains: A society in which each individual produces 1,600 pounds of MSW a year is consuming too much of our natural resources and is diminishing environmental quality. Today's MSW recycling systems are analogous to the "end-of-the-pipe" emission controls enacted 25 years ago. Air and water discharge standards were designed to stop pollution. They do so, but at a cost of about $150 billion per year. Recycling MSW lowers the amount going into landfills but at too high a cost.

EPA and some progressive companies have stressed "pollution prevention" and "green design" as the only real solution to pollution problems. Just cleaning up Superfund waste sites has proven extraordinarily expensive. Less expensive but still inefficient is the cost of preventing environmental discharges through better management of hazardous waste. The ideal solution is to redesign production processes so that no hazardous waste is created in the first place and no money is needed for discharge control and remediation.

For MSW, this approach would mean designing consumer products to reduce waste and to facilitate recycling. The potential hazards associated with toxic materials in landfills could be reduced by eliminating the toxic components in many products. For example, stop adding cadmium to plastics to give them a shiny appearance and stop using lead pigments in paints and ink. Another example is choosing packaging to minimize the volume of waste. Finally, products can be designed so that at disposal time the high-value recyclable materials can be easily removed.

Producers and consumers don't have good information to help them make choices among materials. And even when they have the information, they are not sufficiently motivated to use it. Most consumers know that they shouldn't dump used motor oil down the drain and shouldn't put old smoke detectors or half-empty pesticide containers in their trash. If they were charged the social cost of these practices, they would find more environmentally satisfactory ways of handling these unwanted products. In some cases it may be cost effective for manufacturers to include prepaid shipping vouchers to encourage consumers to return highly toxic components such as radioactive materials in smoke detectors before disposing of a product.

The best way to inform consumers and producers and to motivate them to act in socially desirable ways is to establish a pricing mechanism for materials and products that reflects their full social cost, including resource depletion and environmental damage. Full-cost pricing of raw materials would lead producers to make more socially desirable choices of materials and lead them to designs that are easier to reuse or recycle. A major problem with the current system is that product wastes in MSW arrive at the MRF having been manufactured with little or no thought for making them easy to recycle. Full-cost pricing would change the choice of materials and design

so that the MRF was an integrated part of a product's design.

Unfortunately, more research is required to determine the full cost of materials, and after that is done, it will be necessary to develop a means of implementing the concept. Neither task will be easy, but the alternative is to neglect environmental problems or to attempt to regulate every decision.

Even under the best of conditions, improved design and recycling will not eliminate the need for disposal. The waste stream will be smaller and less hazardous, but the total volume will still be daunting. We will have to come back to comparing the merits of landfills, recycling, and incineration. Changes in the waste stream will force us to examine each option with fresh eyes. At present, this might mean reserving recycling for metals, using the plastic and wood product portions of MSW as fuel for energy-producing incineration, and landfilling the rest.

MSW is a systems problem. Any one-dimensional solution, be it mandated recycling, incineration, or something else, is likely to do more harm than good. An assumed preference for recycling flies in the face of economic reality unless mechanisms can be found to greatly lower the costs of collection and sorting. The long-term answer to managing MSW is likely to include green design, materials choice, component reuse, and incineration, as well as recycling. Finding a way to use full-cost pricing so that decisions are decentralized and quickly adaptable will be the key to achieving thoughtful use of resources and improvements in environmental quality.

POSTSCRIPT

Municipal Waste: Should Recycling Efforts Be Expanded?

Readers of these two essays may be mystified by the diametrically opposite conclusions drawn by the authors from their analyses of the results of municipal waste recycling efforts. One factor contributing to this difference is that although Young's article was published only a few months after the article by Hendrickson et al., the data he uses are considerably more recent, and as he points out, the volatile market value of recycled materials had recently risen very sharply. Another fact to bear in mind is that Hendrickson et al. focus on the area around Pittsburgh, Pennsylvania, where the greater availability of unpopulated areas suitable for landfills makes that option considerably more attractive and cheaper than in New York or the New England states. These factors are only partly responsible for the sharply different conclusions. At least as important are differences in the assumptions and methods of analysis used in the complex job of assessing the costs and benefits of recycling. Hendrickson et al. argue that the pollution resulting from the collection and processing of recyclable materials exceeds the environmental benefits associated with recycling. Others who have examined this question maintain that the much lower pollution associated with the manufacture of paper, glass, aluminum, and steel from recycled feedstocks rather than from virgin raw materials makes the recycling of these waste stream components highly beneficial from an environmental perspective.

Two articles that denigrate the recycling of municipal waste materials—"Curbside Recycling Comforts the Souls but Benefits Are Scant," *The Wall Street Journal* (January 19, 1995) and "Recycling Is Garbage," the cover story by John Tierney in the June 30, 1996, issue of *The New York Times Magazine*—have both prompted vociferous responses from environmentalists and environmental organizations. Perhaps the most detailed and well-documented of these are "Advantage Recycling," a response to the *Wall Street Journal* article, and "Anti-Recycling Myths," a commentary on *The New York Times Magazine* article. Both of these are publicly available reports, coauthored by Richard A. Dennison and John F. Ruston of the Environmental Defense Fund, and accessible at the Internet site listed at the end of this postscript.

At the same time that Hendrickson et al. were bemoaning the economic and environmental failings of recycling, waste management research experts William E. Franklin and Marjorie Franklin were presenting a description of a healthy, thriving recycling industry and making optimistic predictions about its future in their article in the March/April 1995 issue of the trade journal *MSW Management*. In the same issue of that journal Delwin Biagi describes the progress that the sprawling city of Los Angeles, California, is making with its ambitious, new recycling program, and in the May/June 1996 issue, Sue Eisenhold describes how the success of urban programs has inspired the development of creative rural recycling efforts throughout the United States and Canada.

In "A Rationale for Recycling," *Environmental Management* (vol. 18, no. 3, 1994), David G. Evans rejects traditional financial analysis as a tool to determine whether or not wastes should be recycled. He proposes what he considers a more rational basis for evaluating the worth of the goals of a proposed recycling program. He argues that if such an analysis supports the program, governmental intervention is appropriate to compensate for the failure of market signals when trying to meet societal objectives.

For an Internet site related to this issue, see http://www.edf.org/pubs/ Reports/, which contains a listing of Environmental Defense Fund research reports available through the Internet, including several concerning waste recycling.

ISSUE 14

Nuclear Waste: Should Plans for Underground Storage Be Put on Hold?

YES: Nicholas Lenssen, from "Facing Up to Nuclear Waste," *World Watch* (March/April 1992)

NO: Luther J. Carter, from "Ending the Gridlock on Nuclear Waste Storage," *Issues in Science and Technology* (Fall 1993)

ISSUE SUMMARY

YES: Nuclear waste researcher Nicholas Lenssen proposes that due to technical uncertainties and political realities, the search for a permanent nuclear waste repository should be delayed until the future of nuclear power is decided.

NO: Science writer Luther J. Carter argues that Nevadans can be persuaded to accept the proposed Yucca Mountain site as safe for surface and underground storage of both civilian and military nuclear waste.

The fission process by which the splitting of uranium and plutonium nuclei produces energy in commercial and military nuclear reactors generates a large inventory of radioactive waste. This waste includes both the "high-level" radioactive by-products of the fission reaction, which are contained in the spent fuel rods removed from the reactors, and a larger volume of "low-level" material, which has been rendered radioactive through bombardment with neutrons—neutral subnuclear particles—emitted during the reaction. "Low-level" waste also includes the refuse produced during medical and research uses of radioactive chemicals.

The amount of highly radioactive material that builds up in the core of a commercial nuclear power plant during its operation far exceeds the radioactive release that results from the explosion of a high-yield nuclear weapon. Because radioactive emissions are lethal to all biological organisms—causing severe illness and death at high doses and inducing cancer at any dose level—it is necessary to make sure that the radioactive wastes are kept isolated from the biosphere. Since some of the nuclear products remain radioactive for hundreds of thousands of years, this is a formidable task.

The early proponents of nuclear reactor development recognized the need to solve this problem. Confident that scientists and engineers would find the solution, a decision was made to proceed with a program, sponsored and funded by the U.S. government, to promote nuclear power before the serious issue of permanent waste disposal had been resolved.

Forty years later, with 100 commercial nuclear power plants licensed in this country, more than 300 in other countries around the world, and hundreds of additional military nuclear reactors piling up lethal wastes in temporary storage facilities every day, the early confidence that the disposal problem could be solved has long since disappeared. Nowhere in the world is there a proven, operating plan for permanent nuclear waste disposal. In the United States, several abortive plans and schedules have been mandated by Congress, only to be abandoned for a variety of technical and political reasons. The most recent Nuclear Waste Policy Act, legislated in 1982, set a step-by-step schedule to complete a permanent, operating "high-level" waste repository by 1998. This schedule has proven impossible to meet. In December 1987, recognizing that serious problems were again developing in implementing the new plan, Congress short-circuited the process by designating Yucca Mountain, Nevada, as the only site to be considered for the first high-level repository.

A solution to the problem of "low-level" waste has been equally elusive. Amendments were passed in late 1985 in an attempt to make the 1980 Low-Level Radioactive Waste Policy Act workable. But political and technological disputes continue unabated, and the timetable established in the legislation has not been met.

The history of the nuclear waste issue illustrates the folly of focusing on technological fixes without recognizing that solutions to real world problems must meet political, socioeconomic, and ecological criteria that are not revealed by isolating the results of laboratory investigations from the other aspects of the issue. The simplistic response of some nuclear scientists is to claim that the technological problems have been resolved and nuclear waste disposal is only a "political" issue. A careful examination of the situation reveals the inappropriateness of adopting such a perspective. The evaluation of a proposed technological solution to a problem is related to social values, which in turn affect the political position of the participants in the process. Serious differences exist as to the degree of isolation and period of time necessary for "high-level" waste containment. How certain need experts be about future geological processes before they can claim that burying wastes in a particular location will result in the required degree of isolation?

Researcher Nicholas Lenssen, author of a Worldwatch paper on nuclear waste, proposes that in view of the uncertainty about the future of nuclear power, and because of the scientific and political difficulties with geological burial, above-ground "temporary" storage is likely to remain the only viable option well into the twenty-first century. Writer Luther J. Carter, author of a book on nuclear waste, sees the urgent need to resolve the disposal problem. He recognizes that present plans for Yucca Mountain are doomed, but he thinks that Nevadans could be convinced to accept a proposal to bury both commercial and military nuclear waste at the site, beginning with underground retrievable storage.

YES

Nicholas Lenssen

FACING UP TO NUCLEAR WASTE

A series of rapid-fire events has recently swept the nuclear field: amidst an almost celebratory atmosphere, *The Bulletin of the Atomic Scientists* rolled back the minute hand of its famed Doomsday Clock; the Soviet Union peacefully closed shop; the U.S. Nuclear Regulatory Commission's new chief pronounced an emphasis on "safety, safety, safety"; and the nuclear power industry made plans for a happy-days-are-here-again ad campaign proclaiming the virtues of the "new" nuclear power. The cumulative effect suggests that the atomic-age fears of the past are now safely behind us.

In fact, nothing could be farther from the truth. While the fall of the Soviet Union may have ended the superpower nuclear arms race, it has left the management of thousands of bombs, bombmaking facilities, nuclear materials, and radioactive waste sites in a state of near-chaos. And while the prospect of nuclear confrontation between superpowers has faded, the likelihood of more Saddam Husseins getting their hands on nuclear bombmaking materials is a growing concern.

But the most underestimated dangers of all may be those of the civilian nuclear power industry, which—after 50 years of costly research—has yet to find a safe and permanent way to dispose of its radioactive waste. In the United States, and possibly in the world as a whole, 95 percent of all radioactivity emitted by nuclear waste comes from the civilian sector—primarily from nuclear electric power plants. The cumulative discharge of irradiated fuel from these plants is fast growing; it is now three times what it was in 1980 and twenty times what it was in 1970.

Despite this increase, not a single one of the more than 25 countries producing nuclear power has found a solution that stands up to close scrutiny. The central problem is that nuclear waste remains dangerous for hundreds of thousands of years—meaning that in producing it, today's governments assume responsibility for the fate of thousands of future generations. Yet, neither technically nor politically has any way been found to assure that those generations—not to mention the present one—will be protected. The most prudent policy under such circumstances—to store waste in long-term temporary storage while searching for more responsible and permanent solutions—is being proposed by environmentalists and independent scientists in numerous countries; but even as that happens, the governments of the major nuclear nations continue their pursuit of more grandiose strategies for deep geologic burial, which also may entail greater long-term risks.

The nuclear waste issue has been marked by a series of illusions and unfulfilled promises. Like mirages, safe and permanent methods of isolating radioactive materials seem to recede from reach as they are examined closely. No government has been able to come up with a course of action acceptable either to advocates or opponents of nuclear power. Proponents insist that adequate permanent burial options have been developed and proved—and that it's time to jump-start the industry. Antinuclear advocates have identified flaws in every burial option proposed so far. They feel that in lieu of a commitment to abandon nuclear power, any waste site will become an excuse to start up the nuclear engine again. A political stalemate of this nature has formed in nearly every country.

Ironically enough, out of concern for the threat of global warming has come a political juggernaut that is being used to try to revive the nuclear power industry. Government officials and nuclear industry executives around the world believe that to achieve this "jump-start" will require a fast resolution of the nuclear waste problem. But just as earlier nuclear power plants were built without a full understanding of the technological and societal requirements, a rushed job to bury wastes may turn out to be an irreversible mistake.

BURY THE PROBLEM?

Since the beginning of the nuclear age, there has been no shortage of ideas on how to isolate radioactive waste from the biosphere. Scientists have proposed burying it under Antarctic ice, injecting it into the seabed, or hurling it into outer space. But with each proposal has come an array of objections. As these have mounted, authorities have fallen back on the idea of burying radioactive waste hundreds of feet below the earth's crust. They argue, as does the U.S. National Research Council (of the National Academy of Sciences), that geologic burial is the "best, safest long-term option."

The concept of geologic burial is fairly straightforward. Engineers would begin by hollowing out a repository roughly a quarter of a mile or more below the earth's surface. The repository would consist of a broadly dispersed series of rooms from which thermally hot waste would be placed in holes drilled in the host rock. When the chamber is ready, waste would be transported to the burial site, where technicians would package it in specially constructed containers made of stainless steel or other metal.

Once placed in the rock, the containers would be surrounded by an impermeable material such as clay to retard groundwater penetration, then sealed with cement. When the repository is full, it would be sealed off from the surface. Finally, workers would erect some everlasting sign post to the future—in one U.S. Department of Energy (DOE) proposal, a colossal nuclear Stonehenge—warning generations millennia hence of the deadly radioactivity entombed below.

Geologic disposal, though, as with any human contrivance meant to last thousands of years, is little more than a calculated risk. Future changes in geology, land use, settlement patterns, and climate all affect the ability to isolate nuclear waste safely. As Stanford University geologist Konrad Krauskopf wrote in *Science* in 1990, "No scientist or engineer can give an absolute guarantee that radioactive waste will not someday leak in dangerous quantities from even the best of repositories."

According to a 1990 National Research Council report on radioactive waste disposal, predicting future conditions that could affect a burial site stretches the limits of human understanding in several areas of geology, groundwater movement, and chemistry. "Studies done over the past two decades have led to the realization that the phenomena are more complicated than had been thought," notes the report. "Rather than decreasing our uncertainty, this line of research has increased the number of ways in which we know that we are uncertain."

THEY CALL IT DISPOSAL

In Germany and the United States, where specific burial sites have been selected for assessment and preparation, the work to date has raised more questions than answers about the nature of geologic repositories. German planners have targeted the Gorleben salt dome, 85 miles from Hanover in northern Germany, to house the country's high-level waste from irradiated fuel. But groundwater from neighboring sand and gravel layers is eroding the salt that makes up the Gorleben dome, making it a potentially dangerous location.

Groundwater conditions at the U.S. site at Yucca Mountain, a barren, flat-topped ridge about 100 miles north of Las Vegas, Nevada, are also raising concerns. According to the current plan, the waste deposited in Yucca Mountain would stay dry because the storerooms would be located 1,000 feet above the present water table, and because percolation from the surface under current climatic conditions is minimal.

But critics, led by DOE geologist Jerry Szymanski, believe that an earthquake at Yucca Mountain, which is crisscrossed with more than 30 seismic faults, could dramatically raise the water table. Others disagree. But if water came in contact with hot waste containers, the resulting steam explosions could burst them open and rapidly spread their radioactive contents. "You flood that thing and you could blow the top off the mountain. At the very least, the radioactive material would go into the groundwater and spread to Death Valley, where there are hot springs all over the place," University of Colorado geophysicist Charles Archambeau told the *New York Times*.

Other geologic forces could threaten the inviolability of underground burial chambers. For instance, in 1990 scientists discovered that a volcano 12 miles from Yucca Mountain probably erupted within the last 20,000 years—not 270,000 years ago, as they had earlier surmised. Volcanic activity could easily resume in the area before Yucca Mountain's intended lethal stockpile is inert. It is worth remembering that less than 10,000 years ago, volcanoes were erupting in what is now central France, the English Channel did not exist 7,000 years ago, and much of the Sahara was fertile just 5,000 years ago.

POLITICAL HOT POTATO

Since the early days of nuclear power, scientists have issued warnings about the long-lived danger of radioactive waste. In 1957, a U.S. National Academy of Sciences (NAS) panel cautioned that "unlike the disposal of any other type of waste, the hazard related to radioactive wastes is so great that no element of doubt should be allowed to exist regarding safety." In 1960, another Academy committee urged that the waste issue be resolved *before* licensing new nuclear facilities.

Yet such recommendations fell on deaf ears, and one country after another plunged ahead with building nuclear power plants. As government bureaucrats and industry spokespeople went about promoting their new industry, they attempted to quiet any public uneasiness about waste storage with assurances that it could be dealt with. However, early failures of waste storage and burial practices engendered growing mistrust of the secretive government nuclear agencies that were responsible. For example, three of the six shallow burial sites for commercial low-level radioactive waste in the United States—in Kentucky, Illinois, and New York—have leaked waste and been closed.

Trust also faded around the world as the public came to view government agencies as more interested in encouraging the growth of nuclear power than in resolving the waste problem. Grassroots opposition has sprung up against nearly any attempt to develop a radioactive waste facility.

The United States has perhaps the most dismal history of mismanaging waste issues; from the 1950s onward, the U.S. Atomic Energy Commission (AEC) and its successors have swept nuclear waste problems under the rug. Only following a stinging 1966 NAS critique of the AEC's waste policy (suppressed by the AEC until Congress demanded its release in 1970), and a 1969 fire at the U.S. government's bomb-making facility at Rocky Flats, Colorado (which created vast amounts of long-lived waste in need of storage), did the AEC concoct a rushed attempt to solve the problem by planning to bury nuclear waste in a salt formation in Lyons, Kansas.

By 1973, the AEC was forced to cancel the Lyons project because serious technical problems had been overlooked. For example, the ground around the site was a "Swiss cheese" of old oil and gas wells through which groundwater might seep. The Lyons failure set off a decade of wandering from potential site to potential site, and of growing opposition from apprehensive states.

A number of states, led by California in 1976, responded by approving legislation that tied future nuclear power development to a solution of the waste problem. Suddenly, the future of nuclear power seemed threatened. The nuclear industry pushed the AEC's successor, the Department of Energy (DOE), to bury waste quickly. But DOE had no better success in finding a state amenable to housing the nation's waste.

The department's repeated failures prompted Congress to pass the Nuclear Waste Policy Act of 1982. A product of byzantine political bargaining, the law required DOE to develop two high-level repositories, one in the western part of the country and the other in the east.

From the outset, the department was hampered in its response by an unreasonable timetable and its own insistence on considering sites that were technically and politically unacceptable. As DOE failed to gain public confidence, the process became embroiled in political conflicts at the state level. Finally, when the uncooperative eastern states forced the cancellation of the unsited eastern repository in 1986, the legislation fell apart. With the whole waste program in jeopardy, and over the strong objections of the Nevada delegation, Congress ordered DOE in 1987 to study just one site—Yucca Mountain, adjacent to the federal government's nuclear weapons test area.

While the federal government is determined to saddle Nevada with the country's waste, the state is vigorously seeking to disqualify the site, claiming in part that DOE—given that Yucca Mountain is the only site being investigated—cannot conduct research objectively. So vehement are the objections of Nevadans that the state legislature in 1989 passed a law prohibiting anyone from storing high-level waste in the state. Former U.S. Nuclear Regulatory Commissioner Victor Gilinsky describes Yucca Mountain as a "political dead-end."

GOING IN REVERSE

Although most of the countries using nuclear power are now preparing for geologic burial of their waste, almost every disposal program is well behind its own schedule. In 1975, the United States planned on having a high-level waste burial site operating by 1985. The date was moved to 1989, then to 1998, 2003, and now 2010—a goal that still appears unrealistic. Likewise, Germany expected in the mid-1980s to open its deep burial facility by 1998, but the government waste agency now cites 2008 as the target year. Most other countries currently plan deep geologic burial no sooner than 2020,

with a few aiming for even later [see Table 1].

So charged is the atmosphere surrounding the waste disposal issue that it's questionable whether any government has the political capacity to build and operate nuclear waste repositories. In most countries, even the study of a location as a potential nuclear waste burial site brings people to the streets in protest, as in South Korea and the former Soviet Union. So far, most governments have made short-term decisions on waste while leaving their long-term plans vague, hoping to muddle through.

Even in France, the acknowledged leader in European nuclear power generation, the waste issue defies ready solution. In 1987, the French waste agency, ANDRA, selected four potential sites for burying high-level radioactive wastes. Officials in those locales, disturbed that they had not been consulted, joined with farmers and environmentalists to paralyze the research program. Blockades obstructed government technicians at three of the four sites, and work proceeded only with police protection. In January 1990, in one of the country's largest antinuclear demonstrations since the late 1970s, 15,000 people marched in Angers against one site. By February, then-Prime Minister Michel Rocard had imposed a nationwide moratorium on further work, providing the government a cooling-off period to try again to win public support.

The French Parliament approved a new plan in June 1991. The number of sites to be investigated was reduced from four to two, and the government claims the selection process will be more open this time around. Also, ANDRA officials have a new approach for winning support. They will pay the two communities contending for the site up to $9 million a year for

Table 1

Selected Programs for High-Level Waste Burial

Country	Earliest Planned Year	Status of Program
Argentina	2040	Granite site at Gastre selected.
Canada	2020	Independent commission conducting four-year study of government plan to bury irradiated fuel in granite at yet-to-be-identified site.
China	none announced	Irradiated fuel to be reprocessed; Gobi desert sites under investigation.
Finland	2020	Field studies being conducted; final site selection due in 2000.
France	2010	Two sites to be selected and studied; final site not to be selected until 2006.
Germany	2008	Gorleben salt dome sole site to be studied.
India	2010	Irradiated fuel to be reprocessed, waste stored for twenty years, then buried in yet-to-be-identified granite site.
Italy	2040	Irradiated fuel to be reprocessed, and waste stored for 50–60 years before burial in clay or granite.
Japan	2020	Limited site studies. Cooperative program with China to build underground research facility.
Netherlands	2040	Interim storage of reprocessing waste for 50–100 years before eventual burial, possibly in another country.
Soviet Union	none announced	Eight sites being studied for deep geologic disposal.
Sweden	2020	Granite site to be selected in 1997; evaluation studies under way at Äspö site near Oskarshamn nuclear complex.
United States	2010	Yucca Mountain, Nevada, site to be studied, and if approved, receive 70,000 metric tons of waste.
United Kingdom	2030	Fifty-year storage approved in 1982; exploring options including sub-seabed burial.

Source: Worldwatch Institute, based on various sources.

"the psychological inconvenience" of being studied, according to then-Industry Minister Roger Fauroux. However, parliament has delayed any decision on a final burial site for 15 years. In that time, the country's high-level waste inventory will more than triple.

In Germany, the controversy over radioactive waste mirrors that surrounding nuclear reactor construction, which has come to a standstill. Local opposition to any nuclear project appears deeply entrenched, and there is a general inability of the major political parties to agree on nuclear policy.

The German waste controversy erupted in 1976, when the federal government's investigation of three sites in Lower Saxony created such an uproar among local farmers and students that the state government rejected every one. The following year, the federal government selected another site in Lower Saxony—the salt dome at Gorleben.

Large protests erupted even before the official announcement; 2,500 people took over the drilling site for three months before police hauled them off and set up a secure camp from which scientific work could be conducted. Although the federal government has put all its bets on Gorleben, continuing technical problems and strong opposition from the Lower Saxony government make plans to bury waste by 2008 highly improbable. Critics have warned that the site's geology is unstable. Public confidence in the project sank even lower when a worker was killed by collapsing rock during a 1987 drilling accident.

In Sweden, nuclear issues have been —erupting since the 1970s, when two governments were thrown out of office following attempts to promote nuclear energy. Only after a national referendum in 1980 to limit the number of reactors in the country to 12 and to phase even these out by 2010, was the country able to focus on the waste issue. One immediate dividend from the agreed phase-out was a clarification of exactly how much waste would eventually need to be dealt with: 7,750 tons of irradiated fuel, and 7.2 million cubic feet of other radioactive waste.

Sweden's high-level waste program has won international praise for relying not simply on deep burial but on a system of redundant engineering barriers, starting with corrosion-resistant copper waste canisters that have four-inch thick walls with an estimated lifetime of 100,000 years or longer if undisturbed by humans or geologic forces. Even with the announced phase-out and international scientific praise, Swedish public support has not been forthcoming for burial. Protests halted attempts to site a permanent high-level burial facility 12 years ago, and efforts to explore other sites have met determined local opposition.

The Japanese government also has run into public opposition to its burial plans. In 1984, planners selected an amenable village, Horonobe, near the northern tip of Hokkaido island. But opposition from the Hokkaido Prefecture governor and diet and from nearby villages and farmers has blocked the government from constructing a waste storage and underground research facility there.

There are signs that Japan is now looking beyond its borders for a high-level waste disposal site. Since 1984, China has shown interest in importing irradiated fuel or waste for either a fee or in return for assistance with its own fledgling nuclear program. In November 1990, China and Japan agreed to build an underground facility in China's Shanxi province, where research is to be undertaken on high-level waste burial.

WALK, DO NOT RUN

Because of the scientific and political difficulties with geologic burial, above-ground "temporary" storage is likely to remain the only viable option well into the 21st century. Fortunately, there need be no rush to bury nuclear waste, other than for public relations reasons. As a result, rather than continue focusing on developing controversial and potentially dangerous burial sites, governments can still choose a course of action that will buy time—and gain public support—to continue the search for a dependable long-term solution.

To choose this course requires, first, that nations employ safer methods of temporary storage for radioactive waste, particularly irradiated fuel. For instance, most spent radioactive material is stored in cooling ponds at nuclear power plants —an inherently risky proposition, since electric pumps are needed to circulate cooling water to prevent the fuel from overheating. Yet both governments and independent analysts believe that storage technologies such as dry casks, that rely on passive cooling and are capable of containing materials for at least a century are safer than water-based systems. Such storage would allow radiation levels to fall 90 percent or more.

Even with improved temporary storage systems, however, an institution for the careful monitoring and safeguarding of the waste will be needed to prevent catastrophic accidents or even terrorism. But no government can guarantee the durability of an institution whose responsibilities must continue many times longer than any human institution has ever lasted.

Temporary storage does not solve the problem of nuclear waste, but it could allow time for more careful consideration than is now witnessed in many countries of longer-term options, including geologic burial, seabed burial, and indefinite storage. It also could permit long-term, in-situ experiments with promising technologies such as the Swedish copper canisters.

But addressing the waste problem demands much more than a reduction of technical uncertainties. It also requires a fundamental change in current operating programs as well as new measures to regain public confidence. A lack of credibility plagues government nuclear agencies in most countries. Public distrust is rooted in the fact that the institutions in charge of nuclear waste cleanup also promote nuclear power and weapons production—and have acquired reputations for equivocation, misinformation, and secrecy.

In the United States, the U.S. Office of Technology Assessment, the National Research Council's Board of Radioactive Waste Management, and private research groups have called for an independent government body to take over the task of managing the country's nuclear wastes from DOE. So far, Congress has responded merely by requiring more oversight of DOE. Forming autonomous and publicly accountable organizations to manage nuclear waste would go a long way toward regaining public support, and getting waste programs on track.

BEYOND ILLUSION

In the end, some observers believe that the nuclear waste issue is a hostage of the overall debate on nuclear power, which increasingly tears at nations. "If industry insists on generating more waste, there will always be confrontation. People just won't accept it," believes David Lowry, a British environmental consultant and coauthor of *The International Politics of Nuclear Waste*. Because the political controversies are so intense, true progress on the waste issue may only come about when nations come to decisive resolutions, once and for all, of the nuclear power issue.

Sweden, which has perhaps the broadest (though not universal) public support for its nuclear waste program, made a national decision to phase out its twelve nuclear power reactors by 2010. Without such a decision, public skepticism toward nuclear technologies and institutions could grow only stronger.

While most countries do not have formal policies requiring phase-out of nuclear power, there is a de facto phase-out of new plants imposed by rising costs and concern over safety. Worldwide, roughly 50 nuclear power plants are under construction today—fewer than at any other time in the last 20 years.

Despite this trend, nuclear advocates continue to call for a rapid expansion of atomic power. They've seized upon the threat of global warming and public anxieties about dependence on Middle Eastern oil, aroused by the Gulf War, to push their point.

Yet a world with six times the current number of reactors, as called for by some nuclear supporters, would require opening a new burial site every two years or so to handle the long-lived wastes generated —a gargantuan financial, environmental, and public health problem that nuclear power proponents conveniently continue to ignore. President Bush's 1991 National Energy Strategy, for example, proposed a doubling in the number of U.S. nuclear power plants over the next 40 years, but did not discuss the need for future waste sites.

As experience with nuclear power plants has demonstrated, it will not necessarily become any easier to site and construct future geologic burial facilities once the first is opened. A single accident could set back government and industry efforts for decades. While waste is but one of the problems still facing nuclear power, it is clearly the longest-lasting one.

NO

Luther J. Carter

ENDING THE GRIDLOCK ON NUCLEAR WASTE STORAGE

In light of the nation's hard-won experience with the political and technical realities of nuclear waste storage and containment, it's time to take another hard look at the Nuclear Waste Policy Act (NWPA) of 1982. The U.S. Department of Energy's existing program to investigate Yucca Mountain at the Nevada Test Site (NTS) for use as a geological repository for nuclear waste is in trouble. The costs are huge, the progress is slow and uncertain, and the anticipated benefits are not up to emerging needs.

With exploratory excavation of the site about to begin, we need to reconsider the fundamental parameters of this federal program. Is it possible to evaluate the suitability of the site for *permanent* storage under the proposed schedule, or should we set our sights on a *retrievable* storage facility for now? Should facilities for surface as well as underground storage be located at the NTS? Should the site be considered for deposit only of irradiated (or "spent") fuel from commercial power reactors and glassified high-level waste from past production of plutonium for the military stockpile, as now planned, or should we also include surplus plutonium recovered from dismantled warheads?

Answering these questions is made the more difficult because at the heart of our nation's nuclear waste policies lies a profound ambivalence: the desire to achieve at least a rough consensus in siting a repository versus the recognition that the only way to serve the nation's best interest may be to act without consensus. The original NWPA reflected this ambivalence: It sought to establish a consensus of sorts by screening many sites, providing for public participation and environmental assessments, seeking regional equity, and assuring veto rights for prospective host states. Yet Congress granted the Department of Energy (DOE) the authority to make all the key siting decisions and explicitly kept for itself the right to override a state veto.

The NWPA produced not consensus but conflict. Loud and bitter protests arose across the country in response to DOE's widespread search for sites. In late 1987, Congress was forced to rescue the waste program from a state of

From Luther J. Carter, "Ending the Gridlock on Nuclear Waste Storage," *Issues in Science and Technology* (Fall 1993), pp. 73–79. Copyright © 1993 by The University of Texas at Dallas, Richardson, TX. Reprinted by permission.

political paralysis by drastically amending the NWPA, abruptly limiting the investigation for a geological repository to Yucca Mountain in Nevada.

The decision met with strong disapproval among Nevadans, not to mention a pervasive cynicism about the perceived sacrifice of principle in favor of political expediency. As a sop to an angry Nevada congressional delegation, Congress provided that a surface monitored retrievable storage (MRS) facility for interim placement of spent reactor fuel could not be located with the permanent repository project at the NTS—even though establishing an MRS facility there would have been the surest way for DOE to meet its obligation to begin accepting utilities' spent fuel in 1998. Instead, the siting of a surface MRS facility was put on a purely voluntary basis.

Today, nearly six years later, the Yucca Mountain plan is at a pivotal point. At long last, the deep exploratory testing of Yucca Mountain is near at hand. A 12-acre North Portal support facility is being built for a state-of-the-art tunnel boring machine, similar to one used for the English Channel Tunnel. Next summer, the machine will begin excavating a five-mile long "loop" tunnel through Yucca Mountain from north to south.

However, the program as now defined cannot possibly meet the schedule that's been set for it and, indeed, seems doomed to frustration. The goal set by the sponsors of the 1982 act—establishing a licensed operational repository by 1995 —was never a serious possibility. The date has twice been readjusted, first to the year 2003, then to 2010. Similarly, the costs of "characterizing" the site— that is, determining its suitability—have escalated astronomically. Cost estimates have gone from about $100 million in 1982 to $6.3 billion today, of which about $1.4 billion already has been spent.

To arrive at a realistic schedule and budget for characterizing the site actually is not possible today because the NWPA was drafted on an erroneous assumption. That is, the act reflects a mistaken belief that geologic isolation and containment of nuclear waste are within the known state of the art and, hence, are now licensable under standards established by the U.S. Nuclear Regulatory Commission (NRC) consistent with Environmental Protection Agency criteria. But in reality, developing a geologic repository and credible containment system for long-lived, heat-generating waste is exploratory and experimental. It calls for an iterative, design-as-you-go approach, as advocated by the National Research Council's Board on Radioactive Waste Management in its July 1990 report "Rethinking High-Level Radioactive Waste Disposal." Legislative goals and requirements need to be adjusted in light of this technological reality.

TAKING AN EXPERIMENTAL APPROACH

One major shortcoming of the existing program is that the current schedule allows only four to five years for collecting data crucial to the first licensing application, a constraint sharply criticized by the Nuclear Waste Technical Review Board (NWTRB). Created in 1987 by Congress to look over DOE's shoulder, the NWTRB recently warned that the project is "driven by unrealistic deadlines" and noted that certain key questions about the Yucca Mountain site could take decades to resolve.

An independent reevaluation of the Yucca Mountain plan now appears inevitable. Two senior program officials recently issued a report highly critical of the plan. Rep. Philip R. Sharp (D-Ind.), chairman of the House Energy and Power Subcommittee, the General Accounting Office, and the NWTRB have also called for a thorough program review.

At the urging of Nevada's Gov. Bob Miller, Secretary of Energy Hazel O'Leary has promised to at least review the project's costs and financing. But what Miller and the Nevada congressional delegation really want is for DOE to stop everything. In the view of the state and its allies among the antinuclear and environmental groups, Congress should change course just as drastically as it did in 1987 and abandon the repository and MRS siting programs in favor of continued, and indeed indefinite, storage of spent fuel at the reactor stations. This is the alternative also favored by some academic critics of the present program.

A sharp change of course is now in order, but not in the direction proposed by the state of Nevada. Indeed, Congress has more cause than ever to understand, and to make everyone else understand, that the nation's need for a solution to the nuclear waste problem must now be put ahead of the desire not to impose that solution on an unwilling host state. What is required is to make the NTS the national center for surface as well as deep underground nuclear storage. This would be an important new mission to replace the weapons-testing mission that is fading away.

WHY YUCCA MOUNTAIN?

When Congress decided to make Yucca Mountain, a barren desert ridge formation of volcanic tuff that straddles the southwest boundary of the NTS, the sole candidate site for the first repository, it was picking the location that DOE had rated the best, technically and economically, of the five sites that had been selected as most promising. In many ways, the NTS, where more than 709 nuclear weapons tests have been conducted since 1951, is uniquely suited to nuclear storage. The site is large; at 1,350 square miles, it is bigger than Rhode Island. Its geology, dry climate, and geographical location in a remote area of a sparsely populated desert region offer important advantages. And it has a ready-made infrastructure that includes hundreds of miles of roads and a tradition of tight security.

Scientists at the U.S. Geological Survey see a signal advantage for waste isolation in Yucca Mountain and similar sites in and around the NTS. It's that a repository can be built hundreds of feet above the water table, so that casks of radioactive materials can be kept relatively dry and that retrieval will be relatively easy. As these scientists see it, this advantage offsets what is probably the site's principal drawback—the fact that over geologic time the NTS and the larger Great Basin region have been racked by earthquakes and vulcanism.

Nuclear materials storage in Yucca Mountain should be made robustly defensible by adopting new policies for dealing with the uncertainty inherent in safely containing and isolating radioactive materials for thousands of years. To this end, the repository should be limited, at least initially, to underground retrievable storage (URS). The URS concept, which Lawrence Livermore Laboratory's L. D. Ramspott probably has done more than anyone else to define, is based on the use of massive, self-shielded storage casks containing corrosion-resistant inner canisters. The casks would rest on the floor of the emplacement tunnels, possibly on rail carriages to ease moving them in and out. As Eugene H. Roseboom, Jr., an adviser to the director of the U.S. Geological Survey on the Yucca Mountain project and a URS advocate, describes it, "The repository could be essentially an underground railroad switchyard with canisters on flatbed rail cars parked in the tunnels." Temperatures inside the tunnels would increase from the heat of radioactive decay but could be kept within tolerable limits by means of a ventilation system.

If necessary, the casks could be brought up out of the repository by the access ramps to form a storage array at the surface. For the longer term, however, storage deep underground offers a major advantage over surface storage because if the repository were ever abandoned, as in the case of a societal collapse, the radioactive materials sequestered there would be more likely to remain secure and safely contained.

Location of a surface MRS with a geologic repository makes sense because each adds credibility to the other. Just as storage at an MRS facility cannot be deemed temporary unless progress is being made toward an underground repository, deep geologic storage cannot truly be termed retrievable without a convenient place at the surface for storage of any spent fuel or high-level waste that may be retrieved.

Accordingly, Congress should direct DOE to make preparations for the necessary licensing applications. Most urgently, DOE should ask the NRC for permission to build an MRS facility at the NTS in time to begin receiving spent fuel in 1998. DOE should also begin revising its Yucca Mountain program plans to support a licensing application to

cautiously begin introducing spent fuel into a Yucca Mountain URS and test facility, say by the year 2005.

Development of a URS system could give vital support to scientific investigation of the site's suitability for permanent isolation of nuclear materials. Consider, for instance, these two separate but closely related questions: Will the Ghost Dance Fault zone, which runs through the mountain, prove to be so extensive that a repository of the size now contemplated cannot benefit? Will a "hot repository" or a "cool repository"—as determined by the density of spent fuel emplacement—best keep waste casks free from the corrosive effects of moisture? If the fault zone turns out to be much larger than now expected, the adequacy of the site for a full-scale repository might turn on the hot versus cool repository question and the density of fuel storage. Extensive testing with retrievably emplaced spent fuel could be essential to providing an answer.

MEETING AN EMERGING NEED

The need for surface and deep underground nuclear materials storage at the NTS is now proving pressing indeed. Consider the three principal categories of nuclear materials that should go there.

Spent commercial fuel. Spent fuel is generated by 110 reactors at nearly 70 commercial nuclear stations in 33 states. The existing spent-fuel inventory comes to roughly 27,000 metric tons; by 2010, this figure is expected to rise to nearly 59,000 tons. Nearly all of the spent fuel is kept at the reactors in pools used for cooling and storage. Many of these pools are nearing their capacity, forcing the utilities to look to storage of their older, cooler fuel in dry vaults or casks at the nuclear station.

The NRC regards this as a safe means of temporary storage for up to a century. The state of Nevada and others thus can argue that continued "at-reactor" storage affords a ready alternative to deep geologic storage and indeed buys time for developing safer, more acceptable methods for waste disposal. This argument is open to several objections. First, the belief that a better solution will turn up is entirely speculative. Second, the nuclear waste program is funded by a fee on nuclear electricity. This funding may not last indefinitely—particularly if existing nuclear plants are decommissioned without being replaced. Finally, indefinitely continued at-reactor storage will almost certainly meet with strong public opposition. In the absence of a long-term geological repository or a DOE-operated MRS facility for temporary central storage, at-reactor storage is likely to be seen —and rejected—as a *de facto* permanent solution.

Two current disputes in the upper Midwest bear on this point. In Minnesota, an appellate judge ruled in June against a Northern States Power Company plan for dry-cask storage at its Prairie Island station on the grounds that such storage might in fact be permanent. In Michigan, Consumers Power, which recently went to dry-cask storage at its Palisades station on Lake Michigan, has met opposition from the state Attorney General and from environmental activists who chanted, "We don't want your cask(et)s."

High-level military waste. Use of a Yucca Mountain repository to receive high-level waste from the nuclear weapons production sites is of central importance to the effort to clean up these sites.

Given the huge sums devoted to it (about $6 billion this year alone), the defense site cleanup surely ranks as a national priority and should be lending urgency to the need for greater progress at Yucca Mountain.

The Savannah River Plant's inventory of 34 million gallons of high-level waste, now stored in tanks, is all to be processed into about 7,000 canisters of borosilicate glass, possibly beginning next year. These canisters can be kept in temporary surface storage at Savannah River but will not be securely isolated for the long term until committed to an underground repository. The Yucca Mountain repository could in the longer term receive an even larger consignment of high-level waste from DOE's Hanford reservation in Washington state, and even an impressive amount from the Idaho National Engineering Laboratory. The volume of high-level waste stored at Hanford is nearly twice that kept at Savannah River, and most of it would be many times more difficult to recover, process, and reduce to a vitrified form. DOE's preliminary cost estimates for recovering and glassifying all the Hanford high-level waste run to nearly $50 billion, and there would also be the risk of significant radiation exposures to workers. Clearly, taking on so formidable and expensive a task would make no sense at all unless the waste recovered is to be securely isolated and contained in a geologic repository.

Warhead plutonium. A growing amount of plutonium is being recovered from the decommissioning of warheads required by recent arms-reduction agreements. About 1,800 warheads are being disassembled at DOE's Pantex plant in the Texas Panhandle, near Amarillo, each year, and a total of some 15,000 must be disassembled over the coming decade if the United States is to honor its arms-reduction obligations. By the early part of the next century, surplus warhead plutonium could amount to as much as 50 metric tons, which would be about half the existing military stockpile but less than a tenth of the plutonium present in the spent fuel of a fully loaded Yucca Mountain repository....

But DOE would have the plutonium kept as warhead pits or finished weapons parts and retained essentially as part of the military stockpile to await future decisions as to its disposition, which might include a return to weapons use. This policy defies convincing explanation because the existing plutonium stockpile is several times what will be needed for the downsized U.S. nuclear arsenal expected after the turn of the century. It is also at odds with U.S. policy to have the Russians remove surplus nuclear explosives from *their* military stockpile, and it weakens the moral force of U.S. appeals for the Nuclear Nonproliferation Treaty to be made permanent when it comes up for renewal in 1995....

Chris Whipple, chairman of the National Research Council's Board on Radioactive Waste Management, observes that, "By bringing the plutonium and the spent fuel to the same repository, you would be taking a further step toward international management of the spent fuel as well. The technical challenges are slightly different but the overall requirements for secure isolation of spent fuel, high-level waste, and weapons plutonium seem to be similar. I can't see anything but merit in the idea."

Princeton University's Frank von Hippel, a leading arms control expert recently appointed assistant director for national security in the White House Office of Science and Technology Policy, personally would prefer to see plutonium blended with high-level waste (HLW) for glassification and permanent geologic disposal. But he believes that retrievable storage, with the containers of plutonium placed together with canisters of HLW in the same storage casks, would be a "good compromise" with those (including Russian nuclear specialists) who believe that some day the plutonium will be valuable as a fuel for reactors.

CHANGING THE POLITICAL DYNAMIC IN NEVADA

There is, to say the least, the possibility of a wholly negative and outraged response by the state of Nevada to a federal initiative designating the NTS as the national center for storage of spent fuel, high-level waste, and surplus warhead plutonium. Indeed, state leaders in Nevada have been able to profit politically by crying "Never!" They spurn all federal efforts to enlist state cooperation and point to opinion polls showing that a large majority of Nevadans are opposed to nuclear waste storage at Yucca Mountain, never mind their own considerable part in shaping that opinion.

Nevada's Sen. Richard Bryan and Governor Miller, in particular, have told their constituents that the so-called waste dump is not inevitable, that time is on the state's side in opposing the Yucca Mountain project, and that appeals to negotiate for federal benefits in return for state cooperation must be flatly rejected. The Republican majority leader of the Nevada Senate and several other legislators actually would welcome such negotiations, but on this issue Bryan and

Miller have kept them in the minority and on the defensive.

Yet Nevadans know that, despite all its problems, the Yucca Mountain project has persisted and, with exploratory drilling soon to begin, may gain a new momentum. They also realize that, in the end, Nevada could have the repository but no benefits and no real part in deciding the outcome of safety issues.

Congress could break up the political dynamic that has favored all-out state resistance by declaring unequivocally that the NTS is to become the nation's center for nuclear storage and by directing that a spent-fuel surface storage facility be built and ready to operate by 1998. Elected state officials might suddenly find their political survival in jeopardy unless they are resourceful in having the state gain a critical but seriously constructive and well-rewarded role with respect to such nuclear storage.

To make the project more palatable, Congress could give Nevada and the counties principally affected a significant new place in the nuclear storage program. They could, for example, be invited to appoint a number of appropriately qualified scientists and engineers to product design teams. They might also be allowed a leading role in setting up a Nevada-based, but rigorously independent, project oversight agency similar to New Mexico's highly respected Environmental Evaluation Group (EEG), which oversees, and has significantly influenced, DOE's Waste Isolation Pilot Plant project—a geologic repository near Carlsbad for low-level plutonium-contaminated waste from past production of nuclear weapons. For emergencies, a Nevada EEG might be given authority to stop further loading of nuclear materials or even order the retrieval of materials already emplaced. Nevada has long had a nuclear waste project oversight group but, being answerable to the governor, it is far too politicized to have scientific credibility.

Nuclear storage at the NTS could also be made more palatable by joint federal/state high-technology ventures bringing Nevada important economic benefits. The expected loss of thousands of jobs from the ending of nuclear weapons testing is already cause for deep apprehension among some labor groups in southern Nevada and would be felt by the larger regional economy. To counter this disturbing trend, a Nevada Technology Development Trust could be established with money from the Nuclear Waste Fund, which is now collecting well over a half-billion dollars a year from a fee imposed on nuclear electricity....

Nevada, it should be noted, not so very long ago viewed nuclear storage as an opportunity, not a scourge. In 1977, faced with the threat of job losses due to a proposed nuclear test ban, the Nevada Legislature actually petitioned to have nuclear waste stored at the NTS. This receptive attitude did not, in the main, survive the national uproar over repository siting in the 1980s. Even today, however, rural counties in and around the NTS do not, by and large, go along with the state's categorical rejection of the Yucca Mountain project. For these counties, the critical considerations are whether the project can be built safely and whether the state and federal governments will respect their interests. What Congress and the Clinton administration have an opportunity to do now is to act firmly to give the NTS a new nuclear storage mission while letting all Nevadans know that, in carrying out this mission, the government will indeed respect their legitimate interests.

POSTSCRIPT

Nuclear Waste: Should Plans for Underground Storage Be Put on Hold?

Carter states that U.S. Geological Survey scientists are convinced that a repository built at Yucca Mountain can be kept dry. As Lenssen points out, other scientists disagree with this conclusion and fear that a future rise in the water table could disperse the stored waste. Carter acknowledges that local opposition is one of the key problems with the present plan, but he does not fully explain why expanding the proposal to include a much larger quantity of nuclear waste would enhance its political viability.

Nevada's former governor Richard Bryan's outspoken rejection of the congressional decision to designate Yucca Mountain as the permanent storage site set the stage for the state's continued opposition. For an elaboration of Bryan's arguments, read his article "The Politics and Promises of Nuclear Waste Disposal: The View from Nevada," *Environment* (October 1987). For a less politically partisan evaluation of the Yucca Mountain proposal, see Chris Whipple, "Can Nuclear Waste Be Stored Safely at Yucca Mountain?" *Scientific American* (June 1996).

A very pessimistic assessment of the effort to resolve the low-level waste problem is contained in "The Deadliest Garbage of All," by Susan Q. Stranahan, *Science Digest* (April 1986).

On the optimistic side is a report by researchers George Wicks and Dennis Bickford entitled "Doing Something About High-Level Nuclear Waste," *Technology Review* (November/December 1989). They describe the process of "glassifying" nuclear waste, which they claim is the key to permanent safe disposal. (Glassifying means to form a glass that incorporates the radioactive metallic ions and thereby immobilizes them; this would prevent leaching.)

The U.S. nuclear weapons program has created an ongoing disposal and cleanup controversy. For background information about this problem, see William F. Lawless's article in the November 1985 issue of *Bulletin of the Atomic Scientists*. In the October 1990 issue of the same journal, Scott Saleska and Arjun Makhijani present a frightening assessment of ongoing nuclear waste storage and treatment practices at the large military nuclear reservation in Hanford, Washington. Equally distressing is the history of incompetence in building the Waste Isolation Pilot Plant in New Mexico for permanent storage of military nuclear waste, as told by Keith Schneider in "Wasting Away," *The New York Times Magazine* (August 30, 1992). For a chilling exposé of the hazardous nuclear waste disposal practices of the former Soviet Union, see William Broad's article, which begins on the front page of the November 21, 1994, issue of *The New York Times*.

For an Internet site related to this issue, see `http://www.skb.se/skb/eng/default.htm`, which contains information about all aspects of the radioactive waste management problem from the Swedish Nuclear Fuel and Waste Management Company.

PART 4

The Environment and the Future

In addition to the many serious environmental problems of today, there are several potential future crises that might be averted or diminished if preventive measures are taken now: the destruction of tropical rain forests, which play a life-sustaining role in the biosphere; pollution of the atmosphere, which could raise the average global temperature or destroy much of the protective ozone layer; and the continued use of developmental strategies based on nonsustainable technologies, which could deplete resources, increase pollution, and exacerbate world hunger.

- Can Green Marketing Save Tropical Rain Forests?

- Do the Projected Consequences of Ozone Depletion Justify Phasing Out Chlorofluorocarbons?

- Are Aggressive International Efforts Needed to Slow Global Warming?

- Are Major Changes Needed to Avert a Global Environmental Crisis?

ISSUE 15

Can Green Marketing Save Tropical Rain Forests?

YES: Thomas A. Carr, Heather L. Pedersen, and Sunder Ramaswamy, from "Rain Forest Entrepreneurs: Cashing in on Conservation," *Environment* (September 1993)

NO: Jon Entine, from "Let Them Eat Brazil Nuts: The 'Rainforest Harvest' and Other Myths of Green Marketing," *Dollars and Sense* (March/April 1996)

ISSUE SUMMARY

YES: Economics professors Thomas A. Carr and Sunder Ramaswamy and mathematics teacher Heather L. Pedersen describe three projects to promote sustainable use of rain forest products, which they argue help to preserve the forest and support the local economy.

NO: Investigative reporter Jon Entine asserts that most green marketing programs do nothing to slow forest destruction and, moreover, frequently result in the mistreatment of employees, vendors, and customers.

The area of the Earth that is covered by forests has decreased by approximately 33 percent as a result of human activity. The clearing of land for crop production or animal grazing, the harvesting of timber, and the gathering of wood for fuel have been the principal human activities that have shrunk the world's forests.

Rapid regional decimation of tree cover is not a new phenomenon. By the end of the eighteenth century, France had cleared almost 85 percent of its forested land over a period of less than two centuries. Other contemporary industrialized countries, including the United States, have engaged in wholesale deforestation. Until recently, however, these practices have had relatively minor deleterious effects on human welfare.

Today, hundreds of millions of poor people in South and Central America, Africa, and Asia find their principal source of fuel for cooking and home heating threatened by the accelerating clear-cutting of tropical forests. Natives of the forested areas are being uprooted and driven from their only available source of sustenance. The economic forces that promote this plague are large lumbering, cattle ranching, and land speculation entrepreneurs. The beneficiaries include foreign investors as well as local elites with strong ties to the entrenched minority who maintain political control in much of the developing world.

The problem is exacerbated by the displaced forest dwellers who contribute to Third World urbanization. In the cities, charcoal, which is easier to transport, replaces wood as the predominant fuel. In the process of converting wood to charcoal, half of the fuel value of the wood is lost. Thus, the movement of rural villagers to city slums results in a doubling of per capita fuel wood needs.

The recognition that as much as one-third of the annual contribution to the increase in atmospheric carbon dioxide, which contributes to global warming, comes from deforestation has greatly heightened worldwide concern about forest depletion. (The global warming connection is a result of the fact that the cutting and combustion of trees release carbon dioxide that would only be balanced by an equal number of new trees removing that same amount of carbon dioxide as they grow.) Since global warming is an issue of universal concern, there is hope among environmentalists that it will serve to mobilize the enormous number of people needed to save the forests.

Tropical forests supply many useful commercial products and are the source of a wide variety of chemicals, including natural products that are used in the pharmaceutical industry. Among the serious consequences of rain forest destruction would be the loss of a principal source of organic chemicals used in medical research.

Designing and implementing appropriate and effective strategies for reducing or reversing rain forest decimation has produced heated controversy, both within the tropical nations where the destruction is occurring and in the international community. Among the proposals that have been advanced are many "green marketing" strategies whose goal is to enhance the economic worth of goods that can be produced from the forests in a sustainable manner. This is a means of motivating entrepreneurs to favor forest preservation over using forest land for other money-making schemes.

Economics professors Thomas A. Carr and Sunder Ramaswamy of Middlebury College and mathematics teacher Heather L. Pedersen of the Colorado Springs School describe two projects involving the use of forest products and one ecotourism initiative, which they argue are the types of endeavors that "may be key to preserving the vital and fragile resources of the tropical rain forests." Jon Entine is a National Press Club and Emmy Award–winning investigative reporter. He discusses green marketing schemes, such as Ben and Jerry's promotion of Rainforest Crunch ice cream and Body Shop International's tropical skin and hair care products. He argues that, while encouraging consumers to "shop for a better world," these enterprises frequently mistreat employees, vendors, and customers, and do little or nothing to help preserve the forests or support the indigenous peoples.

YES

Thomas A. Carr, Heather L. Pedersen, and Sunder Ramaswamy

RAIN FOREST ENTREPRENEURS: CASHING IN ON CONSERVATION

Each year, nearly 17 million hectares of rain forest—an area roughly equal to that of Wisconsin—are lost world-wide as a result of deforestation. Because more than half of all species on the planet are found in rain forests, this destruction portends serious environmental consequences, including the decimation of biological diversity. Another threat lies in the fact that rain forests serve as an important sink for carbon dioxide, a greenhouse gas that contributes to global warming. The Amazon region alone stores at least 75 billion tons of carbon in its trees. Furthermore, when stripped of its trees, rain forest land soon becomes inhospitable and nonarable because the soil is nutrient-poor and ill-suited to agriculture. Under current practices, therefore, the forests are being destroyed permanently.

Economic forces result in exploitation of the rain forest to extract hardwood timber and fuel and in clearcutting the land for agriculture and cattle ranching, which are primary causes of the devastation. Mounting evidence shows that these conventional commercial and industrial uses of the rain forest (see Table 1) are not only ecologically devastating but also economically unsound. These findings have inspired an innovative approach to save the rain forest. Environmental groups are now targeting their efforts toward developing commercially viable and sustainable uses of the rain forest. Their strategy is to create economic incentives that encourage local inhabitants to practice efficient stewardship over the standing forests. These environmental entrepreneurs no longer view the market as their nemesis but as an instrument to bring about constructive social and environmental change. In theory, the strategy promotes win-win solutions: Environmentalists gain by preserving the rain forests, and local inhabitants gain from an improved standard of living that is generated by enlightened, sustainable development. In practice, the challenge lies in implementing such programs.

Three applications of environmental entrepreneurship in the rain forests have been particularly successful. Conservation International's "The Tagua Initiative," Shaman Pharmaceutical's search for useful drugs in the rain forest, and the management of ecotourism in Costa Rica are three projects that together provide an interesting cross section of the efforts under way to promote sustainable use of rain forest products. A number of common issues and challenges confront these environmental entrepreneurs.

RESPONDING TO DEFORESTATION

Although people everywhere may benefit from preserving the rain forest, the costs of preservation are borne mainly by the local inhabitants. Usually, the inhabitants' immediate financial needs far outweigh the long-term benefit gained by forgoing the traditional extractive methods of forestry or land conversion for agriculture. In many of these countries, high levels of poverty, rapid population growth, and unequal distribution of land encourage migration into the forest regions. Local inhabitants, confronted with the tasks of daily survival, cannot be expected to respond to appeals for altruistic self-sacrifice. Consequently, forests are cut and burned for short-term economic gains. This problem is often exacerbated by misguided government policies in many countries, such as government-sponsored timber concessions that promote inefficient harvest levels, tree selection, and reforestation levels. Governments may charge a royalty far below the true economic value of the standing forest. Such low royalties and special tax breaks raise the profits of logging companies, which thereby stimulate timber booms. In addition, some governments provide special land tenure rules or tax benefits to individuals who "improve" the land by clearing the forest. These rules encourage development in the rain forest region because they impel poor settlers to seek land for agriculture and wealthy landowners to look for new investments.

Environmental entrepreneurs can create commercial alternatives to the traditional damaging uses of rain forest resources, but several factors must first be taken into consideration. For example, commercial development cannot be allowed to harm the ecological integrity of the ecosystem. This can be a difficult challenge as the scale of production increases for many projects. Also, if existing firms are profitable, new firms will be attracted into the industry, thus placing additional pressure on the fragile ecosystem. Of course, the product must also pass the test of the market; consumers must be willing to pay a price that covers the full cost of production. Some environmentally conscious consumers may be willing to pay a premium for sustainably harvested rain forest products. The size of this "green premium" would depend upon these consumers' willingness and ability to pay, as well as on the prices of other products competing with the rain forest products. To maintain the green premium over time, environmental entrepreneurs need to devise a strategy that differentiates their products from others through advertising and some type of institutionalized labeling system. These entrepreneurs must also anticipate the effect of expanding output on market prices. Previous studies have examined the market value of sustainable products from a single hectare. One study in the Amazonian rain forest in Peru found that sustainably harvested products such as fruit, nuts, rubber latex, and selectively logged timber yield more net value than do plantation forestry and cattle ranching. If harvests are expanded, however, market prices may be pushed down, and the profitability of the pro-

Table 1

Commercial and Industrial Products Derived from Tropical Rain Forests

Product	Value of imports by region (millions of U.S. dollars)	Marketshare of rain forest products (percent)	Region receiving imports	Year of estimate
Commercial products				
Fruit and vegetable juices	4,000	100	World	1988
Cut flowers	2,500	100	World	1985
Food additives	750	100	United States, European Community	1991
Spices	439	small	United States	1987
Nuts	216	100	World	1988
Food colorings	140	10	World	1987
Vitamins	67	small	United States	1990
Fiber	54	100	United States	1983/4
Industrial Products				
Fuel	60,000	< 1	United States	1984
Pesticides	16,000	1	World	1987
Natural rubber	666	100	United States	1978
Tannins	170	large	United States	1980
Construction material	12	1	United States	1984
Natural waxes	9.3	100	United States	1985

Note: James Duke, an economic botanist at the U.S. Department of Agriculture, has been compiling estimates of the economic value of hundreds of key commerical and industrial rain forest products. Some of the important estimates are summarized here. Although not all of the imported products are derived from tropical rain forest countries, Duke claims that they all have the potential to be sustainably harvested from these regions.

Source: James Duke, "Tropical Botanical Extractives" (Unpublished manuscript, U.S. Department of Agriculture, Washington, D.C., April 1989).

gram reduced. Another consideration is that entrepreneurs may be able to avoid the expense of developing extensive distribution networks and other marketing costs by forming alliances with established commercial firms. These firms typically have retail outlets and experienced business personnel that can assist the small entrepreneur.

Finally, the environmental entrepreneur must channel income back to the effective owners of the rain forests—the local indigenous people. This return raises the issue of rain forest property rights. The property rights over rain forest resources are not well defined or enforced. Rain forest land is often held collectively, and government-owned land marked as a reserve is not always protected. Even private landowners have a difficult time preventing landless squatters from using their property. Without the enforcement of property rights, rain forests become an open-access resource that is over exploited. This result is not inevitable, however. History suggests that, when the benefits of establishing new property rights exceed the costs, societies often devise new ways to define property rights and improve the allocation of resources.

In addition to the question of physical property rights, there is the problem of defining intellectual property rights. Indigenous people possess a wealth of esoteric knowledge about local plants and animals and their usages. Conservation groups argue that the wisdom of the local inhabitants must be given an economic value or else that knowledge will disappear amidst the destruction of the forest. At the same time, scientists and entrepreneurs also contribute value to rain forest products by discovering useful medicinal compounds in the plants. If these interests are not protected, there will not be sufficient economic incentive to develop new products. During the Earth Summit in Rio de Janeiro [in June 1992], the Bush administration refused to sign an international treaty on biodiversity on the grounds that it would harm the interests of biotechnology firms. (The Clinton administration signed the biodiversity treaty on 4 June 1993.) A key challenge is to develop an institutional mechanism that recognizes the value of both the natives' knowledge and the scientists' and entrepreneurs's contributions, and therefore rewards both types of intellectual property rights in the development of rain forest products.

The Tagua Initiative

Conservation International is an environmental organization based in Washington, D.C., that works to conserve biodiversity by supporting local rain forest communities world-wide. Through a project entitled "The Tagua Initiative," Conservation International is attempting to synthesize "the approaches of business, community development, and applied science to promote conservation through the marketing of non-timber forest products." The tagua nut is an ivory-like seed that is harvested from tropical palm trees to make buttons, jewelry, chess pieces, carvings, and other arts and crafts. Conservation International links button manufacturers in the United States and other countries with rural tagua harvesters in the endangered rain forests of Esmeraldas in Ecuador. The organization works independently with participating companies to design unique marketing strategies tailored to those companies' individual images, product offerings, and marketing campaigns.

In 1990, Conservation International began expanding the market for tagua products and developing a local industry around tagua. Today, tagua buttons are being used by 24 clothing companies, including such major manufacturers as Smith & Hawken, Esprit, J. Crew, and L. L. Bean. The current distribution network links the Ecuadorian tagua producers to the clothing companies through four wholesale button manufacturers. Conservation International collects a royalty based on a percentage of sales to wholesale button manufacturers and uses the proceeds to support local conservation and community development programs in the rain forest. It has also focused its efforts on developing a viable local tagua industry that includes harvesting and manufacturing. A primary objective of The Tagua Initiative is to provide the 1,200 local harvesters with an attractive price for tagua so that they have an economic incentive to protect the standing forest. Recent figures indicate that the price paid to tagua collectors has risen 92 percent since the program began (a 32 percent real price increase after adjusting for the estimated inflation rate). To increase the flow of income to the native economy, Conservation International encourages the development of new tagua products that can be manufactured locally. Currently, the tagua production line has expanded to include eight manufacturers of jewelry, arts and crafts, and other items.

The Tagua Initiative provides a tremendously successful example, at least in the initial stages of development. Since February 1990, 850 tons of tagua have been delivered directly to factories, and the program has generated approximately $2 million in button sales to manufacturers in North America, Europe, and Japan. According to Robin Frank, tagua product manager at Conservation International, the organization is collaborating with about 50 companies worldwide, and many others have expressed interest. Moreover, The Tagua Initiative in Ecuador has become a role model for new projects in Colombia, Guatemala, Peru, the Philippines, and a number of other countries. In all of these cases, Conservative International is working with local organizations to identify and develop sustainable commercial products in a manner that protects sensitive ecosystems. These projects are expanding the rain forest product line to Brazil nuts and pecans from Peru, fibers for textiles, and waxes and oils for the personal health and hygiene market.

In addition to creating marketable rain forest products, Conservation International cooperates with conservation and community development programs, such as the Corporacion de Investigaciones para el Desarrollo Socio/Ambiental (CIDESA) in Ecuador. Ecologists, economic botanists, and conservation planners affiliated with Conservation International help CIDESA to identify critical rain forest sites and monitor harvesting practices to ensure their sustainability, among other things. The province of Esmeraldas in Ecuador is considered a critical "hot spot" because it contains some of the highest levels of biodiversity in Latin America and harbors some of Ecuador's last remaining pristine tracts of western Andean rain forest. Coincidentally, it is one of Ecuador's poorest communities, with a meager annual average per-capita income of $600, about one-half of the national average. The community of Comuna Rio Santiago in Esmeraldas has a population of 70,000, which grows dramatically at an annual rate of 3.7 percent. Four out of every 10 children suffer from malnutrition, and the infant mortality rate is 60 per 1,000 births. There is a high level of alcoholism, and drug addiction is a growing problem. Life expectancy is just 50 years, and the illiteracy level is near 50 percent. All of these actualities indicate an urgent need to protect the natural resources found in this region, not only to maintain biodiversity but also to ensure the economic welfare of the local inhabitants. If these needs are addressed, the program will have the potential to change the current low standard of living in Ecuador by promoting both conservation and economic development.

Over the next 10 years, Conservation International plans to increase the use of numerous rain forest products, such as medicines, furniture, and baskets. These efforts can serve as a role model for firms in the industrial world that seek to create rain forest products and improve the well-being of rain forest inhabitants.

Shaman Pharmaceuticals

Shaman Pharmaceuticals, Inc., draws its name from rain forest *shamans*, traditional medicine men who possess a vast amount of knowledge about the use of plants for medicinal purposes. The shamans' ability to cure a variety of illnesses is founded on centuries of practice and an intimate association with, and dependence upon, indigenous plants. By tapping the knowledge of the shamans, scientists hope to reduce the research costs of identifying plants with beneficial medicinal properties. Furthermore, investigating plant species already known to possess healing characteristics yields a much higher chance of success in the screening process. This ethnobotanical approach—which combines the skills of anthropology and botany to study how native peoples utilize plants—is the basic premise by which Shaman Pharmaceuticals functions. By innovatively combining the disciplines of ethnobotany, isolation chemistry, and pharmacology with a keen market-driven strategy, the company hopes to create a more efficient drug-discovery program.

Shaman has formed strategic alliances with the pharmaceutical industry to enhance its prospects of turning a pharmaceutical discovery into a financial gain. "Shaman feels it is in a strong position to strike such alliances because the company is not only formed around a handful of products, but also around an efficient, ongoing process for generating compounds with a greater likelihood of being active in humans." The company has two main objectives in building these alliances: generating research funds through cooperative arrangements and gaining access to a larger marketing network. Three major pharmaceutical manufacturers have entered into agreements with Shaman: Inverni della Beffa, an Italian manufacturer of plant-derived pharmaceuticals, has signed licensing and marketing agreements and invested $500,000 in Shaman; Eli Lilly committed $4 million to Shaman and collaborates in developing drugs for fungal infections; and Merck & Company is working with Shaman on projects tar-

geting analgesics and medicines for diabetes. (For more on this topic, see "Making Biodiversity Conservation Profitable: A Case Study of the Merck/INBio Agreement," by Elissa Blum, in the May 1993 issue of *Environment*.)

To address the question of intellectual property rights and needs of the indigenous population, Shaman Pharmaceuticals created a nonprofit conservation organization called "The Healing Forest Conservancy" to protect global plant biodiversity and promote sustainable development. The company initially donated 13,333 shares of its own stock to the conservancy and plans to channel future product profits into projects that benefit the people of the source country. The first conservancy project provided health care benefits for the indigenous peoples of Amazonian Ecuador, a region that supplies valuable medicinal plants to Shaman. In return for information about these plants, physician Charles Limbach extended his medical services to three communities and treated 30 children during a whooping cough epidemic. Additionally, the conservancy seeks to create sustainable harvesting techniques for plants with commercial medicinal value. These programs have the task of reconciling the ecological constraints on plant extraction with the economic realities of producing a marketable product. This strategy reflects Shaman's concern that both the physical and intellectual property rights of the indigenous population are protected and that the inhabitants benefit from the research on these products.

As a result of its research efforts over the past few years, Shaman Pharmaceuticals has a pipeline full of active plant leads. Two antiviral products are currently being tested in clinical trials and are expected to reach the market in 1996: Provir is an oral treatment for respiratory viral infections that are common in young children; Virend is a topical treatment for the herpes simplex virus. Both products use the ingredient known as SP-303, a compound that was derived from a medicinal plant that grows in South America and was isolated by the company's discovery process. Patents have been filed on both the pure compounds and the methods of use for these products, which have a target market greater than $1 billion worldwide. Another consequential find is an antifungal agent found in an African plant that is traditionally ingested to treat infections. Shaman is using this compound to make a product that treats thrush, a fungal infection of the mouth, esophagus, and gastrointestinal tract. Given this discovery, the company hopes to find new treatments for other types of fungal infection. Shaman has strategically targeted its product development to address problems for which few effective treatments exist, such as viral and fungal infections. Moreover, there is a growing demand to find treatment for herpes and thrush because the increasing population of immunocompromised patients (including AIDS, chemotherapy, and transplant patients) is particularly vulnerable to these ailments. A third promising line of product development is in the area of analgesics. Shaman has found two plants exhibiting special binding properties that raise the prospect of creating a nonaddictive pain-relief drug. The company is conducting laboratory tests to identify the pure compounds responsible for this analgesic activity and is expanding its screening process by collaborating with Merck.

The raw materials for the screening all come from plants that are either presently harvested or sustainably collected. This discovery process has been quite successful at identifying plants with potential medicinal properties. Based on thousands of field samples collected by ethnobotanical field researchers and on reviews by a scientific strategy team, the company has screened 262 plants and found 192 to be active—a "hit rate" of 73 percent in the discovery process. Future products will be developed from some of these "hits."

According to company president Lisa Conte, "Shaman's well-defined strategic focus and outstanding, dedicated scientists will create a successful business by uniquely combining the newest in technology with the oldest of tribal lore." As a leader in ethnobotanical investigations, Shaman hopes that its initial success will translate into the development of a market for plant-based drugs from rain forest countries. The goal here is to use the revenue generated by these medicines as an economic incentive to preserve the forests and the wisdom of the native healers.

Ecotourism in Costa Rica

Ecotourism has been defined as "purposeful travel that creates an understanding of cultural and natural history, while safeguarding the integrity of the ecosystem and producing economic benefits that encourage conservation." Successful ecotourism creates economic opportunities in terms of both employment and income for the local people. These benefits furnish the local community with a strong incentive to practice good stewardship over their natural resources.

In Costa Rica, ecotourism has become a large and growing industry. In 1986, tourism generated $132.7 million and ranked as Costa Rica's third largest source of foreign exchange. In 1989, more than 375,000 tourists visited Costa Rica, 36 percent of whom were motivated by ecotourism. Tourism to Costa Rica's parks increased 80 percent between 1987 and 1990 and surged another 25 percent in 1991. Costa Rica offers the ecotourist diverse rain forests, abundant biodiversity, and breathtaking scenery. To protect these valuable resources, a national park system was established in 1970, which now comprises 34 parks and covers 11 percent of the total Costa Rican land area. Some of the most popular sites for ecotourism in Costa Rica, such as the Monteverde Cloud Forest Reserve and the La Selva Biological Station, are also centers for important biological research. Recently, these areas have attracted thousands of visitors each year, primarily because of the rich flora (more than 2,000 plant species) and fauna (some 300 animal species).

During the mid 1980s, the Costa Rican government sought to reconcile conservation and development interests by pursuing a strategy of sustainable development. Ecotourism was viewed as a clean source of development that might facilitate the preservation of the natural resource base. The actual implementation of this strategy was left to the private sector. The early environmental entrepreneurs in Costa Rica's ecotourism industry included Costa Rica Expeditions, Tikal, Horizontes, and the Organization for Tropical Studies. The growth of the ecotourism industry has since put strains on the fragile resource base. For example, the large number of visitors at popular parks is causing such problems as erosion and water pollution. Given the attraction of tourist revenues and the danger of overcrowding, environmental entrepreneurs are finding it difficult

to create ecotourism programs that are consistent with the principles of sustainable development. Efforts to control ecotourism in Costa Rica are still in the early stages, and more research is needed soon if the industry is to serve its original purpose.

One firm that is striving to attain this balance is International Expeditions. This 11-year-old, Alabama-based company operates 30 travel programs on 6 continents. Company president Richard Ryel and Tom Grasse, the director of marketing and public relations, contend that the ecotourism industry needs to forgo short-run profits and adopt a four-part conservation ethic that includes increasing public awareness about the environment, maximizing economic benefits for local people, encouraging cultural sensitivity, and minimizing the negative impacts on the environment. International Expeditions applies these principles to business practices: For example, to create a flow of money into the local economy, the company uses the host country's airline when possible, employs local tour operators, and uses other services within the rain forest community. The company's tour of Costa Rica begins in San Jose and proceeds through the country's national parks. The tour organizers hire Costa Rican guides who are familiar with the local habitat, and both guides and tourists stay at accommodations close to the parks whenever possible. These steps are designed to prevent tourist revenue from leaking outside the local communities that live near the parks.

To minimize detrimental impacts on the ecosystem and to promote respect for the rain forests, International Expeditions arranges small, manageable groups, educates participants about the ecosystem, avoids fragile habitats, and minimizes disruptions to the wildlife. In keeping with its objective of promoting natural history and conservation education, International Expeditions has designed a series of workshops in Costa Rica. The workshops are led by some of the world's leading experts on life in the rain forest, including Alwyn Gentry of the Missouri Botanical Garden, Donald Wilson of the National Museum of Natural History, and James Duke of the U.S. Department of Agriculture. Participants join in small group sessions to engage in hands-on field experience, such as nature walks, boat trips, and bird watching, and visit such sites as the Monteverde Cloud Forest and Tortuguero National Park on the Caribbean coast. Various sites feature canopied walkways up to 125 feet off the forest floor, which allow participants to walk among the treetops and closely observe the flora and fauna. The local guides also educate tourists about the history, culture, and socioeconomic conditions of indigenous peoples.

During the 1992 season, the cost of the 10-day, general nature tour throughout Costa Rica was $1,998 per person, and the 8-day workshop cost $1,498 per person. Because roughly 50 percent of these expenditures go to Costa Rica, these trips create the dual benefits of educating the nature traveler and generating income for the local economy.

A KEY TO PRESERVATION

Clearly, sustainable development of rain forest products has the potential to bring about positive change, preserve biodiversity, and improve the welfare of local communities. Because deforestation is spiraling out of control, the efforts of organizations like Conservation International, Shaman Pharmaceuticals, Inc., and International Expeditions have become imperative. E. O. Wilson of the Museum of Comparative Zoology at Harvard University calculates that deforestation of the rain forest is responsible for the loss of 4,000 to 6,000 species a year —an extinction rate 10,000 times higher than the natural extinction rate before the emergence of humans on Earth. Furthermore, the unwritten knowledge of forest peoples is rapidly disappearing. Thomas Lovejoy, assistant secretary for external affairs at the Smithsonian Institution, asserts that the rain forest "is a library for life sciences, the world's greatest pharmaceutical laboratory, and a flywheel of climate. It's a matter of global destiny." The need to develop methods to deal with the issue is urgent, and environmental entrepreneurs may be key to preserving the vital and fragile resources of the tropical rain forests.

NO

Jon Entine

LET THEM EAT BRAZIL NUTS: THE "RAINFOREST HARVEST" AND OTHER MYTHS OF GREEN MARKETING

"Business is our new universal community," says the speaker, and there is an immediate murmur of agreement. With eyes closed, the scene echoes of a Rotary Club luncheon in a genial, Midwestern town. There is an air of optimism that everyone seems to share.

"Religion and government no longer work as forces for community and change. We are in the era of business, it defines our relationships and values, and it doesn't have to be driven by the bottom line." The burly, ruby-faced speaker is clearly taken by his own message. The all-white, well-heeled crowd is entranced. "We are the leaders who can turn business into a positive social force."

The audience rises from its seats and breaks into applause. Although the words ring of Des Moines, the audience is forty-something L.A. Aging baby boomers in khaki sportcoats and designer jeans mix with business executives in Ann Taylor power suits. One man with stylishly long hair, a black silk shirt, black pants and sunglasses whispers into a cellular phone. Judging by the cars in the parking lot, this crowd long since traded in its Beetles for BMWs and Broncos.

This was a June celebration to open the Los Angeles chapter of Business for Social Responsibility, a trade group that promotes itself as environmentally and socially progressive, and they have come to hear their hero. The slightly rumpled, three-time college dropout holds the audience spellbound with his prescription for 'saving the world through business.' Their affection, indeed the adulation, is tangible.

The object of their rapt attention is Ben Cohen, who, in the late 1970s, starting mixing batches of ice cream at an abandoned gas station in Burlington, Vermont, with his high school buddy Jerry Greenfield. Today, Ben & Jerry's Rainforest Crunch, Chunky Monkey, and Cherry Garcia are indulgences of choice for baby boomers. Although he no longer runs the company day-today, Cohen, 44, remains Chairman and eccentric corporate symbol of Ben & Jerry's Homemade, the 18-year-old, $160 million publicly traded company.

Ben & Jerry's is the best known of the "good guy" entrepreneurs with quixotic corporate personas and New Age social philosophies. Skin-and-hair-care franchiser The Body Shop International (BSI), eco-friendly apparel makers Patagonia and Esprit, Tom's of Maine natural toothpaste and personal-care wholesaler, and Reebok athletic shoes are a few of the companies which have sliced a sizable niche out of the retail pie by turning "green" issues—such as the rainforest, "natural" ingredients and an opposition to animal testing—into their points-of-difference in a fickle, ultra-competitive consumer market. Many of these companies started with non-existent advertising budgets but were run by executives with an intuitive understanding of how to play the media dominated by baby boomers like themselves. And no company has benefited more from friendly press coverage than Ben & Jerry's.

In Los Angeles, Cohen rails on about the greedy, soulless character of Corporate America, and then boasts about his special flavor of New Age business. "Rainforest Crunch," he says, "shows that harvesting Brazil nuts is a profitable alternative for Amazon natives who have seen their lands ravaged to create grazing areas or for mining." The crowd is on its feet.

Yet, Ben & Jerry's own annual report carries the not-so-socially responsible details of what some anthropologists now call the rainforest fiasco. Despite Cohen's rhetoric that buying Rainforest Crunch helps preserve the fragile Amazon environment and the aboriginals who live there—a theme repeated uncritically by most of the media—his Third World project offers a lesson in the dangers of paternalistic capitalism. In fact, many anthropologists believe the rainforest harvest has led to the worst possible scenario: an increase in clear-cutting and mining, and a greater dependence among Amazon natives on selling land for subsistence income.

GREEN MARKETING OR GREEN WASHING?

Cohen & Company preach an oxymoronic message: the generation that wanted to change the world now encourages consumers to "shop for a better world," the title of a best-selling "green" consumer guide. It's a two-for-one sale that rings up big profits: 'buy our not-tested-on-animals Brazil nut hair rinse or ice cream and get social justice for free.'

U.S. consumers spend upwards of $110 billion on products from companies they perceive as socially or environmentally progressive. According to a study last summer by the Social Investment Forum, $150 billion in teacher, union, church and other pension funds is held by investment managers using social screens; another $12 billion is invested in mutual funds which follow various "ethical" or "green" formulas. More than 45 funds in the U.S. alone screen out companies for manufacturing "sin" products such as cigarettes, while they include firms that promote social policies such as making "cruelty-free" products.

For years, The Body Shop was the favorite of the ethical investing community. Its founder, Anita Roddick, is the most visible and outspoken of the green marketing executives. Since opening a tiny shop in 1976 offering "one-stop ear piercing" and a range of natural-sounding lotions, Roddick has grown BSI into an $800 million multinational company with 1300 mostly-franchised stores in 45 countries. She has cultivated a reputation for promoting the latest politically-correct social campaign: saving the whales, recycling, animal rights, AIDS research, and most prominently, preserving the environment and indigenous cultures by sourcing ingredients from the Third World. Roddick dubbed these micro-projects "Trade Not Aid," popularizing the eco-liberal concept of using capitalism instead of aid projects to reduce Third World dependency.

Despite rhetoric of good intentions, BSI has had a string of fair trade fiascos. For instance, over a year ago in Ghana, The Body Shop bought $20,000 worth of shea-butter from 10 villages for use in its creams. According to a front-page article in the *Toronto Globe & Mail*, the creams didn't sell, and today, the project is abandoned and the local economy is in tatters. BSI made no follow-up orders and left villages with thousands of dollars of unsold butter and no buyers.

The Body Shop's fair trade program has been plagued with problems. Richard Adams, who has founded two fair trade organizations, remembers seeing leaflets at BSI's stores in 1987 promoting its first import, foot massagers made by orphan boys in India. As director of Traidcraft in the early 1980s, Adams had briefly carried wood carvings made by the same group of orphans, who lived in a home called The Boys' Town. "Joe Homan, its director, was sourcing carvings from child labor sweat shops," he recalls discovering after poor quality shipments prompted an investigation. Worse, the local community said boys were being molested. Adams immediately sent the Roddicks a letter. "I never heard back,"

he says. Homan, it turns out, had been kicked out of a Christian Brothers sect. Two alarmed members of the Jesuit order visited the Roddicks after getting wind of the project. Still, nothing was done.

"Gordon [Roddick] was aware of his reputation," says Anne Downer, former head BSI franchisee for much of Asia. Downer, who attended the christening of The Boys' Town with the Roddicks in 1987, remembers Gordon saying that he had heard the rumors but didn't believe them. "He didn't seem unduly concerned and didn't seem to take it seriously."

Over the next few years, as Homan went about stealing charity funds and molesting orphan boys, the Roddicks sent out glowing reports to their franchisees. "Joe's work in The Boys' Town is ceaseless, he cares for the boys and girls and they really appreciate what he is doing for them," gushed one account in 1989. The roof caved in the next year when the English and Indian press ran exposes of Homan's escapades. The Roddicks first tried to suppress the scandal and then attempted to turn it into a public relations advantage by claiming credit for exposing him. "This story has not hit the Canadian Press yet but could erupt at any time," read one memo. "It is important that you know your facts. Anita... blew the whistle on Joe." A similar bulletin went to all of its American franchisees.

Not one of the Body Shop's dozen "Trade Not Aid" projects has been accurately promoted. And by its own statistics, they represented just 0.165% of the company's business as recently as 1993, at the height of its self-promoting rhetoric. Yet, despite their tiny size and frequent problems, these projects have generated overwhelmingly favorable media coverage—including much of the 10,000 positive mentions the company says it averages each year.

RAINFOREST FIASCO

Over the past decade, the "rainforest harvest," as it has come to be called, has been the most publicized international fair trade program and a defining symbol of social activism. The marketing of the rainforest blends three cultural trends: the environmentalist struggle to protect the forest against clear-cutting, the movement to preserve indigenous peoples, and baby boom narcissism.

The rainforest movement gathered momentum after the annual Brazilian Peoples Conference in 1989. Roddick and various journalists, environmentalists and eco-celebrities, from Jane Fonda to Sting, gathered in Altamira for the event, which garnered headlines around the world. Not long after, BSI introduced rainforest bath beads made with babassu nut oil, and hair conditioner from nuts harvested and processed by two Kayapo villages in the eastern Amazon.

BSI attached a bright Trade Not Aid sticker to its rainforest bead display, although babassu nuts are not grown in the Amazon, and the beads were made mostly from super-refined oil sourced from the Croda Chemical company— tested on animals in 1986. The hair conditioner uses a tiny fraction of Brazil nut oil at what cosmetic experts say are ineffective levels. According to a study by UK-based Survival International, BSI pays the workers $1.33 per kilo of nuts collected—an average of $500 for a five month harvesting season. Yet in its public relations hand-outs, BSI has claimed that workers in its projects are paid "first world wages." Little money trickles down to the villages. The young Kayapo leaders ("socios") who run the project continue to sell off land rights to profiteers cutting down mahogany trees. The village has been nicknamed Kayapo, Inc. for cashing in their timber dollars for cars, Western-style homes and even an airplane.

HARVEST MOONSHINE

Ben & Jerry's rainforest project, which was more ambitious, has a serendipitous history. In 1988, at a party after a Grateful Dead rainforest fundraising concert, Ben Cohen casually mentioned that he was developing a new brittle for an ice cream using something more exotic than peanuts. According to those present, Jason Clay, an ambitious anthropologist with the Cambridge indigenous rights group Cultural Survival, lit up like a video game. He regaled Cohen with his pet project to market renewable non-timber rainforest products such as fruits, nuts and flowers. A few days after the concert, Cohen's new friend headed to Vermont carrying a 50-pound bag of rainforest nuts. "We mixed up the first batch of brazil nut crunch in Ben Cohen's kitchen and served it to the board of directors that night," recalled Clay, "and we were off."

Within months, Cohen founded and became half-owner of Community Products Inc. CPI was set up to source Brazil nuts from Cultural Survival (CS) and turn them into brittle for ice cream, and cosmetic products and candy made by other companies. His intentions were no doubt benevolent; CPI promised to pay harvesters a 5% "environmental premium" and give 60% of any profits to charity, a third of that to Cultural Survival.

Ben & Jerry's has long been a favorite of both green-oriented consumers and investors. It does set an impressive standard of ethical innovation: it has published state-of-the-art social audits, gives an astonishing 7.5% of pre-tax profits to charity and buys local dairy products to help preserve the family farm. But the company is most readily identified with its flagship Rainforest ice cream.

Ben & Jerry's launched Rainforest Crunch early in 1990. "Money from these nuts," read the label, "helps to show that rainforests are more profitable when cultivated for traditional harvest than when their trees are cut and burned for short-term gain." The Third World ice cream was an overwhelming, overnight success—for Ben & Jerry's, which reaped tens of millions of dollars in profits and free publicity. But the view from Amazonia was not nearly so sanguine.

Critics found little evidence to support the central premise of the harvest—that foraging for nuts could ever approximate the income natives collect by selling off land rights to miners and foresters. "Marketing the rainforest... perpetuates the process of leaving to the forest dwellers the resources of the least interest to the broader society," wrote anthropologist Michael Dove for the East-West Center in Honolulu, in a typical critique.

Outside of Cultural Survival, where founder David Maybury-Lewis and Jason Clay were positioned to reap fame and perhaps fortune as consultants if the harvest took off, anthropologists quietly urged a go-slow strategy on Ben & Jerry's and BSI, but were ignored.

The worst case scenario was soon realized. There was no established supply chain for Amazon nuts. Most natives such as the Kayapo, long since corrupted by Western interests and fighting a losing battle to alcoholism, were not about to stop selling land rights to meet the expectations of social activists in London and Cambridge. Ben & Jerry's anticipated source for the nuts, the Xapuri cooperative (which had no native workers but was comprised of white rubber tappers, mostly of Portuguese ancestry) in western Brazil, never could meet the quality standards or quantity demands of the fad product.

To meet the sudden explosion in demand, market forces took hold and agri-businesses were drawn in to meet it. The harvest proved to be a windfall for landowners, who have long monopolized trade in this region. "That first year, we had to source all of our nuts from commercial suppliers," concedes Michelle McKinley, the former general manager of CS who left in November after reassembling the pieces of an organization nearly bankrupted by the ill-conceived harvest. Agri-barons elbowed out native suppliers and flooded the market. Nut prices, already soft, plummeted, cutting the incomes of tribes who did collect nuts. Amanakáa, a Brazilian peoples rights group, took Ben & Jerry's to task for sourcing directly from the Mutran family, a notorious Latin American agri-business convicted of killing labor organizers.

While the project was spinning out of control, harvest hype developed into a New Age business mantra. Sting set up the now-defunct Rainforest Foundation and began singing the praises of the free market. Usually-vigilant social critic Alexander Cockburn even became a convert; he attacked the UK-based indigenous rights organization Survival International after its director, Stephen Corry, published "Harvest Moonshine," a meticulously documented critique of the project which criticized Cockburn's friends at Cultural Survival.

Based in large measure on Roddick's self-promotion as a fair trade leader, Ralph Nader dubbed her "the most progressive business person I know," *Mother Jones* invited her onto its board, *USA Today* called her "The Mother Theresa of Capitalism," and the yuppie business magazine *Inc.* put Roddick on its cover with the headline, "This Woman Has Changed Business Forever."

The Brazilian and Bolivian governments took advantage of the harvest hype to justify cutting expensive, politically unpopular financial aid to native populations. A confidential report by the Alliance of Forest Peoples (a coalition including the Xapuri) attacked Cultural Survival for its "minimal" concrete support. "Their negative repercussions have been enormous," read the report. "We have not seen any return." Brazilian peoples groups, cowed at first by the Cohen-Roddick marketing barrage, gradually became more vocal. "A thriving market in forest products," said Julia Barbosa, president of the national Rubber Tappers Council which represented the Xapuri workers, "is no substitute for a political program that protects the forests and people who live in it."

To cover the economic shortfall, some native communities even sold off more land rights. In the end, the celebrated harvest has created a Brazil nut business dominated by some of Latin America's most notorious capitalists. Over the years, more than 95% of Ben & Jerry's Brazil nuts have been purchased on agri-business dominated markets; today, almost 100% are commercially sourced. According to Cultural Survival's McKinley, the so-called progressive retailers had been increasingly unwilling to pay the 5% environmental premium; last year only $22,000 was collected. "We rushed into this project recklessly," she now says. "We created a fad market overnight and the hard sell promotions have contributed to a lot of confusion. The harvest just didn't work."

In retrospect, early optimistic projections by rainforest capitalists seem almost ridiculous. Clay had estimated a $20–25 million market by 1996 with the benefits flowing to the rubber tappers and native communities. The business peaked in 1991 at $1.3 million, dropped to $250,000 in 1995, and has nearly sunk Cultural Survival. Clay was forced out. By the spring of '94, the Xapuri had cut off all supplies to CS. The project has run in the red for four years, generating no profits for Community Products and no charity.

NO WHALES HAVE BEEN KILLED BY MY COMPANY

Ironically, despite Ben Cohen's attempts to brush off the fiasco, his company did release an independent social audit documenting it. Paul Hawken, the environmentalist, author and businessman, published his analysis as part of Ben & Jerry's annual report released last summer. "It is a legitimate question," wrote Hawken, "whether representations made on Ben & Jerry's Rainforest Crunch package give an accurate impression to the customer." He quoted sharp criticism from Amazon rights groups, then concluded: "There have been undesirable consequences which some say were predictable and avoidable."

So, why have social activists, academics and journalists been caught off guard by the ethical contradictions of socially responsible business and New Age adventures such as the rainforest fiasco?

Does buying ice cream or hair rinse with Brazil nuts promote progressive social change or merely inure the public to the profligacy, and elitism, that has gradually coopted the green consumer movement?

The Sixties did inspire a new morality-based social philosophy that emphasizes the individual's responsibility to speak out against injustice and corruption. It drew its social vision from the civil rights movement, anti-Vietnam activism, environmental consciousness and feminism, and it continues to inspire social and environmental reforms. But there is an underside to the legacy of the counter-culture: narcissism, arrogance and self-indulgence.

Baby boomers—people born from the mid-1940s to 1960—are beginning to dominate the business and political landscape. Since 1990, their share of national leadership—Congress and governorships—has more than doubled from 21% to 45%, and will reach more than 70% within the decade. They are gradually becoming the American political and business establishment.

Yet, many conspicuous baby boom business leaders seem convinced of their socially responsible credentials, in large measure because they came of age in the Sixties. The visionaries at the vanguard of this movement—from Cohen and Roddick to Mo Siegel at Celestial Seasonings and Paul Fireman at Reebok—are loath to admit that "social responsibility" is in part a margin game. When profits are rolling in, as they were in the 1980s, progressive gestures are painless.

But facing growing pains and intense worldwide competition, many are firing workers, closing inner city stores, cutting back on charity projects, and making their products in overseas sweatshops.

Just last November, Reebok received reams of positive press when it gave a Human Rights Award, an annual event. Yet, it was curiously silent a few days later when reports surfaced that its workers in Thailand make 25 cents an hour for 18 hour days. Asked about the contradiction, Reebok's Paul Fireman told the UK newspaper *The Observer* that he will not "impose U.S. culture on other countries... 'when in Rome, do as the Romans.'" In other words, Reebok, BSI and other New Age entrepreneurs frequently act much like any business with bottom line challenges.

The not-so-pristine consequences of green consumerism have been largely absent from business reporting, since many journalists who have so slavishly profiled these successful entrepreneurs share with them common cultural pretensions. Many have convinced themselves that growing up protesting Vietnam and supporting Earth Day forever marks them as progressives, though today their closest brush with social responsibility may consist of little more than enjoying a Ben & Jerry's Peace Pop.

On close scrutiny, progressive business if often a land of alchemy where promises are easy to make, workers are frequently treated with indifference, and environmental reforms are superficially attempted. At best, the relatively small number of consumers with a high tolerance for high-priced goods—most of the products in question command a hefty premium over ordinary brands—play a modest role in raising awareness of social problems. (And even so, it's just a prosperous sliver of baby boomers affected.) At worse, cause-related marketing, as it is called, is little more than baby boom agitprop, masking serious ethical lapses. "Many socially responsible companies have noble corporate philosophies," observes Jon Lickerman, a social researcher with the Calvert Group of socially responsible mutual funds, "but mistreat their own employees, vendors, and customers."

They've also inspired a wave of green marketing by mainstream firms. Guardians of free speech and public health such as Philip Morris take out full-page ads decrying the sale of cigarettes to minors while railing against Big Government; Chevron brags that its sunken oil rigs are havens for Gulf fisheries; oil drillers, developers and natural gas companies band together to form the National Wetlands Coalition, complete with a logo featuring a duck flying over marshes, to front their attacks on environmental reform. Madison Avenue has embraced greenwashing with a vengeance, and the green business movement, with its facile posturing on complex issues, must bear some of the responsibility.

ICE CREAM POLITICS

"It's really a disingenuous marketing strategy to say if you spend $2.99, you'll help save the rainforest," warns Michelle McKinley, formerly of Cultural Survival, which no longer sources Brazil nuts for Ben & Jerry's. But her criticism hasn't dampened Ben Cohen's enthusiasm for hawking Rainforest Crunch. Today, Cohen and co-founder Jerry Greenfield spend little time running the company that has grown far beyond their man-agerial expertise. They can be found on a college ice cream tour. At the Wharton Business School in Philadelphia, Ben and Jerry sermonized on their usual topics: the crazy fun of starting a business, corporate ethics and of course Rainforest Crunch. "After the speech, I talked with both Ben and Jerry personally," wrote Ritu Kalra, an MBA graduate, in a recent e-mail discussion about the controversy. "Neither of them knew much about the harvest. When it came down to it, they didn't want to comment on it and didn't feel responsible at all for any misleading labeling or for telling half-truths to about 300 college students."

In the case of the rainforest, Cohen still seems oblivious to or afraid to admit the real impact of his now-collapsed pet project. "We have created demand for rainforest products," he boasted at the annual meeting of Business for Social Responsibility in San Francisco in November. There was no mention of the rapacious agri-businesses that supply most of his nuts.

The BSR members—many personal friends of Cohen and part of an informal intelligentsia of the "progressive" business community—were reluctant to press their wounded hero. They were far more eager to munch on Ben & Jerry's Rainforest Crunch donated for the event. "It's so inspiring," one BSR member was heard to say as she licked her spoon clean, "to know that business can make money and still do so much good."

POSTSCRIPT

Can Green Marketing Save Tropical Rain Forests?

Jon Entine makes a scathing denunciation of the false promises used to promote the green marketing schemes he assesses. This does not preclude the possibility that more appropriate forms of the incentive programs advocated by Carr, Pedersen, and Ramaswamy could be valuable components of a multidimensional rain forest preservation strategy. A general point made by many rain forest activists in response to proposals formulated by academic researchers, government planners, or industrial entrepreneurs from developed nations is that such plans are not likely to have a significant impact on deforestation unless they fully recognize the complex needs of the Third World people. For an elaboration of this concern in the context of a critique of several proposed tactics, see "Rainforest Crunch: Combating Tropical Deforestation," by Hannah Finan Roditi and James B. Goodno, *Dollars and Sense* (November 1990).

An even more fundamental precondition for the design of an effective strategy to save the rain forests is a clear understanding of the causes of tropical forest destruction. That is the principal message of John Vandermeer and Ivette Perfecto in their highly informative book *Breakfast of Biodiversity: The Truth About Rain Forest Destruction* (Food First Books, 1996). Vandermeer and Perfecto argue that there is a "web of causality" linking several significant factors that together explain the assault on the forests. For a concise presentation of this analysis, see their feature article "Rethinking Rainforests: Biodiversity and Social Justice" in the Summer 1995 issue of the *Food First Backgrounder*, available from Food First, 398 60th Street, Oakland, CA 94618.

One type of incentive program to induce tropical countries to take actions designed to protect their forests are so-called debt-for-nature swaps through which lender nations cancel certain outstanding debts. Many of the initial examples of this strategy have been criticized as unattractive to debtor nations. In the June 1994 issue of the *Journal of Forestry*, Dana R. Vissar and Guillermo A. Mendoza argue that the latest versions of these programs are designed to meet this objection and have been more successful.

Rain forest preservation was one of the key environmental problems discussed at the 1992 Earth Summit in Rio de Janeiro. The chances of success in dealing with this issue based on these discussions is the subject of the optimistic article "After Rio—Our Forests, Ourselves," by Sandra Hackman *Technology Review* (October 1992). For an Internet site related to this issue, see http://www.ran.org/ran/, the home page of the Rainforest Action Network.

ISSUE 16

Do the Projected Consequences of Ozone Depletion Justify Phasing Out Chlorofluorocarbons?

YES: Don Hinrichsen, from "Stratospheric Maintenance: Fixing the Ozone Hole Is a Work in Progress," *The Amicus Journal* (Fall 1996)

NO: Patricia Poore and Bill O'Donnell, from "Ozone," *Garbage: The Independent Environmental Quarterly* (September/October 1993)

ISSUE SUMMARY

YES: *Amicus Journal* contributing editor Don Hinrichsen argues that chlorofluorocarbons (CFCs) and other chemicals that destroy stratospheric ozone are a serious threat to terrestrial life and that, despite the considerable progress to date, the international community needs to take further action to protect the ozone layer.

NO: *Garbage* magazine's editor and publisher Patricia Poore and associate publisher Bill O'Donnell argue that their analysis of conflicting evidence leads to the conclusion that ozone depletion is not a crisis requiring an outright ban on CFCs.

In 1974 a short paper by M. J. Molina and F. S. Rowland was published in *Nature* magazine. Based on laboratory experiments, the paper warned of a potential threat to the stratospheric ozone layer resulting from the rapidly expanding use and release of a family of synthetic chemicals. This speculative prediction gave rise to an immediate controversy among the scientific, environmental, and industrial communities because of the essential role played by atmospheric ozone in shielding human beings, as well as other terrestrial flora and fauna, from the harmful effects of the high-energy ultraviolet radiation emitted by the sun.

The molecules in question, chlorofluorocarbons (CFCs), were developed by the chemical industry as inert, volatile nontoxic fluids. They have been used as the working fluids in refrigeration and air conditioning systems, as the propellants in pressurized spray cans for a variety of industrial and consumer products, as foaming agents for plastic foams, and as cleansing solvents in the electronics industry. Ultimately, CFCs find their way into the atmosphere where, because of their chemical inertness and insolubility in water, they neither decompose nor get washed out in rainfall. Molina and

Rowland proposed that CFCs would, over a period of about a decade, rise to levels in the stratosphere where they would be exposed to the UV radiation that fails to reach the lower atmosphere because of ozone absorption. They would then photodecompose, producing atomic chlorine, which laboratory studies have shown would act as an effective catalytic agent in destroying ozone.

The predictions of Molina and Rowland met with much skepticism and stimulated intense activity on the part of scientists, particularly those associated with companies and industries that had a vested interest in selling or using CFCs, who tried to disprove the dire prediction of serious ozone depletion. Rowland has devoted much of his professional and private life to defending and substantiating his prediction as well as seeking an international response to the need to phase out the use of CFCs. Gradually, through both laboratory work and environmental sampling, data accumulated that supported the ozone depletion prediction and refuted proposed alternative mechanisms for the removal of CFCs from the atmosphere.

Predictions of the extent of ultimate ozone loss from the continued use of CFCs rose and fell as new data accumulated. Then in 1985 came reports of large-scale seasonal losses of ozone over the Antarctic. Follow-up studies have resulted in a growing consensus that this effect is indeed a result of the increasing atmospheric concentrations of CFCs and related compounds. Furthermore, estimates of the health and environmental consequences (including the increased incidence of human skin cancers and phytoplankton destruction) if CFC use is not drastically curtailed are again on the rise. In 1995 Rowland and Molina received the ultimate vindication of the importance of their predictive research. They shared the first Nobel Prize in chemistry ever given for environmental research with Paul Crutzen, who had also made significant early contributions to understanding ozone layer chemistry.

The first action to reduce ozone destruction was the unilateral banning of CFCs in aerosol spray cans by the United States, Canada, and Scandinavia in 1976–1978. Stimulated by the Antarctic findings, international conferences on the problem have been held since 1985. In 1987, in Montreal, a landmark agreement was reached to phase out the use of ozone-depleting chemicals. Subsequent meetings have broadened the scope and accelerated the implementation of these actions. But are they really necessary?

Don Hinrichsen, a contributing editor to *The Amicus Journal,* researched the following article under a grant awarded by the University of Maryland's Center for Global Change. He argues that recent data indicate that ozone-destroying chemicals are causing faster depletion than previously predicted, justifying more stringent measures than have already been agreed to by the international community. Patricia Poore and Bill O'Donnell, respectively the publisher and editor and associate publisher of *Garbage* magazine, assert that a "rational analysis of the facts" leads to the conclusion that ozone depletion is not an urgent crisis that justifies the economic disruption that will result from the planned rapid phaseout of ozone-depleting chemicals.

YES

Don Hinrichsen

STRATOSPHERIC MAINTENANCE: FIXING THE OZONE HOLE IS A WORK IN PROGRESS

There is a Texas Instruments plant in McKinney, Texas, that produces 3,000 electronic circuit boards every year. In 1989, the annual cost of raw materials used for a single cleaning process in this plant came to more than $350,000. In 1995, that cost was down to $14,000. In 1989, the use of lead solder produced thousands of pounds of hazardous waste, which had to be disposed of at considerable expense; in 1995, the amount of lead waste had been cut by 3,000 pounds a year. In 1989, cleaning and maintenance of the equipment required a full eight-hour shift every two weeks; by 1995, it took ten minutes a day. As if all this were not enough, in 1995, workers at the plant were producing circuit boards in half the time they used to take in 1985.

What happened at Texas Instruments was not, strictly speaking, the result of technological innovation driven by free-market forces. It was the result of the Montreal Protocol.

Until the 1990s, Texas Instruments (TI) used chlorofluorocarbons (CFCs) to clean its circuit boards. CFCs were considered "miracle compounds" when they were discovered in 1928; they were chemically stable, harmless, and had several highly useful commercial applications. By the 1970s, this family of chemicals was central to a number of major industries. They were used as coolants in refrigerators and air conditioners, as propellants in spray cans, and as feedstocks to blow Styrofoam and similar foams. At TI and other manufacturers of circuit boards—which can be rendered worthless by the tiniest defect—the substances were used in enormous quantities as solvents, to clean off the residue left after soldering: the boards were first immersed in CFC baths, and then mechanically sprayed with still more CFCs to wash off the last of the debris. By 1989, TI's 133 plants around the world were consuming close to two million pounds of CFCs and related chemicals annually. Throughout the mid-1980s, companies in the United States as a whole were using CFCs to manufacture more than $100 billion worth of products a year.

But in 1974, University of California scientists F. Sherwood Rowland and Mario Molina had hypothesized that the very stability of CFCs would enable them to rise intact into the upper reaches of the atmosphere, where ultraviolet radiation would break them down, releasing chlorine. Chlorine ordinarily combines with other substances at much lower altitudes; released into the stratosphere, reasoned Molina and Rowland, it could destroy molecules of the ozone gas that surrounds the earth in a widely dispersed band. That layer of ozone, roughly ten to thirty miles overhead, serves as a vital shield for all terrestrial life by blocking ultraviolet radiation.

[In 1995], Molina and Rowland received the Nobel Prize for their work, along with Paul Crutzen, a meteorologist who also worked on the chemistry of the ozone layer. At the time, however, their theory created an environmental controversy of titanic proportions. During the decade after it came out, scientists expressed growing concern, governments worried, and citizens grew increasingly alarmed—but industry, represented by the trade group known as the "Alliance for Responsible CFC Policy," argued vehemently that there was not enough evidence to restrict CFC use, and that restrictions would do appalling economic damage. "CFC producers and users argued for a delay of any regulations affecting their use," recalls Alan Miller, former director of the Center for Global Change at the University of Maryland. "Most CFC-dependent industries claimed that no alternatives were possible, that any alternative would be too expensive, or that alternatives would surely compromise worker and environmental safety."

Supporting evidence, however, trickled in bit by bit. In 1981, NASA satellites found the first concrete signs of ozone depletion. In 1984, a British team found the frightening "ozone hole" over Antarctica. In 1986, a U.S. team sponsored by the National Oceanic and Atmospheric Administration found strong evidence that the cause of the seasonal hole was a chemical process rather than wind or solar activity, as some had theorized. In the same year, under mounting public pressure, the Alliance for Responsible CFC Policy reversed its stand against limits of CFC use.

That capitulation was followed in short order by the landmark Montreal Protocol of 1987. This extraordinary international agreement was endorsed initially by forty-nine industrialized countries; today there are 150 signatories. The Protocol called for the elimination of half of all ozone-depleting substances by mid-1996, a major industrial phaseout, and it was binding, not voluntary. Moreover, at their second meeting in 1990, the parties responded to further evidence —and to the pressure of a highly organized coalition of environmental groups from around the world—by unanimously agreeing to phase out all CFCs by the turn of the century. They assigned similar phaseout dates for other chemicals now known to destroy ozone in the stratosphere: halons and carbon tetrachloride by the year 2000, methyl chloroform by 2005. And in February 1992, alarmed at reports that the ozone layer was thinning still faster than predicted, the European Community and the United States announced that they would push forward their phaseout deadline to the end of 1995.

David Doniger, an attorney for NRDC [National Resources Defense Council] in the 1980s and a major player in the environmentalists' push for a global ban, believes that the key to securing a binding international agreement was the concept of a phaseout. In practical, commercial terms, the phaseout represented a business opportunity: in setting a deadline by which everyone had to be using something else, it created an incentive for CFC producers to be the first to discover and market that something else. Most importantly, however, eliminating ozone depleters was simply "not something that industry could do overnight," Doniger says. The phaseout concept "ended the gridlock between those who said the chemicals had to be eliminated and those who said there were no alternatives."

* * *

At Texas Instruments, the phaseout gave engineers at the McKinney plant time to search for the alternatives. What they found was a process called controlled atmosphere soldering, an advanced soldering technique used extensively in Europe but virtually unknown in the United States. A German company, Seho, provided the first unit on a test basis so that TI engineers could evaluate its performance.

They were "amazed" by the results, says Jeff Koon, a process engineer at McKinney. Controlled atmospheric soldering produced virtually no waste, so it used materials much more efficiently and left the final product clean. Hence the elimination of 3,000 pounds of hazardous lead waste, along with an entire step—washing the finished boards in solvents—in the manufacturing process. "We were able to reduce costs and cycle time, and produce a better product by using fewer chemicals and by eliminating the need to dispose of hazardous wastes," says Koon. "What began as an environmental solution soon became a business solution." The European technique was eventually implemented throughout the company.

This kind of cooperation between companies is extremely rare, for good reason; rival business concerns are not usually in a position to let down their competitive guard. What made it possible for Texas Instruments and for many others was, above all, the phaseout deadline, which created an overriding common interest. But there was another factor: a new forum specifically designed to serve as the neutral ground where engineers from different companies could meet and exchange information.

This forum was the brainchild of Stephen Andersen, an enterprising economist at the Stratospheric Protection Division of the U.S. Environmental Protection Agency (EPA). Andersen was appointed to chair the UN Environment Program's Solvents Technical Options Committee. In 1989, at a meeting in Washington, D.C., he persuaded a number of key U.S. companies, including Texas Instruments, Nortel, and AT&T, to become founding members of the International Cooperative for Ozone Layer Protection (ICOLP). Established as a partnership between government and industry, ICOLP had grown to fifteen corporate members by 1992. Its official mission was to "promote and coordinate the worldwide exchange of nonproprietary information on alternative technologies, processes, and substances for ozone-depleting solvents."

"It was clear to me that companies needed each other in order to accomplish the goals in the time period set," says Andersen now. "We realized that if all the stakeholders were to cooperate, they could move much faster down the road towards a complete phaseout."

And with a binding deadline already in place to drive the process, Andersen was free to structure the partnership so as to allow industry members the maximum freedom to maneuver. Cooperation was voluntary; progress was to come from company-led technological breakthroughs, with a minimum of government interference. Committees of government and industry scientists and technical experts were appointed to study different technical problems, and each committee set its own agenda and timetable. At the end of the day, the manuals used by EPA as guidelines for the phaseout would be largely written by these industry-led committees.

It was an unusual arrangement, and it produced some unusual results. "As company representatives worked on these committees, they were stunned by each company's contribution," says Andersen. "Some of the big companies thought they had all the skills they'd ever need, but it just wasn't the case. Some people had their best engineering experiences working on these committees, because there were remarkable breakthroughs."

Digital Equipment Corporation, for instance, developed one of the first water-based cleaning processes for electronic circuit boards. Digital donated the technology to ICOLP, and more than 600 companies requested information on the process. The Ford Motor Company managed to phase out its annual consumption of 1.95 million pounds of CFCs and other ozone depleters, which were used mostly as solvents and in automobile air conditioning units, at a cost of $9 million. IBM, which topped the list of U.S.-based multinationals as a yearly consumption level of 13 million pounds, succeeded in eliminating all of them for a modest investment

of $10 million—one of the most cost effective operations in the company's history.

Though the transformation involved pain and cost for many companies, particularly for small retail businesses such as auto repair shops, it was hardly the commercial disaster predicted by the Alliance for Responsible CFC Policy. According to Stephen Andersen, the "leadership" companies report investments of one to thirty million dollars each, with their savings in production costs offsetting all or a large part of that initial investment. "More importantly, the new ozone-safe technologies have reduced manufacturing defects, increased product reliability, and allowed production of miniaturized circuits that could not be cleaned with CFCs," he adds. "One measure of this remarkable success is that electronics companies have nothing but praise for the CFC phaseout." To David Doniger, who is now Counsel to EPA's Assistant Administrator for Air and Radiation, the phaseout "is a clear illustration of the difference between what companies say they can do ahead of time and what they can in fact accomplish."

* * *

Serious unsolved problems remain, however, and the fact that ozone depletion continues to escalate at rates above and beyond what scientists have predicted means that we cannot afford to be complacent. There is an international contraband market in CFCs that is believed to be bringing many thousands of tons of the substances into the developed world every year. Then there are the ozone-depleting chemicals that have yet to be phased out in the developed world. In an important delaying tactic, the CFCs once used universally as refrigerants have been replaced largely by HCFCs (hydrochlorofluorocarbons) which are significantly less harmful to the ozone layer. HCFC-22, for instance, is only 2 percent as destructive as CFCs. Recognizing, however, that enough of it in the stratosphere will destroy the ozone layer just as surely as unfettered CFC use, the Protocol signatories agreed in December 1995 that the developed world would phase out production by 2020 and the developing world by 2040. But there is as yet no ideal substitute in sight for HCFCs, and much will hinge on the research that continues in that quarter.

Another problem is methyl bromide. A pesticide used extensively as a soil fumigant, methyl bromide was the last ozone depleter to be recognized as such. Pound for pound, however, it is even more damaging than CFCs. A single chlorine ion released by the breakdown of a CFC molecule can devour 100,000 molecules of ozone in the stratosphere through a catalytic reaction —but when methyl bromide breaks down it releases bromine, which is thirty to sixty times as destructive. And traditionally, agricultural chemicals have proved more difficult to take off the market than industrial chemicals. The United States has already delayed its phaseout deadline by a year, to 2001, under pressure from agribusiness lobbyists. The rest of the industrialized world will not phase it out until 2010. The developing world has promised only to freeze its use by 2002. Fortunately, there are some alternatives in sight. One option is methyl iodide, a chemical cousin that does not damage the ozone layer. Other options include modifications in processes for growing and harvesting.

But the biggest challenge of all may lie in the developing world and Russia. In 1985, the world produced about 1.1 million tons of CFCs. By the end of 1995, that figure had been whittled down to less than 400,000 tons. Most of that remaining production of CFCs is being used in Russia and the newly independent states of the former Soviet Union—in violation of their treaty obligations. Third World countries, which account for a smaller share, have another decade to phase out CFCs. And their use is predicted to grow enormously as countries like China continue to develop toward a consumer-oriented industrial economy, expanding in population size all the while. Household appliance companies in both China and India, for instance, are planning to produce millions of refrigerators and freezers using CFCs, as well as HCFCs, over the next few decades. Rajendra Shende, Coordinator of UNEP's Ozonaction Program, observes that because of this growth in developing countries, "the phaseout in developed countries could be undone in a relatively short time."

The problem in both regions is lack of resources to make the transition. ICOLP, of course, is sharing its technological breakthroughs with developing countries. But despite the multiple advantages and relatively short payback periods of many of these advances, eliminating CFCs requires some hefty upfront investments. It cost Texas Instruments more than $27 million to eliminate CFCs and other ozone-damaging chemicals from its production processes; the Hitachi Corporation of Japan invested close to $160 million in finding safer substitutes. Many companies in developing countries cannot raise that kind of capital in the span of a few years.

In theory, there is a mechanism in place to help them do it. During the negotiations for the original Montreal

Protocol, the issue of the phaseout costs was a serious one for developing countries, which argued that they had not created the ozone emergency and should not be stuck with the bill. One of the provisions hammered out during the long, often acrimonious sessions was a special Multilateral Fund, to be paid for by the industrialized world, which would help poorer countries offset the costs of the phaseout.

To date, the Fund has financed more than 1,000 projects at a total cost of $440 million. These projects, which are already in place and working, will eliminate 30 percent of all ozone depleters used in the Third World by the turn of the century. Much of the investment has been used to finance suitable alternatives to CFCs, especially as coolants, solvents, and degreasers. "In 1995, we approved $205 million worth of projects to phase out 22,000 metric tons of these chemicals in Third World countries," says Omar El-Arini, head of the Fund. "If we kept that up, we could replace all the chemicals the developing countries are committed to phase out by 2010, if they continue their current rate of consumption."

That last qualification, however, is a big one. It is virtually a given that developing countries will increase their rate of consumption, and that they will need even more help than the framers of the Montreal Protocol originally envisioned. But as the ozone emergency has dropped off the front pages and out of the public's consciousness, the resolve of the signatories has wavered. The Multilateral Fund has been receiving about 20 percent less money than was pledged for 1996. Italy, which owes $19 million this year, has paid nothing at all. In the United States, a recalcitrant Congress has authorized the payment of only $23 million out of the $38 million promised. That is a victory, perhaps, given the current anti-environmental Congress, where one elected official declared not long ago that the reason Molina and Rowland received the Nobel Prize for their ozone work was that Sweden is "an environmental extremist country."

* * *

But while governments drag their feet, the companies that have eliminated CFCs continue to benefit. At Texas Instruments, the phaseout was such a convincing demonstration of the advantages of using fewer resources that, one manager says, "TI's whole philosophy of doing business changed." According to this executive, Shaunna Sowell, Vice President and Manager of the company's Environmental, Safety and Industrial Hygiene Program, TI has decided to aim for "zero wasted resources" by the turn of the century. "We now want to avoid the costs of compliance to government regulations by taking the initiative," Sowell says. "We intend to be so far down the road with clean technologies that compliance with new regulations will not even be an issue."

The company has plans to recapture and recycle much of its chemical feedstock, saving millions of dollars in treatment and disposal costs. Toxic wastes, Sowell claims, have been reduced by close to 80 percent. Most of TI's far-flung manufacturing plants, operating in twenty countries, now conserve or recycle process water. In addition, through a program initiated by employees, TI recycles nearly 75 percent of all paper, cardboard, wood, plastics, and metal.

And so it is ironic that, after successes like these, the world barely noticed when it achieved the first major milestone in the history of ozone protection policy recently. They said it could never by done —but on December 31, 1995, the United States and Europe stopped making CFCs. It is an example environmentalists must point to over and over again, as the international community moves reluctantly to address the continuing tasks of saving the ozone layer.

NO

**Patricia Poore and
Bill O'Donnell**

OZONE

No journalistic "lead" for this story. No weary scientists peering through the frozen antarctic mist after a restless night spent dreaming of blind rabbits. No international chemical-industry conspiracies. We won't try to hook you. We won't promise an easy read, either. But we will try to remain neutral, even as we suggest that conventional wisdom may be deeply flawed.

We have spent the better part of two months deeply engrossed in the literature of ozone depletion. Our editorial interest had been aroused by the recent popular books[1] which present vastly different interpretations of science. We moved in further with the original scientific papers of Dobson, Rowland and Molina, Teramura, et al. We then read expert reviews of the literature by Elsaesser, Singer, et al.

We found compelling arguments on both sides, only to find credible contradictory information in the next day's reading. Let us warn you up front, anything resembling a final conclusion eludes us.

Although the science around ozone depletion is a continuum—an as-yet incomplete mosaic of postulates and findings—politics and media hype have transformed the argument into a battle between philosophical adversaries: Camp Apocalypse and Camp Hogwash. We may be accused of adding to the confusion by developing our arguments around this artificial divide, but there is really no choice. The escalating volley of counterpoints and rebuttals has given rise to overstatement, simplification, and a growing tendency to lie by omission, suppressing information that doesn't fit. It is to that situation that this article must be written.

Representing Camp Apocalypse are Sharon Roan, author of *Ozone Crisis*, and Vice President Al Gore, author of *Earth in the Balance*. They were preceded by, and continue to find support from, the environmental group Greenpeace and other environmentalist public-interest groups.

Representing Camp Hogwash, we found Rogelio (Roger) Maduro, primary author of *The Holes in the Ozone Scare*, and, less hysterically but just as dismissively, Dixy Lee Ray, primary author of *Trashing the Planet and Environmental Overkill*.

From Patricia Poore and Bill O'Donnell, "Ozone," *Garbage: The Independent Environmental Quarterly* (September/October 1993). Copyright © 1993 by *Garbage: The Independent Environmental Quarterly*, 2 Main St., Gloucester, MA 01930. Reprinted by permission.

From our reading, we find that the truth may lie in the middle—in this arena, a radical place to be. Our views echo those of Ronald Bailey in his book *Eco-Scam*,[2] and Dr. S. Fred Singer (*Global Climate Change*), a physicist and climatologist oft-quoted by both camps.

We are comfortable making these statements for the record: (1) Both camps are engaging in hyperbole and lies of omission. (2) The chemical industry is not "dragging its feet" in coming up with substitutes for CFCs [chlorofluorocarbons] indeed they are responding deftly to market demand and will make huge profits from the phase-out. (3) There is currently no "crisis," nor any documented threat to human health, inasmuch as (a) the so-called ozone hole is an ephemeral disturbance over a mostly unpopulated area; (b) ozone thinning over populated latitudes, if it exists, is within the range of natural fluctuation and is seasonal; (c) no documentation exists for actual sustained increase in UV-B radiation at ground level.

We believe, however, that there may be cause for concern. We are skeptical of the debunkers' claims. No, it is not chlorine from oceans and volcanoes which is responsible for creating the effect seen in the polar region; yes, chlorine from CFCs does apparently make it to the stratosphere and does destroy ozone.

We consider the lack of disclosure and debate regarding the real costs of a precipitous halocarbon phase-out to be near-criminal. The costs that will be involved (monetary, opportunity, and human) receive scant coverage, in spite of the fact that the "threat" of ozone depletion is demonstrably lesser than any number of real threats both worse in scope and more immediate.

WHAT WAS THE QUESTION?

Let's review briefly the points of debate, both to define the scope of our discussion and to inform those who have not been reading carefully the science sections of newspapers in the past four years.

A theory advanced in 1973 by F. Sherwood Rowland and Mario Molina (Univ. of California-Irvine) holds that chlorofluorocarbons (CFCs) and related molecules, owing to their tremendous stability, eventually reach the stratosphere and, photolyzed by intense ultraviolet radiation, split to release energized chlorine atoms that then destroy ozone (O_3) molecules. Obviously, O_3 is always being created and destroyed, but it is thought that the increased destruction from man-made chemicals has tipped the balance and caused a temporary net depletion in the O_3 concentration. This is potentially harmful because O_3 is one mechanism that controls the amount of UV-B radiation reaching the biosphere (UV-B is an ultraviolet wavelength that affects the body, in ways that are both life-sustaining and, in excess, damaging.)

The "ozone hole" is the graphic name given to a phenomenon that so far exists only seasonally over the Antarctic region; namely, a thinning of the concentration of O_3 molecules that represents a depletion of up to two-thirds for a limited amount of time. Scientists on all sides of the debate agree that preexisting conditions unique to the Antarctic zone create the possibility of the "ozone hole."

Those scientists and politicians calling for an immediate CFC ban believe that very recent minor, unsustained, localized depletion of ozone in the stratosphere in some areas outside the polar regions is caused by CFCs, and is a harbinger of increasing future depletion. The issue was presented strongly enough that a phase-out was planned in 1987 in an international treaty called the Montreal Protocol; the dissemination of certain findings since that time resulted in a decision for a near-total ban by 1996.

In the meantime, a strong counterpoint to the ozone theory and the proposed ban has been presented, which many people refer to as a "backlash." Regardless of the personal political motivations of the skeptics, good reasons for this "backlash" include the discovery of information suppressed in the politicking for a ban, as well as a growing realization of the extraordinary costs inherent in phasing out the relatively safe, useful and ubiquitous chemicals.

POINTS OF CONTENTION

Each camp purports to interpret the original data. Only since the publication of the popularized books, or since about 1989, has the debate escalated into a war, with each side battling the other point by point. Let's look at Camp Apocalypse first, as it gained favor earlier and still holds sway. Here are their major points:

1. CFCs, HCFCs, and halons are proven to be responsible for a sudden (in a 40-year period) depletion of stratospheric ozone, which created the "ozone hole" over Antarctica. The effect of CFCs on the stratosphere will lead to a similar hole over the Arctic, and will change the ozone layer over populated areas for at least 100 years, even with a phase-out and ban.
2. The "ozone hole" gets worse every year, starting sooner or growing in area or breaking up later.
3. Ozone loss causes increased UV-B at ground level, which has resulted

in severe sunburns and will cause increases in skin cancer, cataracts, and immune deficiency.
4. Increased UV-B at ground level will affect the food chain, from phytoplankton to soybeans, and may have apocalyptic results.

As you can see, their points are a mix of the known and the projected. Context is often missing from the arguments of both camps, as well. For example, saying "the ozone hole gets worse every year" sounds definitive (and terrifying), but the period referred to is only 14 years —an insufficient baseline from which to chart real deviation. Now, the salient points from Camp Hogwash, themselves a mixture of red herrings and truth:

1. CFCs are heavier than air and therefore can't get up into the stratosphere.
2. In any case, chlorine from CFCs pales in comparison to the chlorine released by the oceans and volcanic eruptions.
3. There has always been an ozone hole, we just didn't know how to look for it.
4. There is no long-term "thinning" of the ozone layer.
5. The relationship between stratospheric ozone concentration and UV-B at ground level is unknown, and no sustained increase in UV-B at ground level has been demonstrated.

* * *

Both camps bring up the same topics; only their conclusions differ. Let's look at those topics, one by one, with a more neutral perspective, based on a reading of both and reference to some of the original documents.

THE OZONE HOLE

The argument regarding whether or not the "ozone hole" existed before CFCs remains murky. The question, apparently, is what did ground-breaking researcher Gordon Dobson really find when he examined ozone concentration in the 1950s (i.e., before the proliferation of CFCs). Did he discover the ozone hole or not? Some in the hogwash camp have publicly asserted that Dobson found ozone levels as low as 150 Dobson Units [D.U.] over Halley Bay [on the Antarctic continent at approx. 75° S].

We looked it up ourselves. Here is Gordon Dobson reviewing his findings of the late 1950s in a paper written for *Applied Optics* in March 1968—long before the controversy erupted.

"One of the more interesting results on atmospheric ozone which came out of the IGY [International Geophysical Year] was the discovery of the peculiar annual variation of ozone at Halley Bay. The annual variation of ozone at Spitzbergen [a Norwegian Island at approx. 80° N.] was fairly well known at that time, so, assuming a six months difference, we knew what to expect. However, when the monthly telegrams from Halley Bay began to arrive and were plotted alongside the Spitzbergen curve, the values for September and October 1956 were about *150 units lower than we expected.* [our emphasis] We naturally thought that Evans had made some large mistake or that, in spite of checking just before leaving England, the instrument had developed some fault. In November the ozone values suddenly jumped up to those expected from the Spitzbergen results. It was not until a year later, when the same type of annual variations was repeated, that we realized that the early results were indeed correct and

that Halley Bay showed most interesting difference from other parts of the world. It was clear that the winter vortex over the South Pole was maintained late into the spring and that this kept the ozone values low. When it suddenly broke up in November both the ozone values and the stratosphere temperatures suddenly rose."

So, while Dobson's group didn't find levels as low as those measured in the mid 'eighties, it's clear from his language that he was shocked at how low ozone concentrations were over Halley Bay, and at a loss to explain how such a phenomenon could exist. Whether or not the "hole" (that is, levels as low as 150 D.U.) is a recent occurrence, it is clear that the physical environment particular to Antarctic had depleted ozone in the austral spring before CFCs could be credibly implicated.

Dobson's group didn't have converted spy planes, high-tech satellite imagery, and countless researchers available to them. They had one instrument in one place. Today, we see the exact position of maximum ozone depletion shifting location from year to year. Could it be that Halley Bay was outside of the "hole" in '56 and '57? We can never know.

CAN CFCs MIGRATE TO THE STRATOSPHERE?

"CFCs are much heavier than air, and so could never reach the stratosphere." It is clear to us that this is a bogus argument. While it's true that CFCs weigh anywhere between four and eight times as much as air, and will sink to the floor if spilled in a laboratory, in the real world, they won't stay on the ground. Our atmosphere is a very turbulent place. Says Rowland: "The atmosphere is not a quiescent laboratory and its mixing processes are dominated to altitudes far above the stratosphere by the motions of large air masses which mix heavy and light gaseous molecules at equal rates. Throughout most of the atmosphere, all gaseous molecules go together in very large groups, independent of molecular weight.

"By 1975, stratospheric air samples… had been shown regularly to have CFC-11 present in them. During the past 17 years, CFC-11 and more than a dozen other halocarbons have been measured in literally thousands of stratospheric air samples by dozens of research groups all over the world."

WHAT ABOUT NATURAL SOURCES OF CHLORINE?

Say the skeptics: "The amount of chlorine hypothetically released by CFCs pales in comparison to that available from natural sources." They are talking about seawater evaporation and volcanoes. Dixy Lee Ray tells us in *Trashing the Planet:* "The eruption of Mount St. Augustine (Alaska) in 1976 injected 289 billion kilograms of hydrochloric acid directly into the stratosphere. That amount is 570 times the total world production of chlorine and fluorocarbon compounds in the year 1975."

The hogwash camp has said that one billion tons of chlorine are released into the atmosphere from natural sources, as compared to a theoretical 750,000 tons from man-made sources. Taken at face value, these seemingly scientifically arrived-at proportions would lead one to believe that man-made sources are insignificant.

Most unfortunately for the hogwash camp, Ray had made a terrific blunder.

Her calculation came not from Alaska in 1976, but from a theoretical extrapolation of the total HCL released (not necessarily reaching the stratosphere) by a mammoth eruption 700,000 years ago. She may have made the same argument (which rested on a 1989 paper by Maduro) even with accurate numbers, but noise over the mistake has eclipsed the question.

Indeed, what about volcanoes, spewing chlorine compounds at high velocities? Again, the amount released by volcanoes is not the same as the amount reaching the stratosphere. Yet Maduro insists: "No matter what figure is used, the basic point remains that the amount of chlorine emitted by Mother Nature through volcanoes dwarfs the amount contained in man-made CFCs."

Ozone-depletion researchers counter that whatever the amount of chlorine compounds released through natural sources, all of it is washed out in the lower atmosphere through precipitation —before it has reached the stratosphere.

In summary, the hogwash camp is vastly overstating the importance of natural sources of chlorine. The apocalyptic camp entirely dismisses the importance of natural sources of chlorine because it is removed by rainfall, with negligible amounts reaching the stratosphere.

Whom to believe? Is it really true that only organic, water-insoluble compounds (e.g., CFCs) can deliver chlorine to the stratosphere? Are we really to believe that there's enough precipitation in the antarctic night to wash out all the chlorine being emitted by Mount Erebus (a volcano, continuously active since 1972, six miles from the monitor station at McMurdo Sound)—before any of it can move up to the stratosphere in the great, turbulent polar vortex?

GLOBAL OZONE DEPLETION?
FROM WHAT BASELINE?

For the record, no solid evidence exists to suggest ozone depletion over the northern latitudes poses any health hazard. Are you shocked? It's no wonder. Environmental groups and the popular press tell us the threat is now.

Case in point: On February 3, 1992, NASA "interrupted their research" to announce their prediction of a full-scale ozone hole over much of the U.S. and Europe: the infamous "hole over Kennebunkport" referred to by then-Senator Al Gore. It didn't happen. The October 1992 Greenpeace report entitled *Climbing Out of the Ozone Hole* claimed: "The formation of an ozone hole over the Northern Hemisphere in the near future, and possibly as early as 1993, now appears inevitable." Greenpeace's "inevitable hole" over the Northern Hemisphere didn't materialize, either.

That the alarms were false didn't stop them from becoming common knowledge. The July 1993 issue of the women's fashion magazine *Vogue* tells us that "thorough sun protection is the cornerstone of any summertime beauty strategy. As government scientists report ozone over the Northern Hemisphere is at its lowest level in fourteen years." The ominous warning appears in a feature article called "Beauty and the Beach," which shows page after page of bathing beauties soaking up the summer sun in the latest bikinis.

What the article fails to mention is that the 10 to 15% reduction government scientists reported occurred in March and April, when the amount of UV-B reaching the northern latitudes was but a small fraction of what the summertime sun delivers. We have to be careful when we interpret these diminished percentage-point results. A ten percent depletion over Kennebunkport in April (and its corresponding as-yet theoretical increase in UV-B) is still but a small fraction of that received in New York or Boston in June— when people really are out on the beach. We also must be careful to understand what baseline is being used to report these "depletions."

Of those who either discredit the degree of ozone thinning or differ on its range of effects, few carry greater weight or generate more controversy than S. Fred Singer, who holds a doctorate in physics from Princeton University and is now president of an Arlington, VA-based think tank called Science and Environmental Policy Project.

Dr. Singer is skeptical about claims by other scientists that, on average, global ozone levels are falling: "One cannot estimate whether there has been any long-term change from short-range observations because the natural fluctuations are so large." According to Singer, long-term analyses are compounded by daily ozone fluctuations that double naturally from one day to the next [without any cataclysmic outcome, by the way]. "Seasonal fluctuation, from winter to summer, are as much as 40% and the eleven-year solar cycle is three to five percent, on a global average. Extracting long-term variations from a few percentage points of change in a decade is like observing temperatures for one season and judging whether climate has changed over the long term. It can't be done.

"It is not possible to eliminate the chance that what we are seeing is a natural variation.

"The Antarctic hole is a genuine phenomenon," Singer concedes. "But it is nothing much to worry about because it lasts such a short while and has already stabilized. Besides, it is controlled more by climate than by CFCs."

THE UV-B QUESTION

The scary part of ozone depletion is, of course, the correlation to increased UV-B penetration. The most often-cited theoretical relationship is that for every 1% decrease in stratospheric ozone, we can expect a 2% increase in ground-level UV-B. It would seem a good check of diminishing ozone claims would be to quantify the penetration of UV-B. Problem is, the few who are looking can't find any increase at the Earth's surface.

Despite the analysis of TOMS (Total Ozone Mapping System) satellite data released by former EPA-administrator William Reilly indicating *springtime* average ozone levels over the United States have dropped 8% in the last decade, there are no data to suggest increased penetration of UV-B on the ground. In fact, a report published in the September 28, 1989, issue of *Nature* cites a study that found a 0.5% average *decrease* in UV-B between 1968 and 1982, despite an overall decrease in ozone column density of 1.5% over the same period.

Ozone doomsayers counter by arguing: 1) The monitors used are not capable of making distinctions between UV-A and UV-B radiation, and 2) UV-B is not reaching the surface because it's being absorbed in the troposphere by man-made pollutants. They reason that we shouldn't count on our fouling of the lower atmosphere to protect us from damage we're inflicting above.

If the monitors are antiquated, you'd think we'd be funding new ones, given our fear of the sky. The second argument is a red herring. The reported 8% depletion in stratospheric ozone (which should theoretically create a hard-to-miss 16% increase in UV-B) occurred during a decade when tropospheric pollution was decreasing over the U.S.—courtesy of the Clean Air Act.

The Connection to Human Health

All claims regarding human health risks associated are related not to ozone thinning *per se*, but to increased UV-B exposure. So far, researchers have not in fact tied increases in skin cancer and cataracts to increased UV-B exposure due to thinning ozone. There is no epidemiological evidence of suppressed immune function due to UV-B exposure caused by thinning ozone.

(No one questions that people get more UV exposure than in the past. Only a few generations ago, a tan was considered unhealthy. Only since the 1950s have so many people had the leisure and desire to be out in the sun, wearing scant clothing. And only with technological advances have so many white people been living in previously inhospitable "sunbelts.")

But is there more UV-B, overall, sustained, at ground level? What would it mean if we can find ozone depletion without a corresponding rise in UV-B penetration to ground level?

WHERE WE ARE—AS OF AUGUST '93

Public policy is driven by the public, not by scientists. A recent survey gave these results: 67% of Americans consider themselves "extremely concerned about the environment." But only one in five is aware that CFCs are used in refrigeration, and only one in 30 is aware that CFCs are used in air conditioning. Are a well-meaning public and the politicians who serve them not well enough informed to make global decisions that will cost hundreds of billions of dollars? Will future generations look back at the "ozone crisis" as the greatest waste of resources in human history? Or will they thank us for taking lifesaving action without delay? (The apocalyptics talk about political foot-dragging "for 14 years," but the Montreal Protocol is perhaps the fastest, largest non-military global response to a perceived threat in human history.)

The following observations are based not on our own scientific experiments, of course, but rather on a rational analysis of the facts following a great deal of reading. We have no vested interest in either camp.

1. Attributing the Antarctic "ozone hole" to CFCs is overstatement to the point of fallacy. Natural conditions have always existed which deplete the concentration of ozone in that region during a specific time of year. However, scientific data do support the theory that stable, man-made chlorinated molecules are implicated in a localized net ozone loss during the natural cycle.

2. Ozone depletion is not an epic crisis. Remember, even if ozone maintains 100% of its "normal level," skin cancers will still occur. On a day when ozone levels over Punta Arenas, Chile, are reduced by 50% because of the "hole," the theoretical maximum increase of UV-B levels would be equal to only 7% of what reaches

the ground at the equator on the same day.

3. We must monitor UV-B at ground level to see if in fact there is any correlation with stratospheric ozone fluctuations.

4. A outright ban on CFCs and other useful halocarbons (before adequate substitutes are available) would cause more human suffering and economic mayhem than the theoretical increase in ozone depletion under a more managed phase-out. In the U.S. we have the financial means and perhaps the political will to accept the challenge —albeit at tremendous cost and lost opportunities. In other parts of the world, an already insufficient supply of affordable refrigeration would be exacerbated. The result will be more disease from food-borne bacteria, and greater hunger.

What do you think?

NOTES

1. *The Holes in the Ozone Scare/The Scientific Evidence That the Sky Isn't Falling* by Rogelio A. Maduro and Ralf Schauerhammer. 21st Century Science Associates, Washington, D.C., 1992. *Ozone Crisis/The 15-Year Evolution of a Sudden Global Emergency* by Sharon Roan. John Wiley & Sons, New York, 1989. *Trashing the Planet/How Science Can Help Us Deal with Acid Rain, Depletion of the Ozone, and Nuclear Waste (Among Other Things)* by Dixy Lee Ray with Lou Guzzo. Regnery Gateway, Washington, D.C., 1990. *Earth in the Balance/Ecology and the Human Spirit* by Al Gore. Houghton Mifflin Co., Boston, 1992.
2. *EcoScam/The False Prophets of Ecological Apocalypse* by Ronald Bailey. St. Martin's Press, New York, 1993.

POSTSCRIPT

Do the Projected Consequences of Ozone Depletion Justify Phasing Out Chlorofluorocarbons?

Poore and O'Donnell claim that public policy is driven by the public, not by scientists. Scientists have a difficult time getting a response from political leaders to their pleas for action on environmental threats. But for many years, it was not the public who opposed warnings about ozone layer depletion. It was CFC producers and other powerful economic interests who attempted to refute the accumulating evidence that was doggedly presented to world leaders. For two articles that support Hinrichsen's position about the seriousness of the ozone threat and that deride efforts supported by some U.S. Congress members to roll back rather than strengthen existing regulations, see Kevin Robert Gurney's article "Saving the Ozone Layer Faster," *Technology Review* (January 1996) and the cover story by Janet S. Wager in the Winter 1995/1996 issue of *Nucleus*.

Simply negotiating a treaty does not ensure compliance. Greenpeace and other environmental organizations are continuing to mobilize public pressure to guarantee enforcement of the provisions of the agreement. In "The World Can't Wait for DuPont," *Greenpeace* (July/August 1990), Judy Christrup accuses the principal U.S. producer of CFCs of hedging on its commitment to cooperate in efforts to end ozone depletion. Jack Doyle's article "Hold the Applause: A Case Study of Corporate Environmentalism," *The Ecologist* (May/June 1992) supports this accusation.

For an in-depth analysis of the provisions of the original Montreal Protocol, see "The Montreal Protocol: A Dynamic Agreement for Protecting the Ozone Layer," by Jamison Koehler and Scott Hajost, *Ambio* (April 1990). The ozone "hole" that was discovered over the Antarctic poses a specific threat to the Antarctic food chain. For a discussion of this local, but significant, aspect of the problem, see "Fragile Life Under the Ozone Hole," by S. Z. El-Sayed, *Natural History* (October 1986).

For an Internet site related to this issue, see http://www.epa.gov/docs/ozone/resource/center.html, which contains the U.S. EPA's Ozone Depletion Resource Center home page.

ISSUE 17

Are Aggressive International Efforts Needed to Slow Global Warming?

YES: Moti Nissani, from "The Greenhouse Effect: An Interdisciplinary Perspective," *Population and Environment: A Journal of Interdisciplinary Studies* (July 1996)

NO: Thomas Gale Moore, from "Why Global Warming Would Be Good for You," *The Public Interest* (Winter 1995)

ISSUE SUMMARY

YES: Interdisciplinary studies professor Moti Nissani argues that action should be taken to reduce the potentially grave impacts of greenhouse-induced global warming, despite current uncertainties about the magnitude of the effect, because the actions will be beneficial in any event.

NO: Economist Thomas Gale Moore maintains that since most of the likely effects of global warming will be beneficial to humankind, it makes no sense to invest in expensive efforts to reduce greenhouse gas emissions.

The likelihood of a major worldwide meteorological disturbance that would drastically affect climate and thus profoundly alter the balanced web of ecological cycles has provoked speculation by scientists as well as authors of science fiction. A currently prominent theory proposes that the age of dinosaurs was brought to a sudden and spectacular end as a result of just such an event. Supporters of this theory have pointed to evidence that an asteroid or comet may have struck the earth, causing an enormous dust cloud to blanket the planet for many years, blocking much of the incident solar radiation. The lush tropical forests of the time would have been decimated by the reduction of sunlight. The resulting loss in the dinosaurs' primary food source, coupled with the climate change, could have produced sufficient stress to cause short-term massive extinctions.

Only recently, however, has there been serious scientific concern that significant changes in the average surface temperature or other worldwide meteorological effects could result from intentional or inadvertent human intervention. Although it is generally accepted that the per capita production of energy would have to increase by a factor of 100 or more before a direct, observable atmospheric heating could occur, there are other aspects of present industrial activity that are widely believed to be potential causes of calamitous atmospheric effects.

Many atmospheric scientists now predict that our environment may be altered in a dramatic way as the result of the increase in carbon dioxide and other trace gas concentration in the air due to the burning of fossil fuels, destruction of forests, and other agricultural and industrial practices. Trace gases transmit visible sunlight but absorb the infrared radiation emitted by the earth's surface, much as the glass covering of a greenhouse does. A continued increase in these gases could cause sufficient heat to be trapped in the lower atmosphere to raise the world's average temperature by several degrees over the next 50 to 100 years. This would result in major alterations in weather patterns and perhaps melt part of the polar ice cap. The rising ocean would then submerge vast low-lying coastal areas of all continents.

There is now little doubt that atmospheric carbon dioxide and other trace gas levels are rising. Most meteorologists now agree that there will be some resultant warming; but due to the complexity of the many interacting phenomena that affect climatological patterns, there is much uncertainty about how large the temperature increases will be and whether or not they will actually be sufficient to cause the apocalyptic effects that some predict.

The prolonged periods of extremely high temperature experienced during the summers of 1988 and 1989 in many regions of the United States and other parts of the northern hemisphere led to public speculation that this unusual weather was due to the onset of greenhouse warming. A few climatologists and meteorologists supported this view, but most claimed that there was insufficient evidence for such a conclusion. In November 1995, however, the Intergovernmental Panel on Climate Change (IPCC) issued its second major study on global warming in the next 100 years and beyond, concluding that "the balance of evidence suggests that there is a discernible human influence on climate." The 1995 report, based on an evaluation of over 20,000 scientific papers, predicts that global average temperatures are likely to increase by between 1.8 and 6.3°F before the end of the twenty-first century. The United States originally declined to accept the goals for reducing greenhouse gas emissions that were negotiated as part of the Framework Convention on Climate Change resulting from the 1992 Earth Summit in Rio de Janeiro. A reversal of this position was announced following the release of the IPCC study.

Moti Nissani is a professor in the interdisciplinary studies program at Wayne State University. While admitting that uncertainty remains about the severity of the consequences of greenhouse-induced global warming, he argues that failing to take protective measures that are ecologically beneficial and economically profitable is sheer folly. Thomas Gale Moore is an economist and a senior fellow at the Hoover Institution. Moore argues that the effects of any significant global warming are likely to be primarily beneficial and that it would therefore be foolish to take measures to prevent it, which he claims would be very difficult and costly.

YES

Moti Nissani

THE GREENHOUSE EFFECT: AN INTERDISCIPLINARY PERSPECTIVE

Now we can only wait till the day, wait and apportion our shame.
These are the dykes our fathers left, but we would not look to the same.
Time and again were we warned of the dykes, time and again we delayed:
Now, it may fall, we have slain our sons, as our fathers we have betrayed.

—Rudyard Kipling

INTRODUCTION

A recent, rather typical, review (Beckerman & Malkin, 1994) argues that even if the greenhouse threat is real, even if temperatures rise and low-lying lands must be protected forever by an enormous system of dikes, such unlikely occurrences do not justify "imposing vast costs on the present generation rather than helping developing countries overcome the environmental problems that they are facing today" (for similar views, see Moore, 1995, Nordhaus, 1994, p. ix; Singer, Revelle, & Starr, 1993). The present essay argues that anyone willing to cross disciplinary boundaries can easily ascertain that this surprisingly popular viewpoint is mistaken.

NATURE OF GREENHOUSE EFFECT

Sunlight can go through the atmosphere—that is why we see the Sun. Sunlight then warms the ground and lower atmosphere, which then emit heat, a form of radiation we can feel but not see. In physical terms, heat radiation has a longer wavelength than visible light. On the spectrum it falls just below visible red, hence it is called *infrared radiation.*

Now, CO_2 (carbon dioxide) and a few other *greenhouse gases* in the atmosphere allow most sunlight to go through them. When this light reaches the ground or lower atmosphere, it is converted in part into heat which is then reflected back towards space. CO_2 and other greenhouse gases trap some of

Adapted from Moti Nissani, "The Greenhouse Effect: An Interdisciplinary Perspective," *Population and Environment: A Journal of Interdisciplinary Studies,* vol. 17, no. 6 (July 1996). Copyright © 1996 by Human Sciences Press. Reprinted by permission.

this heat and irradiate it back to the ground, thereby delaying its escape into space.

Earth, then, is livable thanks to its naturally occurring greenhouse gases: water vapor, carbon dioxide, methane (natural gas), nitrous oxide (laughing gas), and ozone (Hare, 1993, p. 11). Like the glass of a car with rolled-up windows (but through a different physical process), these gases trap more heat than light. Our planet is thus a sleeping giant, comfortably blanketed by its own set of greenhouse gases. Without these atmospheric gases, Earth would be some 63°F colder than the current average of 59°F, hence lifeless.

The chief culprit in changing Earth's greenhouse balance is CO_2. Our civilization is burning enormous quantities of coal, gas, oil, and wood, thereby releasing CO_2 into the atmosphere. Forest burning similarly releases CO_2 and transforms trees from long-term consumers of CO_2 to short-term producers. As a result, since 1800 CO_2 levels have gone up by more than 27%, with more than half of this increase taking place since 1959! (Brown, Kane, & Ayres, 1993, p. 68).

In the future, other factors may further exacerbate this problem. For instance, ozone-related increases in ultraviolet light (Smith, 1995), as well as rising pollution levels, may reduce the capacity of the world's oceans to sustain small, floating aquatic plants, thereby further disturbing the CO_2 balance on Earth.

Some human-made CFCs (chlorofluorocarbons) are still being discharged into the atmosphere, and CFCs trap heat too. Other important enhanced greenhouse gases are methane and nitrous oxide. In absolute terms, the increase in CFCs, methane, and nitrous oxide has been comparatively small, but pound for pound, some of these gases are more powerful heat absorbers than CO_2. Their combined warming effect is equivalent to that of a 15% rise in CO_2. So the Earth's atmosphere contains now the equivalent of 42% more CO_2 than it did in 1960 (Beckerman & Malkin, 1994).

EVIDENCE FOR ENHANCED GREENHOUSE EFFECT

Ecosystems are comprised of numerous living and nonliving elements. We are often ignorant of the existence of some of these elements, and we only partially comprehend others. All these elements, in turn, form an intricate web of interconnections and feedbacks, a web which often eludes our grasp. As if this is not enough, we have also good reasons to suspect that ecosystems often behave chaotically—a change in one or another of their seemingly insignificant components may, in the long run, profoundly alter them.

For these reasons, we can never be absolutely sure that the biosphere is changing in the direction predicted by the greenhouse theory. There is, however, a growing body of evidence suggesting that this may be the case. Here we can only mention some developments which can be reasonably viewed as harbingers of global warming (Kerr, 1995):

- Rising levels of CO_2 and other greenhouse gases in the atmosphere.
- A 1°F increase in average temperatures at the surface of the Earth in this century (Hare, 1993, p. 13).
- Apparent acceleration of this warming trend (1995, 1990, 1991, and 1994 are the first, second, third, and fourth warmest years on record).

- Cooling of the stratosphere—a striking confirmation of theoretical predictions (Santer et. al., 1996).
- Unusual weather extremes in recent years (more numerous and severe storms, floods, and droughts; cf. Houghton, 1994; Monastersky, 1995).
- A possibly unprecedented rate of change, since 1945, in the timing of the seasons in the Northern Hemisphere (Thomson, 1995).
- A longer growing season of Northern Hemisphere's terrestrial plants (Keeling, Chin, & Whorf, 1996).
- Melting of Arctic and Antarctic ice and retreat of the Antarctic ice shelf (Beardsley, 1995).
- Retreat of some Alpine, Himalayan, Chinese (Guoan et al, 1994), and other mountain glaciers.
- Shifts towards the poles and to higher elevations of the Edith's checkerspot butterfly (Parmesan, 1996), and an expanded range of a few other animal and plant species (Flavin & Tunali, 1996, pp. 15-16).
- Spread of tropical diseases like malaria and cholera (Stone, 1995).
- Destruction of coral reefs.
- Rising ocean temperatures (Regalado, 1995).
- Steadily rising levels of water vapor in the stratosphere.
- Rising sea levels (Nerem, 1995).

CONSEQUENCES OF ENHANCED GREENHOUSE EFFECT

These continuing trends would likely have some favorable outcomes. For instance, because low CO_2 levels currently limit the pace of photosynthesis, all other things being equal, rising levels of this gas may increase the productivity of farms, forests, and marine systems. Likewise, Siberians, Greenlanders, and other northerners might welcome a warmer climate.

The best scientific bet, however, is that, on balance, the effects would be troublesome. Temperatures may have already risen by about 1°F, explaining perhaps the unusually hot summers and weather extremes of recent years. In fifty years, if we continue the unbridled release of greenhouse gases into the atmosphere, temperatures might go up by some 3°F. This increase may lead ocean water to expand and rise. Ocean water may rise, as well, because higher temperatures may melt the polar ice caps. Sea levels may thus rise by 17 inches by the year 2070 (Brown, Kane, & Ayres, 1993, p. 68), submerge low-lying areas such as Louisiana, and force hundreds of millions to permanently abandon their homes and communities. Unable to cope with the unprecedented pace of climatic fluctuations and change, some wild species might perish (Gates, 1993). Climates may shift, perhaps converting once-prosperous agricultural areas into deserts. Humanity may be visited more often by devastating storms, droughts, and other weather extremes. Higher temperatures, weather extremes, flooding of coastal areas, regional changes in rainfall patterns, and an unstable seasonal cycle (Thomson, 1995, p. 66) may reduce agricultural, forest, and natural productivity (Manning & Tiedemann, 1995; Rosenzweig, 1994). Tropical climates and diseases may spread and summer heat waves may become more common (Stone, 1995). The incidence of heatstroke and asthma may go up. Oxygen levels in the atmosphere and oceans may decline. History likewise shows that, at times, global and regional temperatures profoundly affect human affairs;

climatically, economically, or politically stressed societies are especially vulnerable (Brown, 1994).

An even worse specter cannot be altogether ruled out. As the Earth heats up, more water would turn into vapor, and vapor is a greenhouse gas. Stored CO_2 might likewise escape from ocean rocks and shells, and stored methane might escape from vast permafrost regions (Cherif & Adams, 1994, p. 30). Beyond a certain point, the process may get out of control:

> Until recently, we have been lucky. Earth has just as much carbon as Venus, but most of it is still locked away harmlessly in rocks.... Is it possible that we will someday destroy Earth's good health and turn our home into a runaway greenhouse? Will the human volcano heat Planet Earth until all the seas go dry and lead melts in the sunlight? Are we already on the downhill path to Venus? We simply do not know enough yet about Venus, or even about Earth, to be sure of the answer. But judging by our neighboring world, we are playing with fire (Weiner, 1986, p. 174).

WHAT SHOULD HUMANKIND DO?

Owing to the complexities of Earth's biosphere and climate, all predictions are shrouded in doubt. It could be that, as I revise these words, our planet's temperatures are imperceptibly rising. For argument's sake, let us arbitrarily say that there is a 1 in 2 chance that this is occurring. If this warming continues, in a few decades it may lead to adverse (say, 1 in 10), beneficial (say, 1 in 10), or neutral (say, 8 in 10) consequences for the quality of life on this planet. Finally, there is the specter of consequent extinction of life on Earth within a few centuries as a result of human-caused,

unchecked global warming (say, 1 in 100). Amidst all these uncertainties and arbitrary numbers we can be sure of one thing: the uncertainties will remain. Should we then cross our fingers, allow present trends to continue, and let chance decide our fate?

Given the stakes, some people feel that we ought to avert the *possibility* of disaster, regardless of cost. Should we, they ask, reduce the suffering of malaria victims, or the beauty of ancient forests, to dollars and cents? They are troubled by questions of justice: Should we cling to profitable production technologies which risk the well-being of our contemporaries and descendants? These people also remind us that massive government spending can often improve economic performance and *material* quality of life —as it did, for example, in Germany and America in the 1930s.

As we have seen, others insist that we should act only if the requisite policies do not divert resources from even more urgent tasks. No one, however, openly argues that we should do nothing if the requisite policies not only avert the greenhouse threat, but if they also have many other beneficial environmental, public health, and aesthetic consequences *and* if they can save our species billions of dollars every year. If such policies were shown to exist, the greenhouse debate would, in principle, come to an end. Who could oppose beneficial and remunerative policies? Uncannily enough, although such policies have been readily available for decades, they are not being followed.

CFCs have contributed to as much as 24% of the suspected warming. Because they are also the chief cause of ozone layer depletion, they are being phased out. Over the next century, their concentrations in both the lower and upper atmosphere will decline, thereby slowing down the suspected warming trend.

The needed additional steps have been championed for decades by many writers. Among the most indefatigable, articulate, and insightful advocates of this soft path is Amory Lovins. Here is a typical refrain:

> Global warming is not a natural result of normal, optimal economic activity. Rather, it is an artifact of the economically inefficient use of resources, especially energy. Advanced technologies for resource efficiency, and proven ways to implement them, can now support present or greatly expanded worldwide economic activity while stabilizing global climate—and saving money. New resource-saving techniques—chiefly for energy, farming, and forestry—generally work better and cost less than present methods that destabilize the earth's climate (Lovins & Lovins, 1991, p. 433).

Such steps, soft path advocates say, could cut emissions of CO_2 by more than 60%, of methane, by 17%, and of nitrous oxide by 75%. Such claims are usually dismissed by politicians and journalists who believe that the greenhouse threat is a chimera requiring no action whatsoever, by reputable economists who believe that it might cost as much as 4 trillion dollars to avert the greenhouse danger (Schneider, 1990, p. 188), *and also* by many informed science writers who are committed to removing the greenhouse threat (Franck & Brownstone, 1992, pp. 145-6).

Such widespread dismissals seem to make a mockery of Lovins' claims that increased energy efficiency can solve the greenhouse problem *and* save money. Are his claims absurd? My answer to this is simple. I have been studying science, environmental issues, and the human condition for twenty years, and I would gladly pledge my life, fortune, and sacred backgammon set on this proposition: Lovins' claims are not absurd, but entirely correct.

To begin with, assertions of combined savings and safety are supported by many other researchers. Also, the worst greenhouse offender—the United States —does not use energy as efficiently as some other equally prosperous countries. By catching up with *existing* Swedish standards, for instance, the United States could vastly reduce greenhouse emissions, save trillions, and begin to heal its citizens and trees, fields and streams, water and air.

A similar point concerns history. Compared to real energy expenditures in 1973, and thanks to conservation measures implemented since then, energy conservation is already saving the United States at least $100 billion a year. Twenty years ago many economists opposed energy conservation for 1001 reasons. They have thus managed to slow down this historical process, but common sense, and the logic of a mixed economy, tilted the balance and proved them wrong.

Thus, the soft path position boils down to nothing more outlandish than a plea to all nations to accelerate this salutary historical trend, in part by following the proven examples of prosperous, energy-efficient, countries like Sweden and Japan.

The soft path package is comprised of numerous measures, of which only a few can be mentioned here:

- "Removing a 75-watt incandescent lamp [the familiar household light bulb] and screwing into the same socket a 15-watt compact fluorescent lamp will provide the same amount of light for 13 times as long, yet save enough coal-fired electricity over its lifetime to keep about a ton of CO_2 out of the air (plus 8 kg of [polluting and acid rain-causing] sulfur oxides and various other pollutants).... Yet far from costing extra, [in the long run each lamp]... saves tens of dollars more than it costs" (Lovins & Lovins, 1991, pp. 437-8; see also National Academy of Sciences, 1994, pp. 217).

- A 1989 study by the U.S. Department of Energy describes "15 proven, readily available, improvements in car design. These, plus two more equally straight-forward improvements," would not involve any changes in car size, safety standards, or acceleration, yet they could reduce fuel consumption by 35%. And this is a mere drop in the tank. Already available prototypes such as the Toyota AXV (89 mpg city; 110 mpg highway), prove that cars more than three times as efficient as the world's fleet can be at least "as comfortable, peppy, safe, and low in emissions as today's typical" new car (Lovins & Lovins, 1991, p. 446).

- According to the National Academy of Sciences, "a consensus is emerging in the engineering, utility, and regulatory communities that, even when past efficiency gains and projected population and economic expansion are considered, an additional, significant reduction can be made in U.S. residential and commercial electricity consumption. This reduction is not expected to sacrifice comfort levels and will cost less—in many cases, substantially less —than the purchase of new sources of power" (1992, p. 204). The savings in both carbon emissions and dollars

can be readily accomplished through such simple steps as adding triple pane windows to existing buildings and improving the design of hot water tanks. For the United States alone, such measures would cut total CO_2 emissions by some 18%, and would save some $56 billion per year (National Academy of Sciences, 1994, p. 240). By itself, this figure is striking: Every year, the average American household could save hundreds of dollars through this step alone.

Space does not permit the completion of this magic list (cf. Nissani, 1996). At this point, suffice it to mention recycling (Commoner, 1990; Lovins & Lovins, 1991, p. 474; Miller, 1994, p. 402), cogeneration (Miller, 1994, p. 450), reduction of wasteful methane emissions (Heilig, 1994, p. 131), chemical-free agriculture (Commoner, 1990), reconstruction of new small-scale hydroelectric plants (Miller, 1994, p. 464), solar cells (Keepin, 1990, p. 316), solar methane (Commoner, 1990), and other solar technologies (Smith, 1995, p. 40, Asimov & Pohl, 1991, pp. 226, 230).

Scoffers at the soft path often treat the greenhouse problem in isolation from everything else that ails our planet and species. They forget that while academia can be gainfully fragmented into disciplines, the world cannot: reality is a web, not a collection of parallel lines. The recently-negotiated CFC ban would markedly aid both the ozone depletion problem and the greenhouse threat, but this combined effect is a mere peanut in Santa Lovins' famous briefcase. Besides averting the greenhouse and ozone threats, the soft path would entail worldwide savings of untold billions of dollars and countless natural resources.

It would improve our material quality of life, reduce pollution, cut severe environmental and health impact of coal use (e.g., black lung disease, land subsidence), improve human health, eliminate future acid rain problems (which are currently aging buildings and monuments, damaging forests, and killing fish in thousands of lakes and streams). Furthermore, this path would diminish urban smog and help clean up our air, water, and food. It would reduce the incidence of tragic and costly floods, storms, and, perhaps, other natural disasters. It may improve the quality of topsoil and farmland, thereby increasing long-term agricultural productivity. It would gradually lead to the elimination of costly and unsafe nuclear power. "In sum, informal estimates (of EPA)... suggest that most—perhaps around 90% —of the problems EPA deals with could be displaced, at negative cost, just by energy efficiency and by sustainable farming and forestry. That is a pleasant by-product of abating global warming at a profit" (Lovins & Lovins, 1991, p. 518). Moreover, the soft path would considerably slow down the worrisome prospect of massive species extinction. It would raise economic competitiveness (for instance, greater energy efficiencies partially explain low production costs of Japanese cars). And it would reduce dependence on foreign energy supplies.

CONCLUDING REMARKS

The closest parallel to the greenhouse tale can perhaps be found in science fiction. For instance, in Karel Capek's humorously pessimistic *War with the Newts*, exceptionally clever and prolific salamanders are encountered in some far off bay. At first their discoverers offer them knives and protection from sharks in exchange for pearls. Gradually, however, many of the world's nations avail themselves of these creatures for other purposes, including war. In a few years, the salamanders run out of living space. To accommodate their growing numbers, they flood countries, one at a time. To do this, they need supplies from countries elsewhere and from merchants of the soon-to-be ravaged country itself. Needless to say, the salamanders have no trouble securing everything they need. At the end, humanity is on the verge of sinking and drowning; not so much by the newts, but by its greed, shortsightedness, and colossal stupidity.

This and other tales (e.g., Capek's *R.U.R*, Kurt Vonnegut's *Cat's Cradle*) imply that the world is not a wholly rational place. Indeed, the place and date of publication of *War with the Newts*— Czechoslovakia, 1935—throw some light on the origin of this tale. At that time, or a short time earlier, a few English, French, or American divisions could have invaded Germany, sent Hitler into early retirement, and saved humanity from disaster. Others besides Capek appealed for preemptive action. But Western politicians worried about the next elections and disregarded the more distant future. They remembered their petty quarrels and forgot their common, and far more sinister, foe.

Humankind's greenhouse policies similarly defy common sense. If the technical solutions are so easy, profitable, and beneficial, why are they not adopted? Why did President Clinton, when announcing his administration's greenhouse position in late 1993, agree to do virtually nothing? Is it mere ignorance on the part of politicians, as Lovins & Lovins suggest (1991, p. 525)? Is it greed (humanity spends one trillion dollars a year on coal, oil, and gas alone; cf. Leggett, 1990, p. 4)? Is it yet another manifestation of Garrett Hardin's (1968) tragedy of the commons? Is it inertia? The answers to these important queries—answers which rival in number and ingenuity Lovins' energy-saving gizmos—cannot be explored here (cf. Nissani, 1992, 1994).

In the meantime, it would appear that the greenhouse threat is real; the recipe for health and wealth simple; the wisdom to use it, absent. To justify their faith in humanity's luck, the optimists can rightly cite the historical record. But to maintain their faith in humanity's rationality, they must show that the probability of disaster is close to zero and that the costs of prevention are well above zero. Until this feat is accomplished, skeptics would go on insisting that all but the details of humankind's environmental follies had been predicted long ago in Capek's *War with the Newts*.

The last chapter in humanity's greenhouse saga remains to be written, perhaps long after cacti have grown over our cheeks. Until then, one's future projections depend less on science and more on one's temperament: on whether one sees the world as turning towards dawn or dusk. Who knows? We may continue to emit greenhouse gases forever and remain as cool and comfortable as we have ever been. We may come to our senses in time, act, and vanquish the threat. We may inadvertently remove the threat. We may sweat and survive. Or we may sink and drown.

ACKNOWLEDGMENTS

... I thank Donna Hoefler-Nissani, Virginia Abernethy, and my students for their patience, encouragement, and criticism.

REFERENCES

Asimov, I. & Pohl, F. (1991). *Our angry earth.*
Beardsley, T. (1995). It's melting, it's melting. *Scientific American, 272* (7), 28.
Beckerman W. & Malkin, J. (1994). How much does global warming matter? *The Public Interest*, Winter, 3–16.
Brown, L., Kane, H., and Ayres, E. (1993). *Vital signs.*
Brown, N. (1994). *Climate change: a threat to peace.*
Cherif, A. H. & Adams, G. E. (1994). Planet Earth. *The American Biology Teacher, 56*, 26–36.
Commoner, B. (1990). *Making peace with the planet.*
Flavin, C. & Tunali, O. (1996). *Climate of hope.*
Franck, I. & Brownstone, D. (1992). *Green encyclopedia.*
Gates, D. M. (1993). *Climate change and its biological consequences.*
Guoan, Z., et al. (1994). climatic change and its environmental effects during this century in Xinjiang, China. In R. G. Zepp (Ed.). *Climate-biosphere interactions* (pp. 279–291).
Hardin, G. (1968). The tragedy of the commons. *Science, 162*, 1243–1248.
Hare, F. K. (1993). The challenge. In H. Coward and T. Hurka (Eds.). *Ethics and climate change: the greenhouse effect.*
Heilig, G. K. (1994). The greenhouse gas methane (CH_4): sources and sinks, the impact of population growth, possible interventions. *Population and Environment: A Journal of Interdisciplinary Studies, 16* (2), 109–137.
Houghton, J. (1994). *Global warming.*
Keeling, C. D., Chin, J. F. S. & Whorf, T. P. (1996). Increased activity of northern vegetation inferred from atmospheric CO_2 measurements. *Nature* 382 (July 11), 146–149.
Keepin, B. (1990). Nuclear power and global warming. In J. Leggett (Ed.). *Global warming* (pp. 295–316).
Kerr, R. A. (1995). Studies say—tentatively—that greenhouse warming is here. *Science, 268* (June 16), 1567–1568.
Kipling, R. (1964), "The Dykes." In R. F. Niebling (Ed.). *A journey of poems* (pp. 138–140).
Leggett, J. (1990). Introduction. In J. Leggett (Ed.). *Global warming.*
Lovins, A. & Lovins, L. H. (1991). Least-cost climatic stabilization. *Annual Review of Energy and the Environment, 16*, 433–531.
Manning, W. J. & Tiedemann, A. V. (1995). Climate change: potential effects of increased atmospheric carbon dioxide (CO_2), ozone (O_3), and ultraviolet-B (UV-B) radiation on plant diseases. *Environmental Pollution, 88*, 219–245.

Miller, G. T. (1994; 8th edition). *Living in the environment.*

Monastersky, R. (1995). Dusting the climate for fingerprints. *Science News,* 147 (June 10), 362–363.

Moore, T. G. (1995). Why global warming would be good for you. *The Public Interest,* 118 (winter), 83–99.

National Academy of Sciences. (1992). *Policy implications of greenhouse warming.*

Nerem, R. S. (1995). Global mean sea level variations from TOPEX/POSEIDON altimeter data. *Science,* 268 (June 2), 708–710.

Nissani, M. (1992). *Lives in the balance,* Chapter 9.

Nissani, M. (1994). Conceptual conservatism: an understated variable in human affairs? *Social Science Journal,* 31, 307–318.

Nissani, M. (1996). The greenhouse effect: an interdisciplinary perspective. *Population and Environment: A Journal of Interdisciplinary Studies,* 17, 459–489.

Nordhaus, W. D. (1994). *Managing the global commons.*

Parmesan, C. (1996). Climate and species range. *Nature,* 382 (August 29), 765–766.

Regalado, A. (1995). Listen up! The world's oceans may be starting to warm. *Science,* 268 (June 9), 1436–1437.

Rosenzweig, C. (1994). Predicted effects of climate change on agricultural ecosystems. In R. G. Zepp (Ed.). *Climate-biosphere interactions* (pp. 253–269).

Santer, B. D. et. al. (1996). A search for human influences on the thermal structure of the atmosphere. *Nature,* 382 (July 4), 39–46.

Schneider, S. H. (1990). The costs of cutting—or not cutting—greenhouse gas emissions. In J. Leggett (Ed.). *Global warming.*

Singer, F. S., Revelle, R., & Starr, C. (1993). What to do about greenhouse warming: look before you leap. In R. A. Geyer (Ed.). *A global warming forum* (pp. 347–355).

Smith, C. (1995). Revisiting solar power's past. *Technology Review,* 98 (5), 38–47.

Smith, R. C. (1995). Implications of increased solar UV-B for aquatic ecosystems. In G. M. Woodwell and F. T. Mackenzie. *Biotic feedbacks in the global climatic system* (pp. 263–277).

Stone, R. (1995). If the mercury soars, so may health hazards. *Science,* 267 (February 17), 957–958.

Thomson, D. J. (1995). The seasons, global temperature, and precession. *Science,* 268 (April 7), 59–68.

Weiner, J. (1986). *Planet earth.*

NO

Thomas Gale Moore

WHY GLOBAL WARMING
WOULD BE GOOD FOR YOU

In his book *World on Fire: Saving on Endangered Earth*, Senator George Mitchell prophesied that:

> Climate extremes would trigger meteorological chaos—raging hurricanes such as we have never seen, capable of killing millions of people; uncommonly long, record-breaking heat waves; and profound drought that could drive Africa and the entire Indian subcontinent over the edge into mass starvation.... Even if we could stop all greenhouse gas emissions today, we would still be committed to a temperature increase worldwide of two to four degrees Fahrenheit by the middle of the twenty-first century. It would be warmer then than it has been for the past two million years. Unchecked it would match nuclear war in its potential for devastation.

Senator Mitchell's forecast and his history are both wrong. Warmer periods bring benign rather than more violent weather. Milder temperatures will induce more evaporation from oceans and thus more rainfall—where it will fall we cannot be sure, but the earth as a whole should receive greater precipitation. Meteorologists now believe that any rise in sea levels over the next century will be at most a foot or more, not twenty.

Mitchell also flunks history: around 6,000 years ago, the earth sustained temperatures that were probably more than four degrees Fahrenheit hotter than those of the twentieth century, yet mankind flourished. The Sahara desert bloomed with plants, and water-loving animals such as hippopotamuses wallowed in rivers and lakes. Dense forests carpeted Europe from the Alps to Scandinavia. The Midwest of the United States was somewhat drier than it is today, similar to contemporary western Kansas or eastern Colorado. In contrast, Canada enjoyed a warmer climate and more rainfall.

Raising the specter of disaster as well, Vice President Al Gore has called the threat of global warming "the most serious problem our civilization faces." He has styled those who dispute it as "self-interested" and compared them to spokesmen for the tobacco industry who have questioned the relation of smoking to cancer. However, Gore is misinformed; many disinterested scien-

From Thomas Gale Moore, "Why Global Warming Would Be Good for You," *The Public Interest*, no. 118 (Winter 1995), pp. 83–99. Copyright © 1995 by National Affairs, Inc. Reprinted by permission of the author and *The Public Interest*.

tists, including climatologists with no financial interest other than preventing wasteful expenditures of society's limited resources, question the evidence and the models that underlie the warming hypothesis.

In fact, the evidence supporting the claim that the earth has grown warmer is shaky. Moreover, the theory is weak and the models on which the conclusions are based cannot even replicate the current climate. It is asserted, for example, that over the last 100 years, the average temperature at the earth's surface has gone up by 0.5°C (Celsius) or about 1°F (Fahrenheit). However, given evidence that in the United States temperatures have failed to rise, and British naval records that find no significant change in temperatures at sea since the mid-1800s, the public is entitled to be wary. Moreover, even the National Academy of Sciences is skeptical of the validity of the computer models and warns that the modeling of clouds—a key factor—is inadequate and poorly understood.

The dire forecasts of global warming hinge on a prediction that human activity will provoke a continued upsurge in atmospheric carbon dioxide. Many environmentalists believe that the burning of fossil fuels, the release of methane from agricultural activities, and the escape of other chemicals into the air over the next few decades will lead to an effective doubling of greenhouse gases sometime in the next century....

What is well known is that climate changes: from the Mesozoic era, when the earth appears to have been about 18°F warmer than now, to the ice ages, when huge glaciers submerged much of the Northern Hemisphere. One paleoclimatologist estimated that, during the Precambrian period, the polar regions were about 36°F colder than they are in the contemporary world. During the last interglacial, about 130,000 years ago or about when modern man first explored the globe, the average temperature in Europe was at least 2°F to 5°F warmer than at present. Indeed, during the last 12,000 years, that is, since the end of the last glacial period, the global climate has alternated between substantially warmer and noticeably cooler temperatures.

EXPECTED EFFECTS OF GLOBAL WARMING

Although most of the forecasts of global warming's repercussions have been dire, an examination of the likely effects suggests little basis for that view. Climate affects principally agriculture, forestry, and fishing. Manufacturing, most service industries, and nearly all extractive industries are immune to climatic shifts. Factories can be built in any climate. Banking, insurance, medical services, retailing, education, and a variety of other services can prosper as well in warm climates (with air-conditioning) as in cold (with central heating).

A few services, such as transportation and tourism, may be more susceptible to weather. A warmer climate will lower transportation costs: less snow and ice will torment truckers and automobile drivers; fewer winter storms will disrupt air travel; a lower incidence of storms and less fog will make water transport less risky. A warmer climate could, however, change the nature and location of tourism. Many ski resorts, for example, might face less reliably cold weather and shorter seasons. Warmer conditions would mean that fewer northerners would feel the need to vacation in Florida or the Caribbean. On the other hand, new tourist opportunities might develop in Alaska, northern Canada, and other locales at higher latitudes or in upper elevations.

A rise in world-wide temperatures will go virtually unnoticed by inhabitants of the industrial countries. As modern societies have developed a larger industrial base and become more service oriented, they have grown less dependent on farming, thus boosting their immunity to temperature variations. Warmer weather means, if anything, fewer power outages and less frequent interruptions of wired communications.

Only if warmer weather caused more droughts or lowered agricultural output would even Third World countries suffer. Should the world warm, the hotter temperatures would enhance evaporation from the seas, producing more clouds and thus more precipitation world wide. Although some areas might become drier, others would become wetter. Judging from history, Western Europe would retain plentiful rainfall, while North Africa and the Sahara might gain moisture. The Midwest United States might suffer from less precipitation and become more suitable for cattle grazing than farming. On the other hand, the Southwest would likely become wetter and better for crops.

A warmer climate would produce the greatest gain in temperatures at northern latitudes, with less change near the equator. Not only would this foster a longer growing season and open up new territory for farming, but it would mitigate harsh weather. The contrast between the extreme cold near the poles and the warm atmosphere on the equator drives storms and much of the earth's climate. This difference propels air flows; if the disparity is reduced, the strength of winds driven by equatorial highs and arctic lows will be diminished.

As a result of more evaporation from the oceans, a warmer climate should intensify cloudiness. More cloud cover will moderate daytime temperatures while acting at night as an insulating blanket to retain heat. The Intergovernmental Panel on Climate Change has found exactly this pattern to hold for the last 40 years, indeed for the whole of the twentieth century. For the Northern Hemisphere in summer months, daytime high temperatures have actually fallen; but in the fall, winter, and spring, both the maximum and especially the minimum temperatures (night time) have climbed.

Warmer night-time temperatures, particularly in the spring and fall, create longer growing seasons, which should enhance agricultural productivity. Moreover, the enrichment of the atmosphere with CO_2 will fertilize plants and make for more vigorous growth. Agricultural economists studying the relationship of higher temperatures and additional CO_2 to crop yields in Canada, Australia, Japan, northern Russia, Finland, and Iceland found not only that a warmer climate would push up yields, but also that the added boost from enriched CO_2 would enhance output by 17 percent. Researchers have attributed a burgeoning of forests in Europe to the increased CO_2 and the fertilizing effect of nitrogen oxides.

Professor of Climatology Robert Pease writes in the *Wall Street Journal* that we may now be living in an "icehouse" world and that a warming of about two degrees Celsius, which is what his model indicates, may actually make the earth more habitable. The higher temperatures combined with more carbon dioxide will favor plant and crop growth and could well provide more food for our burgeoning global populations.

Geologic history reveals that warmer global temperatures produce more, not less, precipitation, a fact reflected by a recent scientific investigation that shows the Greenland icecap to be thickening, not melting. So much for the catastrophic prediction that our coastlines will be flooded by a rise in sea level from polar meltwaters.

The United States Department of Agriculture, in a cautious report titled *Climate Change: Economic Implications for World Agriculture*, reviewed the likely influence of global warming on crop production and world food prices. The study, which assumed that farmers fail to make any adjustment to mitigate the effects of warmer, wetter, or drier weather —such as substituting alternative or new varieties of crops, increasing or decreasing irrigation—concludes that:

> The overall effect on the world and domestic economies would be small as reduced production in some areas would be balanced by gains in others, according to an economic model of the effects of climate change on world agricultural markets. The model ... estimates *a slight increase* in world output and a *decline in commodity prices* under moderate climate change conditions. [Emphasis added.]

HISTORICAL METHOD

The best evidence for the effect of climatic change on humans, plants, and animals comes from history. Since statistics on the human condition are unavailable except for the most recent centuries, I shall use indirect methods to demonstrate the influence of climate on man's well-being. A growth in the population, major construction projects, a significant expansion in arts and culture—all indicate that society is prosperous. If the population is expanding, food must be plentiful, disease cannot be overwhelming, and living standards must be satisfactory. If building, art, science, and literature are vigorous, the civilization must be producing enough goods and services to provide a surplus available for such activities. Renaissance Florence was rich; Shakespeare flourished in prosperous London; wealthy Vienna provided a welcome venue for Haydn, Schubert, Mozart, and Beethoven.

Clearly climate is far from the only influence on man's well-being. Governments that extort too much from their people impoverish their countries. A free and open economy stimulates growth and prosperity. War and diseases can prove catastrophic. On the other hand, a change in climate has frequently been a cause of war or aided the spread of disease. A shift to more arid conditions, for example, impelled the Mongols to desert their traditional lands to invade richer areas. A cold, wet climate can also confine people to close quarters, which can abet contagion. Moreover, a shift towards a poorer climate can lead to famine and disease.

Throughout history, climatic changes probably forced technological innovations and adaptations. The shift from warm periods into ice ages and back again likely accelerated the evolution of modern man. Each shift would have left small groups of hominoids isolated and subject to pressures to adapt to new weather conditions. These shifts, especially to the more adverse conditions created by the spread of extreme cold, would put strong selection pressure on the human forebears that ultimately led to modern man. Even after *Homo sapiens* started spreading across the earth, climatic shifts fostered new technologies to deal with changed circumstances.

The influence of climate on human activities has declined with the growth in wealth and resources. Primitive man and hunter-gatherer tribes were at the mercy of the weather, as are societies which are still bound to the soil. A series of bad years can be devastating. If, as was the usual case until very recently, transportation is costly and slow, even a regionalized drought or an excess of rain can lead to disaster, although crops may be plentiful a short distance away. Thus, variation in the weather for early man had a more profound influence on his life and death than do fluctuations in temperature or rainfall in modern times when economies are more developed. Since the time of the industrial revolution, climate has basically been confined to a minor role in human affairs.

IN THE BEGINNING

Since its origins, the earth has experienced periods significantly warmer than the modern world—some epochs have been even hotter than the most extreme predictions of global warming. Today's cool temperatures are well below average for the globe in its more-than-four-billion-year history. During one of the warmest such eras, dinosaurs and a rich ecological world flourished. Studies of climatic history show that sharp changes in temperatures over brief periods of time have occurred frequently without setting into motion any disastrous feedback systems that would lead either to a heating that would cook the earth or a freezing that would eliminate all life.

Modern man apparently evolved into his current genotype between 40,000 and 200,000 years ago, probably in Africa during an ice age. Around 150,000 years ago, the extent of ice coverage reached a maximum; around 130,000 years before the present (YBP), a rapid deglaciation occurred. The warm interglacial era, during which temperatures may have exceeded those forecast under a doubling of greenhouse gases, lasted about 15,000 years until the onset of renewed glaciation at 115,000 YBP. Over the next 100,000 years, the glaciers fluctuated with the climate, but at no time did the average temperature equal the level of the previous interglacial epoch or reach the warmth of the last 10,000 years.

Human advancement—basically a few improvements in hunting tools and some cave art—was incredibly slow during the Ice Age, a period whose length dwarfs the centuries since. Over the last 12 millennia of interglacial warmth, however, modern man has advanced rapidly. The advancement in technology and living standards required a climate that was more hospitable than during that frozen period.

After the Ice Age, the sea level rose as much as 300 feet, hunters in Europe roamed through modern Norway, and agriculture developed in the Middle East. For about 3,000 to 4,000 years, the globe enjoyed what historians of climate call the Climatic Optimum period—a time when average world temperatures were significantly hotter than today. At its height between 4000 B.C. and 2000 B.C., H. H. Lamb, a leading climate historian, estimates that the world was 4°F to 5°F warmer than during the twentieth century. During the relatively short period since the end of glaciation, the climate has experienced periods of stability separated by "abrupt transition." Lamb estimates that, at its coldest, during the Mini Ice Age, the temperature in central England for January was about 4.5°F colder than today.

If modern humans originated 200,000 years ago, why did they not develop agriculture for the first 190,000 years? Even if *Homo sapiens* originated only 40,000 years ago, people waited 30,000 years to grow their first crops, an innovation which yielded a more ample food supply. Farming developed first in the Middle East, immediately after the end of the last Ice Age. From 11,000 to 9,000 years ago, the climate became warmer and wetter in the Middle East, shifting the ecology from steppe to open woodland. This led to the domestication of plants and animals, probably because the warmer, wetter weather made farming possible. From its origins around 8000 B.C., agriculture spread northward, appearing in Greece about 6000 B.C., Hungary 5000 B.C., France 4500 B.C., and Poland 4250 B.C. Is it a coincidence that this northward spread followed a gradual warming of the climate that made agriculture more feasible at higher latitudes?

During the ice ages, Europe was covered with tundra and populated by large herds of wild animals. Hunting was easy and game was plentiful. As the climate warmed and rainfall increased, forests spread northward, driving the animals toward the higher latitudes. The population of Europe had either to follow or to develop a new source of sustenance —farming. The connection between a less cold and wetter climate and the spread of agriculture seems inescapable.

Over history, the number of humans has been expanding at ever more rapid rates. Around 25,000 years ago, the world's population may have measured only about three million. Fifteen thousand years later, around 10,000 B.C., the total had grown by one-third, to four million. It took 5,000 more years to jump one more million, but in the 1,000 years after 5000 B.C., it added another million. Except for a few disastrous periods, the number of humans has mounted with increasing rapidity. Only in the latter half of the twentieth century has the escalation slowed. However, in propitious periods, that is, when the climate was warm, the population swelled faster than during less clement eras.

THE FIRST CLIMATIC OPTIMUM

During the period from 9,000 to 5,000 years ago, the earth was warmer than today; perhaps 4°F hotter, about the average of the various predictions for global warming after a doubling of CO_2. Although the climate cooled after 3000 B.C., it stayed relatively warmer than the modern world until sometime after 1000 B.C., when chilly temperatures became more common.

The invention of agriculture coincided with the end of the last Ice Age and the melting of the glaciers. Archaeologists have found the earliest evidence for husbandry and farming in Mesopotamia around 9000 B.C. As the earth warmed, the Middle East was becoming wetter and the Iranian plateau was shifting from an open, dry plain with roving bands of game to a more wooded environment with less reliable food sources. No one really knows how man first domesticated animals and developed farming, but the coincidence in time suggests that the warmer, wetter weather, especially in the mountains, may have encouraged new techniques.

The Optimum period may have been the origin of the Garden of Eden story. In Europe, this warmer period produced an expansion of civilization and a technological revolution. The Bronze Age replaced the New Stone Age. The more benign climate with less severe storms encouraged trade by sea. During this epoch, Europe enjoyed mild winters and warm summers. With the reduced size of glaciers and less snow in the Alps, travel from southern to northern Europe became considerably easier. The northern reaches traded tin for manufactured bronze in the south. Alpine people mined gold and traded it for goods produced around the Mediterranean. Baltic amber found its way to Scotland.

Notwithstanding the less stormy weather, rainfall was more than adequate to produce widespread forests. Western Europe, including parts of Iceland and the Highlands of Scotland, was mantled by great woods. The timber, until European average temperatures dipped temporarily for about 400 years between 3500 B.C. and 3000 B.C., consisted of warmth-demanding trees, such as elms and linden in North America and oak and hazel in Europe. These species have never regained their dominant position in American and Europe. Not only did Europe enjoy a benign climate with adequate rainfall, but the Mediterranean littoral, including the Middle East, apparently received considerably more moisture than it does today. The Indian subcontinent and China were also much wetter during this Optimal period.

During the warm period prior to 3000 B.C., China enjoyed much warmer temperatures. In particular, mid-winters were as much as 9°F hotter and rice was planted a month earlier than today. Bamboo, valued for food, building material, writing implements, furniture, and musical instruments, grew much farther north than is now possible.

The Southern Hemisphere also seems to have flourished during the warm millennia after the most recent Ice Age. Lamb reports that the southern temperate zone enjoyed both warmer weather and more moisture than it does currently. Scholars have found that Australia was consistently wetter than today in both the tropical and temperate regions. Since the end of that epoch, the great deserts of Australia have expanded and the climate has become cooler and drier. Apparently, most of the other great desert regions of the world had more rainfall during the Climatic Optimum than they do now.

Lamb contends that the period of temperature maximum was also a period of moisture maximum in subtropical and tropical latitudes. During this warm era, Hawaii experienced more rainfall than in the twentieth century. Even Antarctica enjoyed warmer weather, about 4°F to 5°F higher, and during the summer in some of the mountains the weather was warm enough to produce running streams and lakes, which have subsequently frozen.

Less is known about civilizations that flowered and died in the Indian subcontinent. One of the first, which flourished in an area that is now virtually desert, disappeared around 1500 B.C., when the climate became distinctly drier and the earth cooler. Historians and archaeologists also attribute the failure of this civilization to poor agricultural techniques that may have exacerbated drought.

From the end of the Optimum period of sustained warmth until around A.D. 800 to A.D. 900, the world's climate and, in particular, the European climate, varied between periods of warmth and cold. The period from 500 B.C. to A.D. 600 was one of varied temperatures, although cooler on average than the previous 4,500 years. During these centuries of varied weather, classical Greece flourished and then declined; the Roman Empire expanded, only to be overrun by barbarians from central Asia who may have been driven out of their homeland by an increasingly cold and dry climate.

Europe became wetter, with the formation of peat bogs over northern areas. The population abandoned many lakeside dwellings while mountain passes became choked with ice and snow, making transportation between northern Europe and the south difficult. The Mediterranean littoral and North Africa dried up, although they remained more moist than now.

SOME LIKE IT HOT

From around A.D. 800 to 1200 or 1300, the globe warmed and civilization prospered. This Little Climatic Optimum generally displays, although less distinctly, any of the same characteristics as the first. Greenland was 4°F to 7°F warmer than at present. The Mediterranean, the Near East, and North Africa, including the Sahara, enjoyed more rainfall than they do today. From Western Europe to China, East Asia, India, and the Americas, mankind flourished as never before.

In the West, Charlemagne, creator of the Holy Roman Empire, may have inaugurated this climatic era while Dante, writing *The Divine Comedy*, may have closed it. In *A History of Knowledge*, Charles Van Doren contended that the "three centuries, from about 1000 to about 1300, became one of the most optimistic, prosperous, and progressive periods in European history." All across Europe, an unparalleled building spree ensued: construction began on the Abbey of Mont-Saint-Michel (1017), St. Marks in Venice (1043), Westminster Abbey in London (1045), and a vast number of other major structures.

European commerce expanded and traders reached the Middle East, bringing back not only exotic goods but new ideas and information about classical times as well. St. Thomas Aquinas defined medieval Christian doctrine in his *Summa Theologica* in 1258; possibly the oldest continuous university in the world was founded in Bologna in A.D. 1000 for the study of the law; and the early twelfth century saw the inauguration of the University of Paris. By 1167, Oxford University became a flourishing educational institution, and less than half a century later (1209), Cambridge was founded.

Technology grew rapidly during this period. New techniques expanded the use of the water mill, the windmill, and coal to provide energy and heat. Sailing improved through the invention of the lateen sail, the sternpost rudder, and the compass. Roads were built and new techniques developed for the use of stone in construction. New iron-casting techniques led to the development of better tools and weapons. The textile industry began employing wool, linen, cotton, and silk and, in the thirteenth century, the spinning wheel was developed. Soap, essential for hygiene, came into use in the twelfth century. Mining, which had declined since the Romans, at least partly because the cold and snow had made access to mountain areas difficult, was revived after the tenth century.

The warmth of the Little Climatic Optimum made territory farther north cultivable. In Scandinavia, Scotland, and the high country of England and Wales, farming became common in areas which neither before nor since have yielded crops reliably. Greater crop production meant that more people could be fed, and the population of Scandinavia exploded. The rapid growth in numbers in turn propelled and sustained the Viking explorations and the Norman conquests that ravaged the coasts of England, Ireland, Holland, and France, leading as well to the foundation of colonies in Iceland and Greenland.

Europe's riches enabled and emboldened its rulers to take on the conquest of the Holy Land through a series of Crusades starting in 1096 and ending in 1291. The Crusaders, probably stimulated in party by a mushrooming population with an economic surplus large enough to spare men for the invasion of the Muslim empire, captured Jerusalem in 1099—a feat not equaled until the nineteenth century.

Even southern Europe around the Mediterranean enjoyed a more moist climate than currently exists. In the reign of the Byzantine Emperor Manuel I Comnenus, art and culture flourished. Under the control of the Fatimid caliphate, Egypt cultivated a "House of Science" where scholars worked on optics, described the circulation of the blood, and compiled an encyclopedia of natural history. For the first time in the West, block printing appeared. The caliphate effectively turned Cairo into a brilliant center of Muslim culture.

MULTICULTURAL HEAT WAVE

In Persia, Omar Khayyam published astronomical tables, a revision of the Muslim calendar, a treatise on algebra, and his famous *Rubáiyát*. Farther south

in Africa, the kingdom of Ghana and its capital, Kumbi, reached its apogee in the tenth century. Its subsequent decline may be attributable to a reduction in rainfall that led to the area's increased barrenness. In the fourteenth century, the Mandingo Empire, which controlled most of West Africa and Timbuktu, luxuriated in a brilliant culture.

Looking back on the economic performance of China since 200 B.C., Chinese economist Kang Chao has discovered that real earnings rose from the Han period (206 B.C. to A.D. 220) to a peak during the Northern Sung Dynasty (A.D. 961 to 1127). This coincides with other evidence of longer growing seasons and a warmer climate. The wealth of this period gave rise to a great flowering of art, writing, and science. During the 300 years of the Sung Dynasty, farmers invented 35 major farm implements—that is, over 11 per century, a significantly higher rate of invention than in any other era. In the middle of the eleventh century, the Chinese invented movable type employing clay pieces.

During the Northern Sung Dynasty, Chinese landscape painting with its exquisite detail and color reached a peak never again matched. The Southern Sung produced pottery and porcelains unequaled in subtlety and sophistication. Literature, history, and scholarship flourished as well. Scholars prepared two great encyclopedias, compiled a history of China, and composed essays and poems. Mathematicians discovered the properties of the circle. Astronomers devised a number of technological improvements to increase the accuracy of measuring the stars and the year.

Chinese civilization has waxed and waned for about 3,500 years; yet, during all those centuries, only once has it ventured to spread its culture or its people beyond its normal borders. Beginning with the twelfth century A.D., at the height of the medieval warm period, Chinese explorers and merchant ships plied the Indian Ocean and landed on the East African coast. Although favorable weather may not have motivated these voyages, which ended in the fourteenth century, they coincided with both the warmest temperatures and the time of the richest per-capita incomes. Certainly, the more clement climate meant fewer storms and easier sea travel.

Japan also prospered during the Little Climatic Optimum. In the Heian Period (A.D. 794 to 1192), the arts thrived as emperors and empresses commissioned the construction of vast numbers of Buddhist temples. Murasaki Shikibu, perhaps the world's first female novelist, composed Japan's most famous book, *The Tale of Genji*. Other classical writers penned noteworthy essays: Sei Shonagon, a court lady, wrote *Makura-no-Soshi* (The pillow book). The Japanese aristocracy vied to compose the best poems. This attests to the existence of a prosperous economy with ample food stocks to support a leisured and cultivated upper class.

Between A.D. 800 and 1200, the peoples of the Indian subcontinent prospered as well. Society was rich enough to produce colossal and impressive temples, beautiful sculpture, and elaborate carvings, many of which survive to this day. The Madurai Temple, one of the finest Hindu shrines, as well as the Tanjore Temple, date from this period. Seafaring empires existed in Sumatra, which reached its height around 1180, and in Java. Ninth-century Java erected the vast stupa of Borobudur; other temples, the Medut, Pawon, Kelasan, and Prambana, also originated in this era. In the early twelfth century, the Khmers, predecessors of the Cambodians, built the magnificent temple of Angkor Wat. In the eleventh century, Burmese civilization reached a pinnacle. In and around its capital, Pagan, succeeding kings constructed vast numbers of sacred monuments. Today, the area is a dusty plain littered with the crumbling remains of nearly 13,000 temples and pagodas, implying that the climate was once more hospitable.

Less is known about civilizations in the Americas during this period, or even how the climate changed. Around A.D. 900, the Chimu Indians in South America developed an extensive irrigation system on Peru's coast, and their capital contained 100,000 to 200,000 people. The Toltec civilization, which occupied much of Mexico, reached its apogee in the thirteenth century. By 1200, the Aztecs had built the pyramid of Quetzalcoatl near modern Mexico City. The Anasazi civilization of Mesa Verde apparently flourished during the warm period, but the cooling of the climate at the end of the medieval warmth, around 1280, may have led to its disappearance.

Thus, warmer times brought benefits to most people and most regions. As is always the case with a climatic shift, the changes benefited some while adversely affecting others. Indeed, every change is usually feared since it makes current practices obsolete and requires the adoption of new techniques and, often, new technology. Change is always disruptive; at the same time, it produces new ideas and new ways of coping with the world. Nevertheless, for most of the known world, the Little Climatic Optimum of the ninth through the thirteenth centuries brought significant benefits.

NO Thomas Gale Moore / 339

THE LITTLE CHILL

The earth cooled substantially from around 1300 to 1850, especially after 1400, with temperatures falling some 2°F to 4°F below those of the twentieth century. This indicates that temperatures may have fallen by as much as 9°F in the two-hundred years from 1200 to 1400, a drop of approximately the same magnitude as the maximum rise forecast under global warming. These frigid times did bring hardships, and population growth slowed. For much of these centuries, famine and disease stalked Europe and Asia.

The fourteenth century experienced extremely variable weather with very cold spells followed by warm but very dry conditions. Between 1347 and 1348, famine struck northern Italy, followed by the Black Death which decimated the population. Between 1348 and 1350, the Bubonic Plague killed about one-third of northern Europe's people. Life expectancy fell 10 years in little over a century, from 48 years in 1280 to 38 years in the period 1376 to 1400.

Notwithstanding the cooling climate and the ravages of disease after 1300, European civilization recovered in the fifteenth century with the advent of the Renaissance. This burst of cultural activity represented an expansion of the artistic and intellectual activity of the High Middle Ages.

Ironically, the outpouring of art, science, and literature that made up the Renaissance may have been sustained by the Plague. The colder climate made agriculture more chancy, reduced the territory available for farming, and lowered yields. Yet, without the one-third drop in Europe's population caused by the Black Death, food supplies would have been too meager to support a large cultivated class that promoted the arts. The reduced agricultural output, however, was still large enough to support the even more diminished population.

From around 1550 to 1700, the globe suffered from the coldest temperatures since the last Ice Age. Lamb estimates that in the 1590s and 1690s, the average temperature was 3°F below the present. Grain prices increased sharply as crops failed. Famines were common. In Scotland, between 1693 and 1700, crops failed in seven out of eight years. The Continent suffered from cold and rain, which produced poor growing conditions, food shortages, famines, and finally riots in the years 1527 to 1529, 1590 to 1597, and the 1640s. The shortages between 1690 and 1700 killed millions and were followed by more famines in 1725 and 1816.

WARMER IS BETTER

If mankind had to choose between a warmer or a cooler climate, they would be better off with the former. Whether the climate will warm is far from certain; that it will change is unquestionable. Human activity is likely to play only a small and uncertain role in these changes. The burning of fossil fuel may generate an enhanced greenhouse effect, or the release into the atmosphere of sulfates may cause cooling. It is simply hubris to believe that *Homo sapiens* can significantly affect temperatures, rainfall, and winds.

It is much easer for a rich country such as the United States to adapt to any long-term shift in weather than it is for poor countries, most of which are considerably more dependent on agriculture than the rich industrial nations. Such populations lack the resources to aid their flora and fauna in adapting, and many of their farmers earn too little to survive a shift to new conditions. These agriculturally dependent societies could suffer real hardship if the climate shifts quickly. The best preventive would be a rise in incomes which would diminish their dependence on agriculture. Higher earnings would provide them with the resources to adjust.

Preventing the predicted global warming would be very difficult, particularly since the cost of trimming emissions of CO_2 could be extremely high. William Cline of the Institute for International Economics, a proponent of regulatory initiatives to reduce the use of fossil fuels, has calculated that the cost of cutting emissions from current levels by one-third by 2040 would be 3.5 percent of World Gross Product. In terms of the estimated level of world output in 1992, this would amount to roughly $900 billion annually, an amount that could slow growth and impoverish some who survive on the margin. These resources could be better spent on promoting investment in the poorer countries of the world.

Should warming become apparent at some time in the future, creating more difficulties than benefits, policymakers may have to consider preventive measures. Based on history, however, global warming is likely to be positive for most of mankind while the additional carbon, rain, and warmth should also promote plant growth that can sustain an expanding world population. Global change is inevitable—warmer is better, richer is healthier.

POSTSCRIPT

Are Aggressive International Efforts Needed to Slow Global Warming?

Moore's essay and subsequent testimony before a congressional subcommittee, in which he made similar arguments, set off a storm of reactions and rebuttals from geophysicists, meteorologists, and other environmental scientists. These responses, many of which are accessible through the Internet site referenced at the end of this postscript, include critiques of Moore's analysis. One criticism, for example, is that Moore's claim that atmospheric carbon dioxide levels have been much higher at times during the past 8,000 years is based on his misreading of a reference that presented data about carbon-14 isotope levels, not total atmospheric carbon. Another criticism is that those who, like Moore, claim that there may have been historical periods when the climate was warmer are not really addressing the issue posed by the threat of rapid global temperature changes. The highly populated world that we live in is dependent on intensive agriculture, which will surely be negatively impacted by any significant, persistent change in climate or precipitation patterns that occurs over a period as short as a few decades.

S. Fred Singer is a member of the group of scientists who dismiss the seriousness of greenhouse-induced global warming. Singer presents a succinct summary of his arguments in "Warming Theories Need Warning Labels," *The Bulletin of the Atomic Scientists* (June 1992). Richard Elliot Benedick was the chief U.S. negotiator of the 1987 Montreal Protocol on protecting the ozone layer. In "Equity and Ethics in a Global Warming Convention," *America* (May 23, 1992), Benedick advocates using the experience gained in negotiating the ozone protection treaties as a model for agreements on reducing greenhouse gas emissions.

The case for using energy taxes to mitigate climate change is made by Frank Muller in "Mitigating Climate Change: The Case for Energy Taxes," *Environment* (March 1996). Robert White explores the general prospect for overcoming the political barriers that prevent effective international actions to reduce greenhouse gas emissions in the Fall 1996 issue of *Issues in Science and Technology*. For reactions to the Intergovernmental Panel on Climate Change's 1995 report, see the articles by Darren Goetze in the Spring 1996 issue of *Nucleus* and by Colum F. Lynch in the Spring 1996 issue of *The Amicus Journal*.

For an Internet site related to this issue, see http://www.mnsinc.com/richp/moore_warming.html, which contains links to critiques of Moore's paper and a response by Moore.

ISSUE 18

Are Major Changes Needed to Avert a Global Environmental Crisis?

YES: Hilary F. French, from "Forging a New Global Partnership to Save the Earth," *USA Today Magazine* (May 1995)

NO: Julian L. Simon, from "More People, Greater Wealth, More Resources, Healthier Environment," *Economic Affairs* (April 1994)

ISSUE SUMMARY

YES: Worldwatch Institute senior researcher Hilary F. French calls for an international effort to stabilize the planet by switching to sustainable technologies before environmental deterioration becomes irreversible.

NO: Professor of economics and business administration Julian L. Simon predicts that over the long term enhanced brainpower coupled with the market forces of a free economy will lead to improved standards of living and a healthier environment.

In 1972 the results of a study by a Massachusetts Institute of Technology computer modeling team triggered an avalanche of controversy about the future course of worldwide economic growth. The results appeared in a book entitled *The Limits to Growth* (Universe Books, 1972). The book's authors— Donella Meadows, Dennis Meadows, Jorgen Randers, and William Behrens —predicted that exponential growth in population and capital, accompanied by increasing pollution, would culminate in sudden resource depletion and economic collapse before the middle of the next century. The sponsors of the study, a group of rich European and American industrialists called the Club of Rome, popularized its conclusions by distributing 12,000 copies of the book to prominent government, business, and labor leaders.

Critiques of the study emerged from all sectors of the political spectrum. Conservatives rejected the implication that international controls on industrial development were necessary to prevent disaster. Liberals asserted that no-growth policies would hurt the poor more than the affluent. Radicals contended that the results were only applicable to the type of profit-motivated growth that occurs under capitalism. Among the universal criticisms of the study were the simplicity of the computer models used and the questionable practice of making long-term extrapolations based on present, increasing growth rates. The book's authors admitted that no attempt was made to incorporate the complex sociopolitical interactions that can profoundly affect the type and level of international industrial activities.

Although the debate about the specific catastrophic predictions of Meadows et al. has died down, the questions raised during that controversy continue to receive attention. In 1980 a three-volume publication entitled *The Global 2000 Report to the President* was released by the U.S. government. This report, which has sold over 500,000 copies, is the result of a joint study by the Department of State and the Council on Environmental Quality under President Carter of trends in population growth, natural resource development, and environmental quality through the end of the twentieth century. The dire projections of this study include increased environmental degradation, continued abuse of natural resources, and a widening of the gap between the rich and the poor.

This study, like its predecessors, has had its share of methodological criticism. For example, anticipated changes in energy use during the period of the study are not taken into account. Despite these flaws, the *Global 2000 Report* has contributed to the growing consensus that present patterns and rates of worldwide industrial growth are likely to cause intolerable environmental stress. This issue, the potential for conflict between the need for development and the need for environmental protection, was the central focus of the 1992 United Nations Earth Summit in Rio de Janeiro, which, in turn, was organized in response to a recommendation of the World Commission on Environment and Development, established by the UN in 1983 to produce a "global agenda for change." The concept of sustainable development, which requires a fundamental change in the technologies used by the world's economies in order to meet their energy, transportation, agricultural, and industrial production needs, has received increasing attention in the aftermath of the Rio meeting.

Hilary F. French, vice president for research of the Worldwatch Institute, summarizes the widespread concerns about developmental practices that are resulting in global environmental deterioration. Her assessment is that the responses to these dire problems have thus far been inadequate. She concludes that a sweeping public commitment to sustainable development is needed to prevent ecological disaster and social disintegration. Prominent among the ecological and environmental optimistis is Julian L. Simon, professor of economics and business administration at the University of Maryland. Simon claims that there is no evidence that environmental degradation, health problems, or world hunger are increasing, and he predicts that unless governments restrict the free market trends, the world can look forward to an improved standard of living and a cleaner environment.

YES

Hilary F. French

FORGING A NEW GLOBAL PARTNERSHIP TO SAVE THE EARTH

In June, 1992, more than 100 heads of state and 20,000 non-governmental representatives gathered in Rio de Janeiro for the United Nations Conference on Environment and Development (UNCED). It resulted in the adoption of Agenda 21, an ambitious 500-page blueprint for sustainable development. In addition, Rio produced treaties on climate and biological diversity, both of which could lead to domestic policy changes in all nations. Significantly, the conference pointed to the need for a global partnership if sustainable development was to be achieved.

Since Rio, a steady stream of international meetings have been held on the many issues that were on its agenda. For instance, the September, 1994, International Conference on Population and Development in Cairo put the spotlight of world attention on the inexorable pace of population growth and the need to respond to it through broad-based efforts to expand access to family planning, improve women's health and literacy, and ensure child survival.

The pace of real change has not kept up with the increasingly loaded schedule of international gatherings, though. The initial burst of international momentum generated by UNCED is flagging, and the global partnership is called for is foundering due to a failure of political will. While a small, committed group of individuals in international organizations, national and local governments, and citizens' groups continues trying to keep the flame of Rio alive, business as usual largely is the order of the day in the factories, farms, villages, and cities that form the backbone of the world economy.

As a result, the relentless pace of global ecological decline shows no signs of letting up. Carbon dioxide concentrations are mounting in the atmosphere, species loss continues to accelerate, fisheries are collapsing, land degradation frustrates efforts to feed hungry people, and the Earth's forest cover keeps shrinking. Many of the development and economic issues that underpin environmental destruction are worsening. Income inequality is rising, Third World debt is mounting, human numbers continue growing at daunting rates, and the amount of poor people in the world is increasing.

From Hilary F. French, "Forging a New Global Partnership to Save the Earth," *USA Today Magazine* (May 1995). Copyright © 1995 by The Society for the Advancement of Education. Reprinted by permission.

The global partnership that is needed to reverse these trends will have several distinct features. It will involve a new form of relationship between the industrialized North and the developing South. Another feature will be a division of responsibility among different levels of governance worldwide. Problems are solved best at the most decentralized level of governance that is consistent with efficient performance of the task. As they transcend boundaries, decision-making can be passed upward as necessary—from the community to the state, national, regional, and, in some rare instances, global level. A third requirement is the active participation of citizens in village, municipal, and national political life, as well as at the United Nations.

Above all, the new partnership calls for an unprecedented degree of international cooperation and coordination. The complex web of ecological, economic, communication, and other connections binding the world together means that no government can build a secure future for its citizens by acting alone.

PROTECTING THE GLOBAL ENVIRONMENT

One of the primary ways the world community has responded to the environmental challenge is through the negotiation of treaties and other types of international accords. Nations have agreed on more than 170 ecological treaties—more than two-thirds of them since the 1972 UN Conference on the Human Environment. In 1994, the climate and biological diversity conventions as well as the long-languishing Law of the Sea treaty received enough ratifications to enter into force. In addition, governments signed a new accord on desertification and land degradation.

These agreements have led to some measurable gains. Air pollution in Europe has been reduced dramatically as a result of the 1979 treaty on transboundary air pollution. Global chlorofluorocarbon (CFC) emissions have dropped 60% from their peak in 1988 following the 1987 treaty on ozone depletion and its subsequent amendments. The killing of elephants has plummeted in Africa because of the 1990 ban on commercial trade in ivory under the Convention on International Trade in Endangered Species of Wild Flora and Fauna. Mining exploration and development have been forbidden in Antarctica for 50 years under a 1991 accord.

The hallmark of international environment governance to date is the Montreal Protocol on the Depletion of the Ozone Layer. First agreed to in September, 1987, and strengthened significantly twice since then, it stipulates that the production of CFC's in industrial countries must be phased out altogether by 1996. It also restricts the use of several other ozone-depleting chemicals, including halons, carbon tetrachlorides, methyl chloroform, and hydrochlorofluorocarbons. Developing countries have a 10-year grace period in which to meet the terms of the original protocol and its amendments.

While this is a momentous international achievement, the world will have paid a heavy price for earlier inaction. Dangerous levels of ultraviolet radiation will be reaching the Earth for decades to come, stunting agricultural productivity and damaging ecological and human health.

The lessons learned in the ozone treaty are being put to a severe test as the international community begins to confront a more daunting atmospheric challenge—the need to head off climate change. Less than two years after it was signed in Rio, the Framework Convention on Climate Change became international law in March, 1994, when the 50th country (Portugal) ratified it. The speed with which the treaty was ratified was in part a reflection of the fact that it contains few real commitments.

The pact's deliberately ambiguous language urges, but does not require, industrial nations to stabilize emissions of carbon—the primary contributor to global warming—at 1990 levels by the year 2000. Developing nations face no numerical goals whatsoever, though all signatories must conduct inventories of their emissions, submit detailed reports of actions taken to implement the convention, and take climate change into account in all their social, economic, and environmental policies. No specific policy measures are required, however.

As of Late 1994, most industrial countries had established national greenhouse gas targets and climate plans, but they vary widely in effectiveness. Among the most ambitious and comprehensive are those of Denmark, the Netherlands, and Switzerland, none of which have powerful oil or coal industries to contend with. Through the use of efficiency standards, renewable energy programs, and limited carbon taxes, these plans are likely to limit emissions significantly in those nations.

According to independent evaluations by various nongovernmental organizations (NGOs), most of the climate plans issued so far will fall short of stabilizing national emissions and the other goals they have set for themselves. For example, Germany and the U.S., two of the largest emitters, have issued climate plans that fail to tackle politically difficult policies—the reduction of coal subsidies in German and the increase of gasoline taxes in the U.S. Neither country is likely to meet its stated goals. Reports from Japan suggest that it, too, is unlikely to achieve its stabilization target. In another failure of will, long-standing efforts by the European Union to impose a hybrid carbon/energy tax have failed so far, despite strong support from the European Community.

Even if the goal of holding emissions to 1990 levels in 2000 is met, this falls far short of stabilizing atmospheric concentrations of greenhouse gases, which will require bringing carbon emissions 60–80% below the current levels. As a result, several European countries and the U.S. have voiced cautious support for strengthening the treaty to promote stronger actions, though they have not said exactly how.

As with protecting the atmosphere, preserving biological diversity is something all nations have a stake in and no one country effectively can do alone. One of the most important achievements of the 1993 Convention on Biological Diversity was its recognition that biological resources are the sovereign property of nation-states. When countries can profit from something, they have an incentive to preserve it.

Genetic diversity is worth a lot. The protection that genetic variability affords crops from pests, diseases, and climatic and soil variations is worth $1,000,000,000 to U.S. agriculture. Over all, the economic benefits from wild species to pharmaceuticals, agriculture, forestry, fisheries, and the chemical industry adds up to more than $87,000,000,000 annually—over four percent of the U.S. gross domestic product. Though international pharmaceutical companies have been extracting genes from countries without paying for years, the convention says that gene-rich nations have a right to charge for access to this valuable resource and encourages them to pass legislation to set the terms.

One widely publicized model of this is a 1991 agreement between Merck, the world's largest pharmaceutical company, and Costa Rica's National Institute of Biodiversity (INBIO). Merck agreed to pay the institute $1,000,000 for conservation programs in exchange for access to the country's plants, microbes, and insects. If a discovery makes its way into a commercial product, Merck has agreed to give INBIO a share of the royalties. Discussing how to replicate such agreements likely will be a high priority for countries that have signed the convention.

Besides providing a forum for future negotiations, the convention calls for a number of actions by governments to preserve biological wealth. Possible steps in the future include discussions of a protocol on biotechnology, as well as deliberations on international standards for biodiversity prospecting agreements.

The oceans are another natural resource whose protection requires international collaboration. Not only did the Law of the Sea receive sufficient ratifications to enter into force in 1994, agreement also was reached on modifications to the original agreement that are expected to mean that the U.S. and other industrial countries will join in. The rebirth of this treaty comes just in time for the world's oceans and estuaries, which are suffering from overfishing, oil spills, land-based sources of pollution, and other ills.

The Law of the Sea contains an extensive array of environmental provisions. For instance, though countries are granted sovereignty over waters within 200 miles of their shores (called Exclusive Economic Zones, or EEZs), they also accept an obligation to protect ecological health there. The treaty contains pathbreaking compulsory dispute resolution provisions, under which nations are bound to accept the verdict of an international tribunal.

Just as the Law of the Sea is coming into force, however, its rules are being overtaken by events in one important area—over-fishing. In particular, the original treaty failed to resolve the issue of fish stocks that straddle the boundaries of EEZs and species that migrate long distances. The UN has convened a series of meetings to discuss possible international action to deal with a situation that has seen seafood catch per person fall eight percent since 1989.

CURBING LAND DEGRADATION

The latest addition to the international repertoire of environmental treaties is a convention intended to curb land degradation, adopted in June, 1994. According to the UN Environment Program, the livelihoods of at least 900,000,000 people in about 100 countries are threatened by desertification, which affects about one-quarter of the Earth's land area. The degradation—caused by overgrazing, overcropping, poor irrigation practices, and deforestation, and often exacerbated by climatic variations—poses a serious threat to efforts to raise agricultural productivity worldwide.

The desertification treaty supplies a framework for local projects, encourages national action programs, promotes regional and international cooperation on the transfer of needed technologies, and provides for information exchange and research and training.

Protecting the environment and combating poverty are recognized to be interlinked priorities. The Cairo conference looked at the complex interconnections among population growth, deteriorating social conditions, sexual inequity, environmental degradation, and a range of other issues. A sustainable future can not be secured without an aggressive effort to fight poverty and meet basic social needs.

Trends during the last several decades suggest a mixed record on improving human welfare. Even though impressive progress has been made in boosting immunization rates, reducing infant mortality, and increasing life expectancy, one in three children remains malnourished, more than 1,000,000,000 people lack safe water to drink, and about 1,000,000,000 adults can not read or write. The share of the world's population living in poverty has declined steadily, but the actual numbers continue to rise to more than 1,000,000,000 individuals. Rather than shrinking, the gap between the rich and the poor is growing. In 1960, the richest 20% of the world earned 30 times as much income as the poorest 20%; by 1991, the difference had risen to 61 times as much.

A crucial first step toward turning these statistics around was taken in Cairo, when more than 150 countries approved a World Population Plan of Action aimed at keeping human numbers somewhere below 9,800,000,000 in 2050. It covers a broad range of issues, including the empowerment of women, the role of the family, reproductive rights and health, and migration. The plan calls for expenditures on population programs to more than triple by 2000—from

$5,000,000,000 to $17,000,000,000. Of the total, $10,000,000,000 is intended for family planning programs; $5,000,000,000 for reproductive health; $1,300,000,000 for prevention of sexually transmitted diseases; and $500,000,000 for research and data collection. The action plan also calls for accelerating existing UN initiatives aimed at expanding women's literacy and improving their health—though it fails to provide spending targets for doing so.

Vatican opposition to proposed language on abortion rights captured headlines during the conference, but the real news was the consensus forged between the industrial and developing worlds and among representatives of population, women's, and human rights groups during two years of preparation for the meeting. Key elements of this include a recognition that slowing population growth and making progress on a range of social fronts are inextricably linked challenges. It follows from the new consensus that reaching population stabilization goals will require a far different approach than in the past and that family planning programs alone will be insufficient to do so. Equally important are investments in changing the conditions that generate demand for large families—such as illiteracy and a low status of women. In addition, there was widespread agreement that family planning efforts must be noncoercive and integrated broadly with reproductive health programs.

At the Cairo conference, 10 diverse developing nations representing Muslim, Buddhist, and Christian religious traditions joined together to share their experiences with others. Each has achieved considerable success in recent years in bringing fertility rates down. In Indonesia, for instance, the birth rate dropped from 5.6 births per woman in 1971 to three in 1991. In Colombia, it declined from 7.1 to 2.9 over 30 years.

As for poverty, unemployment, and social integration, efforts to combat these problems have decreased in recent years, as recession-ridden nations have found it harder and harder to appropriate funds. Few countries have reached the international target of devoting .07% of their gross national product to development assistance, and the amounts that are spent often are not targeted well. Because donor nations have tended to skew their disbursements toward their own security interests, the 10 countries that are home to two-thirds of the world's poorest people get just 32% of total aid expenditures. The richest 40% of the developing world receives twice as much aid per person as the poorest 40%.

Under the proposed 20:20 Compact on Human Development, developing countries would agree to devote 20% of their domestic resources to human priorities and donors would target 20% of their aid funds for such purposes. If this initiative succeeds, it will be making a major contribution to a more sustainable world.

Additional priorities include progress toward alleviating debt burdens and addressing unfavorable terms of trade for developing countries. Though the financial crisis has been eased for some of the largest debtors, such as Brazil, it remains very much alive in many of the poorest nations. The total external debt of developing countries has grown sevenfold during the past two decades, from $247,000,000,000 in 1970 to more than $1.7 trillion in 1993.

Though the ratio of debt-service payments to foreign-exchange earnings has been declining globally in recent years, it still is on the rise in sub-Saharan Africa, which spends some 25% of export receipts on debt repayments. For many countries, this number is far higher.

To generate the hard currency required to pay back loans, the International Monetary Fund (IMF) and others have urged debtor nations to undertake export-promoting reforms, such as devaluing exchange rates, and fiscal reforms to reduce public-sector deficits. The strategy has been only partially successful. A handful of countries in East Asia and Latin America have boosted exports dramatically, but others with the poorest 20% of humanity have not, accounting for just one percent of world trade.

Trade barriers to developing-country products continue to be a major impediment to boosting exports. Restrictions on textiles and clothing alone are estimated to cost the Third World $50,000,000,000 in lost foreign exchange annually. Though recent negotiations under the General Agreement on Tariffs and Trade (GATT) made modest inroads into the problems, developing countries and the former Eastern bloc are expected to account for a mere 14–32% of the projected global income gains from the revised GATT by 2002. Africa is projected to lose $2,600,000,000 a year as a result of the agreement, as rising world agricultural prices due to the mandated subsidy cuts will boost its food import bill.

Where the push to expand exports has been successful, the benefits often have been unequally distributed. In Latin America, for instance, economic growth has picked up in recent years, but the share of the population living in poverty is projected to hover near 40% through the end of the decade. For some, the strategy is a net loss. Subsistence farmers—frequently women—often are displaced from their land so it can be devoted to growing crops to please the palates of consumers in distant lands. Indigenous peoples are forced from their homelands as forests are felled for foreign exchange revenue.

GRASSROOTS OPPOSITION TO SELLING RESOURCES

The uprising in the Mexican state of Chiapas in early 1994 was a wake-up call to some of the failures of this development model. In terms of resources, Chiapas is rich, producing 100,000 barrels of oil and 500,000,000,000 cubic meters of natural gas daily; supplying more than half of the country's hydropower with its dams; and accounting for one-third of the nation's coffee production and a sizable share of cattle, timber, honey, corn, and other products. However, the benefit from selling these resources is not flowing to many of the people who live there. According to Mexican grassroots activist Gustavo Esteva, "Rather than demanding the expansion of the economy, either state-led or market-led, the [Zapatista rebels] seek to expel it from their domain. They are pleading for protection of the 'commons' they have carved out for themselves.... The [Zapatistas] have dared to announce for the world that development as a social experiment has failed miserably in Chiapas." World leaders would do well to heed his warning that the existing economic orthodoxy needs some fundamental rethinking.

Achieving sustainable development requires protecting the rights of local people to control their own resources —whether it be forests, fish, or minerals. Yet, nations and individuals also are discovering that, if today's transnational challenges are to be mastered, a wider role for international institutions is inevitable.

To respond to this need, considerable reforms are necessary in the United Nations to prepare it for the world of the future. The UN Charter, for example, was written for a different era. Neither "environment" nor "population" even appear in the document. Moreover, though the need for more effective international institutions is clear, people the world over justifiably are worried by the prospect of control of resources being centralized in institutions that are remote from democratic accountability.

As the 50th anniversary of the UN approaches, many ideas are being floated for changes to prepare the world body for the future. Some proposals concern the need to expand membership on the Security Council to make it more broadly representative of today's world. Others focus on the economic and social side of the organization's operations. The UN Development Program (UNDP), for instance, is advocating a Development Security Council—a body of about 22 members to promote the cause of "sustainable human security" at the highest levels.

While these proposals are being debated, another idea merits consideration —the creation of a full-fledged environmental agency. The UN Environment Program (UNEP) has contributed a great deal considering a limited budget which until recently was smaller than that of some private U.S. environmental groups. UNEP does not enjoy the stature within the UN system of a specialized agency, meaning it has few operational programs of its own. Though charged with coordinating the UN response to environmental issues, it has little ability to influence the programs of other agencies with much larger budgets. The time has come either to upgrade UNEP to specialized agency status or create a new environmental agency.

In considering what the functions of such an organization might be, Dan Esty of Yale University suggests that a Global Environmental Organization (GEO) might develop basic environmental principles analogous to widely recognized trade principles advanced by GATT, such as most-favored-nation status and nondiscrimination. High on such a list would be full-cost pricing, the idea that environmental costs should be internalized in the prices of products, rather than passed on to taxpayers. Other proposals include the precautionary principle—that decisions to take preventative action sometimes can not await conclusive scientific proof—and a right to public participation. Governments already have endorsed those ideas and others in the Rio Declaration, but have not given an organization the task of seeing that they are respected.

In addition, a GEO could play a critical role by serving as an information clearinghouse—as UNEP's Global Environmental Monitoring System already does on a small scale. It also might serve as the implementing agency for some UNDP-financed projects. A GEO could be a partner in recycling or land reclamation. It also might elaborate some common minimum international environmental production standards.

Finally, the time has come for governments to create some form of dedicated funding mechanism to finance investments for the transition to a sustainable society—including environmental expenditures, social initiatives, and peacekeeping costs. Among the possibilities are a levy on carbon emissions, international air travel, or flows of money across national borders. To discourage destabilizing currency speculation, Nobel-laureate economist James Tobin has suggested that a .5% tax be placed on foreign-exchange transactions. This would raise more than $1.5 trillion annually. Even a smaller levy would raise far more funds than are available today. A tax of .003% of daily currency transactions would raise $8,400,000,000.

Even in the best of circumstances, the slow pace of international diplomacy and the rate at which environmental and social problems are growing worse are difficult to reconcile. The best hope for improving the process of global governance lies with people. Just as national policymaking can not be considered in isolation from public pressure, global policymaking increasingly must consider an organized and influential international citizenry.

The most familiar role for nongovernmental organizations and grassroots groups is within national borders. Around the world, there is an encouraging growth in such activities. In addition to this critical work, citizens' groups are beginning to make their influence felt in international forums. In Rio, the 20,000 concerned citizens and activists who attended from around the globe outnumbered official representatives by at least two to one. More than 4,000 NGOs participated in the Cairo conference, where they widely were credited with helping to share the terms of the debate. Some of the organizations at these meetings—such as Friends of the Earth, Greenpeace, the International Planned Parenthood Federation, and the World Wide Fund for Nature —represent global constituencies rather than parochial national interests. Taken together, all this activity adds up the creation of a bona fide global environmental movement.

Working through international coalitions such as the Climate Action Network and the Women's Environment and Development Organization, these groups are a powerful force. Daily newsletters produced by citizens' groups, including *Eco* and the *Earth Negotiations Bulletin*, have become mainstays of the international negotiating process. Widely read by official delegates and NGOs during international meetings, they reveal key failures in negotiations and prevent the obscure language of diplomacy from shielding governments from accountability for their actions.

The participation of the international scientific community also is critical. International panels of scientists convened to study both ozone depletion and climate change played instrumental roles in forging the consensus needed to push these political processes forward. The treaties on these two problems created scientific advisory groups that meet regularly and offer advice on whether the agreements need to be updated in light of new scientific information.

The interests of the business community sometimes can be harnessed to positive effect. The Business Council for Sustainable Development, 50 chief executives from the world's largest corporations, were active in the lead-up to the Earth Summit. Though the council opposed language that would have advocated developing standards to regulate multinational corporations, it argued persuasively in its report, *Changing Course*, that sound environmental policies and business practices go hand in hand. The U.S.-based Business Council for Sustainable Energy—a coalition of energy efficiency, renewable energy, and natural gas companies that favor taking action to avert global warming—has begun to participate in international climate negotiations, counterbalancing the lobbying efforts of oil and coal companies.

FORMIDABLE OBSTACLES

Despite their impressive contributions, citizens' groups working at the global level face formidable obstacles. International law traditionally has functioned as a compact among nations, with no provisions for public participation comparable to those that are taken for granted at the national level in democracies around the world. There is nothing yet resembling an elected parliament in the United Nations or any of its agencies. Though the UN has begun to experiment with occasional public hearings on topics of special concern, these continue to be rare events. No formal provisions are made for public review and comment on international treaties or is there a mechanism for bringing citizen suits at the World Court. International negotiations often are closed to public participation, and access to documents of critical interest to the public generally is restricted.

The UN Economic and Social Council is reviewing the rules for the participation of citizens' groups in the UN system at large. Some of those involved in the debate advocate making it easier for groups to be involved, taking the Rio experience as their guide. Others resist this view, worrying about the system being overwhelmed by sheer numbers or about whom the citizens' groups are accountable to. The outcome of these deliberations remains to be seen, but it seems likely that the UNCED process has set a new standard for participation that the UN system will have difficulty backing away from.

When it comes to openness and accountability, GATT has been subject to particularly strong criticism for its secretive procedures. When a national law is challenged as a trade barrier under GATT, the case is heard behind closed doors by a panel of professors and bureaucrats steeped in the intricacies of world trade law, but not in the needs of the planet. Legal briefs and other critical information generally are unavailable to the public, and there is no opportunity for citizens' groups to testify or make submissions. Governments are discussing rules on public participation for the Trade and Environment Committee of GATT's successor, the World Trade Organization. Preliminary reports suggest that the fight for public access will be a long and hard-fought battle.

Despite a checkered history regarding openness, the World Bank has instituted two new policies that others would do well to emulate. Under an information policy, more of its documents will be available publicly and an information center has been established to disseminate them. The second change—the creation of an independent inspection panel —will provide an impartial forum where board members or private citizens can raise complaints about projects that violate the financial organization's policies, rules, and procedures. Though both initiatives were watered down in the negotiating process, they nonetheless represent sizable chinks in the World Bank's armor. It will be up to the concerned public to test the limits of these new policies and to press for them to be strengthened— and replicated elsewhere.

Besides access to information, the public must become a fuller partner in the development process itself. All too often, "development" has served the purposes of a country's elite, but not its poorest members. A growing body of evidence suggests that, for a project to succeed, the planning process must include the people it is supposed to benefit. In other words, aid should be demand-driven, rather than imposed from above. Several bilateral aid agencies have developed new ways of fostering widespread participation in the development planning process, and the World Bank has come up with a new strategy along these lines. The challenge, as always, will be moving from words to action.

Despite public support for far-reaching changes, the international response to the interlinked threat of ecological collapse and social disintegration remains seriously inadequate. Fifty years ago, with large parts of Europe and Asia in shambles in the wake of World War II, the world community pulled together with an impressive period of institution-building that set the tone for the next half-century. The time has come for a similar burst on innovation to forge the new global partnership that will enable the world to confront the daunting challenges that await it in the next millennium.

If the changes called for in this article are made and the power of public commitment to sustainable development is unleashed, the planet can head off global ecological collapse and the social disintegration that would be sure to accompany it. However, if complacency reigns and international forums generate lots of talks and paper, but little action, the future does not look bright. The choice is ours to make.

NO

Julian L. Simon

MORE PEOPLE, GREATER WEALTH, MORE RESOURCES, HEALTHIER ENVIRONMENT

This is the economic history of humanity in a nutshell. From 2 million or 200,000 or 20,000 or 2,000 years ago until the 18th century there was slow growth in population, almost no increase in health or decrease in mortality, slow growth in the availability of natural resources (but not increased scarcity), increase in wealth for a few, and mixed effects on the environment. Since then there has been rapid growth in population due to spectacular decreases in the death rate, rapid growth in resources, widespread increases in wealth, and an unprecedently clean and beautiful living environment in many parts of the world along with a degraded environment in the poor and socialist parts of the world.

That is, more people and more wealth have correlated with more (rather than less) resources and a cleaner environment—just the opposite of what Malthusian theory leads one to believe. The task before us is to make sense of these mind-boggling happy trends.

The current gloom-and-doom about a 'crisis' of our environment is wrong on the scientific facts. Even the US Environmental Protection Agency acknowledges that US air and water have been getting cleaner rather than dirtier in the past few decades. Every agricultural economist knows that the world's population has been eating ever-better since the Second World War.

Every resource economist knows that all natural resources have been getting more available not more scarce, as shown by their falling prices over the decades and centuries. And every demographer knows that the death rate has been falling all over the world—life expectancy almost tripling in the rich countries in the past two centuries, and almost doubling in the poor countries in only the past four decades.

POPULATION GROWTH AND ECONOMIC DEVELOPMENT

The picture is now also clear that population growth does not hinder economic development. In the 1980s there was a complete reversal in the consensus of thinking of population economists about the effects of more people. In

1986, the National Research Council and the National Academy of Sciences completely overturned its 'official' view away from the earlier worried view expressed in 1971. It noted the absence of any statistical evidence of a negative connection between population increase and economic growth. And it said that 'The scarcity of exhaustible resources is at most a minor restraint on economic growth'. This U-turn by the scientific consensus of experts on the subject has gone unacknowledged by the press, the anti-natalist [anti-birth] environmental organisations, and the agencies that foster population control abroad.

LONG-RUN TRENDS POSITIVE

Here is my central assertion: Almost every economic and social change or trend points in a positive direction, as long as we view the matter over a reasonably long period of time.

For a proper understanding of the important aspects of an economy we should look at the long-run trends. But the short-run comparisons—between the sexes, age groups, races, political groups, which are usually purely relative—make more news. To repeat, just about every important long-run measure of human welfare shows improvement over the decades and centuries, in the United States as well as in the rest of the world. And there is no persuasive reason to believe that these trends will not continue indefinitely.

Would I bet on it? For sure. I'll bet a week's or month's pay—anything I win goes to pay for more research—that just about any trend pertaining to material human welfare will improve rather than

get worse. You pick the comparison and the year.

Let me quickly review a few data on how human life has been doing, beginning with the all-important issue, life itself.

THE CONQUEST OF TOO-EARLY DEATH

The most important and amazing demographic fact—the greatest human achievement in history, in my view—is the decrease in the world's death rate. Figure 1 portrays the history of human life expectancy at birth. It took thousands of years to increase life expectancy at birth from just over 20 years to the high twenties in about 1750. Then life expectancy in the richest countries suddenly took off and tripled in about two centuries. In just the past two centuries, the length of life you could expect for your baby or yourself in the advanced countries jumped from less than 30 years to perhaps 75 years. What greater event has humanity witnessed than this conquest of premature death in the rich countries? It is this decrease in the death rate that is the cause of there being a larger world population nowadays than in former times.

Then starting well after the Second World War, the length of life you could expect in the poor countries has leaped upwards by perhaps 15 or even 20 years since the 1950s, caused by advances in agriculture, sanitation, and medicine (Figure 2).

Let me put it differently. In the 19th century the planet Earth could sustain only 1 billion people. Ten thousand years ago, only 4 million could keep themselves alive. Now 5 billion people are on average living longer and more healthily than

Figure 1

History of Human Life Expectancy at Birth (3000BCE–2000CE)

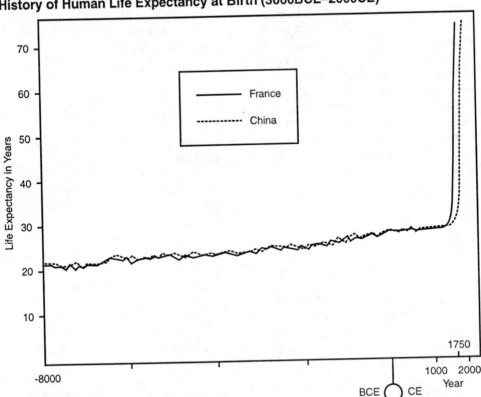

BCE: Before the Christian Era.

ever before. The increase in the world's population represents our victory over death.

Here arises a crucial issue of interpretation: One would expect lovers of humanity to jump with joy at this triumph of human mind and organisation over the raw killing forces of nature. Instead, many lament that there are so many people alive to enjoy the gift of life. And it is this worry that leads them to approve the Indonesian, Chinese and other inhumane programmes of coercion and denial of personal liberty in one of the most precious choices a family can make—the number of children that it wishes to bear and raise.

THE DECREASING SCARCITY OF NATURAL RESOURCES

Throughout history, the supply of natural resources has worried people. Yet the data clearly show that natural resource scarcity—as measured by the economically-meaningful indicator of cost or price—has been decreasing rather than increasing in the long run for all raw materials, with only temporary exceptions from time to time: that is, avail-

Figure 2
Female Expectation of Life at Birth

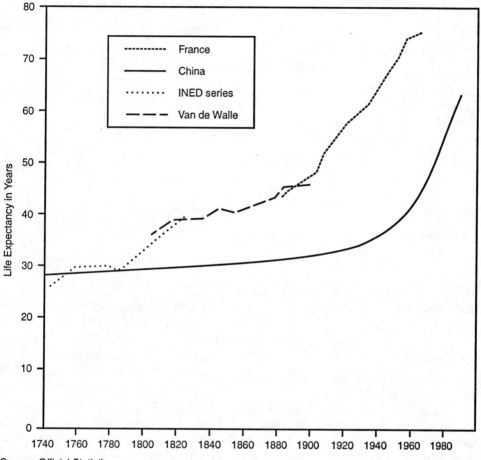

Source: Official Statistics

ability has been increasing. Consider copper, which is representative of all the metals. In Figure 3 we see the price relative to wages since 1801. The cost of a ton is only about a tenth now of what it was two hundred years ago.

This trend of falling prices of copper has been going on for a very long time. In the 18th century BCE in Babylonia under Hammurabi—almost 4,000 years ago—the price of copper was about a thousand times its price in the USA now relative to wages. At the time of the Roman Empire the price was about a hundred times the present price.

In Figure 4 we see the price of copper relative to the consumer price index. Everything we buy—pens, shirts, tyres—has been getting cheaper over the years because we have learned how to make them more cheaply, especially during the past 200 years. Even so, the extraordinary fact is that natural

Figure 3
Copper Prices Indexed by Wages

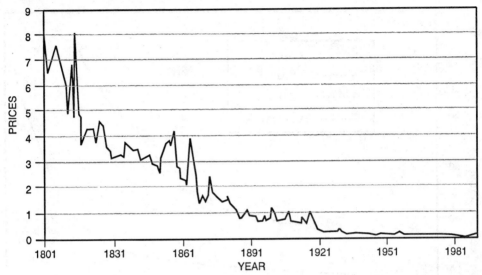

resources have been getting cheaper even faster than consumer goods.

So, by any measure, natural resources have been getting more available rather than more scarce.

In the case of oil, the shocking price rises during the 1970s and 1980s were not caused by growing scarcity in the world supply. And indeed, the price of petroleum in inflation-adjusted dollars has returned to levels about where they were before the politically-induced increases, and the price of gasoline is about at the historic low and still falling. Taking energy in general, there is no reason to believe that the supply of energy is finite, or that the price of energy will not continue its long-run decrease indefinitely. . . .

FOOD—'A BENIGN TREND'

Food is an especially important resource. The evidence is particularly strong for food that we are on a benign trend despite rising population. The long-run price o food relative to wages is now perhap only a tenth as much as it was in 180 in the USA. Even relative to consume products, the price of grain is dow because of increased productivity, as wit all other primary products.

Famine deaths due to insufficient foo supply have decreased even in absolut terms, let alone relative to population, i the past century, a matter which pertain particularly to the poor countries. Pe person food consumption is up over th last 30 years. And there are no dat showing that the bottom of the incom scale is faring worse, or even has failed t share in the general improvement, as th average has improved.

Africa's food production per perso is down, but by 1994 almost no-on any longer claims that Africa's sufferin results from a shortage of land o water or sun. The cause of hunger i Africa is a combination of civil wa

Figure 4
Copper Prices Divided by CPI

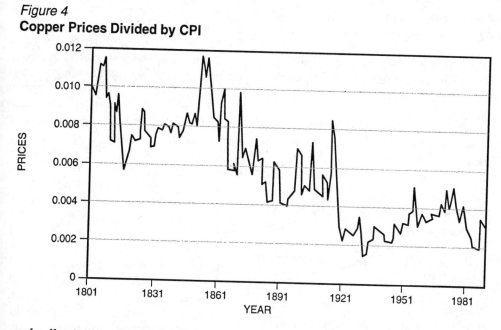

and collectivisation of agriculture, which periodic droughts have made more murderous.

Consider agricultural land as an example of all natural resources. Although many people consider land to be a special kind of resource, it is subject to the same processes of human creation as other natural resources. The most important fact about agricultural land is that less and less of it is needed as the decades pass. This idea is utterly counter-intuitive. It seems entirely obvious that a growing world population would need larger amounts of farmland. But the title of a remarkably prescient article by Theodore Schultz in 1951 tells the story: 'The Declining Economic Importance of Land'.

The increase in actual and potential productivity per unit of land has grown much faster than population, and there is sound reason to expect this trend to continue. Therefore, there is less and less

reason to worry about the supply of land. Though the stock of usable land seems fixed at any moment, it is constantly being increased—at a rapid rate in many cases—by the clearing of new land or reclamation of wasteland. Land also is constantly being enhanced by increasing the number of crops grown per year on each unit of land and by increasing the yield per crop with better farming methods and with chemical fertiliser. Last but not least, land is created anew where there was no land.

THE ONE SCARCE FACTOR

There is only one important resource which has shown a trend of increasing scarcity rather than increasing abundance. That resource is the most important of all—human beings. Yes, there are more people on earth now than ever before. But if we measure the scarcity of people the same way that we measure the scarcity of other economic goods—by how much we must pay to obtain their services—we see that wages and salaries have been going up all over the world, in poor countries as well as rich. The amount that you must pay to obtain the services of a barber or cook—or economist—has risen in the United States over the decades. This increase in the price of people's services is a clear indication that people are becoming more scarce even though there are more of us.

Surveys show that the public believes that our air and water have been getting more polluted in recent years. The evidence with respect to air indicates that pollutants have been declining, especially the main pollutant, particulates. With respect to water, the proportion of monitoring sites in the USA with water of good drinkability has increased since the data began in 1961.

Every forecast of the doomsayers has turned out flat wrong. Metals, foods, and other natural resources have become more available rather than more scarce throughout the centuries. The famous Famine 1975 forecast by the Paddock brothers—that we would see millions of famine deaths in the US on television in the 1970s—was followed instead by gluts in agricultural markets. Paul Ehrlich's primal scream about 'What will we do when the [gasoline] pumps run dry?' was followed by gasoline cheaper than since the 1930s. The Great Lakes are not dead; instead they offer better sport fishing than ever. The main pollutants, especially the particulates which have killed people for years, have lessened in our cities. Socialist countries are a different and tragic environmental story, however!

... But nothing has reduced the doomsayers' credibility with the press or their command over the funding resources of the federal government....

With respect to population growth: A dozen competent statistical studies, starting in 1967 with an analysis by Nobel prizewinner Simon Kuznets, agree that there is no negative statistical relationship between economic growth and population growth. There is strong reason to believe that more people have a positive effect in the long run.

Population growth does not lower the standard of living—all the evidence agrees. And the evidence supports the view that population growth raises it in the long run.

Incidentally, it was those statistical studies that converted me in about 1968 from working in favour of population control to the point of view that I hold today. I certainly did not come to my current view for any political or religious or ideological reason.

The basic method is to gather data on each country's rate of population growth and its rate of economic growth, and then to examine whether—looking at all the data in the sample together—countries with high population growth rates have economic growth rates lower than average, and countries with low population growth rates have economic growth rates higher than average. All the studies agree in concluding that this is not so; there is no correlation between economic growth and population growth in the intermediate run.

Of course one can adduce cases of countries that seemingly are exceptions to the pattern. It is the genius of statistical inference, however, to enable us to draw valid generalisations from samples that contain such wide variations in behaviour. The exceptions can be useful in alerting us to possible avenues for further analysis, but as long as they are only exceptions, they do not prove that the generalisation is not meaningful or useful.

POPULATION DENSITY FAVOURS ECONOMIC GROWTH

The research-wise person may wonder whether population density is a more meaningful variable than population growth. And, indeed, such studies have been done. And again, the statistical evidence directly contradicts the common-sense conventional wisdom. If you make a chart with population density on the horizontal axis and either the income level or the rate of change of income on the vertical axis, you will see that higher density is associated with better rather than poorer economic results....

The most important benefit of population size and growth is the increase it brings to the stock of useful knowledge. Minds matter economically as much as, or more than, hands or mouths. Progress is limited largely by the availability of trained workers. The more people who enter our population by birth or immigration, the faster will be the rate of progress of our material and cultural civilisation.

Here we require a qualification that tends to be overlooked: I do not say that all is well everywhere, and I do not predict that all will be rosy in the future. Children are hungry and sick; people live out lives of physical or intellectual poverty, and lack of opportunity; war or some new pollution may finish us off. What I am saying is that for most relevant economic matters I have checked, the aggregate trends are improving rather than deteriorating.

Also, I do not say that a better future happens automatically or without effort.

It will happen because women and men will struggle with problems with muscle and mind, and will probably overcome, as people have overcome in the past—*if the social and economic system gives them the opportunity to do so.*

THE EXPLANATION OF THESE AMAZING TRENDS

Now we need some theory to explain how it can be that economic welfare grows along with population, rather than humanity being reduced to misery and poverty as population grows.

The Malthusian theory of increasing scarcity, based on supposedly fixed resources (the theory that the doomsayers rely upon), runs exactly contrary to the data over the long sweep of history. It makes sense therefore to prefer another theory.

The theory that fits the facts very well is this: More people, and increased income, cause problems in the short run. Short-run scarcity raises prices. This presents opportunity, and prompts the search for solutions. In a free society, solutions are eventually found. And in the long run the new developments leave us better off than if the problems had not arisen.

To put it differently, in the short run more consumers mean less of the fixed available stock of goods to be divided among more people. And more workers labouring with the same fixed current stock of capital means that there will be less output per worker. The latter effect, known as 'the law of diminishing returns', is the essence of Malthus's theory as he first set it out.

But if the resources with which people work are not fixed over the period being analysed, the Malthusian logic of diminishing returns does not apply. And the plain fact is that, given some time to adjust to shortages, the resource base does not remain fixed. People create more resources of all kinds.

When we take a long-run view, the picture is different, and considerably more complex, than the simple short-run view of more people implying lower average income. In the very long run, more people almost surely imply more available resources and a higher income for everyone.

I suggest you test this idea against your own knowledge: Do you think that our standard of living would be as high as it is now if the population had never grown from about 4 million human beings perhaps 10,000 years ago? I do not think we would now have electric light or gas heat or cars or penicillin or travel to the moon or our present life expectancy of over 70 years at birth in rich countries, in comparison to the life expectancy of 20 to 25 years at birth in earlier eras, if population had not grown to its present numbers....

THE ROLE OF ECONOMIC FREEDOM

Here we must address another crucial element in the economics of resources and population—the extent to which the political-social-economic system provides personal freedom from government coercion. Skilled people require an appropriate social and economic framework that provides incentives for working hard and taking risks, enabling their talents to flower and come to fruition. The key elements of such a framework are economic liberty, respect for property, and fair and sensible rules of the market that are enforced equally for all.

The world's problem is not too many people, but lack of political and economic freedom. Powerful evidence comes from an extraordinary natural experiment that occurred starting in the 1940s with three pairs of countries that have the same culture and history, and had much the same standard of living when they split apart after the Second World War—East and West Germany, North and South Korea, Taiwan and China. In each case the centrally planned communist country began with less population 'pressure', as measured by density per square kilometre, than did the market-directed economy. And the communist and non-communist countries also started with much the same birth rates.

The market-directed economies have performed much better economically than the centrally-planned economies. The economic-political system clearly was the dominant force in the results of the three comparisons. This powerful explanation of economic development cuts the ground from under population growth as a likely explanation of the speed of nations' economic development.

THE ASTOUNDING SHIFT IN THE SCHOLARLY CONSENSUS

So far I have been discussing the factual evidence. But in 1994 there is an important new element not present 20 years ago. The scientific community of scholars who study population economics now agrees with almost all of what is written above. The statements made above do not represent a single lone voice, but rather the current scientific consensus.

The conclusions offered earlier about agriculture and resources and demographic trends have always represented the consensus of economists in those fields. And the consensus of population economists also is now not far from what is written here.

In 1986, the US National Research Council and the US National Academy of Sciences published a book on population growth and economic development prepared by a prestigious scholarly group. This 'official' report reversed almost completely the frightening conclusions of the 1971 NAS report. 'Population growth [is] at most a minor factor....' As cited earlier in this paper, it found benefits of additional people as well as costs.

A host of review articles by distinguished economic demographers in the past decade has confirmed that this 're-visionist' view is indeed consistent with the scientific evidence, though not all the writers would go as far as I do in pointing out the positive long-run effects of population growth. The consensus is more towards a 'neutral' judgement. But this is a huge change from the earlier judgement that population growth is economically detrimental.

By 1994, anyone who confidently asserts that population growth damages the economy must turn a blind eye to the scientific evidence.

SUMMARY AND CONCLUSION

In the short run, all resources are limited. An example of such a finite resource is the amount of space allotted to me. The longer run, however, is a different story. The standard of living has risen along with the size of the world's population since the beginning of recorded time. There is no convincing economic reason why these trends towards a better life should not continue indefinitely.

The key theoretical idea is this: The growth of population and of income create actual and expected shortages, and hence lead to price rises. A price increase represents an opportunity that attracts profit-minded entrepreneurs to seek new ways to satisfy the shortages. Some fail, at cost to themselves. A few succeed, and the final result is that we end up better off than if the original shortage problems had never arisen. That is, we need our problems though this does not imply that we should purposely create additional problems for ourselves.

I hope that you will now agree that the long-run outlook is for a more abundant material life rather than for increased scarcity, in the United States and in the world as a whole. Of course, such progress does not come automatically. And my message certainly is not one of complacency. In this I agree with the doomsayers—that our world needs the best efforts of all humanity to improve our lot. I part company with them in that they expect us to come to a bad end despite the efforts we make, whereas I expect a continuation of humanity's history of successful efforts. And I believe that their message is self-fulfilling, because if you expect your efforts to fail because of inexorable natural limits, then you are likely to feel resigned; and therefore literally to resign. But if you recognise the possibility— in fact the probability—of success, you can tap large reservoirs of energy and enthusiasm.

Adding more people causes problems, but people are also the means to solve these problems. The main fuel to speed the world's progress is our stock of knowledge, and the brakes are (a) our lack of imagination, and (b) unsound social regulation of these activities.

The ultimate resource is people—especially skilled, spirited, and hopeful young people endowed with liberty—who will exert their wills and imaginations for their own benefit, and so inevitably benefit not only themselves but the rest of us as well.

POSTSCRIPT

Are Major Changes Needed to Avert a Global Environmental Crisis?

It is tempting to accept Simon's rosy predictions for the future and his faith in the ability of human beings to solve whatever problems they confront. However, Simon undermines his argument early in his essay by suggesting that environmental degradation is a problem only in poor and socialist parts of the world. He claims that the U.S. Environmental Protection Agency acknowledges that air and water in America have generally been getting cleaner. However, satellite photographs reveal a growing region of constant hazy air pollution over much of the northeastern United States.

Simon's view that increasing world population is positive rather than problematic is fully explicated in his book *The Ultimate Resource* (Princeton University Press, 1981). For a more recent look at Simon and his worldview, his controversial standing among ecologists, and additional background to this debate on the earth's future, see John Tierney's "Betting the Planet," *The New York Times Magazine* (December 2, 1990).

The issue of resource depletion has recently been incorporated into the more general debate about the concept of "sustainable development." The World Commission on Environment and Development published a much publicized report, entitled *Our Common Future*, on many aspects of this issue in 1987. Commission chairperson Gro Harlem Brundtland, prime minister of Norway, has actively publicized its findings and recommendations. Her keynote address at the 1989 Forum on Global Change, "Global Change and Our Common Future," was published in *Environment* (June 1989).

For a discussion of the important concept of "carrying capacity," which is centrally related to this issue, see the chapter by Sandra Postel in the Worldwatch Institute book *State of the World 1994* (W. W. Norton, 1994). Among the many informative articles about sustainable development and how it might be achieved that have been published in the journal *Environment* are those by Tanvi Nagpal in the October 1995 issue, and by Molly Harris Olson in the May 1996 issue. Two encouraging descriptions of cities that have made some progress toward sustainability are contained in Steve Learner's article about Chattanooga, Tennessee, in the Spring 1995 issue of *The Amicus Journal* and in the article by Nicholas Gertler and John Ehrenfeld in the February/March 1996 issue of *Technology Review*.

For an Internet site related to this issue, see http://iisd1.iisd.ca/, which is the home page of the International Institute for Sustainable Development, a multimedia resource for environment and development policymakers.

CONTRIBUTORS
TO THIS VOLUME

EDITOR

THEODORE D. GOLDFARB is a professor of chemistry at the State University of New York at Stony Brook. He earned a B.A. from Cornell University and a Ph.D. from the University of California, Berkeley. He is the author of over 35 research papers and articles on molecular structure, environmental chemistry, and science policy, as well as the book *A Search for Order in the Physical Universe* (W. H. Freeman, 1974). He is also the editor of *Sources: Notable Selections in Environmental Studies* (Dushkin/McGraw-Hill). Dr. Goldfarb is a recipient of the State University of New York's Chancellor's Award for Excellence in Teaching. In addition to teaching undergraduate and graduate courses in environmental and physical chemistry, he has taught summer institutes and special seminars for college and secondary school teachers and for undergraduate and graduate research students on a variety of topics, including energy policy, integrated waste management strategies, sustainable development, and ethics in science. He is presently directing a program funded by the National Science Foundation that is designed to promote the incorporation of ethics and values issues in the teaching of secondary school science. Dr. Goldfarb has served as consultant and adviser to citizens' groups, town and city governments, and federal and state agencies on environmental matters. He is an active member of several professional organizations, including the American Chemical Society, the American Association for the Advancement of Science, and the New York Academy of Sciences.

STAFF

David Dean   List Manager
David Brackley   Developmental Editor
Ava Suntoke   Developmental Editor
Tammy Ward   Administrative Assistant
Brenda S. Filley   Production Manager
Juliana Arbo   Typesetting Supervisor
Diane Barker   Proofreader
Lara Johnson   Graphics
Richard Tietjen   Publishing Systems Manager

AUTHORS

ROBERT W. ADLER is a senior attorney and director of the Clean Water Project at the Natural Resources Defense Council in Washington, D.C., a national, nonprofit organization staffed by attorneys, scientists, and resource specialists dedicated to the protection of public health and the environment. He is also an adjunct professor at the University of Virginia School of Law.

IVAN AMATO is an author who frequently writes about environmental issues. His work has been published in *Science* and *Garbage: The Independent Environmental Quarterly.*

RONALD BAILEY, an environmental journalist, is the producer of *TechnoPolitics,* a weekly PBS television series. As a staff writer for *Forbes,* he has covered science and technology policy issues. His publications include *Eco-Scam: The False Prophets of Ecological Apocalypse* (St. Martin's Press, 1993).

CHRISTOPHER BOERNER is a Jeanne and Arthur Ansehl Fellow at the Center for the Study of American Business at Washington University in St. Louis, Missouri.

THOMAS A. CARR is an assistant professor in the economics department at Middlebury College in Middlebury, Vermont.

ED CARSON is a staff reporter for *Reason.* He has written on a variety of subjects, including taxation, school choice, affirmative action, and Generation X. In 1993 he was the recipient of the Madison Center for Educational Affairs Award for Best News Coverage.

LUTHER J. CARTER is an independent, Washington, D.C.–based journalist. He is the author of *Nuclear Imperatives and the Public Trust: Dealing With Radioactive Waste* (Resources for the Future, 1987), which received the Special Forum Award from the U.S. Council on Energy Awareness in 1988. He is a former writer for *Science,* a journal of the American Association for the Advancement of Science, specializing in energy and the environment.

JOHN DANIEL is the poetry editor for *Wilderness* magazine.

RICHARD de NEUFVILLE is chair of the technology and policy program at the Massachusetts Institute of Technology in Cambridge, Massachusetts. He specializes in analyzing transportation systems.

JON ENTINE is a journalist specializing in business ethics, sports, and culture. His reporting over 20 years has won many awards, including two Emmys. He has served as adjunct professor of journalism at New York University and has lectured at Columbia University.

JEFFERY A. FORAN is executive director of the Risk Science Institute in Washington, D.C., and a former associate professor and director of the Environmental Health and Policy Program at George Washington University.

HILARY F. FRENCH is a senior researcher at the Worldwatch Institute in Washington, D.C. She is the author of *Clearing the Air: Worldwatch Paper 94.*

ROBERT W. HAHN is an adjunct professor of economics with the Heinz School at Carnegie Mellon University and in the Department of Engineering and Public Policy. He is also a resident scholar at the American Enterprise Institute in Washington, D.C., a privately funded public policy research organization, and cochair of the U.S. Alternative Fuels Council.

DOUG HARBRECHT is a correspondent for *Business Week* in Washington, D.C.

PAUL HARRISON is the author of *The Third Revolution* (Penguin Books, 1993), which won a Population Institute Global Media Award.

BETSY HARTMANN is director of the Hampshire College Population and Development Program in Amherst, Massachusetts, and has been a fellow of the Institute for Food and Development Policy. She is the author of *Reproductive Rights and Wrongs: The Global Politics of Population Control*, rev. ed. (South End Press, 1995).

CHRIS HENDRICKSON is a professor of civil engineering in and associate dean of the College of Engineering at Carnegie Mellon University in Pittsburgh, Pennsylvania.

DON HINRICHSEN is a contributing editor of *The Amicus Journal*.

THOMAS LAMBERT is a Clifford M. Hardin Fellow at the Center for the Study of American Business at Washington University in St. Louis, Missouri.

DAVID LANGHORST is an executive board member of the Idaho Wildlife Federation.

LESTER LAVE is a James H. Higgins Professor of Economics at Carnegie Mellon University in Pittsburgh, Pennsylvania, with appointments in the Graduate School of Industrial Administration, the School of Urban and Public Affairs, and the Department of Engineering and Public Policy. He received a Ph.D. in eco-

nomics from Harvard University and was a senior fellow at the Brookings Institution from 1978 to 1982.

NICHOLAS LENSSEN is a research manager at E Source. Based in Boulder, Colorado, E Source conducts research in energy technologies and publishes a wide range of reports. His research and writing focus on energy policy, alternative energy sources, nuclear power, radioactive waste, and global climate change, and he has testified before the U.S. Congress and the European Parliament on energy issues. His publications include *Power Surge: Guide to the Coming Energy Revolution* (W. W. Norton, 1994).

JON R. LUOMA is a widely published environmental writer and a regular contributor to such magazines as *Audubon*, *Wildlife Conservation*, the *New York Times Magazine*, and *Discover*. His articles also appear frequently in the "Science Times" section of the *New York Times*. His publications include *Troubled Skies, Troubled Waters* (Viking Penguin, 1984) and *A Crowded Ark: The Role of Zoos in Wildlife Conservation* (Houghton Mifflin, 1988).

FRANCIS McMICHAEL is a Blenko Professor of Environmental Engineering at Carnegie Mellon University in Pittsburgh, Pennsylvania.

THOMAS GALE MOORE, an economist and educator, is a senior fellow of the Hoover Institution on War, Revolution, and Peace at Stanford University. A former professor at Michigan State University, Stanford Graduate School of Business, and the University of California, Los Angeles, he was a member of President Ronald Reagan's Council of Economic Advisers from 1985 to 1989. He is an adjunct scholar of the Cato Institute.

MOTI NISSANI is a professor in the Interdisciplinary Studies Program at Wayne State University in Detroit, Michigan.

BILL O'DONNELL is a former associate publisher of *Garbage: The Independent Environmental Quarterly*.

HEATHER L. PEDERSEN is a mathematics teacher at the Colorado Springs School in Colorado.

MARK L. PLUMMER is a senior fellow at the Discovery Institute, which is a nonpartisan center for national and international affairs. He specializes in environmental issues, and he is coauthor, with Charles C. Mann, of *The Aspirin Wars: Money, Medicine, and 100 Years of Rampant Competition* (Alfred A. Knopf, 1991).

PATRICIA POORE is a former publisher and editor of *Garbage: The Independent Environmental Quarterly*.

SUNDER RAMASWAMY is chairman of the economics department at Middlebury College in Middlebury, Vermont. He received his Ph.D. from Purdue University.

BERNARD J. REILLY is the corporate counsel at DuPont, where he has been managing the legal aspects of the company's Superfund program since 1986.

RUTH ROSEN is a professor of history at the University of California, Davis. She writes regularly on politics and culture, and she is the author of *The Lost Sisterhood: Prostitution in America, 1900–1918* (Johns Hopkins University Press, 1984).

STEPHEN H. SAFE is in the Department of Veterinary Physiology and Pharmacology at Texas A&M University in College Station, Texas. He is the founding principal of Wellington Environmental Consultants, now Wellington Laboratories, and he is a member of the American Association for Cancer Research and the American College of Toxicology.

LYNN SCARLETT is vice president of research for the Reason Foundation, a nonprofit, public policy research organization in Santa Monica, California. Her research centers on environmental and land-use regulations, solid waste, and recycling issues, and air quality. She has testified on environmental and solid waste issues before the Federal Trade Commission, the U.S. House Subcommittee on Transportation and Hazardous Waste, and the California Senate Committee on the Environment. She received her B.A. and M.A. in political science from the University of California, Santa Barbara, where she also completed her Ph.D. in political science and political economy.

JULIAN L. SIMON is a professor of economics and business administration in the College of Business and Management at the University of Maryland at College Park. His research interests focus on population economics, and his publications include *Population Matters: People, Resources, Environment, and Immigration* (Transaction Publishers, 1990), *The Ultimate Resource*, 2d ed. (Princeton University Press, 1994), and *The Economics of Population: Key Modern Writings* (Edward Elgar, 1997).

KATHERINE R. SMITH, a former analyst and acting director of the U.S. Department of Agriculture's Economic Research Service, is director of the policy studies program at the Henry A. Wallace Institute for Alternative Agriculture in Greenbelt, Maryland.

DANIEL SPERLING is director of the Institute of Transportation Studies at the University of California, Davis, where he is also a professor of civil engineering and environmental studies. He chairs a National Research Council committee on alternative transportation fuels, and he is a member of the National Academy of Sciences committee on transportation and a sustainable environment.

JOE THORNTON is research coordinator for the Greenpeace Toxics Campaign in New York City.

BRIAN TOKAR is an associate faculty member at Goddard College in Plainfield, Vermont. A regular correspondent for Z magazine, he has been an activist for over 20 years in the peace, antinuclear, environmental, and green politics movements. He is the author of *The Green Alternative: Creating an Ecological Future*, 2d. ed. (R & E Miles, 1987).

WILLIAM TUCKER, a writer and social critic, is a staff writer for *Forbes* magazine. His publications include *The Excluded Americans: Homelessness and Housing Policies* (Regnery Gateway, 1989), which won the 1991 Mencken Award for best nonfiction, and *Zoning, Rent Control, and Affordable Housing* (Cato Institute, 1991).

TED WILLIAMS has been a regular contributor to *Audubon* for over 15 years, during which he has covered a variety of topics, including gold mining in Alaska and the Northern Forest of the Northeast.

JOHN E. YOUNG is a senior researcher at the Worldwatch Institute and a contributing researcher of *State of the World 1995* (W. W. Norton, 1995).

INDEX